FRAGMENTED CITIZENS

Fragmented Citizens

The Changing Landscape of Gay and Lesbian Lives

Stephen M. Engel

NEW YORK UNIVERSITY PRESS
New York

NEW YORK UNIVERSITY PRESS
New York
www.nyupress.org

References to Internet websites (URLs) were accurate at the time of writing. Neither the author nor New York University Press is responsible for URLs that may have expired or changed since the manuscript was prepared.

Library of Congress Cataloging-in-Publication Data
Names: Engel, Stephen M., author.
Title: Fragmented citizens : the changing landscape of gay and lesbian lives / Stephen M. Engel.
Description: New York : New York University Press, [2016] |
Includes bibliographical references and index.
Identifiers: LCCN 2015047147 | ISBN 9781479809127 (cl : alk. paper)
Subjects: LCSH: Gay rights—United States. | Gays—Political activity. | Homophobia—United States. | Citizenship—United States. | United States—Politics and government.
Classification: LCC HQ76.8.U5 E54 2016 | DDC 323.3/2640973—dc23
LC record available at http://lccn.loc.gov/2015047147

New York University Press books are printed on acid-free paper, and their binding materials are chosen for strength and durability. We strive to use environmentally responsible suppliers and materials to the greatest extent possible in publishing our books.

Manufactured in the United States of America

10 9 8 7 6 5 4 3 2 1

Also available as an ebook

To Teddy, Emily, Evan, and Josh, for reminding me why

Justice grows out of recognition of ourselves in each other.
—President Barack Obama,
    Eulogy for Reverend Clementa Pinckney,
    June 26, 2015

CONTENTS

ACKNOWLEDGMENTS

I wrote this book to bring together two areas of interest: gay and lesbian politics and American political development (APD). The initial idea developed in the waning days of graduate school at Yale when I was approached by Rick Valelly to present on an American Political Science Association (APSA) panel in August of 2009. The panel was meant to generate ideas about connections between sexuality and state development. In those early remarks was the kernel of this endeavor, what my friends and colleagues have come to know as "Engel's gAyPD" project. Over the past few years, many have nurtured this project with me.

Writing may be a solitary act, but the development of a book is rarely so. From that first APSA panel to the completion of the final draft, this book would have been impossible without the intellectual encouragement, friendship, and helpful criticism of so many. Rick Valelly has proven a strong advocate of this project as we pursued similar questions. Julie Novkov found something valuable in that initial APSA essay, offering to publish it in a 2010 issue of the newsletter of the APSA sexuality and politics section. Doing so gave me the courage to keep at the project, even when I wasn't quite sure where it would go or what the argument might be. Julie further supported my research when she, Priscilla Yamin, and Kathleen Sullivan invited me to present material that would ultimately become chapter 5 of this book at a conference in May 2011 at Ohio University.

Stephen Skowronek and Suzanne Mettler offered invaluable criticism on this book's theoretical core: the notion of distinctly identifiable modalities of regulatory recognition of homosexuality. Mettler pushed me to consider how these frameworks might overlap and exist in tension, and Steve nudged me to always attend to agency when I kept reverting back to describing structures, institutions, and contexts. Indeed, I am deeply indebted to Steve for whatever intellectual and academic success I have achieved. He introduced me to American political development just when I was losing faith in pursuing political science. By bringing me on as editorial assistant of *Studies in American Political Development* while I was in graduate school, Steve offered me an intellectual home and a place where I might rediscover what I loved about the study of politics, power, and the dynamics of social change.

Work on this project straddled three homes. First, in the midst of my early research, I left Marquette University for a position at Bates College. Each experience proved formative. In my last year at Marquette I drafted and lobbied for legislation to bring equitable benefits to LGBT-identified faculty and staff. Doing so spurred my interest in the way private authorities regulate and structure citizens' lives. Second, at Bates, I was able to offer an APD seminar and quickly came to realize how challenging it was to teach some of the theoretical foundations of the field to undergraduates. As a pedagogical tool, this book was inspired by my Bates students in my APD seminar and my course "Sexuality Movements and the Politics of Difference." It aims to bring central ideas of APD and sexuality studies into conversation and to make them accessible to a broader audience. Third, I could not have completed this project without the intellectual community and deep friendship offered by colleagues at the American Bar Foundation. The ABF offered a year-long fellowship during 2013–14 so that I could write, present ideas, and gain critical feedback, all without the pressures of maintaining an active teaching schedule. This gift of time (as well as a very helpful research grant) was immeasurably valuable. In particular, I thank Laura Beth Nielsen, Quinn Mulroy, Robert Nelson, Terence Halliday, Jothie Rajah, Christopher Schmidt, Victoria Saker Woeste, Jill Weinberg, Jeff Kosbie, and Joanna Grisinger for comments and support on early ideas and drafts.

My time at the ABF afforded opportunity to present different sections of this project at conferences and universities across the country, where I was challenged and encouraged. Thanks to Daniel Galvin, Tom Ogorzalek, Anthony Chen, Alvin Tillery, Ken Kersch, Aziz Rana, Emily Zackin, Megan Francis, Steven Epstein, Jeffrey Isaac, Nicole Kazee, Stephen Kaplan, Abbey Steele, Alex Kirshner, Shatema Threadcraft, Amin Ghaziani, Rob Finn, Benjamin Gunning, McGee Young, Julia Azari, Paul Frymer, Tom Keck, David Brookman, Ryan Mack, and Lucas Schluesener for their support and critiques.

Bates has proven to be a wonderful place to grow as a teacher and scholar, and I could not be more thankful for having landed in such an intellectually fertile and collegial institution. Thanks to John Baughman and Rebecca Herzig for sharing their ideas about this project with me from my first days at Bates. Thanks to Aslaug Asgeirsdottir, Leslie Hill, Bill Corlett, Jim Richter, and Arlene MacLeod for seeing ideas and arguments in this project to which I had been blind and for daring me to make it richer, more multidisciplinary, and more accessible to a broader array of possible readers. Thanks to Emily Kane, Erica Rand, Senem Aslan, Jason Scheideman, Clarisa Perez-Armendarez, Caroline Shaw, Ben Moodie, Michael Sargent, Heidi Taylor, David Cummiskey, Theri Pickens, Andrew White, and Timothy Lyle for making my years at Bates so welcoming. And, thanks also to Bates for financially supporting the research for this project, first through a new faculty grant from 2011 to 2014 and then with a faculty development grant for 2014–15.

Four students deserve particular mention. Teddy Poneman, Evan Cooper, Emily Roseman, and Joshua Manson—all members of the Bates class of 2015—each in his or her own way reminded me of why I began this project and why it was important to complete it. I dedicate this book to them. Teddy: for prompting me to always bring theory to practice. Evan: for inspiring me to keep at it even when completing this project seemed nearly impossible. Emily: for reminding me of the importance of leaving some questions unanswered. And, Josh: not only for remarkable research assistance but, more importantly, for teaching me that research without passion is hardly worth the effort.

My editor at NYU Press, Ilene Kalish, has been an enthusiastic supporter since we first discussed this project at the May 2013 New England Political Science Association meeting in Portland, Maine. Pushing me to get a proposal drafted by August, she worked to have it reviewed and a contract offered so that I might have the time and the rigid deadlines necessary to keep me on track. Thanks also to Caelyn Cobb for all of her excellent work in shepherding the manuscript through the publication process. I also thank the editors of *Studies in American Political Development*, *Law & Social Inquiry*, and *Perspectives on Politics* for granting permission to publish materials that appeared in their respective journals. An earlier version of parts of chapter 1 was published as "Developmental Perspectives on Lesbian and Gay Politics: Fragmented Citizenship in a

Fragmented State," *Perspectives on Politics* 13 (June 2015). A much earlier version of a part of chapter 4 was published as "Organizational Identity as a Constraint on Strategic Action: A Comparative Study of Gay and Lesbian Interest Groups," *Studies in American Political Development* 21 (Spring 2007). And, earlier versions of parts of chapter 5 were published as "Frame Spillover: Media Framing and Public Opinion of a Multifaceted LGBT Rights Agenda," *Law & Social Inquiry* 37 (Spring 2013).

Finally, this book would have been impossible without the unflagging love and encouragement of my family. And, because this book is now complete, I can tell my parents that their good Jewish son is ready to find a husband, especially since, as they are so fond of reminding me, our marriage would now be recognized throughout the land.

Introduction

Fragmented Citizens

We're adults, we're contributing to the welfare of society and yet, here's this one thing that just reaches up every year and kind of slaps us in the face.
—Brian Wilpert, on the challenges of filing joint tax returns for same-sex couples[1]

Angie's List is open to all and discriminates against none and we are hugely disappointed in what this bill represents.
—Bill Oesterle, chief executive officer of Angie's List, on his opposition to the Indiana Religious Freedom Restoration Act[2]

Today, hundreds of thousands of children are being raised in same-sex households. . . . Those hundreds of thousands of children don't get the stabilizing structure and the many benefits of marriage.
—Donald Verrilli, solicitor general of the United States, arguing before the Supreme Court, *Obergefell v. Hodges*[3]

The spring of 2015 was, in myriad ways, a disorienting season for gays and lesbians in the United States. Various events reminded us that, even as significant strides toward equal rights for sexual minorities had been achieved and public support for same-sex marriage had hit a record high, our status as equal citizens was hardly consistently recognized.[4] We were (and continue to be) seen differently and unequally depending on who was doing the looking.

This fragmented recognition was brought into stark relief by the springtime ritual of filing taxes. This requirement was "an accounting nightmare for thousands of gay and lesbian couples" because their status as married has been so contingent.[5] Financial services firms, such as Wells Fargo, acknowledge this instability in their marketing to gay and lesbian couples: "You may have taken steps to formalize your domestic partnership where you are, but what if you relocate? The laws that affect your relationship vary from state to state. And, even if you stay where you are, laws constantly change." The advertisement stipulates, "Our future doesn't have to depend on which state we are in."[6] Yet, ironically, Tax Day 2015 indicated the opposite. The material security that same-sex couples can expect depends very much on where they live.

In 2013, when the Supreme Court held in *United States v. Windsor* that the section of the federal Defense of Marriage Act (DOMA) that defined marriage solely as between one man and one woman was unconstitutional, it required the federal government to recognize same-sex marriages where state governments had already done so.[7] In the months after *Windsor* the Internal Revenue Service established that, for federal tax purposes, it would recognize same-sex couples as married if they had first celebrated their marriage in a state where such unions were recognized, i.e., a "place of celebration" standard.[8] However, in the spring of 2015, at least thirteen states did not recognize same-sex marriages; consequently, those states rendered gay or lesbian married couples legal strangers.[9]

These state governments committed a violence of misrecognition and nonrecognition: "there's the insult of filing a legal document that says you're single when you're not."[10] Lesbian, gay, bisexual, and transgender (LGBT) individuals are hardly strangers to the "painful experience of nonrecognition . . . in a heteronormative society."[11] This experience of "social annihilation," as the sociologist Deborah Gould names it, can manifest as feelings of anger, frustration, or sadness, or it may fuel attempts at social change.[12] Either way, it is exposed in the structural variations of governmental recognition and reinforced by a marketplace where financial firms can assist in constructing private architecture that secures against the vagaries of public regulatory acknowledgment. Even after *Windsor*, Wells Fargo responded with an advertisement in the October/November 2013 issue of the LGBT news magazine the *Advocate*. Under the title "Changing Laws Can Change Your Life: Wells Fargo Is Here to Help," the text read,

> Even with the Court's decision [in *Windsor*], a majority of states still have either limited or no recognition of same-sex marriages. This leads to a

"patchwork" approach to equality where each state can determine the rights of LGBT couples under that state's laws. It also raises more questions and requires guidance. Wells Fargo believes it's paramount for ALL LGBT couples to have a team of professionals in place to help them sort through the laws as they currently are, as well as what they will look like in the future. . . . These are people with specific experience who are well-versed in the current set of challenges, along with planning techniques available to help tackle some complexities of existing laws.

By playing on concerns about the instability of recognition, the advertisement explained how private policy architecture can be purchased to create stability for couples and families who have financial means. This possibility carries obvious class implications—those who can afford it can more readily insulate themselves from the pressures of a hostile state—and it triggers concerns about the development of a neoliberal state in which private market transactions replace government-provided services and practices, thereby potentially exacerbating inequalities.[13]

The violence of nonrecognition and misrecognition is emotional and material. In some states where their marriages go unrecognized, same-sex couples had to file up to five separate tax forms. First, for federal taxes, they completed an official joint federal form. Then, for state taxes, they completed but, in some cases, did not file federal and state forms meant to untangle their finances and render them legal strangers. This process yields complicated questions such as how charitable donations are accounted for if the amount is drawn from a joint checking account and, if the couple has children, how they can be recognized as dependents if the couple is considered unmarried in the tax-filing process. These questions are difficult to answer without expert advice, particularly when "[e]ach state can have slightly different rules, but, when asked about them, state employees don't always give consistent answers."[14] Complications are evident in the extra time and expense created. Same-sex married couples "face extra paperwork, heftier tax-prep fees, and tax questions that puzzle even the experts."[15] Exasperation is a prominent response: "There is no way that I, as a Joe Q. Public, who happens to be gay and in a same-gender marriage, would figure out how to file this form out. I mean, it's just impossible."[16]

Tax season is only one instance that illuminates this circumstance of variable recognition. In April 2015, shortly after taxes were filed, the question of whether the Fourteenth Amendment of the United States Constitution requires states to recognize same-sex marriages, and thus whether variable recognition was constitutional, was argued before the Supreme Court in *Obergefell v. Hodges*. At stake were hardly just questions about how one files taxes—although a ruling would certainly clarify that matter—but more fundamental assessments of the balance of state and federal power as well as the state's responsibility to recognize equally all of its citizens. The Court's ruling would clarify a range of rights and responsibilities, including but not limited to parental rights, inheritance, healthcare responsibilities, and survivor benefits rendered unclear by the variable recognition that *Windsor* reinforced.

During oral argument in *Obergefell v. Hodges*, the Supreme Court justices mused on the scope of what was before them. Some were troubled by what they thought they were being asked to consider, to alter the meaning of marriage, an institution that, for Justice Anthony Kennedy, had for "millennia" meant "only heterosexual marriage." This Court was tasked to say something that is "very difficult for the court to say, 'Oh, well, we know better.'"[17] Picking up this argument, Chief Justice John Roberts wondered if ruling in favor of same-sex marriage would do more harm than good because, he remarked to Mary Bonuato, the lawyer representing advocates for same-sex marriage, "If you prevail here, there will be no more debate. . . . [C]losing of debate can close minds." Cautioning that litigating for social change may only inflame public debate, Roberts continued, "and it will have a consequence on how this new institution is accepted. People feel very differently about something if they have a chance to vote on it than if it's imposed on them by the courts."[18]

The irony of the justices' concerns is that they imagined a nation far more divided on marriage equality than public opinion data suggested. Support and institutional recognition proceeded at lightning pace. While majorities had endorsed same-sex-marriage recognition since 2011, a tidal wave of state recognition followed *Windsor*, when state and lower federal judges began to interpret that ruling as invalidating state constitutional bans on marriage recognition.[19] Prior to *Windsor*, twelve states and the District of Columbia recognized same-sex marriage. By the time of oral argument in *Obergefell*, same-sex marriages were recognized in twenty-five more.

But perhaps one of the more dizzying aspects of *Obergefell* as well as of *Windsor* was the prominence of a particular argument in favor of same-sex marriage. Kennedy's ruling for the Court in *Windsor* emphasized how denying same-sex marriage recognition harmed children of same-sex couples. The federal government's refusal to recognize same-sex marriages under DOMA "humiliates tens of thousands of children now being raised by same-sex couples. The law in question makes it even more difficult for the children to understand the integrity and closeness of their own family and its concord with other families in their community and in their daily lives."[20] Kennedy spoke to the material harm government policy inflicted on these children: "DOMA also brings financial harm to children of same-sex couples. It raises the cost of health care for families by taxing health benefits provided by employers to their workers' same-sex spouses. And it denies or reduces benefits allowed to families upon the loss of a spouse and parent, benefits that are an integral part of family security."[21] Kennedy wrote that DOMA "instructs all federal officials, and indeed all persons with whom same-sex couples interact, including their own children, that their marriage is less worthy than the marriages of others."[22]

Solicitor General Douglas Verrilli reiterated this sentiment at oral argument in *Obergefell*. And, Kennedy called opponents of recognition to task. Opponents maintained that expanding marriage recognition beyond opposite-sex couples would undermine the attachment to children. Without the states' commitment to opposite-sex marriage as a unique institution, "men and women would still be getting together and creating children, but they wouldn't be attached to each other in any social institution."[23] But Kennedy contended that this was the exact—and undesirable—situation into which states were compelling same-sex couples with children. Turning the argument on its head, Kennedy contended, "I think the argument cuts against you," for it "assumes that same-sex couples could not have the more noble purpose [of parenting], and that's the whole point."[24] Precisely because the 1970s homophobic campaigns of Anita Bryant, which intended to "Save the Children" from expansion of gay and lesbian rights and which fostered the successful repeal of local ordinances protecting citizens from discrimination on the basis of sexual orientation, are within lived memory, the enlisting of parental rights and the security of children in the service of equality for gays and lesbians is an ironic development.[25]

Supreme Court oral arguments in *Obergefell* came on the heels of public debate that once again raised the question of whether individuals could be legitimately discriminated against on the basis of their sexual orientation. Discussion centered on the passage of a Religious Freedom Restoration Act in Indiana. The law, according to proponents, aimed to protect individuals from being compelled to act contrary to their religious beliefs. But the scope was unclear: would it protect from being forced to provide services to a same-sex wedding or would it enable discrimination against gay, lesbian, bisexual, and transgender persons, and is there a substantive difference between those two questions?[26]

The law was amended, although whether or not the revision ameliorated the prospect of discrimination is open to question, particularly as Indiana has no statute barring discrimination based on sexual orientation or gender identity.[27] Nevertheless, what is remarkable is that public backlash against the Indiana law was spearheaded by the private sector. The most vocal opponents showcased by news media were not state or national gay rights groups but Salesforce.com, whose CEO, Marc Benioff, announced that the company would stop all corporate travel to Indiana, and Angie's List, whose CEO, Bill Oesterle, announced that the company would halt planned expansion in the state. Apple CEO Tim Cook took to the pages of the *Washington Post* to pen an op-ed denouncing the law. The Indiana Chamber of Commerce called the law bad for business, as it "was always going to bring the state unwanted attention." The NCAA, which was holding the finals of the Division I collegiate basketball tournament in Indianapolis, expressed concern.[28] Media showered attention on companies that came out against discrimination, suggesting that the private sector was recognizing the value of LGBT persons far differently and more robustly than public institutions were doing.

These three episodes, all occurring during the spring of 2015, illustrate the variable and contextual meaning of citizenship for LGBT individuals. They reveal how much public opinion has shifted, how much the LGBT rights movements have achieved, and how much remains on the horizon to secure. In particular, they foreground the need to grapple with the way private sector developments affect public or state recognition of the status of LGBT persons. Spring 2015 revealed how much citizenship—that relationship between the individual and state in which the latter acknowledges the former as falling within its responsibility to recognize, protect, and regulate in key sites, e.g., market, military, family, immigration, etc.—is fragmented and contingent for those who identify as gay, lesbian, bisexual, or transgender.

Gay and Lesbian Sexuality, Citizenship Status, and American Political Development

"Citizenship" is not easily defined. The term's multiple meanings create conceptual messiness. Rogers Smith refers to citizenship as "an intellectually puzzling, legally confusing, and politically charged and contested status."[29] Linda Bosniak imposes order by disaggregating the concept into distinct components: (1) enjoyment of rights, (2) legal recognition by a community, (3) social and political engagement, and (4) an identity of belonging.[30] Her definition points to philosophical traditions on which each component draws. Liberal theory focuses on citizenship as conferring rights; civic republicans stress the participatory engagement and sense of belonging to a community that citizenship engenders.[31]

In this book, the citizen is a person subject to the state's sight or recognition, identification, and classification. A citizen is included in and acknowledged by the body politic.[32] Citizenship is not just a legal status of rights but "a claim on the public attention and concern."[33] It connotes a set of power relations in the dynamic between the individual and the governing institution—whether public or private—with which she interacts. To bring focus and emphasis to the centrality of institutional recognition does not replace rights or responsibilities as giving content and meaning to citizenship. It is only to suggest that even if recognition is necessary but not sufficient to establish citizenship, it is prior to any enactment of citizenship status. Recognition connotes dynamics of institutionalized power more than substantive guarantee. It turns the analytical lens away from the rights claimant and toward those institutions that constitute, exercise power over, and enable the citizen.

The actions that give citizenship depth, such as claiming rights or participating in civic life, are not enough to establish citizenship status. These are premised upon and require *recognition* by regulatory authorities. As queer theorist Shane Phelan posits,

Whether an action fosters citizenship depends upon the interplay between the actor and those with and toward whom s/he acts. It is never a matter simply between individuals or even between groups, but is a contest among and within polities concerning the constitution of those polities. . . . Although dissent may be an important vehicle for expressing citizenship, dissent in the face of total rejection is not citizenship but rebellion. Such rebellion becomes citizenship not simply when the rebel claims to be a member of the polity but when the *other* members of that polity *recognize* her as such.[34]

Defining citizenship as grounded in processes of acknowledgment, Phelan writes, "the specific rights and obligations of citizens may vary from state to state, but recognition of members is prerequisite to a claim on any configuration of rights and duties."[35] Citizenship is rendered by "structures of acknowledgment," through which "the polity decides who is eligible" for rights and duties.[36]

This book identifies and examines many such "structures of acknowledgment" with which sexual minorities interact, including administrative agencies, courts, legislatures, executive authorities, and private workplaces. It describes the shifting meanings of gay and lesbian personhood and citizenship by connecting these changes over time to the dynamics and development of different public and private regulatory authorities. Since citizenship is here defined as a relational identity dependent on institutional recognition, I draw on concepts prominent in American political development (APD) scholarship—a field that explores the historical development of institutions, ideas, and processes of the American state—to explain why, even as public opinion shifts to favoring gay and lesbian equality and new rules mandating equal treatment are put into place, inequalities persist.

While citizenship studies has grown,[37] and more of this work overlaps with APD scholarship, particularly with regard to race and gender identity,[38] APD's focus has been elsewhere. According to Suzanne Mettler and Andrew Milstein,

APD research has probed deeply into the processes of state-building and the creation and implementation of specific policies, yet has given little attention to how such development affects the lives of individuals and the ways in which they relate to government. . . . APD scholars, being deeply engaged in questions about institutional development and historical processes, are well equipped to illuminate much about the relationship between citizens and government. The problem is that, to date, they have largely refrained from doing so.[39]

Studying sexuality goes some way toward filling this research gap. The political development of gay and lesbian politics in the United States is important and ought to receive more attention, especially as "some skepticism about its legitimacy and scholarly worth" troublingly persists among political scientists.[40] Such attention would shed light upon more general dynamics of American political development.

Equality and inclusion within the political community as a recognized citizen, much less a recognized person, for any member of a discriminated-against group, has hardly followed a smooth trajectory. Despite myths of progress and rhetoric of how the arc of history bends in the United States, institutional and policy obstacles undermine constitutional ideals. In addition, achieving equal treatment is not only a matter of changing opinions, beliefs, or attitudes. As Rogers Smith expressed, when describing the persistent history of racism and gender bias, "these beliefs were not merely emotional prejudices or 'attitudes.' Over time, American intellectual and political elites elaborated distinctive justifications for these ascriptive systems. . . . Many adherents of ascriptive Americanist outlooks insisted that the nation's political and economic structures should formally reflect natural and cultural inequalities, even at the cost of violating doctrines of universal rights."[41] Generalizing the assessment, Joseph Lowndes, Julie Novkov, and Dorian Warren contend that we limit our understanding of inequality—its sources and the possibility of policy remedies—when we consider it only as an artifact of attitudes.[42]

So, in this book, I do not seek to examine why public opinion toward gay and lesbian rights concerns—decriminalization, marriage, military service, adoption rights, employment and housing protections—has turned favorable in recent years or to question its necessary if not sufficient role in explaining successes of gay rights activism. Instead, I hope not only to show how, given the institutional design of federalism, the dynamics of incomplete political change, and the diverse issues that comprise the contemporary gay rights aims, the citizenship status of gays and lesbians varies across space, time, and issue but also to account for how inequalities persist despite opinion change and despite active attempts and successful alterations in policy and formal rules and statutes that guarantee equal treatment. Doing so, I argue, requires that we shift focus when recounting the dynamics of gay and lesbian politics, from individual rights to institutional recognitions.

My objective to trace changes in the regulatory recognition of gay and lesbian status is animated by two questions, one substantive and one disciplinary. The first: how and why do inequalities for gay and lesbian citizens persist even as formal rules mandating equal treatment are put into effect? The second: what would a political developmental approach to gay and lesbian politics look like and what insights might it provide that are different from those that follow from growing research in history, sociology, economics, and other, particularly behavioral, branches of political science?

TABLE 1.1. Variation in Laws Affecting LGB Persons (as of November 1, 2014)[43]

State	Nondiscrimination Employment Law	Same-Sex Marriage	Joint/Step Adoption
Alaska	No	Yes	Status Undefined
Arizona	No	Yes	Status Undefined
California	Yes	Yes	Yes
Colorado	Yes	Yes	Yes
Connecticut	Yes	Yes	Yes
Delaware	Yes	Yes	Yes
DC	Yes	Yes	Yes
Hawaii	Yes	Yes	Yes
Idaho	No	Yes	Yes
Illinois	Yes	Yes	Yes
Indiana	No	Yes	Yes
Iowa	Yes	Yes	Yes
Kansas	No	Yes	Status Undefined
Maine	Yes	Yes	Status Undefined
Maryland	Yes	Yes	Yes
Massachusetts	Yes	Yes	Yes
Minnesota	Yes	Yes	Yes
Montana	No	Yes	Step/Joint Undefined

Some of the inequalities experienced by gay and lesbian citizens—made evident by the difficulties in tax filing, the ongoing litigation for marriage recognition, and the continued development and implementation of state laws with potential discriminatory effects—can be accounted for by the institutional design of federalism, which is unlikely to produce a common approach to any statutory concern.[44] And, on a range of contemporary concerns, including but not limited to nondiscrimination in employment, adoption access and parental rights, and marriage recognition, the states form a patchwork of dissimilar status across space (see table 1.1).

Nevertheless, this policy variation is not only a consequence of federalism. Rather, as this book aims to show, it stems from the very processes of political change itself. My argument rests on a conception

TABLE 1.1 (*cont.*)

State	Nondiscrimination Employment Law	Same-Sex Marriage	Joint/Step Adoption
Nevada	Yes	Yes	Yes
New Hampshire	Yes	Yes	Yes
New Jersey	Yes	Yes	Yes
New Mexico	Yes	Yes	Status Undefined
New York	Yes	Yes	Yes
North Carolina	*No*	*Yes*	*Obstacles*
Oklahoma	*No*	*Yes*	*Status Undefined*
Oregon	Yes	Yes	Yes
Pennsylvania	*No*	*Yes*	*Step/Not Joint*
Rhode Island	Yes	Yes	Yes
South Carolina	*No*	*Yes*	*Status Undefined*
Utah	*No*	*Yes*	*Yes*
Virginia	*No*	*Yes*	*Status Undefined*
Washington	Yes	Yes	Yes
West Virginia	*No*	*Yes*	*Status Undefined*
Wisconsin	Yes	Yes	Obstacles
Wyoming	*No*	*Yes*	*Status Undefined*

In the fourteen italicized states, getting married—and thus outing oneself as gay or lesbian—could threaten employment, as there are no statutory protections from discrimination on the basis of sexual orientation in those states. All other states not listed do not currently recognize same-sex marriage and do not protect from discrimination in hiring, firing, or promotion in employment.

of the polity offered by APD scholars, particularly Karen Orren and Stephen Skowronek. They describe the normal condition of the polity as fractured, with different policies adopted at different times such that unexpected and unforeseen frictions may arise: "the institutions of a polity are not created all at once, in accordance with a single ordering principle; they are created instead at different times, in light of different experiences, and often for quite contrary purposes."[45] As new policies are layered upon those in place, the juxtaposition and lack of integration creates the "interplay of multiple institutions [which is] a source of both tensions and opportunities."[46] Consequently, attempts to establish equality often expose or foster previously unseen inequities. From this friction-inducing dynamic spring opportunities, which entrepreneurial actors may seize to push for policy, legal, and institutional innovation.[47] Politics is constituted by the interaction of multiple regulatory authorities, constructed at different times and potentially overlapping and conflicting with one another. These authorities are implicated and engaged in the definition of fundamental human attributes and relationships, including sexuality. If they exist in tension, then we might expect the definitions and recognitions they offer to similarly be in tension.

Developmental scholarship also highlights patterns that enable empirical analysis and normative recommendation. Certain regularities emerge over time. By focusing on patterns, APD scholars "locate the key components of a situation and demarcating them helps to identify meaningful points of change."[48] Consequently, "pattern identification is the sine qua non of the enterprise."[49]

These two concepts—the polity as multiple governing authorities in tension and patterns of political change that pinpoint meaningful shifts in political practices, ideas, laws, or institutions—are employed in this book to evaluate changes in the recognized personhood and citizenship status of gay and lesbian Americans since the late nineteenth century.[50] Given the polity's qualities of fragmentation, its acknowledgment or recognition of persons and citizens is likely not to be all at once or of a piece. Rather, as Phelan contends, "we may, then, expect to see that exclusions at certain points coexist with cautious inclusions at some other sites and comfortable equality at yet others."[51] This book provides a developmental accounting of institutional recognitions of gay and lesbian status to illustrate the rendering of fragmented citizenship.

A developmental approach to gay and lesbian politics aims to consider how attention to sexuality as an ordering concern of governance and regulation enriches our explanations of institutional change, partisan behavior, policy development, and state-society interaction. The payoff is at least twofold. First, developmental conceptions of political change can account for the persistence of inequalities in ways that enrich traditional answers, which tend to emphasize the interplay of movement push and countermovement pushback.[52] Second, a developmental approach compels rethinking about citizenship, what it connotes and how it is determined. If the developmental polity is always bound in internal tension among distinct and potentially incongruent governing authorities and if these governing authorities confer recognition upon individuals that gives their citizenship meaning and content, then different governing authorities may offer differing forms of recognition. Consequently, a developmental account of gay and lesbian politics offers a conception of citizenship that is hardly whole. Despite rhetoric of progress toward a constitutionally whole citizen, that ideal is fragmented by the dynamics of political change itself. Citizenship, precisely because it is a relational concept that depends upon the recognition of others, is always negotiated and challenged; its boundaries shift, and change is hardly unidirectional. Citizenship is fractured and fragmented by dynamics that define development of the polity.

A Developmental Approach to Gay and Lesbian Citizenship: Why Now? Why Needed?

When politics scholar Tim Cook assessed the status of gay and lesbian studies in political science for the *American Political Science Review*, he drew attention to an appreciable deficit. During the 1980s and 1990s, when scholars across the humanities and social sciences built a field that asked new questions, uncovered hidden histories, and provided pathways across stifling disciplinary boundaries, "political science was notably absent."[53] Over a decade later the landscape has changed. In a 2012 assessment for the *Annual Review of Political Science*, Richard Valelly noted the transformation. Where Cook had heard silence, Valelly now heard an "exceptionally sophisticated conversation" of "cutting-edge work" in fields as varied as social movement studies, public opinion studies, and analyses of judicial politics.[54] This intellectual development took place despite concerns that research on lesbian, gay, bisexual, transgender, and queer identities remains problematically at the margins of political inquiry.[55] In this context, Valelly noted a silence. Far too little scholarship on LGBT politics evaluates links between sexuality and state development or has employed an APD perspective. As he saw it,

> APD has largely neglected both LGBT politics and the parallel back-lash . . . the silence of APD on the subject of sexuality politics is noticeable. Since they began publishing in the late 1980s, the two leading journals associated with APD, *Studies in American Political Development* and the *Journal of Policy History*, have published fewer articles on LGBT politics (e.g., Bell 2010, Engel 2007) than other leading political science journals.[56]

Other scholars share Valelly's assessment. Dara Strolovitch has contended that social scientists increasingly conceptualize identities as multiple, contextual, and fluid, such that they are "dynamic, simultaneous, and mutually constitutive."[57] Nevertheless, she argues that attention to intersectional identities and the politics of marginalization, particularly along racial, ethnic, and gender lines, has only recently characterized research in American political development.[58] Similarly, while acknowledging that "a small group of scholars has worked in recent years to consider LGBT issues as they relate to politics, public opinion, and the state," Julie Novkov writes that "scholars have not yet produced a full historical institutional analysis of the relationship between LGBT identity and the state comparable to the literature on the relationship between processes of racialization and the state. As in studies of race and the state, we must distinguish between discriminatory individual attitudes (however deeply and structurally embedded) and institutionalized structures of subordination and control."[59]

Exposing this need for research begs a set of questions. What would a political development approach to and account of sexuality politics in the United States look like? What would its unit of analysis be? What kind of data would be gathered? And what methods would be utilized to evaluate that data? Is there an existing literature in APD that already studies sexualities but that we might not see as doing so? There is now an extensive normative and empirical literature on queer citizenship and a large sociological literature on LGBT movements, and the history of sexuality is, according to eminent historian David Halperin, finally "a respectable academic discipline."[60] Does this scholarship not qualify as APD and, if not, why not? How might APD studies of sexuality be different from the burgeoning sexuality studies in history, sociology, law, normative theory, political behavior, etc.? How might sexuality studies cue off APD explorations of race, ethnicity, and gender, be distinct from such approaches, and intersect with them? Why is an explicitly developmental account of sexuality politics needed, and how would it contribute to developing insight into mechanisms of change of interest to historical scholars, e.g., path dependence, institutional/policy layering, drift, feedback, etc.?

This book tries to answer these questions. It provides a framework within which to explore how regulatory authorities in the United States recognized gay and lesbian sexuality, how that recognition has changed over time, and how distinct modalities of recognition by different governing authorities have fractured the status of gays and lesbians across space, over time, and by issue. It draws attention to pattern identification as a central principle of APD scholarship. And, it rests on the core definition of the polity that development scholars endorse—the polity as comprised of multiple governing authorities in tension—to reveal insights into changing content and meaning of personhood and citizenship status for gays and lesbians. Attending to how distinct modalities of recognition operate through distinct orders of governance can reveal why, even as formal rules of equality for gays and lesbians are established, inequalities persist and unseen challenges to equality come to the fore.

Chapter Overview

This book details the way public and private regulatory authorities have defined lesbian and gay personhood and citizenship status over time. It explores citizenship as a relational status conferred in the recognition of the individual by regulatory authorities. By using this definition, coupled with a developmental approach to politics, it aims to explain how inequalities persist for lesbian and gay citizens even as formal rules banning discrimination and indicators of public support for equality have increased. It develops an account of gay citizenship as constructed, fragmented, contingent, contextual, and temporally and spatially unstable. It does not offer a comprehensive history of gay, lesbian, and bisexual rights mobilization, and it is not about the rise and life of these movements in the United States. Instead, it identifies distinct modalities through which governing authorities have defined homosexuality over time and examines episodes of regulatory, legal, and policy congruence and incongruence among these authorities to illustrate the ongoing fragmented status of gay and lesbian Americans. By shifting analytical focus from rights mobilization to recognition of status, it aims to provide an intervention in political developmental scholarship to promote and value the study of sexualities.

Chapter 1 provides more detailed discussion of central concepts in developmental scholarship—pattern development, governing orders in tension, and path dependency—as frameworks for conceptualizing change over time in institutional recognitions of gay and lesbian status. It begins by articulating why reconceptualizing citizenship as grounded in recognition rather than rights and/or responsibilities is a necessary move for a developmental study. Grappling with the way governing regulatory authorities may define citizenship differently across time, space, and issue—how they may see an individual distinctly depending on temporal, spatial, and issue contexts—will foster a richer notion of citizenship, one that views citizenship as more than a status that protects natural or liberal rights or confers republican responsibilities.

Chapter 2 examines varieties of same-sex intimacies prior to the political construction and recognition of the modern homosexual person. Paying particular attention to the administrative state as a site of recognition, it points to evaluations of immigration and civil service policy that illustrate how identifying and excluding homosexuals from the United States encouraged the growth of administrative state capacities. The chapter draws attention to Progressive Era (1880–1920s) concerns with sexual otherness expressed in the private and public sectors, an otherness inextricably bound with extant discourses and assumptions of gender and racial inferiorities. It integrates Progressive fears of sexual otherness and aberrant gender presentation within a broader project that included scientific racism, eugenics, and democratic institution building to cultivate a particular national community and democratic citizen. It details the policy shifts taken to move from homosexual sodomy as a criminal act toward establishing a generally consistent form of recognition of the homosexual as a dangerous person threatening to healthy civic growth and national security.

Chapter 3 describes the tensions that emerged when gays and lesbians began to define themselves and to be seen as an unjustly persecuted minority. This transition is borne out in dissent within the early homophile organizations as to whether to frame homosexuality as analogous to race, such that remedies against discrimination would require active state intervention, or to frame homosexuality as a private act, such that the primary remedy would be decriminalization and thus call for existing beyond the purview of state regulation altogether. And, this new recognition of discrimination and of a clearly defined minority class was reflected back from institutional authorities as varied as the Supreme Court, municipal governments, and the human resource policies of private sector firms.

Chapter 4 examines how two national LGBT interest organizations—the National LGBTQ Task Force and the Human Rights Campaign—premised their work on the recognition of gays and lesbians as a distinct persecuted minority group. That identity underlay different strategies for social change, and the tactics employed created distinct organizational identities. This chapter focuses on that organizational self-definition, and it assesses the way reputations—or the way these groups have identified themselves and are seen by others—constrain and enable strategies and abilities to secure political and legal reform. A particular organizational identity may conform or clash with the regulatory recognition offered by state and private institutions. Conformity may enable more incremental shifts toward some LGBT equality claims. Clashes or misfits between organizational identity and regulatory recognition may not foster immediate or incremental change, but may serve long-term aims of establishing foundations for a regulatory recognition not yet widely adopted. Consequently, congruence between regulatory recognition and self-definition may undermine more expansive aims of social change.

Chapter 5 explores simultaneous trends in public opinion, public policy, and jurisprudential development at the end of the twentieth century that supported the privatization and closeting of gays and lesbians. It begins with a discussion of patterns in public opinion that illustrate support for gay rights when they are conceptualized within a framework of private liberty but opposition when those rights are considered as a matter of public recognition and equality. It examines how television news media framings of these rights claims exhibit similar patterns. The chapter then evaluates federal statutes and Supreme Court rulings that parallel and reinforce this privatization and closeting imperative. These policies and rulings reveal a refusal to see LGBT citizens at all. While no longer criminalized, these citizens were left beyond the boundaries of state recognition.

Chapter 6 examines how the recognition that gays and lesbians constitute an unjustly discriminated-against minority, which is an element of the jurisprudential doctrine of suspect class and tiered scrutiny, has been used by executive officials and state and federal judges from the mid-1990s through the present day to promote same-sex marriage. Recognition of a history of discrimination and political powerlessness are two characteristics that comprise suspect-class status and the corresponding tiered-scrutiny doctrine, which has been developed by the Supreme Court over the latter half of the twentieth century. That doctrine is a central vehicle through which the Court has recognized discrimination, promoted equal protection against racial and sexual discrimination, and defined its own role in reenforcing pluralist democracy.

Chapter 7 examines the Supreme Court's refusal to recognize gays and lesbians as a suspect class or discriminated-against minority within the parameters of its tiered-scrutiny doctrine even as it has decriminalized homosexual conduct, ruled against state-based discrimination against gays, lesbians, and bisexuals, and required federal and state recognition of same-sex marriages. Those victories for gay rights rest on an emerging doctrine of human dignity that, while perhaps rhetorically appealing, fosters an abstract notion of liberty blind to social, political, and historical contexts. This doctrine may supplant the tiered-scrutiny doctrine, which was historically premised on the Court's responsibility to recognize and counter actively the deficiencies of majoritarian democracy that rendered minorities oppressed and voiceless. Recognition of suspect-class status, of a deeply contextualized history of discrimination and political powerlessness, has given way to an abstract and ill-defined notion of "dignity" as the foundation for gay rights claims. Nowhere is this more clearly stated than in the Court's ruling in *Obergefell* that the Constitution's guarantee of due process liberty requires all states to recognize same-sex marriages. And yet, this amorphous concept of dignity may provide only limited support as gay and lesbian rights move beyond marriage recognition and may sharpen clashes with others who claim that antigay stances fall within their own guarantees of dignity.

The conclusion begins by assessing the contemporary status of policies affecting gay and lesbian equality. Prior to 2014, two distinct regimes of recognition were evident. One group of states had established policies protecting gays, lesbians, and bisexuals (and, to a lesser extent, transgender individuals) from workplace, housing, and other forms of discrimination and creating stable relationship and familial recognition. Another set had tended to offer none of these protections. Yet, as state bans on same-sex-marriage recognition have failed to withstand judicial review since *Windsor*, states have been compelled to recognize same-sex marriage even as they do not provide other protections from discrimination. The Court's ruling in *Obergefell*—which nationalizes marriage equality—only reinforces the instability of status for gays and lesbians since their recognized marital status may leave them vulnerable to discrimination grounded in their sexual identity. The fragmented status of lesbian and gay citizens continues, and the incoherence of variable recognitions is further revealed. Finally, the chapter summarizes the themes and main contention of this book: Examining gay and lesbian politics from a developmental perspective yields insights not only into how state development and social construction of sexuality overlap and interlock but also into how tracing distinct modalities of regulatory recognition of sexuality across distinct sites of authority illustrates developmental claims about the nature of political change as not comprehensive, creating unexpected results, and often not moving in a singularly progressive direction.

This book sketches one developmental account of gay and lesbian status and politics. By drawing attention to the fragmented nature of the polity as its normal condition, the book enables not only fuller examination of the persistence of inequalities but also clearer understanding that the condition of gays and lesbians is fragmented. If citizenship is neither only a comprehensive bundle of rights nor a set of participatory responsibilities but is first constituted by processes of recognition, and if the polity is not stable but is always in tension across multiple institutional sites of authority, then citizenship, as an institutionally granted status, is perhaps just as temporally and spatially contingent and unstable as the polity itself. In short, the fragmented state creates a fragmented citizen. This may be at least one important insight gained by greater attention to sexuality, particularly gay and lesbian sexualities, from a developmental point of view.

1

From Individual Rights to Institutional Recognitions

Toward a Developmental Account of Gay and Lesbian Politics

There is no notion more central in politics than citizenship,
and none more variable in history, or contested in theory.
—Judith N. Shklar, *American Citizenship: The Quest for
Inclusion*, 1991[1]

The institutions of a polity are not created or recreated all
at once, in accordance with a single ordering principle; they
are created instead at different times, in the light of different experiences, and often for quite contrary purposes. . . .
[P]olitics in the United States, like politics elsewhere, con-
sists, in large part at least, in acting out the consequences.
—Karen Orren and Stephen Skowronek, *The Search for
American Political Development*, 2004[2]

LGBT rights are often described and pursued in ways parallel to historical and ongoing struggles for African American civil rights, labor
rights, and women's rights.[3] Such comparisons are drawn in our most
prominent exemplars of civic rhetoric. For example, in his 2012 inaugural address, President Barack Obama stamped the LGBT movement
with the legitimating imprimatur of the civil rights and women's rights
movements that preceded it:

> We, the people, declare today that the most evident of truths—that all
> of us are created equal—is the star that guides us still; just as it guided
> our forebears through Seneca Falls, and Selma, and Stonewall; just as it
> guided all those men and women, sung and unsung, who left footprints
> along this great Mall, to hear a preacher say that we cannot walk alone; to

hear a King proclaim that our individual freedom is inextricably bound to the freedom of every soul on Earth.[4]

By folding the LGBT rights movements into the canon of a national narrative of progress toward yet-unrealized constitutional ideals, Obama embraced a dynamic pluralist vision of democracy. And, his reference to Stonewall—a Greenwich Village gay bar where a multiday riot sparked the modern gay rights movement—would hardly go unnoticed.[5] Media commentators lighted upon it as groundbreaking, a moment when the LGBT rights movement was acknowledged as legitimate, included within the pantheon of the rights struggles at the heart of civic identity, and vital to the realization of liberty and equality.[6]

Since the concept of rights, as a liberal ideal and rhetorical touchstone, is so central to U.S. civic identity, it is hardly surprising that contemporary LGBT movement actors frame their purpose as securing rights or that they define equal citizenship in terms of rights.[7] From Frank Kameny's first organized picket outside the White House in 1965, in which a group of civil servants fired for their homosexuality carried banners proclaiming "Homosexuals Are American Citizens, Too" to today's most well-funded LGBT interest group in the United States, the Human Rights Campaign, which defines itself as "working for lesbian, gay, bisexual, and transgender equal rights," prominent actors—although not all[8]—within these communities have conceived of citizenship as made manifest in rights and of access to rights as indicating inclusion within the civic community.[9]

Even as LGBT rights can be fitted to a pattern of progressive rights attainment, "American political development offers no clear historical trajectory, no inevitable march of rights, no irresistible triumphs of rights and freedom."[10] Law, politics, and policy do not just recognize rights already naturally held by persons; rather, bureaucrats, policymakers, lawyers, and private regulatory authorities such as human resource managers are active agents in shaping the way individuals' identities are recognized and thus in determining the rights that they can access. Such determination is the result of deliberative and contested dynamics of regulatory recognition, and this recognition does not occur at a steady pace or in a single direction. Consequently, inequalities can be built anew or "novel intellectual, political, and legal systems reinforcing racial, ethnic, or gender [or sexuality] inequalities might be rebuilt in America in the years ahead."[11] The state sees and sexualizes its citizens in changing ways over time. Rights are, as an empirical matter, a regulatory construct, hardly stable, hardly perpetual, and always subject to negotiation.

This chapter lays the foundation for a developmental accounting of gay and lesbian politics by shifting the analytical focus from rights claims to institutional recognitions of sexual identities. Redirecting attention from rights claims to differential statuses afforded by regulatory recognition calls attention to the need to examine the way institutional and ideational contexts defining the meaning of gay and lesbian personhood and citizenship have varied over time and across space. The chapter makes sense of this differential recognition by state and private regulatory authorities by drawing on the developmental notion of the polity as made up of multiple, conflicting governing orders. Ultimately, the chapter demonstrates how different governing authorities may adopt distinct modalities simultaneously, thereby creating a fragmented identity, an identity that has different implications for rights claims and civic responsibilities depending on what institution is doing the looking. It utilizes two cases to illustrate this idea: first, Department of Defense efforts to treat soldiers equally, which have grated against other orders of authority concerning family and marital recognition, employment, and religious expression; and second, emerging tensions between marriage recognition and parental recognition.

From Rights to Recognition as the Cornerstone of Citizenship

Rights discourse in contemporary LGBT mobilization draws on two American political traditions. First, one route to sociopolitical and legal reforms runs through the courtroom, and rights talk is the language of litigation.[12] Second, citizenship claims are often articulated through rights discourse because natural rights are central to the liberalism that defines many aspects of American political culture.[13] This discourse calls to mind T. H. Marshall's classic conception of citizenship as a network of mutually constitutive rights. Those who have rights are citizens; those who do not are not. Once one is a citizen, she holds all the rights and responsibilities that all other citizens are recognized to have.[14]

Inclusion in the polity as citizen, by this logic, necessarily makes one equal to all other citizens.

Adding nuance to this conception, Elizabeth Cohen evaluates citizenship's "constitutive elements," which form a "braid of citizenship rights" that need to be "unbundled" to be assessed fully.[15] She contends that the rights of citizens are not only "independent of, rather than contingent upon, each other" but also that such "independently justified rights can be granted in differentiated bundles," giving rise to various types of what she terms "semi-citizenship."[16] Different individuals can have distinct bundles of rights, and thus semi-citizenship can take distinct form depending on the content of the particular bundle granted. Gays and lesbians in the United States, because they may have some rights—they are not criminalized—but lack others—they are not always protected against workplace discrimination on the basis of sexual orientation or gender identity—are semi-citizens.[17]

The concept of rights captures only one way of thinking about citizenship. Beyond the boundaries of the Anglo-American tradition, movements for LGBT equality need not only be framed by referencing rights. For example, in the late 1990s and early 2000s, the debate in France over the creation of the Pacte Civil de Solidarité (PaCS), which established state recognition of any coupling of French citizens regardless of sexual orientation or even romantic status, occurred almost entirely within the bounds of cultural reference to republicanism. French republicanism, with its emphasis on common claims to national identity and compulsion to reject particularistic affiliations, is antithetical to the identity politics that has defined American struggles for racial, cultural, ethnic, and sexual equal rights.[18] Yet, advocates and opponents of the PaCS relied on *republican* tropes to bolster their arguments.[19]

This republican concept of the citizen "integrate[s] the demands of liberal justice and community membership."[20] It emphasizes responsibilities to the democratic community and often relies on either the cultivation of civic virtue or participation in public deliberation to bolster the liberal emphasis on individual right.[21] Judith Shklar rejects the republican participatory model of the ideal citizen since it is an insufficient metric by which to evaluate the historical evolution and contemporary meanings of citizenship: "Whatever the ideological gratifications that the mnemonic evocation of an original and pure citizenry may have, it is unconvincing and ultimately an uninteresting flight from politics if it disregards the history and present actualities of our institutions."[22] Shklar's efforts to historicize citizenship remind us to account for the way citizenship depends on political context and the way that context has changed over time. Tying the meanings and changing configurations of sexual identities—as act, person, and citizen—to the development of state and private regulatory infrastructure is the main objective of this book.

Calling attention to that context shifts the operative focus of citizenship from the individual claiming citizenship to the set of institutions that recognize or confer citizenship status. As Iris Marion Young reminds us, the citizen is constituted by another's gaze and is therefore always in danger of being marked as less than equal: "While the subject desires recognition as human, capable of activity, full of hope and possibility, she receives from the dominant culture only the judgment that she is different, marked, or inferior."[23] Similarly, for Shane Phelan, these others are within the community and yet not recognized as part of that community. Phelan refers to such individuals—and she includes LGBT persons in this category—as strangers who "trouble the border between us and them" precisely because they may have rights in certain contexts and when recognized as occupying certain identities but not have access to rights in other contexts or when their LGBT identity is invoked.[24]

Recognition need not require approval of one's political perspectives or ideas, but it does, for Phelan, demand "an affirmation of one's place in a political community."[25] Citizenship is the status that indicates how one has been rendered not only equal to others in a politico-legal context but how one has been rendered equally legible. It derives from the gaze of public institutions as well as from the recognition offered by private authorities. Examination of private regulatory infrastructure is necessary to produce a fuller sense of the way inclusion within the community of citizens is fostered, especially in the United States, where so many basic welfare rights are provided by private corporate institutions and not by the state.[26] Furthermore, as Shklar reminds us, citizenship is constituted also in the marketplace: "Modern citizenship is not confined to political activities and concerns. . . . It is in the marketplace, in production and commerce, in the world of work in all its forms, and in voluntary associations that the American citizen finds his social place, his standing, the approbation of his fellows, and possibly some of his self-respect."[27] Some conceptions of modern citizenship are deeply grounded in this idea of the citizen as earner (and as consumer).[28] Again, Shklar notes, "This vision of economic independence, of self-directed 'earning,' as the ethical basis of democratic citizenship took the place of an outmoded notion of public virtue, and it has retained a powerful appeal. We are citizens only if we 'earn.'"[29] LGBT individuals are not fully free to engage in free labor. In a majority of states, they are vulnerable to being fired for nothing more than their sexual orientation or gender identity, as no federal law bars such discrimination. Given what Shklar calls "the intimate bond between earning and citizenship" in the United States, LGBT persons remain outside the inclusive scope of Shklar's conception of citizenship.[30]

Redirecting attention from the individual making the rights claim to the governing authority doing the regulatory recognition can bring analysis of citizenship into fuller conversation with some of the ideas that undergird the study of American political development. Political development scholars define the polity as fractured, with different policies adopted at different times such that unexpected and unforeseen frictions may continuously arise. Such fragmentation is a consequence of the way the polity is constructed: piecemeal, over time, and without grand design. Given the polity's qualities of fragmentation and internal institutional and ideational tensions, extensions of acknowledgment by the polity, or the way a person or citizen may be recognized in full dimension, are likely not to be all at once or of a piece. Rather, as Phelan contends, "we may, then, expect to see that exclusions at certain points coexist with cautious inclusions at some other sites and comfortable equality at yet others."[31]

Any institution—whether public or private—that governs the individual over his life cycle must make the individual legible, and therefore it must develop laws, policies, norms, and rules that define the individual's identity as well as establish its relationship to that individual and her identity.[32] Sexuality, particularly same-sex intimacy, has hardly been singularly recognized and defined. Contemporary understandings of homosexuality, which identify, first, a particular class of people who exhibit congruence between biological sex and sexual desire for an individual of the same biological sex and, second, an act that might be performed regardless of any innate orientation, do not capture the myriad forms of homosexualities evident throughout history. David Halperin contends that sexual identity suffers from a definitional incoherence, which has developed due to "accumulation, accretion, and overlay" of functionally distinct kinds of homosexualities that were more or less prominent at particular times.[33] And, as Eve Kosofsky Sedgwick suggests, sexuality is neither innate and unchanging nor constructed at one moment, but defined and redefined in different ways over time.[34]

The idea of such redefinition grounds the pattern of five distinct modalities of recognition explored in this book. Public and private regulatory authorities in the United States have defined and seen sexual minorities since the late nineteenth century as (1) a threat to national community; (2) individuals who commit homosexual acts, which can endanger national security and moral health; (3) people subject to unjust discrimination; (4) a group decriminalized but otherwise privatized and beyond state recognition; and (5) persons dignified through the public and equal recognition of intimate relations once considered morally and physically dangerous. This pattern of modalities is not meant to be fully inclusive of various forms of homosexualities that exist at any one time. It does, however, name distinct dispositions that a given regulatory authority might maintain toward homosexuality at a particular time. Accordingly, these modalities represent boundaries of meaning that constitute homosexuality. These modalities may be thought of as certain settlements of norms or ideas about what lesbian and gay personhood means and entails. Identifying multiple modalities is meant to indicate not only that there is change over time as old prejudices give way but also that different modalities can operate simultaneously in different governing orders, thereby rendering the experience and identity of a gay individual fundamentally fractured across space and issue.

These modalities do not constitute a periodization schema. They capture the way a particular regulatory authority might recognize and define a gay or lesbian person over time as well as across space and issue. Governance does not necessarily wholly shift from one modality to another in an ordered pattern. At any moment, different state and private regulatory authorities may exhibit the disposition of distinct modalities. And, to the extent that there might exist different forms of same-sex intimacy, as historians of sexuality suggest, rather than a unitary modern homosexual personage, different regulatory authorities are implicated in the recognition and indeed construction of those varieties. The challenge, of course, is not only to identify these modalities and their consequences on the contours of political development but also to trace the deliberate processes of how new ideas about homosexuality, new forms of regulatory recognition, are created, voiced, and accepted, if not necessarily wholly displacing alternative modalities. Entrepreneurship and political creativity of various kinds are central to this dynamic.[35]

The Queer Potential of American Political Development

Research in American political development seeks to explain change over long swaths of time. As Orren and Skowronek have characterized this objective, "because a polity in all its different parts is constructed historically, over time, the nature and prospects of any single part will be best understood within the long course of political formation."[36] In addition, this scholarly tradition challenges the so-called iconography of order, or the assumption that political science should aim to explain institutionalized regularities or engage in what Robert Lieberman characterizes as "a quest to find synchronous patterns—equilibria—in political life, [which] often leaves political scientists scratching their heads when asked to account for political change."[37] To explain change, APD scholarship relaxes the assumption that the state is a composite of stable, orderly institutions and regularized behaviors.[38] Instead, the state is made of multiple orders of authority where each order is "a durable mode of organizing and exercising political power . . . with distinct institutions, policies, and discourses."[39] These orders include laws, policies, norms, and discourses that regulate government interaction between church and state, familial relations, or employee-employer dynamics.[40] Each order displays an internal consistency or "a regular, predictable, and interconnected pattern of institutional and ideological arrangements that structures political life in a given place at a given time."[41] Multiple orders existing simultaneously suggest the possibility of "tension or complementarity among patterns that might more plausibly drive the dynamics of political development."[42] Since multiple orders make up the polity, there is no reason to assume that all orders are congruent, are compatible, or fit together in a coherent fashion.

As Desmond King and Rogers Smith define them, institutional orders are "coalitions of state institutions and other political actors and organizations that seek to secure and exercise power in demographically, economically and ideologically structured contexts that define the range of opportunities open to political actors."[43] King and Smith limit discussion to racial orders in which "political actors have adopted (and often adapted) racial concepts, commitments, and aims in order to help bind together their coalitions and structure governing institutions that express and serve the interests of their architects."[44] We might, on this model, conceptualize sexuality orders whereby political institutional rules and actors' behaviors are evidence of a particular view about lesbian, gay, and bisexual sexuality, e.g., as a criminal act only, as a permitted act only, or as a marker of an unjustly discriminated-against class, etc. Such distinct views would constitute different regulatory recognitions, i.e., modalities, and institutional practices with subsequent implications for whether and how institutions acknowledge and maintain lesbian, gay, and bisexual personhood and citizenship status.

The view of a polity as multiple-orders-in-tension arises from the nature of political change, policy innovation, and legal development. First, political arrangements are never set out comprehensively; institutional design is never on a clean slate.[45] New policies are layered upon those already in place. That layering may create unexpected interactions and outcomes.[46] Second, when new policies are set up, they reflect ideas, assumptions, and aspirations of their designers, who may be long since dead, and those policies may produce outcomes antithetical to current ideas, assumptions, and aspirations. If not altered, these policies may drift in directions that do not necessarily cause dysfunction but may serve aims antithetical to original intent.[47]

Consequently, much APD scholarship eschews any functionalist account of institutional design altogether: "Institution-building is disjointed and historically contingent on preexisting relationships, producing historical lags in which, contrary to the expectations of rational choice scholars, the rules and structures of a governing body will reflect multiple layers of interests that diffuse political power in unexpected ways."[48] These multiple orders—these various internally coherent patterns of ideas, assumptions, and institution—clash with one another as each is developed at different times and for different reasons. Political change occurs because the political system—a system of multiple clashing orders—is, by definition, never at equilibrium, and actor intent cannot be taken as congruent with policy or institutional outcome.

APD is not all of a piece even as there are certain topics—administrative state development, policy development, public law—and concepts—path dependence,[49] displacement, feedback loops,[50] layering of new policies upon existing ones,[51] drift,[52] entrepreneurial actors[53]—that unify the research agenda. If APD has a central organizing purpose, it is that it uncovers "the historical construction of politics."[54] According to Orren and Skowronek, "the study of American political development is a substantive inquiry guided by a theoretical precept. The substantive inquiry covers the full range of politics in the United States. . . . The theoretical precept is this: because the polity in all its different parts is constructed historically, over time, the nature and prospects of any single part will be best understood within the long course of political development."[55] Thus, the goal of a developmental account of gay and lesbian politics would be not only to say something about lesbian and gay politics—although it should be that—but also, perhaps more importantly, to suggest that we learn something new and interesting about the polity more broadly—about its institutions, practices, and interactive dynamics between the public and private—when we approach it through the lens of sexuality.

Just as APD scholars have paid increasing attention to identity categories such as race, ethnicity, sex, and gender, their work has not only or even primarily offered insights about identity-based organizing nor have they treated identity as static, constant, or given. This research has illustrated how, by using these categories as a lens, a richer understanding of political change can come into view. For example, Naomi Murakawa's evaluation of the backlash thesis, which views the racialization of law-and-order rhetoric in the 1960s as a response to urban riots and ideology of black power, exemplifies identity-based developmental scholarship. By considering race as an organizing principle of politics—as the lens through which to comprehend strategic political decision making—Murakawa illustrates that the conventional wisdom has the core dynamic backwards: "the U.S. did not confront a crime problem that was then racialized; it confronted a race problem that was then criminalized."[56]

Generalizing this point and drawing on insights from critical race theory,[57] Paul Frymer suggests that racism is not merely "an 'attitude'" grounded in "individual factors such as the racist actor's feelings of resentment and insecurity" but instead an organizing principle of political development.[58] Its logics of domination are embedded in the rules, norms, and institutions that not only incentivize strategic behavior but also frame the options available for rational actors to consider. Similarly, Michael Dawson and Cathy Cohen point to the need to examine "social processes that racialize, categorize, and constrain the life opportunities of different groupings of people in this country. . . . Ignored are the historical and social contexts through which the complicated processes of racialization and categorization utilized in this country have developed and evolved."[59]

In taking developmental studies of race as a model for developmental accounts of sexuality, the objective, to be clear, is not to insert sexuality as a static category for race. Nor does highlighting these studies as a model seek to draw a facile analogy among race, sex, and sexual orientation. When we consider whether and how developmental conceptions of the dynamic, constitutive, and discursive practices of race can be applied to sexuality, it must be maintained not only that the histories of race-based and sexuality-based domination are profoundly different but also that racial and sexuality identities can be embodied in wholly distinct ways. On the first point, queer theory warns against the essentializing of queer identities in the way that racial and ethnic minority-rights models might foster. According to Michael Warner, queer cultures are "not autochthonous," nor can they be considered "even in diaspora, having no locale from which to wander"; as a result, "queer politics does not obey the member/nonmember logics of race and gender."[60] On the second point, sexuality, sex, race, and ethnicity are embodied in distinct ways, in part because some of these identities may be more easily hidden, covered, or disclosed than others.[61]

With this caveat in mind, a developmental approach to the intersection of race with state bureaucratic and policy development, which has revealed new insights into patterns of domination and resistance to state and social power, should be brought to bear on sexuality. Furthermore, treating these identities as wholly separate would undermine necessary attention to the intersectional nature of racial, gender, sexual, and other identity categories. The main point remains that APD has studied racial identities in ways distinct from behavioral political science, particularly in its conception of identity categories as themselves changing over time rather than constituting a given, static, independent variable that might affect a range of dependent variables.[62] There are no obvious reasons why the political construction of sexuality cannot be explored in ways that are similar.

Considering sexuality foundational to institutional and ideational development, rather than treating gays and lesbians as a minority class that wins or loses public support, legislative battles, or legal rulings, tracks a similar impulse in queer studies. In his discussion of how to constitute a queer theory that challenges the extant heteronormativity of social theory, Michael Warner warns against "simply call[ing] for the inclusion of lesbians and gays into a theory that would remain otherwise unaltered."[63] This call to disrupt established forms, to highlight antithetical purposes, and to read politics through identity categories rather than treat identities as concrete forms whose behavior can be observed, tested, and explained is wholly congruent with APD's critique of established approaches and assumptions of political science generally.

Drawing out parallels between queer theory and APD, Dara Strolovich argues that APD's conceptions of time resonate with queer theory's approach to temporality.[64] She contends that queer destabilization of norms, concepts, and rules carries "a sensation of asynchrony" that brings forth "a set of possibilities produced out of temporal and historical difference."[65] Insofar as APD challenges the central tenets of political science by focusing on change rather than equilibrium, by viewing institutions as instigating friction rather than stability, and by treating timelines as multiple, overlapping, and cyclical rather than linear, developmental conceptions of politics, in a sense, queer political inquiry.[66] The developmental definition of the polity as fractured, fragmented, and fundamentally unstable is queer insofar as it challenges disciplinary assumptions and opens possibilities for reconceptualizing the concepts of time, institutional design, and agency. Consequently, the potential for queering politics is hardly as foreign to APD as it might seem at first glance.

How the Normal Condition of the Polity Fragments the Citizen

Even as sexuality rests at the core of personal identity, multiple state and private institutions have played an influential role in constructing and managing the meanings of sexuality. As a result, Orren and Skowronek's definition of the polity as composed of "multiple orders, mutually impinging institutional arrangements and different patterns of change" is particularly useful for thinking about the state's multiple points of contact with and regulation of sexuality.[67] Nevertheless, there are reasons to be skeptical of a developmental approach, and these challenges must be overcome for the animating project of this book to make any sense. If a political development is, as Orren and Skowronek define it, a "durable shift in governing authority," then perhaps the pace of change on LGBT rights is simply too fast and as yet incomplete to register as a durable shift.[68] As Rick Valelly suggests, "LGBT politics may seem to be evolving so rapidly that it is too difficult to perceive and pick out the outcomes, periods, and dynamics that are 'in' that politics."[69]

Arguments against a developmental conception of sexuality politics are premised upon three claims. First, LGBT politics are best conceptualized as they have been to this point: as a politics of social movement and interest organization action. Second, APD research is singularly about state capacity and state institutional change. Third, developmental scholarship—particularly in its attempts to demarcate patterns over time—should continue to divide time into identifiable periods such as party systems, electoral realignments, presidential regimes, judicial regimes, etc.[70] The approach adopted here calls into question each of these claims by (1) reorienting the unit of analysis from movement to person and citizen, (2) broadening the focus of APD into private institutional capacities and powers, and (3) drawing attention to the concept of orders-in-tension as potentially more useful than the concept of regimes or periods.

Insofar as the study of LGBT politics has centered on movement development, strategy, and tactics, an APD approach would seem misguided by definition. According to Orren and Skowronek, social movements are, by definition, not the focus of a developmental study: "The point is not to exclude . . . social movements . . . from their role *in* political development or to deny economic and cultural changes as important influences *on* political development. It is to locate development and nondevelopment as it occurs, to identify changes and continuities in an ongoing organization of authority."[71] In other words, the movement is not the development; it is a means to a policy or legal reform. The policy change is the development; the policy is the manifestation of the durable shift in governing authority. A movement is a tool, not an outcome.

Second, APD scholarship has often examined *state* development, and the durable shifts of interest are those that manifest as "exercise of control over persons or things that is designated and enforceable by the state."[72] Such state-centeredness blinds us to the dynamics and forms of power experienced by gays and lesbians. Elizabeth Armstrong and Mary Bernstein contend that a more robust understanding of power as multisited avoids mischaracterizing gay rights mobilization, which has often viewed the state as not its sole or even its primary target. They contend that power is "anchored in a variety of institutions, including the state. The importance of the state is neither denied nor assumed *a priori*, but is seen as depending upon cultural and historical context."[73] At certain times, the state may be the primary source of domination; however, at other times or in other contexts, nonstate institutions—medicine, science, religion, education, private-sector corporations—may be a primary source of control over citizens' lives. Indeed, given that people's needs and interactions with state and private power shift over the life cycle, i.e., as adult, parental, marital, and employment status changes over time, LGBT citizens' interactions with distinct fields and sources of power, recognition, rights, and domination will also be temporally and spatially contextual.[74]

Third, those APD scholars who have studied gay and lesbian politics have tended to take "regime" as a central organizing concept. A regime is a distinct period of coherent ideas, policies, laws, and institutionalized practices that operate across the polity until wholly replaced or significantly altered. Regimes may not be fully hegemonic; they include within them voices of contestation, but they are comprehensive until wholly disrupted.[75] For example, in one of the most influential studies of the intersection of American political development and homosexuality to date, Margot Canaday bifurcates her analysis into two overarching policy regimes: what she calls an era of "nascent policing" (1890s–1930s), or learning to identify, categorize, and exclude the homosexual, and a later period of "explicit regulation" (1940s–1980s) that is the culmination of this learning process in a clear regulatory regime of homosexual oppression.[76]

Valelly's more recent call to bring sexuality within APD research seems to, at least tacitly, utilize the concept of regime to illustrate how what he calls "straight government" was built and dismantled.[77] His argument rests on the notion that identity is a "contingent and historically evolving construct." He describes how, through distinct federal policies, a government premised on excluding homosexuals from full participation in the civic community was built. According to Valelly, executive, congressional, and bureaucratic action coalesced around a set of policies implemented during the mid-twentieth century that "allocated public stigma and esteem according to sexual orientation," which "influenced state and local policies" as well as "attitudes, behavior, and organizational practices in labor and housing markets, education, and medicine (including psychiatry)."[78] For Valelly, the twentieth century is divided into a period marked by the creation of a comprehensive sexuality regime that identified, stigmatized, and excluded homosexuality from the body politic, and by efforts of LGBT activists since about midcentury to challenge and dismantle this regime, all while building foundations for a new, more inclusive regime.

The regime concept implies a unity of approach, motivation, and outcome across policy and institutional space. However, given the institutionalized dynamics of separation of powers and federalism in the United States, such unity would seem theoretically and empirically unsound. It is far more likely that the polity would be marked by variation and policy incongruities across space and not simply over time.

Therefore, in proposing a developmental approach to the politics of sexuality, I make three conceptual moves. First, taking seriously Orren and Skowronek's definition of what constitutes a development, I shift the unit of analysis from a focus on LGBT movement or movement community to a more explicit focus on individual status as person and/or citizen. Second, to avoid the state-centeredness inherent in many APD studies, I focus on regulatory power more broadly, which can be wielded by state and private institutions. Third, to highlight that ideas, assumptions, discourses, and objectives animating these institutions may coalesce around distinct views of gay sexuality, the conception of the polity as comprised of multiple orders in tension, each potentially operating with a distinct modality of recognizing homosexuality, is applied. This conception is far less unitary than the notion of regime.

As discussed in the introduction, citizenship links the individual to the state and can, if conceptualized as constructed through regulatory recognition, direct analytic focus to the state as one source of power over that individual. As homosexuality has been defined differently over time—as sex act, as personhood, or as person entitled to rights and recognition as citizen—approaching sexuality from this micro level as a changing definition of status helps pinpoint the way different authorities may engage the distinct meanings. Furthermore, since citizenship is a relationship between the individual and state in which the latter acknowledges the former as falling within its responsibility to protect and regulate through key sites, e.g., market, military, family, immigration, etc., it functions as an analytical vehicle to link the individual to state development.[79] A developmental approach to the citizen highlights how that status—defined not only as a set of legal rights conferred by the state but also as a status of visibility that "can be delivered [by the state] in different degrees of permanence or strength"—is imagined and built by the state as part of the state's own construction.[80]

In addition, examining a variety of institutionalized powers beyond the state accomplishes two objectives. First, it brings private regulatory authorities into the analysis. As Cohen notes in her study of semicitizenship, "Administrative rationality may be the province of the state in contemporary politics, but it applies to any political institution charged with governing a population."[81] While Cohen envisions a possible shift from the nation-state as the primary organizing apparatus of citizenship recognition, such projection is not necessary. In the United States, nonstate authorities also regulate citizens' lives. Access to healthcare, life insurance, and other resources of family care are often provided by private employment. These private regulatory authorities should be examined as to how they shape recognition of gay and lesbian persons and citizens as well as how those recognitions interact with, confound, or supplant similar or oppositional state or public policies.

APD scholars have pushed in this direction. Jacob Hacker recommends greater attention to the private sector when accounting for policy changes: "institutionalist analyses must examine the evolution and effects of private as well as government institutions. . . . [I]nstitutionalists need to become even more self-consciously historical in their analyses of politics, and to broaden their inquiries to consider the constraints that the development of private market institutions create for public policy making."[82] While Hacker offered this assessment when evaluating healthcare policy, parallels to other policy arenas, like human resource benefits, including nondiscrimination policies in hiring, firing, promotion, partner health insurance policies, and leave policies to care for loved ones, can be drawn and examined. Since the arc of policy development in the United States, as Hacker has shown, relies upon private-sector provisions and recognitions to disburse healthcare, we can and should consider how other private-sector policies affect the meaning and experience of citizenship, at least to the extent that they promote or inhibit the realization of rights or, indeed, construct parallel institutions that mimic the consequences and security of state sanctioning.

Second, a conception of power as multisited positions each institution, law, or policy as a site of power to be studied. These sites could offer different modalities of recognition simultaneously. Armstrong and Bernstein's multisited conception of power is synchronous with Orren and Skowronek's characterization of the polity as layered and incongruous institutions, policies, and laws, but it also compels us to consider nonstate institutions as sources of authority and recognition of citizens. So, focusing on power rather than the state per se reorients APD toward a broader definition of institutionalized power, which includes but is not limited to the state. And, disaggregating these sites helps to illustrate their potential tension with one another, particularly in the way they recognize LGBT citizens. Each order might engage a distinct modality of recognition, and the consequent tension produces opportunities for political change. The central insight remains: as the polity is made of multiple orders, "changing any aspect of politics entails bumping against authority already in existence."[83]

Developmental Insights into Gay and Lesbian Politics and Law: Persistent Inequalities in Military Policy and Marriage and Family Recognition

The two case studies that follow explore institutions—the military and marriage—rather than examine mobilization for individual rights to military access or marriage recognition, in order to illustrate how different notions or recognitions of citizenship are embedded in different state projects and how those diverse notions can clash, yielding unstable statuses for gays, lesbians, and bisexuals. These two cases were selected for a variety of reasons. First, gay and lesbian interest groups have advocated for military access and marriage equality since the 1990s.[84] Second, the military is one of the primary institutions not only by which state development is measured but also with which citizens directly interact; access and participation within it is one of the key ways in which citizenship is marked and/or conferred.[85] Similarly, despite popular rhetoric and legal discourse framing marriage as a fundamental right, civil marriage, since the late nineteenth century, has functioned as a classificatory tool through which state regulatory authorities define the boundaries and parameters of citizenship. Those whom the state deems capable of marriage not only gain access to rights and benefits but also acquire responsibilities to make and maintain civil community through their marriage.[86] Marriage is not just a right afforded to those considered full citizens; it is an institutionalized regulatory policy through which the state classifies, tracks, and produces citizens. Third, the way marriage and military regulations construct citizen identity as well as the way that regulatory recognition reciprocally often demands further development of each of the two institutions has been a topic of recent interest to many American political development scholars.[87] Finally, the two ideas this book works with—citizenship as a relational and recognized status between the state and the individual and the polity as multiple potentially clashing orders of authority that fracture that status such that it can take on different content across space, time, and issue—are both illustrated by recent developments in military policy and marriage recognition. These two policy areas reveal persistent and previously unseen inequalities even as formal rules of equality in military service are established; they provide useful illustrations of APD principles.

Military Policy

On June 9, 2015, in a speech marking the Department of Defense's celebration of LGBT Pride Month, Secretary of Defense Ash Carter said, "we must start from a position of inclusivity, not exclusivity. Anything less is not just plain wrong; it's bad defense policy, and puts our future strength at risk."[88] The sentiment, similar in tone and intent to Obama's reference to Stonewall in his 2012 inaugural address discussed earlier, was that diversity is a source of strength and that inclusion within the community of full and equal citizens was a necessary goal of the U.S. military. Like so much that occurred in the spring of 2015, this speech was dizzying if only because it marked the abrupt shift from earlier policies and tones on gays' and lesbians' ability to serve openly—policies and rhetoric grounded in the necessity of exclusion.

The strict ban on gays in the military was lifted in 1993 via presidential executive order, and a new policy of silence known as Don't Ask, Don't Tell, Don't Pursue, Don't Harass (DADT) was adopted. Within the pattern of modalities discussed above, DADT reflected a fourth modality of regulatory recognition of gays and lesbians—decriminalized but held from public view—which was a stance all three federal branches would take during the following ten years, and which is further discussed in chapter 5. This policy, which Congress passed into law in 1994, was heavily criticized and ultimately lost public support.[89] It was abolished by congressional statute in 2010.[90] New formal equality of access to service clashed with existing federal marriage law—the Defense of Marriage Act (DOMA)—such that gays and lesbians with spouses were not eligible for various benefits afforded their straight counterparts. The Department of Defense (DoD) developed policies to circumvent DOMA. Ultimately, these workarounds were rendered moot when the Supreme Court struck down the operative section of DOMA in 2013 by its ruling in *United States v. Windsor*.[91] Nevertheless, new inequities continued to emerge. First, some states refused to disburse benefits to same-sex military couples. Second, gay and lesbian soldiers have been deemed ineligible for other services. Despite formal rules of equality being established since 2010, previously unseen challenges to equality have come to the fore. APD's notion of the polity as clashing orders helps to explain why.

When DADT was repealed, new questions arose regarding services that the military provides to these soldiers' partners. As the federal government, under DOMA, did not recognize same-sex marriage, same-sex partners of military personnel did not receive increased housing allowances allotted to their heterosexual counterparts; they did not receive dependent identification cards, so partners faced hurdles to visitation in hospitals; and, they were not entitled to survivor benefits if the service member was killed in action.[92] The military provided services to the families of straight service members, but the move toward equality in one order (military regulation) brought to the surface new inequities given the persistence of and interaction with an established order (marriage regulation) that had not been altered concurrently.

The Office of Personnel Management issued a new rule on July 20, 2012, to go into effect on August 20, 2012, that would resolve some of this tension. The office issued "final regulations to establish that an employee's same-sex domestic partner qualifies as a family member for purposes of eligibility for non-competitive appointment based on overseas employment. The intended effect of this regulation is to ensure that same-sex domestic partners are treated as family members."[93] Nevertheless, due to DOMA, full military benefits extended to the opposite-sex spouses of service members cannot be extended to the same-sex spouses of service members.

On February 13, 2013, the DoD released a memo detailing that an extensive review of benefits provided to the married spouses of service members had been undertaken and that the department would provide same-sex partners a set of benefits including but not limited to dependent ID cards, commissary privileges, exchange privileges, morale, welfare, and recreation programs, surveys of military families, emergency leave, youth programs, family center programs, joint duty assignments, exemption from hostile-fire areas, child care, and legal assistance. The memo asserts,

> At the direction of the President, the Department has conducted a careful and deliberative review of benefits currently provided to the families of Service members. We have now identified additional family member and dependent benefits that we can lawfully provide to same-sex domestic partners of Military Service members and their children through changes in Department of Defense policies and regulations.

These benefits would be extended no later than August 31, 2013. While the memo does not make clear how and why these new recognitions are not in tension with DOMA (although the distinction probably relies on the difference between benefits and statutorily enforced entitlements),[94] it does indicate that full equality is precluded by DOMA: "Additional benefits, such as health care and housing allowances, are by statute currently only available to spouses and therefore cannot be made available to same-sex domestic partners of Service members under current law."[95]

In other words, the memo put into clear policy language the tensions that result when change is not comprehensive at a single moment. Nevertheless, the memo holds out the prospect for bringing the marriage order and the military-access order into alignment through the possible repeal of DOMA: "In the event that the Defense of Marriage Act is no longer applicable to the Department of Defense, it will be the policy of the Department to construe the words 'spouse' and 'marriage' without regard to sexual orientation, and married couples, irrespective of sexual orientation, and their dependents, will be granted full military benefits." Furthermore, the memo stipulates that the tension between marriage and military access may continue even if DOMA is repealed because of state laws and constitutional amendments banning same-sex unions of any kind. It therefore acknowledges that potential problem and highlights an intent to solve it: "In addition, the benefits of changes directed by this memorandum will be re-assessed at that time [when "the Defense of Marriage Act is no longer applicable to the Department of Defense"] to determine whether other changes are needed or appropriate, to include whether unmarried same-sex domestic partnerships should be a basis for eligibility for benefits in the future."[96]

The challenges confronted by the military in its efforts to provide spousal and familial recognition for all service members up to the limits of and, perhaps, in spite of DOMA—in the words of then Secretary of Defense Leon Panetta, to "best to ensure that all Service members are treated equally regardless of sexual orientation"[97]—are responses to what Orren and Skowronek call "the normal condition of the polity," which "will be that of multiple, incongruous authorities operating simultaneously."[98] And, these tensions have hardly been resolved by the *Windsor* ruling. The DoD has interpreted that decision as requiring that all military spousal benefits be extended to same-sex married couples. In a memo released on August 13, 2013, Secretary of Defense Chuck Hagel "welcomes the Supreme Court's recent decision declaring section 3 of the Defense of Marriage Act, which prevented Federal recognition of same-sex marriages, to be unconstitutional." And, he detailed that the DoD would develop new rules so that "all spousal and family benefits, including identification cards, will be made available to all same-sex spouses no later than September 3, 2013."[99]

Even with this policy in place, military couples serving on bases in states with constitutional bans on same-sex marriage faced difficulty accessing the federal benefits. In October 2013, Hagel, responding to pressure from Congress, publicly specified that states taking such action violated federal law.[100] Separately, the Pentagon indicated that these states included Texas, Indiana, Georgia, Florida, Mississippi, Louisiana, Oklahoma, South Carolina, and West Virginia.[101] Some governors maintained that extending benefits would violate their own state constitutional bans on same-sex marriage. Therefore, service members seeking to apply for benefits would have to travel to federal installations to do so; state-maintained bases would not process these benefits.[102] Just as the February memo predicted, the institutionalized fragmentation created by federalism maintained policy incongruities as the older marriage regime was not fully displaced by the *Windsor* ruling. Rather, the newer variable regime of diverse forms of state-based relationship recognition was only further entrenched.

To meet this resistance to the military's attempts to treat all soldiers equally, the military paradoxically enabled what historian Peggy Pascoe called "geographies of evasion."[103] In her study of interracial marriage bans in the United States, Pascoe noted how interracial couples seeking to wed would travel to states with no such ban, marry, and return home hoping that norms of reciprocal marriage recognition—that marriages valid in one state would be treated as valid in others—would compel the home state to recognize the marriage. Pascoe documented how, during World War II, various authorities, including the Red Cross and the Catholic Church, supported this evasion of home state law by funding interracial military couples to travel to states without bans so that they could marry and wives could henceforth be eligible for benefits should husbands be killed in action. After the war, the military reinforced this geography of evasion.[104] The NAACP advised interracial couples that "the present policy of the Department [of the Army] calls for arrangements of such transfers [to bases in northern states without interracial marriage bans] in situations like yours."[105]

Similarly, the DoD, prior to the *Obergefell* ruling, had not directly dealt with states that refused to disburse benefits to same-sex married military couples. Despite calls by members of Congress that the DoD take direct action against these states, the DoD has instead accommodated a geography of evasion. First, in Texas this challenge was overcome when the Pentagon agreed to send federal officials and equipment to state military installations to process benefits requests. Since no Texas state officials would be involved, they could not be held liable for a constitutional violation.[106] In Oklahoma, the state stopped disbursing benefits to all military spouses, whether gay, lesbian, or straight, forcing all service members to apply for those benefits at federal facilities. Oklahoma governor Mary Fallin defended the new policy of blanket nonrecognition: "The state of Oklahoma does not recognize same-sex marriages, nor does it confer marriage benefits to same-sex couples. The decision reached today allows the National Guard to obey Oklahoma law without violating federal rules or policies."[107] Different forms of political creativity within the law are at play when state actors seek to maintain the established modality of regulatory recognition of LGBT citizens.[108]

And, even these policies circumventing recalcitrant states did not solve the problem; more policy innovation was necessary. The August 2013 memo recognized that same-sex couples stationed in states where marriage was not recognized "would have to travel to another jurisdiction to marry" in order to attain federal recognition.[109] The DoD maintains a "place of celebration" standard, but the places where same-sex marriage could be celebrated could be a significant distance from a base where an LGB soldier was stationed. Therefore, because *Windsor* did not compel state recognition of same-sex marriage, because the Obama administration has sought to provide access to federal rights and benefits to as many same-sex couples as possible, and because the DoD has maintained a celebration standard, the military altered its leave policy. On September 4, 2013, the under secretary of defense clarified how long an administrative absence to obtain a marriage license could be. Recognizing that LGB soldiers might be stationed at bases in states where a marriage license could not be obtained, the memo outlined a new policy whereby

the Secretary concerned may grant an administrative absence to a Service member who is part of a couple that desires to get married, but is assigned to a duty station located more than 100 miles from a U.S. state, the

District of Columbia, or other jurisdiction that allows couples to marry. When two service members are part of a couple and desire to get married, both members may be granted an administrative absence, if qualified.[110]

The policy allows for administrative absences to be up to seven days for a service member living in the continental United States, and up to ten days outside the continental United States. The policy responds to the current patchwork state of marriage recognition. It creates a differential leave policy to meet existing circumstances as allowed and created by *Windsor* to maintain "the Department's policy to treat all military personnel equally and to make the same benefits available to all qualified members."[111] In short, the new leave policy accommodates if not encourages the geographies of evasion that same-sex couples must endure given the variable marriage-recognition regime as permitted by *Windsor*. While it meets the needs of individual soldiers trapped in a regulatory recognition regime that creates inequalities rather than resolves them, it also highlights how some form of resolution is ultimately necessary.

Even as gay, lesbian, and bisexual military personnel with married partners have come to expect equal treatment in terms of access to spousal and familial benefits and support programs, they encounter unexpected challenges due to the maintenance not only of the older order of limited marriage recognition but also older orders of employment regulation. For example, the U.S. Army offers spousal counseling through its Chaplain Corps. This corps is a multifaith chaplaincy established in the late eighteenth century and tasked with attending to the spiritual needs of all soldiers.[112] It offers a program known as Strong Bonds, which the U.S. Army describes as

> a unit-based, chaplain-led program which assists commanders in building individual resiliency by strengthening the Army Family. The core mission of the Strong Bonds program is to increase individual Soldier and Family member readiness through relationship education and skills training. Strong Bonds is conducted in an offsite retreat format in order to maximize the training effect. The retreat or "get away" provides a fun, safe, and secure environment in which to address the impact of relocations, deployments, and military lifestyle stressors.[113]

A married lesbian couple, one recognized by the Department of Defense following the *Windsor* ruling as fully qualified to receive spousal benefits, was denied entry into the Strong Bonds program.[114] The couple was considered ineligible due to their sexual orientation. The Chaplaincy Corps operates under constraint of religious authorities from Baptist and Roman Catholic faiths, both of which have announced that ordained chaplains of those faiths would lose their endorsements should they in any way recognize same-sex marriage as legitimate.[115] Therefore, an older regime of religious authority grates against a newer regime of marriage recognition.

Some former military chaplains drafted and published commentary so that these abrasions may be navigated and so that counsel may be given to chaplains on how best to proceed in the wake of DADT's repeal.[116] Chaplain and Major General Douglas Carver, the Twenty-second Army chief of chaplains, considers the repeal of DADT to be broadly representative of the way "the American church stands at the crossroads today perhaps unlike any other generation of Christians in recent history. An increasing tension exists between the church and the culture."[117] This particular volume of commentary assessing the repeal of DADT and the way the military chaplains should respond begins with the statement, "Religious liberty is under attack in America today," and contends that "opponents of homosexual service saw DADT as just the initial step in an all-out assault upon traditional values, and were concerned that it would eventuate in open service of homosexuals."[118] Yet, despite this claim that DADT's repeal violates First Amendment protections of free speech or free exercise, the chaplains admit that this position is unsustainable:

> This argument, while raising legitimate areas of concern for dialogue and debate, is somewhat premature, since the mere presence of homosexuals in the military does not, in itself, constitute a violation of anyone's free speech. The repeal would have to entail some sort of regulation of speech regarding homosexuality, and it does not. Further, legal arguments can only be brought if there is harm, and none exists as yet.[119]

The DADT repeal in no way, at present, forces the chaplaincy to condone homosexuality, despite various concerns voiced by chaplains prior to the repeal.

Access to the Strong Bonds counseling program creates a particular clash of equality versus liberty that is of concern to some within the chaplaincy. Some fear that they could face disciplinary action or lawsuits should they refuse to minister to lesbian or gay couples in this program of marriage-enrichment retreats.[120] For some chaplains, the repeal presaged an attempt by the Obama administration to draft policies "that will result in discharge of Christian Chaplains and troops who cannot 'reconcile' with homosexual sin."[121] Others have dismissed this accusation as "misleading," "unfounded" and a "smoke screen."[122] Laing advises that the chaplains move forward by denying the legitimacy of homosexuality as a public identity that needs to be expressed, or even recognized, thereby raising the religious-expression claim to a higher position in the balancing.[123] But, this tension between religious expression and LGBT rights claims represents more than a philosophical debate between religious liberty and equal rights, as it is so often presented as being.[124] The tension stems not only from a clash between religious order and a newer marital order; it also embodies tensions between a newer marital order and established regulations and policies governing employment.

Despite the repeal of Don't Ask, Don't Tell, gay, lesbian, and bisexual soldiers were not protected by federal law from discrimination. Employment policy within the Department of Defense, which follows federal employment regulation, did not explicitly protect military personnel against discrimination based on sexual orientation; civilian personnel have been protected by the terms of a Department of Defense directive issued in February 2009.[125] In June 2015, Secretary of Defense Carter announced that sexual orientation would be included in the Military Equal Opportunity policy, "ensuring that the department, like the rest of the federal government, treats sexual-orientation-based discrimination the same way it treats discrimination based on race, religion, color, sex, age, and national origin."[126] Of course, the federal policy, as an executive order, is subject to revision or repeal by the next president, and the way this new military policy interacts with claims to free religious exercise by military chaplains remains unclear. In short, through 2015, gay, lesbian, and bisexual military personnel were recognized as married and eligible for some spousal benefits but went unrecognized and ineligible for others due to the frictions created by the layering upon and interaction among multiple orders of regulation: marriage, access, religion, and employment. The polity as multiple incongruent orders resulting from partial and incomplete change and the consequent abrasion between new and existing laws, regulations, policies, and customs is fully evident.

Marriage Recognition

Conceptualizing the polity as multiple orders in tension highlights the clashes and negotiation, the struggles over redefinition, and the rearrangement of priorities and ideas that all come with new policy. The many institutions that comprise the polity are hardly synchronous, and entrenched interests battle new changes at every turn. Not only will new conceptions of citizenship be confronted by countermovements but also, and here is a key point, the regulatory institutions that recognize and define citizenship may operate with different conceptions of citizenship. If the polity is institutionally fragmented and in a continuous state of internal tension, and citizenship is grounded in the recognition that these distinct and probably incongruent institutions might offer, then citizenship itself is likely to be fragmented.

Nowhere is this fragmented status more fully evident than in contemporary marriage recognition. As Michael Warner suggests, when he warns against "speak[ing] of inclusion as if it were synonymous with equality and freedom," the expansion of marriage to include gays and lesbians should be construed not only as the expansion of rights but more as the expansion of state *power*, particularly the power to recognize, construct, define, and limit its citizenry in ever-changing ways.[127] Civil marriage, since the late nineteenth century, has been a tool through which the state defines the boundaries and parameters of citizenship.[128] At stake is not only a right to marry but also a change in status, a status conferred and regulated by the state.

Marriage policy, prior to *Obergefell*, exemplified the policy diversity that can flourish in a federalist system. According to William Eskridge and Darren Spedale, "a regime where different states take different legal stances toward same-sex marriages is where we are heading, and such a regime easily fits within the American tradition of diverse state definitions of marriage."[129] The Supreme Court's ruling in *United States v. Windsor* reinforced this variation. It allowed for full-same-sex-marriage states, non-same-sex-marriage states, and a few state policies of partial recognition, e.g., civil union states such as Colorado or Oregon and limited-domestic-partnership states such as Wisconsin. This situation triggered more questions. For example, if a same-sex couple were married in New York (where the marriage is recognized) but transferred by an employer to Texas or North Carolina (where it is not), would that couple retain federal rights but lose state rights?[130] What if a couple simply decided to move from New York City to Denver? Theoretically, the state of Colorado would recognize the couple's marriage as a civil union, but how would the federal government recognize it?

After the Court ruled in *Windsor*, President Obama directed the Department of Justice to assess the ruling's consequences for a range of federal policy areas. In summarizing the federal government's response in the year since *Windsor*, Attorney General Eric Holder noted that most federal agencies had moved to a standard that would enable federal marriage rights and benefits to apply to citizens married in states that recognize such marriages even if they did not reside in those states. This rule is known as a place-of-celebration standard. While a number of federal agencies already used this standard, others used a place-of-residency standard, such that you were married only if the state in which you currently lived recognized you as such.[131] And, a year out, Holder noted that the move toward a place-of-celebration standard has increased access to more rights:

> The impact of the *Windsor* decision, and the government-wide implementation efforts, cannot be overstated. The Internal Revenue Service [now] permits same-sex couples to file joint tax returns. The Department of Defense permits same-sex spouses of military service members to receive the same benefits as opposite-sex spouses. Our immigration system permits citizens and lawful permanent residents to sponsor same-sex spouses for immigration benefits. And the Department of Justice will recognize the validity of same-sex marriages in courtrooms and proceedings in which its lawyers appear to the greatest extent under the law.[132]

Yet, while these moves had been made, the attempts to implement the *Windsor* ruling via a celebration standard so that the federal government may "recognize lawful same-sex marriages as broadly as possible" exposed persistent barriers to equality.[133] In particular, the Social Security Administration and the Department of Veterans Affairs were banned by statute from utilizing a place-of-celebration standard. Marriage-related benefits conferred by both federal agencies had been "based on the law of the state in which the married couple resides or resided."[134] Accordingly, *Windsor*, in permitting a patchwork of recognition and bolstering the way marital status could shift from state to state, exposed institutions of inequality that derive from the two distinct standards of marital recognition as either celebration or residency.[135]

In addition, as *Windsor* remained agnostic on how states might recognize same-sex couples via policies distinct from cross-sex civil marriage, e.g., civil unions and limited domestic partnerships, the persistent challenge is that no federal civil union law exists. On July 8, 2013, the Obama administration declared that same-sex couples with civil unions remain excluded from federal marriage recognition.[136] However, the Social Security Administration (SSA) has indicated that if the state civil union law permits recognition of the partner as eligible to inherit on the same terms as a married spouse would be, then the SSA will act similarly for federal inheritance tax purposes.[137]

The administration's move to refuse federal recognition of civil unions, while strategically supportive of full marriage recognition, fostered inequities. Consider the hypothetical couple that moved from New York City to Denver. This couple remained married in the eyes of the federal government even as their New York marriage was now viewed by the state of Colorado as a civil union. However, what of their friends who had a civil union in Colorado? This second couple's relationship went unrecognized by the federal government (at least until they could travel to a state with marriage recognition and get a marriage license for that state, which may entail a variety of material burdens). And, what of situations in states, like Vermont, Connecticut, and New Jersey, that have had civil unions for a few years and then established same-sex marriage by state judicial decision? Are the civil unions maintained, or are they automatically converted into marriages to be recognized by state and federal governments? Civil unions are not necessarily automatically recognized as marriages. Rather, as of January 2014, citizens with civil unions have to apply for a marriage license in order to be married in the eyes of both the state and the federal government, thereby placing upon them the financial burden of applying for two licenses (first the civil union and then the marriage license).[138]

This diversity, as Holder's memo indicated, is not just an artifact of federalism. The fallout of *Windsor* highlights the diversity of rules among many federal agencies that confer rights and benefits. And, it exposes the variation in powers that govern these rules in terms of both who has authority to alter them and by what processes they are altered. The variation illustrates not only the vertical federalist relation between the states and the federal government but also the horizontal separation-of-powers dynamic that constrains the abilities of the respective branches to act unilaterally. In short, the *Windsor* ruling cast a bright light on the extent to which the federal administrative state remains a patchwork:

> Federal agencies are not moving in lock step. Instead, they are creating a *patchwork* of regulations affecting gay and lesbian couples. . . . Medicare and Treasury officials have said they would use a "place of celebration" standard for determining whether gay couples are eligible for benefits. That means same-sex couples would receive benefits as long as they are legally married, regardless of where they live. But the Social Security Administration is now using a "place of residence" standard in determining spousal benefits, and a gay couple in Alabama might not receive the same benefits as a gay couple in New York until final determinations are made or Congress acts.[139]

Partial change, rather than comprehensive reform, resulting in patchwork policies is an important dynamic of political development.[140] The state—the composite of regulatory authorities that define and recognize the meaning and content of citizenship—is hardly unified in its regulatory vision. The federal structure of U.S. governance is unlikely to produce a singular regulatory recognition of LGBT citizens. And, such variation is a consequence not only of federal design but also of the dynamics of political change itself, which is never comprehensive and always "proceeds on a site, a prior political ground of practices, rules, leaders, and ideas," that is never fully displaced.[141] New policies are layered upon those already in place, creating potential for unexpected and unintended outcomes.

The unanticipated effects of this layering are evident in clashes between recognizing same-sex marriage and recognizing parental rights of a same-sex couple. At oral arguments in *Windsor* the justices and some amicus briefs focused on whether recognizing same-sex marriage would harm children or whether not recognizing those unions would inflict even more harm on children of same sex-couples.[142] In issuing the Court's ruling, Justice Kennedy focused on the harm of nonrecognition: DOMA "humiliates tens of thousands of children now being raised by same-sex couples. The law in question makes it even more difficult for the children to understand the integrity and closeness of their own family and its concord with other families in their community and in their daily lives."[143]

Even in states that recognize same-sex marriage, this change in the order of marriage recognition has clashed with older regulatory orders governing intimate associations and responsibilities, particularly regarding parenting, creating new tensions and demands for reform. As of June 2014, twenty-three states and the District of Columbia permitted second-parent adoption as an option for same-sex couples, which marked a more than 100 percent increase in less than a decade.[144] Various state-level attempts to prevent same-sex-parent adoption and foster care have failed to pass even as states passed statutory and constitutional bans on same-sex marriage.[145] These attempts have continued even as marriage recognition has spread. For example, in 2007, four states introduced legislation opposing same-sex parenting.[146] And, in 2008, voters in Arkansas approved a ballot measure preventing gay or lesbian couples from adopting, which was later overturned by the state's supreme court in 2011.[147] In more than half the states, same-sex parents face obstacles to being listed on the birth certificates of their children.

Those obstacles were made strikingly evident in June 2014 when a Texas family court judge ruled that the parents of two twin sons could not be named on those children's birth certificates. Jason Hanna and Joe Riggs reside in Dallas, but they were married in Washington, DC, in 2012, and as a result, they are eligible for whatever federal marriage rights follow from "place of celebration" status. They used a surrogate to father two sons. Each father donated sperm, and the twins share an egg donor who is not the surrogate. Only the surrogate, who is not the biological mother since she did not produce the egg but who did carry the fertilized embryos and fetuses to term, is listed on the birth certificate even though Hanna and Riggs are each, by definition, the biological father of one of the twins. Texas is one of nineteen states where the potential for joint adoption by same-sex couples is "unclear," meaning that it can vary from county to county and is at the discretion of the judge.[148] The clash with marriage recognition is obvious: under current Texas law, second-parent adoption is conferred only to married couples. According to Hanna, "In order to grant a second-parent adoption, it has to be between two married people. And so, considering we're not legally married in the eyes of Texas, they don't have to grant that second-parent adoption because they don't recognize our marriage. . . . It's up to the judge's discretion on whether or not to grant it."[149] If *Windsor* had compelled Texas to recognize same-sex marriages as equal to cross-sex marriages, the Texas legislature would have had to pass a law explicitly banning second-parent adoption by same-sex spouses for this situation to have arisen.

As legal scholar Susan Sterett writes, "Expecting that recognition of one's self as a parent requires the stamp of authority on official paper is part of the late modern state, in which registration makes people visible to a plethora of officials. Legality is not dichotomous in a world in which there are extended family members, children's schools, the pediatrician's office, and human resource benefits offices, all of which can recognize one as a parent or not."[150] In other words, official listing of parental status on a birth certificate is a necessary step to secure recognition by public and private regulatory authorities that govern people's access to various necessary services. Without the formal recognition that follows from the state issuance of a birth certificate, the choice of recognition remains with the governing authority. In the absence of clear public policy or private institutional policy to the contrary, a school principal, hospital administrator, or human resource director can choose to recognize a nonbiological lesbian mother or gay father as, in fact, a mother or father to his or her child. And, the emerging regulatory order of marriage that recognizes same-sex marriage has created possible challenges for and limits to parental and same-sex family recognition. One challenge arises as part of a backlash to marriage equality and is illustrated by recent litigation in Iowa. Another, perhaps paradoxically, follows from the requirement of equality that marriage recognition demands; it is illustrated by a recent case in New York.

Tension between a newer order of marriage and an older order of opposite-sex parenting and heteronormative family structures not only creates opportunity for entrepreneurial action—including litigation—but also highlights ongoing attempts by some states to refuse to see same-sex families even as those state governments offer relationship recognition. The Iowa Department of Public Health exemplified this dynamic when it refused to list two people of the same sex, even if married, as parents of a child born to that couple. It maintained this policy—not triggered in a cross-sex context—because of a statute providing that only biological parents can be listed on a birth certificate; this law was on the books well before the state recognized same-sex marriages.[151]

Boundaries of exclusion are redefined but not eliminated. A lower court ruling in the Iowa litigation process, *Gartner v. Department of Public Health* (2012), found in favor of the same-sex couple, ordering the Iowa Department of Public Health to list the same-sex parents as the legal parents of the child in question. Yet, the state appealed, signaling its desire to maintain some zone of community and recognition beyond the reach of LGBT citizens.[152] Ultimately, the Iowa Supreme Court found against the state and ordered that both same-sex spouses be listed as parents on birth certificates.[153]

Since adoption cases are often left to judicial discretion under the best-interests-of-the-child principle, access to and recognition of same-sex parenting varies widely across the United States. Consequently, parents in many states may go unrecognized when in custody disputes with former spouses, partners, or other relatives. This circumstance surfaces not only when the state, like Iowa, actively battles against recognizing same-sex parents but also when the state claims to recognize the full equality of same-sex relationships. Problems of regulatory recognition are not only the consequence of countermovements seeking to halt LGBT rights advances. They also can be the result of implementing principles of formal equality. Therefore, explanations of changes in regulatory recognition of gay and lesbian citizenship are not limited to the interactive dynamics of movement/countermovement mobilization but also stem from the character of political change as always partial. That circumstance is most clearly highlighted presently in New York.

A recent ruling in that state has called parental recognition into question not because the state actively seeks to prevent it but because a judge has ruled that formal adoption recognition is no longer necessary due to the marriage policy in place. The case involves a lesbian couple, married in 2011 when same-sex marriage was legalized in New York. One spouse gave birth to the couple's son, and both parents were listed on the child's birth certificate. The other spouse began the adoption process since, even though she was listed on the birth certificate, she had no biological connection to her son. But, on January 6, 2014, a Brooklyn Surrogate's Court judge ruled that the adoption process could not proceed because the nonbiological mother was already listed on the child's birth certificate.[154]

According to the judge, the adoption was unnecessary and if she did grant it, she would undermine the marriage because the ruling would imply that same-sex married parents need to adopt their children while straight married parents do not. A ruling to this effect would mean that "true marriage equality remains yet to be attained" and that "a same-sex marriage remains somehow insufficient to establish a parent-child relationship."[155] After issuing the ruling, the judge defended the refusal to grant the adoption: "This is a straightforward child born of marriage. Think of all your friends who are married and have children. They don't go to court to seek an adoption. There is a presumption of parentage."[156]

The judge's rationale was premised on the equality that flows from marriage recognition. By contrast, Iowa's refusal to allow the names of the same-sex parents on a child's birth certificate was emblematic of denying equality. Nevertheless, the New York judge's ruling created hardships precisely because of Section 2 of the federal Defense of Marriage Act. That section, not at issue in the *Windsor* litigation, permitted states that did not recognize same-sex marriage to continue to do so, essentially invalidating a marriage of a same-sex couple should the couple be under that nonrecognition state's jurisdiction, for example, by moving or traveling to a nonrecognition state. If a same-sex married couple had a child, their marriage did not translate across state boundaries, and therefore a presumption of parentage also did not carry over. If the child were hospitalized in a nonrecognition state, then the nonbiological parent could be denied access. If the couple splits up, then the nonbiological parent may make no custody claim. Summing up these possibilities, Susan Sommer of Lambda Legal Defense noted that since "we continue to live in a country that has a patchwork of respect and disrespect of same-sex couples," then it becomes imperative "for this couple to have an adoption, because the presumption of parentage may not be respected if they leave the state."[157] The order of family law is hardly unified, and the shift in marriage law by *Windsor* exacerbated that circumstance.

Ironically, then, same-sex families have remained highly unstable from two directions: first, the refusal of states to recognize them (even after the ruling in *Obergefell*), and second, and seemingly ironically, the attempts of state officials, like judges, to follow the principles of formal equality. Indeed, the first dynamic—that of backlash against inroads made by LGBT rights advocates—does not appear to be all that successful. Only a small number of antiparenting backlash efforts were implemented between 1996 and 2006, when about forty anti-marriage-recognition laws were passed. Public law scholar Alison Gash has convincingly argued that this divergence is explained, in part, by the fact that marriage advocacy was far more visible than the struggle for same-sex parenting rights. The latter was confined to family courts, framed in traditional "best interests of the child" rationales rather than in terms of gay and lesbian rights, and tended to rest on statutory rather than constitutional law, dynamics that tended to shield it from public concern.[158] Nevertheless, Gash notes that although same-sex-marriage recognition has spread since 2011, the potential to mobilize anti-same-sex parenting remains on the horizon: "Recent state court rulings in North Carolina, Arkansas, and Kansas certainly validate these fears. Although marriage equality is reaching the point of inevitability, its visibility—and its increased linkages to parenting—may inspire smaller, localized pockets of anti-parenting backlash. Opponents seem to realize that the only way to fight incremental gains in parenting is through incremental opposition—one case at a time."[159]

The instability of same-sex-parenting recognition is not just a consequence of federalism nor only an outcome of countermovement mobilization attempting to halt LGBT rights advances. It is also created by the nature of political change, as the situation in New York reveals. While new rules of marriage recognition develop and alter the marital order, that order has grated against other dimensions of familial recognition, which have not been so altered. Resulting frictions spur confusions and opportunities for political and legal change. Discontinuities among different orders of regulatory recognition create the opportunities for ongoing political change.

Agency and Political Change: Actors in a Developmental Account of Gay and Lesbian Politics

What drives different orders of authority to adopt different modalities of regulatory recognition? If the opportunity for change can arise endogenously through the polity's clashing orders of authority, which might engage distinct modalities of regulatory recognition of gay and lesbian citizens concurrently, then how are these opportunities framed and seized?

It is tempting to suggest that social movement actors fill this role. Many people, from the earliest homophile activists to contemporary leaders, are indispensable in explaining how increased recognition of fundamental notions of equality for gay, lesbian, bisexual, and transgender citizens has become a mainstream political idea. This claim is not incorrect, but it might be considered incomplete. Studies of gay U.S. history have brought many such critical individuals to the fore.[160] They include Harry Hay, who established the Mattachine Society; or Donald Webster Cory, who drafted one of the first manifestos for gay equality, *The Homosexual in America*; or Del Martin and Phyllis Lyon, who established Daughters of Bilitis; or Frank Kameny, who led the first pickets for employment nondiscrimination. Other important actors have been the Gay Liberation Front and the Gay Activist Association of the 1970s; the more formal interest groups of the National LGBTQ Task Force and the Human Rights Campaign that emerged in the 1970s and 1980s; the transformative aims of ACT UP and Queer Nation; or the strategies of legal organizations like Lambda Legal Defense or the Gay and Lesbian Advocates and Defenders, each of which has played a role that compelled state actors to shift from one modality to another. The following chapters will discuss many of these actors and organizations. They built the social movements that, Linda Hirschman declared, perhaps prematurely, executed a "triumphant gay revolution."[161] A variety of inequalities remain, and that reality substantiates the claim of fragmented citizenship.[162]

While movements and interest groups and their innovative leaders and members play a significant role not to be underestimated, there are other actors, hardly formally involved in movement communities, that created, maintained, and recombined the elements of the fragmented polity and thereby altered the content and meaning of citizenship. The case of military policy change suggests as much by pointing out how policies were crafted by lawyers at the Department of Defense. And, as detailed in the chapters to come, these influential actors included bureaucratic agents after World War II who disbursed GI benefits to soldiers discharged from the military for homosexuality even as they were barred from such benefits. They included journalists and other media elites who actively reframed legal rulings as being not about the facts of a case or questions of law but about implications for other rights claims. They included judges, attorneys general, mayors, vice presidents, and presidents who contested the boundaries of marriage. They included private-sector actors such as scientists conducting important research to better understand the nature of homosexuality and to destigmatize it, as well as private corporate human resource officers who, sometimes in response to lobbying by employees and at other times simply reacting to competitive trends in the marketplace, secured equality through employment benefits policy.

Agency can assume different forms, but importantly, opportunities for action develop out of the normal condition of the polity as internally fractured by distinct orders of coherent ideas, institutions, and discourses. As Robert Lieberman posits,

> When stable patterns of politics clash, purposive political actors will often find themselves at an impasse, unable to proceed according to the "normal" patterns and processes that hitherto governed their behavior. . . . Political actors in such circumstances will be induced to find new ways to define and advance their aims, whether by finding a new institutional forum that is more receptive to their ideas or by adapting ideas to take advantage of new institutional opportunities.[163]

Lieberman suggests that old orders are not wholly replaced, but instead that "elements of them are recombined and reconfigured into a new set of political patterns that is recognizably new and yet retains some continuity with the old ones."[164] That dynamic is evident in the brief case study of military regulation. New policies to disburse benefits to families of LGB service members are created, but the fundamental order of government relations with the military are not displaced.

The chapters that follow illustrate moments when entrepreneurial actors took advantage of opportunities afforded by policy gaps and tensions. There were strokes of rhetorical brilliance that relied on fundamental notions of fairness and liberty but put those ideals in the service of ends seemingly antithetical to the ends they had served in the past.[165] There was clear exploitation and leveraging of crisis and exogenous shocks, such as HIV/AIDS, to afford new ways of conceptualizing the meaning of equality, social responsibility, and the protections from discrimination.[166] There were key decisions in legal strategies that hindered future possibilities downstream as well as, alternately, investments in organizational form that expanded the range of options that could be pursued to support the goal of increased rights recognition.[167] Multiple conceptions of agency are leveraged in this book to explain the incomplete shifts in regulatory recognition that create the fragmented citizenship now defining the lived experience of many gay, lesbian, bisexual, and transgender citizens. A developmental account of the polity via the lens of sexuality offers the opportunity to test the robustness of a variety of concepts that APD research seeks to map, including partial displacements, layering, and path dependency. There is no single agent, and the dynamics of recognition are not limited to the well-documented interactions of movement and countermovement. Opportunities for shifts in regulatory recognition arise from the endogenous frictions and tensions that follow from the way political change is always partial, never fully covering all aspects that might be implicated because those aspects may not be apparent at the time a policy change is advocated or implemented. Inequalities emerge and seem to persist because ongoing policy changes bring those previously unseen continuously to light.

Conclusion

This chapter offered a framework for a developmental account of sexuality politics in the United States. It highlighted the need to expand the paradigm through which gay and lesbian politics has traditionally been understood empirically and normatively in political science and sociolegal studies, namely, as a politics of individual and group rights claims demanded by mobilized interests through a range of tactics including but not limited to litigation, legislation, grassroots protest, interest-group lobbying, and expanding popular-culture visibility. A focus on rights and movement politics mires the discussion in whether liberal conceptions of rights have enough breadth and depth to support the types of rights claims LGBT advocates now seek. It also puts the burden of argument on the individual making the rights claim rather than on the order of authority—whether state or private—that must justify the rights denial.

The foundational notion of citizenship is not rights, participation, production, or consumption but recognition. Personhood and citizenship are devices through which the regulatory authorities define and see the individual as able to access rights; as such, these statuses are vehicles by which the state identifies and manages individuals, by which governing authorities understand the individual as able to engage rights that might be understood as "natural." Recognition, then, is, in James Scott's words, a "project of legibility."[168] Similarly, Elizabeth Cohen suggests that citizenship is not only "associated, variously, with statuses, actions, institutions, and rights" but also "a tool of political categorization."[169] And, to the extent that the recognition changes over time, the legibility is altered; the status changes because state and private authorities—sometimes compelled by social movement actors and sometimes not—recategorize the individual.

Considering citizenship as constituted through recognition motivates an exploration of governing authorities. And, the concepts, ideas, and methods that define APD provide a path for empirical evaluation of that authority and its change over time. This chapter has relied on two insights from Orren and Skowronek's definition of American political development. The first is that political change is always partial and incomplete, yielding unanticipated effects. Developmental conceptions of political change help us to understand the persistence of inequalities in ways that enrich traditional answers, which have tended to focus on the interplay between social movement push and countermovement pushback. The second is that the polity is composed of multiple orders, that such orders might exist in tension with one another, and that such tension can provide the political opportunity to motivate change. As APD scholarship has fruitfully demonstrated, laws and policies that structure citizens' lives are never developed all at once; governance is not invented of a piece on a clean slate. More often than not, political change is incremental, limited, and layered. A change in one domain of governance, like marriage laws, might have unanticipated effects on a different, already existing domain of governance, like employment law. Consequently, the various policies, laws, and customs that confer the recognition that defines citizenship may not be fully congruent with one another.

Since rights are not just tangible forms of legal access and guarantee but also function as sites through which the state makes citizens legible to politico-legal institutions and to other community members, any analysis of rights should be coupled with a parallel evaluation of the changing nature of state power. The development of an expanded field of secured gay rights and policy is a matter not only of sociopolitical and legal mobilization but also of the way governing or regulatory authorities have recognized the meaning and content of gay and lesbian citizenship. Citizenship, because it is a status that relies upon recognition by others, can serve as a means to uncover the changing relationship between the individual and the state on various dimensions, including sexuality. In the United States, the status of the lesbian-, gay-, bisexual-, and transgender-identified citizen is far from wholly or consistently recognized. Bringing these ideas together with the patterned schema of five modalities of regulatory recognition yields the central insight into LGBT citizenship that a developmental account offers: since different state and private regulatory authorities may exhibit the disposition of distinct modalities, the citizenship status of an LGBT individual is contingent on the particular authority with which he primarily interacts at any given moment over his life cycle. The rest of this book illustrates the various dimensions and manifestations of that idea.

2

Excluding the Homosexual

Naming Gender and Sexual Transgression

The congenital variety is incurable. All incurable victims should be permanently removed from our social system. They are sources of moral contagion and promoters of sexual crime to whom the right to remain in society should be denied.
—G. Frank Lydston, *The Diseases of Society*, 1904[1]

It was determined that even among the experts there existed considerable difference of opinion concerning the many facets of homosexuality and other forms of sex perversion. . . . For the purpose of this report the subcommittee has defined sex perverts as "those who engage in unnatural sex acts" and homosexuals are perverts who may be broadly defined as "persons of either sex who as adults engage in sexual activities with persons of the same sex." . . . Contrary to common belief, all homosexual males do not have feminine mannerisms, nor do all female homosexuals display masculine characteristics in their dress or actions. The fact is that many male homosexuals are very masculine in their physical appearance and general demeanor, and many female homosexuals have every appearance of femininity in their outward appearance.
—*Employment of Homosexuals and Other Sex Perverts in Government*, 1950[2]

The homosexual is often considered an invention of modernity, a period of rapid industrialization and urbanization in the West dated to the late nineteenth century. This supposition draws, in part, upon Michel Foucault's canonical account of how the homosexual became an object to identify and control:

> As defined by the ancient civil or canonical codes, sodomy was a category of forbidden acts; their perpetrator was nothing more than the juridical subject of them. The nineteenth-century homosexual became a personage, a past, a case history, and a childhood, in addition to being a type of life form, and a morphology, with an indiscreet anatomy and possibly a mysterious physiology. . . . Homosexuality appeared as one of the forms of sexuality when it was transposed for the practice of sodomy onto a kind of interior androgyny, a hermaphrodism of the soul. The sodomite had been a temporary aberration; the homosexual was now a species.[3]

Prior to the late nineteenth century, same-sex sex acts had been lumped together for criminal sanction with a variety of nonprocreative sexual activities outside of wedlock, including masturbation, fornication, sex with animals, sex with children, sexual assault, and cross-sex anal intercourse.[4] By the end of the century, however, same-sex sodomy denoted something fundamental about an individual's personhood.[5] Yet, even then, as this chapter will argue, the sexual invert, as he or she might have been called by the medical and scientific elite, was not the modern homosexual as that identity might be understood in the United States by the mid-twentieth century. Instead, the sexual invert was a conglomeration of multiple transgressive identities that might now be disaggregated into those who are same-sex desirous, those who engage in situational same-sex sexual behavior, and those who cross boundaries of gender expression.

The sexual invert and, later, the homosexual are temporally located identities, each a product of political imperatives of their age. As Jonathan Ned Katz writes, defining sexuality as dichotomously homo or hetero merely "signifies one particular historical arrangement of the sexes and their pleasures."[6] These conceptions are constructed and recognized by regulatory authorities, and the type of recognition conferred, this chapter will show, can serve a variety of aims: tarnishing political opponents, advocating particular nation-building policies, and supporting legal reform. Naming the sexual invert as such—the first modality of regulatory recognition of homosexuality—embodied the fears, aims, and aspirations of Progressive Era reformers of the late nineteenth and early twentieth centuries. The second modality—seeing the modern homosexual, i.e., the narrower identity of an individual sexually attracted to the same sex—provided a foil upon which much of the mid-twentieth-century U.S. security state was predicated.

Identity is not only imposed or created by authorities. Historians have challenged Foucault's focus on scientific classification by detailing how sexual identities were created and maintained by people themselves through the deliberate building of social networks and institutions, which included meeting places and cultural practices.[7] In addition, historians of sexuality have attended to plural forms of same-sex intimacy that belie a homo/hetero distinction.[8] Summarizing these insights, Scott Bravmann contends, "the modernist narrative logic of social constructionist accounts of gay identity formation . . . elides the multiple differences among gay men and lesbians."[9] Consequently, according to Dana Sietler, "the delineations of homosexuality in the early twentieth century are bound up in a circle of meanings that disallow any simple escape into a binary substratum of desire."[10] To render a dichotomous construct of sexuality is to commit the fallacy of imposing contemporary notions of identity upon the past. Doing so obscures both the varieties of self-identification and the processes of definition and articulation by scientific and medical elites, or their gradual dynamic of coming to determine, by the middle of the twentieth century, who was a homosexual. Comprising the turn-of-the-century proto-gay urban subcultures were pansies, fairies, and mollies.[11] And, in the new scientific study of homosexuality, various types were called "Urnings," "psycho-sexual hermaphrodites," "sexual perverts," "sexual inverts," and "persons with contrary sexual feeling."[12] For a developmental study, then, same-sex intimacies are not usefully evaluated by "imposing our own designations which focus primarily on erotic desires and acts."[13] Doing so elides the slow process of observation, description, and categorization of so-called sexual perversities by scientists, bureaucrats, and medical professionals that had to occur in order to *recognize* and thereby produce homosexual identity as grounded first and foremost in same-sex erotic desire.[14]

This chapter describes the project of identifying gender and sexual nonconformity as a threat to nation. That threat was made manifest in two distinct types of regulatory recognition: first, a modality of seeing sexual perversions as a broad category and defining these perversions as counter to Progressive Era national community building and, second, a later, mid-twentieth-century modality that viewed the homosexual more narrowly as same-sex desirous and constructed him or her as a specific threat to national security. Late-nineteenth- and early-twentieth-century sexology was embedded in a broader Progressive imperative to "search for order" and foster national community in the wake of the violence and disruption to nationhood wrought by the Civil War.[15] This goal was particularly evident in immigration policy.[16] As the regulatory identification changed over time to considering same-sex desire a specific threat to national security, government policy shifted toward exclusion and purging homosexuals from military and government during the immediate post–World War II years, often called the "Lavender Scare."[17] Examining the timing of the Lavender Scare provides insights into how identities are recognized by institutional authorities and highlights the importance of recognition as a central concept in a developmental account of sexuality politics.

Sodomy before Homosexuality: Public Order, Public Morality, and the Criminalizing of Nonprocreative and Nonmarital Sex

Regulatory recognition of same-sex intimacy was hardly new by the late nineteenth century. Secular criminal prohibitions on sodomy were a long-standing Anglo American tradition that reached back to the Reformation Parliament of 1533, which punished "buggery," either "committed with mankind or beast," with death.[18] William Blackstone, a central figure in the development of common law principles who first published his *Commentaries on the Laws of England* in the late 1760s, recommended that individuals found guilty of the "infamous *crime against nature*" be subject to capital punishment.[19] But, the crime against nature was not synonymous with homosexual sex. The phrase captured all manner of nonmarital and nonprocreative sexual congress, particularly opposite-sex as well as same-sex rape.

In colonial America, these bans indicate that sodomy was an expansive category hardly limited to same-sex intercourse.[20] The earliest antisodomy statute was adopted in Jamestown in 1610: "No man shall commit the horrible, detestable sins of Sodomie upon pain of death."[21] By 1636, the settlement at Plymouth, Massachusetts, made punishable by death any "solemn compaction or conversing with the devil," which was evident in acts of "sodomy, rapes, [and] buggery."[22] Attitudes toward and punishments for such behavior varied. In Virginia, sodomy was a capital offense; in Pennsylvania, the only capital offense was murder.[23] Enforcement was far from regular, ranging from informal reprimands by town elders to formal trials and convictions.[24] Through the nineteenth century, William Eskridge Jr. notes, "Exactly what constituted sodomy and its various synonyms remained . . . vague and largely unspoken—and therefore rendered it an elastic and dynamic concept."[25] Indeed, not until the 1960s did sodomy laws specifically target same-sex anal and oral sex. The broad language of the antisodomy legal tradition captures the moral opprobrium cast against any nonmarital and nonprocreative sex acts regardless of the sex of the participants.[26]

According to Eskridge, the homosexualization of sodomy law in the United States began in the late nineteenth century, spreading across the statute books of most states during the 1910s and 1920s. Processes of identification were gradual, contested, and traceable. Furthermore, they highlight how same-sex intimacies were differently recognized before the late nineteenth century. Eskridge utilizes the status of American poet Walt Whitman, who celebrates same-sex intimacy in his personal letters as well as, more famously, in his poetry, to illuminate this change over time.[27]

Scholars have documented and critiqued the popular and literary effort to reclaim Whitman as a great gay poet. Regardless of whether Whitman might be classified as gay, the precise nature of his sexuality is rendered less mysterious when contemporary notions of homosexuality are not imposed.[28] Furthermore, it is not at all clear that, if Whitman were gay, he would even have been convicted under nineteenth-century sodomy law in the United States. The legal recognition of same-sex intimacy that existed would not have necessarily criminalized consensual homosexual sex between adults. As Eskridge contends, "Even if Whitman engaged in anal intercourse (for which there is no evidence), it is most unlikely that he would have been arrested for violating the state sodomy law, for its operational purpose was to regulate sexual assaults."[29] Sodomy laws were vaguely specified; they included a range of heterosexual and homosexual sex acts. And, they were applied mostly as a means to maintain public order and discourage the obscene: adultery, heterosexual unwed cohabitation, distribution of obscene literature, and rape.[30] Jonathan Ned Katz identified 105 cases during the nineteenth century that fell under the category of sodomy, buggery, or crimes against nature.

These cases involved sex with animals, sex between an adult man and a male youth, and sexual assaults by men upon both men and women.[31] In Eskridge's review of them, he notes that "it is not clear whether any of these involved conduct we would now consider 'consensual.'"[32] Since sodomy laws were generally meant to maintain public order, it is not even clear that such laws would have criminally sanctioned private consensual same-sex intimate relations between adults. Indeed, oral sex was not criminally defined until 1879, when Pennsylvania became the first state to outlaw the practice. Other states followed with similar expansions to their sodomy bans, but many only after their highest courts restricted the interpretation of extant laws to ban anal sex.[33]

Often the legal naming of the offense followed the prosecution. Men arrested for fellatio were not necessarily charged under sodomy laws because sodomy laws had not yet included oral sex as a crime. Instead, they were sometimes charged with vagrancy until legal codes could be updated: "Most of the individual state statutes were introduced following local scandals in which the public learned that men were engaged in unnatural practices not covered by the traditional crime-against-nature laws."[34] In this way, the development of criminal sanctioning of same-sex behavior followed a similar pattern to the bureaucratic exclusion of homosexuals in immigration policy detailed in the next section: without the proper concepts and language to identify what officials were seeing, they charged men with the tools available in the extant legal discourse. Regulatory enforcement had to learn to recognize the actions and individuals it was seeing. Only later did state legislatures (in the case of sodomy law) or federal officials (in the case of immigration regulation) modify the respective regulatory frameworks to name that with which and whom these officials were coming into contact.

Furthermore, the laws used to attempt to arrest the development of same-sex urban subcultures were not the sodomy bans. Eskridge finds that the state and municipal laws most often utilized against homosexuals were bans on cross-dressing, bans against sexual solicitation and public indecency, which included disorderly conduct and "lewd vagrancy," bans against child molestation, and laws against obscenity. That so many laws targeted same-sex intimacy but did so indirectly speaks to the modality of regulatory recognition in place: it did not clearly identify homosexuality as such. Rather, what was targeted was a loose conception of sexual and gender transgression, still conceptualized mostly in terms of non-consent and the discourse of public health, which seemed increasingly apparent under the newly watchful eye of Progressive urban reform.

Crackdowns on homosexuals in urban centers flourished in the 1920s and 1930s. As Jennifer Terry notes, "Lesbians and homosexual men were subjected to aggressive police raids on gay establishments, to increased arrests for 'homosexual offenses,' and to elaborate extortion schemes," and they "reported being expelled from jobs, evicted from their homes, and threatened by violence."[35] But even in this context, sodomy laws were not the primary mode of persecution and prosecution. Instead, municipalities developed laws targeting gay and lesbian meeting places, particularly bars.[36] And, federal authorities utilized the key institution over which it exerted control: the mail.[37] Homophile publications, a tool used to connect and inform gay men and lesbians prior to and during the early years of gay and lesbian political organizing at midcentury, were censored as obscene. Obscenity, which did not qualify for First Amendment protection, necessarily included any material with homosexual content until the Supreme Court ruled otherwise in *One, Inc. v. Oleson*.[38]

But, municipal, state, and federal persecution of homosexual minorities, as well as the Court's declaration that popular magazines discussing homosexuality were neither criminal nor prurient, required the identification of that minority as more specific than a loose collection of transgressive behaviors. It required seeing a target, and the identification of that target was a gradual process, traceable across multiple orderings of authority—science, medicine, federal immigration policy—which illuminates the tight coupling between changing regulatory recognition and the development of administrative state power.

Making the Democratic Citizen: Progressive Aims Motivate the Naming of the Sexual Threat

This process of identifying and naming the sexual pervert was very much embedded within the animating objectives of Progressivism, particularly the aim of nurturing the growth of a new national community. Sexologists' explanations of same-sex desire and gender nonconformity were grounded in evolutionary theory and utilized prominent Progressive

Era assumptions of scientific racism and eugenic recommendations that animated this objective.[39] The late-nineteenth-century medico-scientific identification of the sexual pervert occurred at a time of intense material dislocation associated with dynamics of industrialization, urbanization, and modernization. In the United States this naming process was also embedded in a simultaneous and unique ideational dislocation. In the aftermath of civil war, an increasingly criticized Reconstruction, and the longest economic depression to that point in the Panic of 1873, faith in national purpose and development faltered.

The Progressive Era was marked by a compulsion to reclaim a faith in exceptional development but to ground it less in divine providence and more in the language of science. As the historian Jay Hatheway notes, "American science became interested in the social behavior of humans in order to ascertain those laws that, if followed, would allow humans to construct a better society consistent with the principles of the national ideology." Clinging to an ideological tradition of difference from Europe, the scientific imperative to "discover the social structures and laws that were conducive to the realization of these principles and the fulfillment of America's earthly mission" was paramount.[40] The discovery, diagnosis, and either exclusion or healing of the sexual pervert were a part of this broader Progressive aim. But, the evolutionary assumptions that underlay the new science suggested that sexual perverts were, ironically, as much evidence of the country's development as they were a threat to it.

Progressives represented an identifiable disposition toward governance, which animated a reform agenda. Progressivism sought reform by relying upon expertise, extolling the benefits of management, and, in response to the fractious trauma of civil war, deliberatively developing a national identity and community, which could voice and govern through an enlightened, educated expression of public opinion.[41] For Progressives, the public opinion they sought to foster was a manifestation of a democratic and national majority's desire as constrained by a simultaneous consideration of the social good, a consideration that could be inculcated through a common civic education. Public opinion was enlightened because it was tempered by education.[42] In a democracy where multiple institutions, including public schools, colleges and universities, the new media of magazine journalism, and civic and voter leagues, were all tasked with educating the public, an enlightened public opinion was possible. Some Progressive reformers imagined a future where "public opinion would (or should) increasingly supplant law and other forms of external coercion in a society."[43]

The cultivation of community was central to all other Progressive reform aims. This community was not only nurtured through civic institutions such as schools, newer media, interest organizations, and voter leagues. It was also nurtured through civic ideas, which would undergird policy innovations, many of which were premised upon the principles of social Darwinism. Social Darwinism, an ideological assumption of racial hierarchy animating political and policy ideas, was grounded in an evolutionary conception of biological development. It explained social and economic inequities and power relations among races and ethnicities, between the two sexes, and between management and labor as natural, unavoidable, and thereby just outcomes of evolution.[44] In essence, all races were inferior to white northern Europeans. In defining what he considered to be "the goal toward which our American commonwealth, the commonwealth of these United States, is making its historic progress," Progressive political scientist John W. Burgess makes this point clear:

> If we regard for a moment the history of the world from the point of view of the production of political institutions, we cannot fail to discern that all great states . . . have been founded and developed by the . . . Aryan race. Indian America has left no legacies to modern civilization; Africa has as yet made no contributions; and Asia . . . has done nothing except in imitation of Europe for political civilization. We must conclude that American Indians, Asiatics and Africans cannot properly form any active, directive part of the political population which shall be able to produce political ideals. They can only receive, learn, follow the Aryan example. . . . I consider, therefore the prime mission of the ideal American Commonwealth to be the perfection of the Aryan genius for political civilization upon the basis of a predominantly Teutonic nationality.[45]

Such scientific racism captures an ironic paradox of Progressivism: its faith in the people to bear broad responsibilities for civic engagement alongside its narrow definition of the proper community of people who could take on such responsibilities.[46]

Scientific racism captured anxieties produced by an increasingly ethnically and racially heterogeneous population, and it justified a range of exclusionary policies, including but not limited to the Chinese Exclusion Acts and extensive marriage regulations that limited citizen access to civil marriage.[47] Progressives saw the specter of degeneracy, a fear of somehow falling off a teleological path of development. Burgess's scholarship captured this fear. It acknowledged that American political development had not always followed the proper path and that much of the political dynamics that led to civil war abandoned the nationalist principles laid by the Framers. For him, the Progressive aim of eradicating the principles that had animated the Confederacy—natural rights and competing sovereignty—put the nation back on the "the plan of universal history."[48]

The medico-scientific naming of the homosexual was very much a part of this Progressive aspiration to cultivate a particular kind of citizen and a robust national community. And, the naming of transgressive sexualities employed similar themes as those that animated scientific racism. In short, the naming of sexual inversion reflected Progressive anxieties and Progressive expertise. Sexual inversion was viewed as a consequence of civilization's development. Just as scientific racists "discovered" physical markers and behavioral characteristics that validated assumptions of race hierarchy, sexologists similarly sought evidence of perversion on the body. David Halperin posits, "There is a remarkably consistent emphasis throughout the history of European sexual representation on the deviant morphology of the invert, his visibly different mode of appearance and dress, his feminine style of self-presentation. Inversion manifests itself outwardly."[49]

The discursive frameworks and ideological assumptions of scientific racism were fitted to the scientific enterprise of homosexual discovery. As Siobhan Sommerville has shown, whether the sexologists' accounts, like those of the Austrian Richard von Krafft-Ebing, the English Havelock Ellis, and the American James Kiernan, were sympathetic to the plight of the homosexual and sought legal reform and decriminalization or were, like the account of George Frank Lydston, more hostile to the sexual invert, they "were steeped in assumptions that had driven previous scientific studies of race."[50] The new sexology named these perversions by utilizing the premises of scientific racism. Such discursive borrowing highlights the extent to which a particular language for coming to know homosexuality's qualities and possible causes had not yet been developed.

In his 1886 opus, *Psychopathia Sexualis with Special Reference to the Contrary Sexual Instinct*, Krafft-Ebing characterized all nonprocreative sexual activity as aberrant and illustrative of degeneracy. Romantic love, made manifest in procreative sex, was evidence of a higher state of human evolution: "In coarse, sensual love, in the lustful impulse to satisfy this natural instinct, man stands on a level with the animal; but it is given to him to raise himself to a height where this natural instinct no longer makes him a slave: higher, noble feelings are awakened, which, notwithstanding their sensual origin, expand into a world of beauty, sublimity, and morality."[51] The underlying assumptions about connections between sexual desire and the more evolved races draw heavily on scientific racism.

The cause of sexual perversion was much debated. Some sexologists, like Kiernan, located it in so-called biological underdevelopment. White urban American men with symptoms of sexual inversion were, according to Kiernan, exhibiting "the original bi-sexuality of the ancestors of the race. . . . The inhibitions on excessive action to accomplish a given purpose, which the race acquired through centuries of evolution, being removed, the animal in man springs to the surface. Removal of these inhibitions produces, among other results, sexual perversions."[52] Kiernan understood sexual inversion as reversion to a previous evolutionary state: "The lowest animals are bisexual and the various types of hermaphroditism are more or less complete reversions to the ancestral type."[53] The sexual pervert was immune to the strictures and influences of contemporary civilization that promoted an evolution beyond animal instinct.

Others characterized this perversion as caused by the stress of civilization's progress. Sexual perversion, for these sexologists, was considered a symptom of a particular disorder such as neurasthenia or nervous exhaustion, which was produced by the pace of change associated with modernity. Neurologists like George Beard, Charles Dana, and Henry Lyman contended that this disease was the price of modern civilization, replete with stressors of various sorts. According to Beard, such nervous exhaustion was made manifest in impotence, masturbation, and desire for same-sex intimacy. It was "more common in America than in any other country" because of the "opportunities and necessities of a rising civilization in a new and immense continent."[54] The cause could not be arrested, for it was progress itself: "The causation of sexual neurasthenia, as of all other clinical varieties, and of modern nerve sensitiveness in general, is not single or simple, but complex; evil habits, excesses, tobacco, alcohol, worry and special excitements, even climate itself—all the familiar excitants being secondary to the one great predisposing cause—civilization."[55]

Charles Gilbert Chaddock, who translated Krafft-Ebing's opus into English and was a well-regarded sexologist in his own right, similarly located sexual inversion in the stresses of modern society.[56] G. Frank Lydston similarly linked modernization with increasing rates of sexual perversion:

> America has for many years furnished conditions peculiarly favorable to degeneracy. The strenuous life of the average American, certainly of every ambitious citizen, has many aspects bearing upon degeneracy in general and vice and crime in particular. Lust for wealth, desire for social supremacy, ambition for fame, love of display, late hours, lack of rest, excitement, the consumption of alcohol, especially by women—these factors combine to cause what Beard termed a distinctively American disease. The body social is growing more and more neuropathic. In the train of this widespread neuropathy comes degeneracy, with all its evil brood of social disorders.[57]

Sexual perversion was always lurking within the body politic as it was a byproduct of the very progress to which political development was wedded. The United States was particularly susceptible because it had, according to Burgess, traveled the furthest on the developmental path. The sexual invert was as much manifestation of progress as it was evidence of civilization's precarious state.

For many, to guard against the possibility of degeneration, specific actions had to be taken. Beard called for a return to a quieter agrarian life, which might provide some rebalancing for the urban white man. His grounding in scientific racism justified the claim that "among the negroes and among the strong, healthy farming population in all civilized countries, . . . those who live out-doors and have well balanced constitutions of the old-fashioned sort are not annoyed by sexual desire when they have no opportunities for gratification, nor to the same degree as the delicate, finely-organized lads of our cities and of the higher civilization."[58] Theodore Roosevelt advocated that "barbarian virtues" not be lost amidst the progress of civilization.[59] He feared that modern society had engendered a less vigorous man, one ultimately incapable of self-governance. He voiced a fear of degeneracy and an articulation of sexual perversion and gender transgression through the discourse of civilization hierarchy associated with scientific racism.

By locating the cause of sexual inversion in the social context of civilization's "progress," some sexologists defined the sexual invert as sick but not criminal, paving the way for some to advocate legal reform, including decriminalization. Hatheway captures the diagnosis: "In so far as inverted sexual perverts were not to be personally held responsible for their unfortunate condition, blame was assigned elsewhere, most frequently the degenerative effects of modern civilization itself. The implication was that society had somehow gone awry, and that the condition of corrupted sexual feeling was merely a symptom of a more fundamental social pathology."[60] In the first English translation of Krafft-Ebing's *Psychopathia Sexualis*, published in 1892, the sexologist prefaces the text with a hope that a new scientific understanding of the condition might foster legal reform and decriminalization: "Even at the present time, in the domain of sexual criminality, the most erroneous opinions are expressed and the most unjust sentences produced, influencing laws and public opinion."[61] While very much wedded to the diagnosis of same-sex attraction as aberrant and indicative of a degenerative pathology, Ellis also undertook his research, in part, to support those he felt were unjustly criminalized:

> The invert is not only the victim of his own abnormal obsession; he is the victim of social hostility. . . . When I review the cases I have brought forward and the mental history of inverts I have known, I am inclined to say that if we can enable an invert to be healthy, self-restrained, and self-respecting we have often done better than to convert him into the mere feeble simulacrum of a normal man.[62]

Echoing this sentiment, Kiernan attempted to build distance between evidence of sexual inversion and a predisposition toward criminal behavior. The invert was no more likely to commit a crime—if same-sex intimacy itself was not criminalized—than the heterosexual. In many ways presaging the findings of mid-twentieth-century psychologist Evelyn Hooker, who found no evidence of mental illness in homosexual men and whose work was used to advocate for and secure the removal of homosexuality from the American Psychological Association's *Diagnostic and Statistical Manual of Mental Disorders*,[63] Kiernan noted that his studies indicated that sexual inverts exhibited "no other evidence of mental deterioration than being homosexual."[64] While homosexuality was considered degenerative within the paradigmatic evolutionary principles of scientific racism, it did not indicate any other criminality. Kiernan recommended that "the mere existence of an alleged perversion should never be admitted as proof of irresponsibility. . . . In full accordance with the spirit of the common law, each case should be tried on its own merits, and the exact mental state of the accused determined."[65] The criminal may be homosexual, but evidence of homosexuality was not evidence of criminality.

Chaddock also sought to decouple homosexuality and criminal predisposition: "that an individual is subject to a perversion of the sexual instinct is not sufficient to establish personal responsibility."[66] While the homosexual might be taken as evidence of the constant strain of the progress of civilization and may be a threat to that civilization if not somehow identified and contained, many of the principal sexologists of the era, including Krafft-Ebing, Ellis, Chaddock, and Kiernan, advocated legal reform at the moment when state legislatures, according to Eskridge, were beginning to consider new criminal sanctions targeted toward same-sex behaviors. The disjuncture between private-sector medico-scientific recognition and public regulatory recognition was, in other words, quite stark.

Not all American sexologists were motivated to support reform. George Frank Lydston, "arguably the leading American specialist on the sexual perversion of contrary sexual instinct within the context of 'diseases of society,'" advocated eugenic treatment for the homosexual.[67] Homosexuality was associated with the rise of modernity, as were any other vices common to urban industrial America. In his text *Diseases of Society*, Lydston describes a number of social ills, including homosexuality, as a "social pathology": "Crime, prostitution, pauperism, insanity in sociologic relations, anarchy, political corruption, and adverse economic and industrial conditions and their causes, congeners, and results will be discussed in this volume as the most important faces of social disease."[68] All such aberrant behaviors had a common cause located in the processes of industrialization and modernization. And, for Lydston, these social pathologies were to be contained and eradicated via some degree of deurbanization and deindustrialization as well as sterilization and euthanasia.[69] In addition, since he considered homosexuality a hereditary trait, marriages could become "the fountain-head to the stream of degeneracy that sweeps through all social systems."[70] Controlling who could be married was a necessary step in curbing the spread of sexual perversion.

In short, the sexual pervert was not only an invention of an increasingly professionalized medico-scientific establishment but also a product of the broader Progressive obsession with cultivating a healthy democratic community. The earliest forms of regulatory recognition of sexual inversion were embedded in a larger sociological concern of devolution and degeneracy, which itself operated within a framework of race hierarchy and an assumption of fragile development. Policy remedies included a more sympathetic call for legal reform, but those who had the greatest public attention—Teddy Roosevelt and George Lydston—sought to counter degeneracy with eugenics. If civilization's development were to continue, then the sexual invert, as much as any of the so-called lower races, had to be better understood and contained. Progressive adherence to scientific racism, eugenics, new civil marriage policies, educational reform, and political institutional reform all fit with the new sexology's conception of the sexual invert as a threat to a robust national community. Each policy was a means to the goal of a healthy citizenry.

Bureaucrats Learn to See the Homosexual

Many sexologists conducted their work to influence the political and legal regulation of sexual perversion. Some, like Ellis, Chaddock, and Kiernan, took a more sympathetic view toward those with same-sex erotic desire and supported decriminalizing same-sex intimacy. Others, like Lydston, who were deeply invested in the Progressive aspiration of cultivating a robust citizenry that might ensure continued development of civilization, were unnerved by the discovery of sexual inverts. Holding fast to assumptions of scientific racism, Lydston saw the invert as foreshadowing America's fall from progress:

> I have said that the higher the race of man, the greater the inhibitions, "under normal conditions." Advance in civilization is, however, not necessarily coeval with progress in ethical standards. After a certain point is reached, the luxury, appetite exhaustion due to satiety, and unhygienic life of civilization bring brain and body degeneracy in their train, and type reversions are more frequent. History shows that extinction of entire social systems may result.[71]

Since civilization's progression held within it the dark circumstances—the stresses of modernization itself—that apparently engendered sexual inversion, Lydston recommended policies that would eradicate and exclude from the national community those persons deemed most susceptible to these stresses. The physician had a particular responsibility to nurture the healthy development of the polity by actively consulting in policy development:

> Upon the physician devolves the major part of the duty of instructing the public in the delicate matters germane to sexual vice and crime. . . . Physicians should be encouraged to write and disseminate among the public dignified and discrete [sic] treatises on various sexual and venereal topics. The more advanced pupils in our boys' schools and colleges should be taught, not only physiology, but elementary principles, at least, of venereal pathology.[72]

Lydston, like all sexologists of the period, operated under the assumption that sexual inversion had physical markers, that those most susceptible could be outwardly recognized. He explicitly detailed these traits:

> They are frequently characterized by effeminacy of voice, dress, and manner. In a general way, their physique is apt to be inferior—a defective physical make-up being quite general among them, although exceptions to this rule are numerous. Sexual perversions, and more particularly inversion, i.e.—homosexuality, or sexual predilection for the same sex,—is

more frequent in the male. . . . Many female inverts are met with, however. For example, there are numerous instances of women of perfect
physique, moving in good society, who have a fondness for women and
are never sexually attracted to men.[73]

These descriptions and Lydston's recommendations for exclusion found
sympathetic ears among bureaucrats developing turn-of-the-century
immigration policy.

In her book, *The Straight State*, Margot Canaday details how the process of recognizing so-called sexual perversions and, later, homosexuality as a personhood status required the simultaneous construction of a
large-scale administrative state. According to Canaday, "the state's identification of certain sexual behaviors, gender traits, and emotional ties as
grounds for exclusion . . . was a catalyst in the formation of homosexual
identity. The state, in other words, did not merely implicate but also
constituted homosexuality in the construction of a stratified citizenry."[74]
Thus, administrative state development is, in part, a story of building an
apparatus to recognize, contain, and exclude the homosexual. Canaday
asks how the United States, characterized by sluggish administrative development, created such an extensive apparatus for policing homosexuality.[75] The answer lies, in part, in the temporal conjuncture of American
state building and medical recognition of homosexuality.

Canaday describes dynamics of bureaucratic learning in which officials created new immigration, military, and welfare policies that
entrenched concerns about homosexuality into administrative state objectives. Over these distinct policy fields a common dynamic is identifiable: a gradual development of discourse through which homosexuality
as a class of persons gains meaning and becomes settled by midcentury.
Yet, before midcentury, bureaucratic action and policy implementation
demonstrate an ambiguity as to what exactly is being identified, contained, and excluded from the body politic. Lacking the terminology to
name precisely the conditions that immigration, welfare, and military
personnel were seeing, early-twentieth-century officials utilized existing categories to justify exclusionary actions taken against gender and
sexual transgressors.

Canaday illustrates this dynamic through immigration policy. Homosexuals were not explicitly banned from immigrating into the United

States until the passage of the McCarran-Walter Act of 1952. But, at the turn of the twentieth century, "aliens were occasionally excluded or deported for sexual perversion . . . and it is possible to see in such cases the development of a rudimentary apparatus to detect and manage homosexuality among immigrants."[76] This system relied on finding the immigrant "likely to become a public charge," or incapable of self-support. Reliance on the already existing category of public charge reveals that immigration policy had "no special legal tool for vetting aliens 'afflicted with homosexuality' in the early years of the twentieth century."[77] Agents of the state "lacked not only an adequate regulatory apparatus but conceptual mastery over what it desired to regulate."[78]

Paralleling the work of contemporary sexologists, immigration officials tended to see sexual perversion as one of many possible indicators of degeneracy. And, immigration officials worked to discover physical indicators of sexual degeneracy, as Lydston and others proposed. Officials at Ellis Island would conduct naked body inspections, often concentrating on immigrants' genitalia, searching for indicators of same-sex attraction.[79] Contemporary sexology suggested that same-sex sexual activity, as it was not procreative, required less energy; therefore, individuals so inclined were generally considered feeble.[80] Consequently, given this lack of energy, so-called inverts were incapable of citizenship insofar as citizenship has been historically predicated, at least in part, upon the idea of "the self-governing individual who could dispose of his labor profitably."[81] The rationale for exclusion was not sexual perversion per se but the way in which sexual perversion indicated likelihood of financial dependence or destitution and thus incapacity for citizenship.

Canaday reviews a number of cases in which the public charge was applied to individuals who did not physically or behaviorally conform to sexual or gender norms, and each bears out the link between sexual defiance and economic dependence.[82] For example, an Italian immigrant, Francesco Spagliano, was denied entry due, in part, to arrested sexual development; the inspecting surgeon noted that Spagliano had a small penis. And, a Public Health Services official interpreted the small penis to indicate sexual perversion: "Persons so affected are liable, owing to inability to satisfactorily perform sexual congress, to become addicted to unnatural practices."[83] Similarly, Nicolaos Xilomenos of Greece was denied entry, although considered physically robust, because his deformed genitals were taken as evidence of lack of sexual development and a precursor to sexual perversion.[84]

Canaday also writes of how gender transgression illustrates the way public charges were not dependent upon discoveries of anatomical abnormalities. Hungarian immigrant Verona Sogan was dressed in female clothes, but medical examiners considered her to be a man.[85] Sogan, like Xilomenos and Spagliano, was characterized as showing "arrested sexual development, which affects ability to earn a living." Again echoing the common sexology tropes of the era, the acting commissioner of the Bureau of Immigration wrote, "He is much undersized and rather effeminate in appearance, and I am informed that persons afflicted such as . . . he are prone to be moral perverts."[86] To make this linkage between sexual inversion and the economic requirements of citizenship transparent, inspectors recommended barring entry because "we doubt whether anyone . . . knowing the circumstances would care to employ him."[87]

The intertwining of sexual perversion with likelihood of economic dependency negated the need for a specific ban on homosexuals. But, it also meant that there was little way to rationalize exclusion for an individual who might demonstrate qualities of sexual deviance while also being economically well off. Canaday provides the example of Reverend Parthenios Colonis, an immigrant who was priest of a Greek Orthodox church in Wheeling, West Virginia.[88] Acting on rumors that he had attempted to have sex with young men, some townspeople contacted immigration officials to investigate Colonis. The Bureau of Immigration recommended that the priest be deported but said that the public charge designation did not apply. Responding to an inquiry as to whether designating an immigrant a moral pervert was grounds for exclusion under the terms of the Immigration Act of 1917, the bureau admitted, "Moral perverts are not specifically excluded by any of the provisions of that act."[89] Bureau officials raised the public charge clause but conceded, "But this alien has no physical disabilities, holds a remunerative position and . . . has plenty of money and is backed by influential friends."[90] Ultimately, the bureau canceled its warrant for deportation.

In these examples, the central claim of Canaday's work is clear: there was no specific ban on homosexual immigrants because regulatory authorities did not see the homosexual. Rather, they saw a sexual and gender transgressor, an individual who behaved or exhibited physical markers that indicated a sexual deviancy that would cause economic dependence and thus an inability to become a fruitful citizen. According to Canaday, "Before the state could equip itself with a provision barring homosexual aliens, the homosexual had to appear to immigration officials."[91] But these officials did not see a homosexual; they saw, as contemporary sexologists would suggest, a broad category of indicators of sexual perversities and deviance.

Furthermore, this recognition was worked out by immigration officials over time through the very nature of the positions they held, through the inspections they conducted, in which they could narrow the scope of qualities they considered indicative of sexual deviance, and through the increase of medical and scientific study of homosexuality, so that by midcentury, government officials—whether in immigration, military, or civil service—would come to see the homosexual defined most prominently as an individual who sexually desires someone of the same sex. Thus, in time, "the state's work of discovery and creation would gel into something much more recognizable as homosexuality."[92] Learning to see homosexuality and to consider the homosexual a threat to community motivated state building. Identification and exclusion required monitoring, which required more state-sponsored research and more officials. By detailing bureaucratic learning, Canaday shows that the state's interest in homosexuality did not commence with a mid-twentieth-century Cold War obsession with an alleged homosexual menace. Cold War–era policies were the culmination of a fifty-year state-building project that defined the boundaries of national community.

"I Am Coming to the Homo Part of It": Homosexuals as Security Threat

Once regulatory agents framed homosexuality as a threat to the national community, many worked to maintain and deepen its exclusion by defining it as a threat to national security. But, as was the case with immigration policy, military and civil service policy exhibited a similar dynamic of *gradually* coming to see the homosexual as threat. The threat of the modern homosexual to national security was not in place until midcentury. Indeed, it was not until World War II that the homosexual person was explicitly barred from military service, and this is precisely because the homosexual person did not exist in the eyes of regulatory authorities.

The military has sanctioned individuals for same-sex sexual behavior. The first recorded discharge for same-sex relations was in 1778.[93] During World War I, discharges were issued when soldiers were found guilty of forcible sodomy.[94] The critical shift that took place in midcentury was a move away from the Progressive conception of sexual perversion as a mark of degeneracy and toward a view of same-sex attraction as an indicator of psychopathology. Indeed, military physicians and psychiatrists were instrumental in recasting homosexuality not as a social disease, as early sexologists maintained, but as an individual mental disorder.[95] Consequently, during World War II, draftees were questioned about homosexual tendencies and excluded if considered homosexual.[96]

American mobilization for the Second World War is central to the emergence of the modern homosexual. Historian John D'Emilio points to the way "the war temporarily weakened the patterns of daily life that channeled men and women toward heterosexuality and inhibited homosexual expression."[97] The military's new policy of explicitly inquiring into a draftee's erotic desires ruptured the silence that shrouded homosexuality among the general public.[98] And, military policy proactively excluded the homosexual as an identity, rather than administering post hoc punishment for discovered sexual behavior. This pattern of increasing exclusion paralleled the trend in other fields from sanctioning particular sexual behaviors toward sanctioning expressed individual identities. Previously, the sexual act was the target, dealt with by the military's criminal justice system; now, in an interesting parallel to Foucault's claim about the creation and control of the homosexual, the military banned not an act but an individual.[99]

During World War II, the army issued about five thousand discharges for homosexuality, while the navy issued about four thousand.[100] Discharged individuals fell into three categories. A violent sexual offender would be court-martialed and, if found guilty, dishonorably discharged. The second category included persons "actually homosexual in their respective inclinations."[101] This homosexual was discharged undesirably.[102] The third category of homosexual included individuals who engaged in homosexual activity, but the activity might be explained as the consequence of "curiosity or intoxication."[103] These individuals were to be treated and returned to duty. The majority of homosexual offenses fell into the second category of undesirable discharge, which could occur under conditions deemed either honorable or dishonorable. Such discharges were issued on blue paper and known as "blue discharges."[104]

The blue discharge was developed as part of a military reform for more humane treatment of homosexuals than existing regulation allowed. Instead of being imprisoned for engaging in banned same-sex behavior, the homosexual would be removed from military service. But, as Canaday points out, the new discharge required yet another layer of bureaucratic apparatus because it bypassed existing formal courts-martial: "the new discharge policy vastly expanded the military's regulatory and surveillance apparatus and made it much easier to remove soldiers suspected of homosexual acts or tendencies."[105] While the new policy made it easier to remove homosexuals because it did not require the high thresholds of evidence that a formal court-martial demanded, it also compelled administrative construction. Newer regulatory recognition—seeing the homosexual as a person rather than just seeing homosexuality as a banned sex act with sanctions already prescribed and apparatus for such sanctions already in place—required more state building.

Despite the military's hunt for and exclusion of homosexuals, its new policy was thwarted by ambiguous terminology and the institutional design of federalism. The ambiguity stemmed from the category of the blue discharge itself. This discharge was issued under multiple circumstances and for various offenses, including homosexuality, drug addiction, bed wetting, and challenges to the military's segregation.[106] A blue discharge, therefore, did not negate a soldier's eligibility for benefits under the new Serviceman's Readjustment Act of 1944, also known as the GI Bill of Rights. Congressional debate on the GI Bill indicates strong disagreement as to whether individuals given a blue discharge and thus discharged "under conditions other than dishonorable" should be eligible for benefits. But, the faction that held for the most liberal distribution of benefits won the argument, particularly because the blue discharge was issued for "minor offenses." The Senate report on the GI Bill concluded, therefore, "it is the opinion of the committee that such offenses should not bar entitlement to benefits."[107]

Eligibility determinations and disbursal of benefits were left to the Department of Veterans Affairs (VA). But, in late 1944, VA administrator Frank Hines admitted that the department was "having considerable difficulty in defining the term 'under conditions other than dishonorable'" that was in the GI Bill and consequently sought guidance on which blue discharge offenses did not negate benefits eligibility.[108] In October 1944, the VA issued guidelines that followed the World War Veterans Act of 1924 and stipulated that any discharge involving "moral turpitude" would be considered dishonorable and would cancel benefits eligibility.[109] But, in rendering that policy, the VA ignored that the act required civil or military conviction, and most homosexuals—those in the second category—were not convicted.

The eligibility of homosexual veterans for benefits was fostered not only by the unclear meaning of discharge "under conditions other than honorable" but also by the federal structure of the department, which relied on local boards for disbursement. This federalism offered not only the potential for policy experimentation but also the possibility and probability of creative defiance of federal authority. Local boards resisted implementing the VA directive that a blue discharge for "moral turpitude" would constitute a dishonorable discharge, perhaps because at the local level, members of the boards knew these discharged men and women personally. As Canaday finds, "A memo from the VA headquarters expressed frustration that local VA officials . . . were awarding benefits to blue discharges so long as they had not been convicted under civil or military law."[110] In April 1945, the department issued another directive, which stated that both homosexual acts and homosexual tendencies were to be treated as a dishonorable discharge and thereby bar the veteran from benefits.[111] The more clearly stated policy furthered the increasing degree to which policy drew a dichotomous distinction between homosexuality and heterosexuality. Nevertheless, local boards resisted and continued to ask for clarification to adjudicate eligibility.[112]

The tension between local and federal authority points not only to the importance of entrepreneurial action and small forms of resistance that follow from opportunity structures implicit in a federal design. It also begs the question as to why the disbursal of federal GI benefits was not centralized. The answer may parallel similar assessments of early patterns of Social Security benefits access in the 1930s and 1940s; these emphasize the desire to maintain systems of racial apartheid. As Robert Lieberman has cogently argued, the New Deal welfare state reinforced entrenched racial biases. National policy aims were supplanted by local control in the pragmatic effort to secure congressional support:

> The Social Security Act of 1935 was a mixture of policies, created in the same formative political impulse, that shared a common underlying goal—providing some measure of economic security for those who found themselves in need through circumstances beyond their control. . . . And yet each of the programs at its origin compromised the inclusion of African-Americans not only through race-laden eligibility requirements but also through administrative arrangements that restricted black access to benefits. Where African-Americans were potentially included among a policy's beneficiaries, Southerners demanded institutional structures that preserved a maximum of local control. Conversely, strong, national social policy institutions were politically possible only when African-Americans were excluded from the center.[113]

By distributing federal benefits via local boards, state governments could exclude African Americans. As Ira Katznelson finds, the GI Bill's "provisions for dispersion of administrative responsibilities . . . were designed to shield Jim Crow."[114] Thus, whereas the local authority enabled discharged homosexuals to sometimes receive benefits, it also fostered exclusion of African Americans. A developmental approach to regulation of sexual citizenship draws attention to this intersection of racial and sexual identity precisely because it attends to the way government—through multiple levels in a federalist system—constructs, includes, and excludes certain identities. Canaday points out the irony: "The decentralized administration of benefits—devised to allow southern states to keep black veterans out of the program—thus may have ironically slowed homosexual exclusion for a time."[115]

The construction of the postwar national security state is inextricably connected to a contemporaneous moral panic over homosexuality. After World War II, the exclusion of homosexuals from military service remained in place, but the rationale for the policy changed. While the military ban had been predicated on the idea that homosexuals were mentally unstable, it shifted to a more general concern that homosexuality posed a security risk.[116] This change paralleled the rationales for purging gay and lesbian civil servants from the federal government, an episode of political homophobia concurrent with the anticommunist Red Scare and referred to as the Lavender Scare.

The Roosevelt and Truman administrations, particularly the Truman State Department headed by Secretary of State Dean Acheson, were plagued by rumors of rampant homosexuality.[117] And, during the early years of the Cold War, the idea of homosexuality as a security risk flourished.[118] Fears of alleged communist and homosexual infiltration overlapped, and anticommunist and antihomosexual propaganda of the period employed similar themes of disease and contagion. Ironically, the demonization of Senator Joseph McCarthy, the face of overzealous efforts to root out alleged communists, relied, in part, upon the "marking as illicit his relationship with another man—an unsurprising rhetorical device, given the ways that homophobia and anticommunism were intertwined in the domestic politics of the time."[119] The Senate's most prominent voice of the Red Scare ironically fell victim to the concurrent Lavender Scare.[120]

Historians point to a June 1947 memo drafted by the Senate Appropriations Committee warning of "a deliberate, calculated program being carried out not only to protect Communist personnel in high places, but to reduce security and intelligence protection to a nullity" as the first articulation of concern. The letter alleged that this program involved "the extensive employment in highly classified positions of admitted homosexuals, who are historically known to be security risks."[121] Secretary of State George Marshall responded by establishing a Personnel Security Review Board, which would ensure that homosexuals and communists, among others, would not be employed within the State Department. Congress further empowered the secretary by attaching to its appropriations for the department the so-called McCarran rider, which gave the secretary absolute discretion to dismiss any government employee who might constitute a security risk.[122]

The State Department review board established guidelines that barred anyone with indicators of weak character, defined as "habitual drunkenness, sexual perversion, moral turpitude, financial irresponsibility or criminal record," from employment within the State Department. The board held that such persons would be more likely to engage with a subversive individual or communist due to their "basic weakness of character or lack of judgment." Between 1947 and 1949, the board identified and removed ninety homosexuals from the department.[123] During this same period, over three thousand military personnel were dismissed from military service for alleged homosexuality.[124] All of this was done prior to Senator Joseph McCarthy's accusations of communist infiltration of the federal government. Consequently, historian David K. Johnson maintains, "Clearly, concern about homosexuals as security risks was neither a creation of Senator McCarthy nor a minor byproduct of the Red Scare."[125]

Three years later, on February 9, 1950, McCarthy famously declared before the Republican Women's Club of Wheeling, West Virginia, that the State Department employed 205 known communists.[126] This accusation cast doubt on the effectiveness of the review board. On February 28, 1950, a Senate subcommittee of the Committee on Appropriations, chaired by Senator Pat McCarran (D-NE), questioned Secretary of State Dean Acheson and John Peurifoy, the personnel chief at the State Department, about the existing policy. At the hearing, Senator Styles Bridges (R-NH) asked how the review board identified individuals who might constitute a security risk. Secretary Acheson summarized those characteristics that raised suspicion: "whether the person has, as a matter of character, any defect which would lead him into any of these difficulties. An example would be a habitual alcoholic or a person who has any other physical or moral defect which could be preyed upon or which might be used by somebody who was attempting to penetrate into the Department." Bridges then inquired as to whether a homosexual or a "person with a criminal record," by which he probably meant someone convicted on a morals charge under existing sodomy or lewdness law, would also fit into this category.[127]

By redirecting the questioning from communist ideology to homosexuality, Bridges sought to provoke a more thorough housecleaning of President Truman's State Department. Indeed, weeks after his hearing, Bridges characterized his goal as identifying any "bad security risks," which he defined by parroting Acheson's definition: "A man doesn't have to be a spy or a Communist to be a bad security risk. He can be a drunkard or a criminal or a homosexual."[128] At the hearing, Bridges asked how many department employees were found to be disloyal, i.e., communist, and dismissed since January 1, 1947. Peurifoy responded that one had been fired and ten were allowed to resign. Bridges then pressed further into the category of homosexuals by asking, "how many other people . . . have been under investigation by the Department or have resigned or have seen fit to sever their service with the Department during that period?" Seeking to clarify to whom Bridges was referring, Peurifoy framed his answer thus: "In this shady category that you referred to earlier, there are 91 cases sir." Bridges then sought further explanation of what this "shady category" included, and Peurifoy responded, "We are talking about people of moral weakness and so forth that we have gotten ridden of." Seeking even more specificity, Senator McCarran then asked, "Now, will you make your answer a little clearer please?" Peurifoy obliged: "Most of these were homosexuals, Mr. Chairman."[129]

Peurifoy's revelation of ninety-one homosexuals dismissed from the State Department, coupled with McCarthy's accusation of over two hundred communists still working at the department, compelled further investigation. Peurifoy's admission was the first public acknowledgment of the dismissal. According to one historian, this "revelation set in motion a chain of events that would have widespread repercussions for governmental security policies and millions of people affected by them for the next twenty years."[130] Prior to Peurifoy's testimony, the Senate had already authorized the Foreign Relations Committee, chaired by Millard Tydings (D-MD), to investigate McCarthy's previous allegations. Now, in the wake of Peurifoy's admission of ninety-one homosexuals, senators called to expand the investigation to include security risks, which included homosexuals, rather than focus on the narrower category of disloyal employees, which included primarily communists.

That debate came to a head in the Senate on April 25, 1950, as Senator William Jenner (R-IN) commented on the disagreement between McCarthy and Tydings:

> The Senator from Wisconsin has asked the Senator from Maryland a question about a homosexual, and the Senator from Maryland has asked the Senator from Wisconsin about how many Communists there are in the State Department. The Senators are using my time in doing so. If the Senators can work out between them in the committee the question of Communists and of "homos," that is what the American people want done.[131]

Tydings, increasingly frustrated and exhausted by the conflation of communists and homosexuals as equivalent risks, refused to shift the investigation's primary focus from communists. He replied,

> I am coming to the homo part of it. The first thing I think we ought to do is to get some of the Communists that we have been hearing so much about, out of the Government, if they are there. . . . That is what we are doing mostly now. I am giving 7 or 8 hours a day to it now, and I am going to give 12 hours a day, if necessary, to it. I am going to get every Communist I can lay my hands on, and I am going to have all the hearings in open session. But I should like to know who the 57 card-carrying Communists known to Acheson now in the State Department are, so I can get hold of them.[132]

Jenner, annoyed by this back and forth between McCarthy and Tydings over who were communists versus who were homosexuals, suggested a compromise: "Maybe I can act as an arbiter. If the Senator from Maryland will tell the Senator from Wisconsin who the homos are, and if the Senator from Wisconsin will tell the Senator from Maryland about the 57 card-carrying Communists—maybe such a trade can be made between the Senator from Maryland and the Senator from Wisconsin." Giving in, Tydings responded, "I will tell the Senator about the homos. I know there is a great desire to shift from Communists to homos." Jenner contended that knowing the names of the homosexuals was of great importance: "I do not know which is worst. Does the Senator?" Tydings appeared to consent. "Let us shift to it," he said. "When I was given this information [about homosexuals at the State Department], I pursued it constantly. I got our force working on it. I have documents in our office—and I am going to talk . . ." But then Tydings switched direction. "No, I will not do that. I will not disclose what the evidence is. But when we get around to it, it will be full and complete for the committee to act on."[133]

Later in the debate, Tydings explained why his committee's focus should remain on disloyal communists rather than expand to a broader category of national security risks, which would include homosexuals. Homosexuality, according to Tydings, constituted a disease but not an obvious security threat, at least not one on a par with communist affiliation. Defending his position against critiques of the Truman administration, Tydings defended his approach to the investigation:

> I try to be fair and impartial. However, if this continued haranguing and heckling continues on the floor of the Senate, it will only prevent us from finding a Communist who might be in the State Department or anywhere else in the Government. I ask Senators to give us a free hand and to give us their cooperation. If they do, Senators can bet their bottom dollar that we will find everything that it is possible to find. . . . I ask my colleagues to stop the continual heckling of the subcommittee about homosexuals and other matters of that kind; and let us get down, first, to the matter of investigating any possible disloyalty. Obviously, a man may have the terrible disease which has been referred to, and yet may not be a party to foreign espionage or may not be a party to deliberately being disloyal to his Government.[134]

Even so, Tydings held that homosexuals should not be employed in government as their condition did threaten the nation, although he could not specify how: "Of course, it is a risk to have in the Government service persons who are afflicted with that disease. Nevertheless, our first job is to get out of the Government service the Communist and the red spies. If we are sincere, we should not obscure that job by bringing in incidental matters, for we can take care of them when we have more time to do so."[135] But, the prioritization of rooting out communists is evident.

Bristling at the idea that homosexuality posed a lesser threat, Senator Kenneth Wherry (R-NE) took the floor. He remained resolute in his quest to ferret out homosexuals even if Tydings refused: "I shall continue as an American citizen and as the junior Senator from Nebraska to do everything I can to clean out moral perverts and subversives from Government; and I am willing to be associated with any man who has the courage of his convictions in an endeavor to accomplish that objective."[136]

Republicans, who had not held the White House in nearly twenty years, capitalized on the increasing panic that homosexuality was rampant in the Truman administration. In April of 1950, Guy Gabrielson, national chairman of the Republican Party, sent a letter to seven thousand party employees suggesting that "perhaps as dangerous as the actual

Communists are the sexual perverts who have infiltrated our Government in recent years."[137] In this first dispatch to party officials in 1950, Gabrielson bemoaned that federal communications regulations as well as prevalent social norms prevented the public from hearing the true nature of the threat: "The country would be more aroused over this tragic angle if it were not for the difficulties of the newspapers and radio commentators in adequately presenting the facts, while respecting the decency of their American audiences."[138] Consequently, he implied, the homosexual menace was gravely underplayed and misunderstood. Similarly, former Republican presidential nominee and governor of New York Thomas Dewey "accused the Democratic national administration of tolerating spies, traitors, and sex offenders in the Government Service."[139]

Ultimately, the Tydings report dismissed McCarthy's accusations as fraudulent, and it made no findings regarding homosexuals employed within the State Department.[140] On July 21, 1950, the day after the Tydings report was published, Senator Jenner criticized it as a "blasphemous perversion of the truth," and perhaps the use of the word "perverse" was deliberate.[141] Days later Jenner maintained that an "army of sexual perverts who are engaged in the filthy immorality of blackmail and degradation" existed in the federal government.[142] He and Wherry would push forward in their quest to root them out.

In the wake of Peurifoy's initial admission, Wherry convinced Senator Lister Hill (D-AL) to convene closed hearings of the Senate subcommittee for appropriations for the District of Columbia to investigate the extent of homosexuality in the executive branch. The committee's report, under Hill's name, found that there was no general problem of rampant homosexuality in the administration and that existing policies to guard against that potential were more than adequate.[143] However, two months prior to the release of the Tydings committee report, Wherry detailed his own findings on the extent of homosexuality within the executive branch as a minority report of the Hill subcommittee.

The reports' respective titles indicate how they framed the issue at hand. The Hill report referenced "Testimony on Subversive Activity and Homosexuals in Government," which both separated the issues as distinct and utilized the medical term "homosexual." By contrast, the Wherry report referenced the "Infiltration of Subversives and Moral Perverts into the Executive Branch." "Infiltration" is a far more menacing term, "moral perverts" was a more inflammatory phrase than the clinical "homosexual," and the specification of the executive branch suggested a particular target: the Truman administration. The Wherry report drew the opposite conclusion from the one offered by Hill and later by Tydings, namely, that Peurifoy's ninety-one homosexuals represented a mere fraction of the problem, and that the existing program established by the Truman administration to secure the executive branch from infiltration was woefully ineffective.[144] Concerned that the homosexuals in the federal government numbered well into the thousands, Wherry ended his report with a proposed resolution that the Committee on the Judiciary establish a subcommittee to investigate the matter further.

On May 19, 1950, Senate Resolution 280 reached the floor. The resolution called for the establishment of a committee that would

> make a full and complete study and investigation of (a) the alleged employment by the departments and agencies of the Government of homosexuals and other moral perverts, and (b) the preparedness of authorities of the District of Columbia, as well as the appropriate authorities of the Federal Government within the District . . . for the protection of life and property against the threat to security, inherent in the employment of such perverts.[145]

This committee, the Senate Investigations Subcommittee of the Committee on Expenditures in the Executive Department, was chaired by Senator Clyde Hoey (D-NC), and its hearings and testimony were conducted in executive session and kept out of the public eye, a circumstance that reflected the Truman administration's attempts to dampen any further accusation of homosexuality within its ranks. The administration sought to work with the Hoey committee to establish procedures that might minimize the administration's exposure while also ensuring that the administration would not appear to stymie the work of the committee.[146]

Aside from attempting to influence the process of the committee, the administration also worked to shape the narrative framework through which homosexuality would be understood. Reiterating ideas put forward by Tydings, the administration tried to minimize discussion of homosexuality as a security risk and sought to frame it as a medical condition. For example, it launched a seminar under the aegis of the National Institutes for Mental Health, titled "Perversion among Government Workers," the central message of which was that homosexuals, if they served in positions that did not require the handling of classified materials, posed no threat to government.[147]

The administration's efforts to frame homosexuality as a medical concern and not a security threat gained little traction. The Hoey committee's chief counsel, Francis Flannigan, was more interested in scheduling testimony that would evaluate the security risk angle rather than the medical concern. Flannigan dismissed medical studies, most notably Alfred Kinsey's *Sexual Behavior in the Human Male*, by saying that "Kinsey doesn't know anything. He's a god-damn statistician," and contending that "[t]he medical experts knew less than anyone else."[148] Instead, Flannigan scheduled testimony from the director of the Central Intelligence Agency, Admiral Roscoe Hillenkoetter, who recounted the story of Colonel Alfred Redl, head of the Austrian intelligence agency before the First World War, who was blackmailed with threats of exposure of homosexuality into spilling national secrets to the Russians. Despite the fact that later witnesses among security officials in the army, navy, and air force cast doubt on blackmail potential and that Hillenkoetter himself suggested that the circumstances of Redl bore little relation to the situation of contemporary civil service officers, the Hoey committee's final report leaned heavily on the blackmail possibility to justify the exclusion of homosexuals from the federal workforce.[149] The committee was far less interested in the more tolerant counternarrative of homosexuality as a medical condition: "By the time the committee got around to hearing testimony from the medical community, only two senators other than the chairman bothered to attend."[150]

The Hoey committee issued its final report in December 1950, and it gave congressional legitimacy to recognizing homosexuality as a threat to national security. The report, "Employment of Homosexuals and Other Sex Perverts in the U.S. Government," claimed,

> Homosexuals and other sex perverts are not proper persons to be employed in Government for two reasons; first they are generally unsuitable, and second, they constitute security risks. . . . [P]erverts are frequently victimized by blackmailers who threaten to expose their sexual devi-

ance. . . . [T]hose who engage in overt acts of perversion lack the emotional stability of normal persons. In addition there is an abundance of evidence to sustain the conclusion that indulgence in acts of sex perversion weakens the moral fiber of an individual to a degree that he is not suitable for a position of responsibility. . . . The lack of emotional stability which is found in most sex perverts and the weakness of their moral fiber, makes them susceptible to the blandishments of the foreign espionage.[151]

The report sealed the discourse through which homosexuality would be framed in the federal government for years to come. When Republicans gained control of the White House in 1952, Eisenhower extended this absolute discretionary authority throughout the federal bureaucracy via Executive Order 10450. The order formally excluded anyone from federal employment who exhibited "any behavior which suggests the individual is not reliable or trustworthy," and such behaviors included "any criminal, infamous, dishonest, immoral, or notoriously disgraceful conduct, habitual use of intoxicants to excess, drug addiction, or sexual perversion." While the order clarified and unified the policies against sexual perversion—the common characterization of homosexuality at the time—David Johnson notes, "the inclusion of the more specific reference to 'sexual perversion' was unprecedented."[152] He further points out the incredible expansion of administrative power that the order permitted:

[T]he Eisenhower administration institutionalized within the executive branch the security concerns that Republican politicians had been railing about since 1950. Security officers rather than legislators would take the lead in overseeing the new security program. . . . The Eisenhower administration expanded the government's security apparatus from a few federal agencies to cover the entire federal workforce while simultaneously broadening its focus from specific concerns about loyalty to vaguer notions of "national security."[153]

In short, concerns about homosexuality contributed to the construction of national security policy; building of the postwar national security state apparatus is inextricably connected with the contemporaneous moral panic over homosexuality. In the sixteen months following the implementation of Executive Order 10450, homosexuals were dismissed from government posts at a rate of forty per month.[154] According to one estimate, by 1958, 20 percent of all adults employed in the country had been screened for potential as a security risk.[155]

A gradual backlash against the campaign to purge homosexuals from federal government began to develop by the late 1950s. Criticism came from foundations such as the Fund for the Republic and the Rockefeller Foundation, as well as from academia, particularly the July 1955 issue of the *Annals of the American Academy of Political and Social Science*.[156] The Supreme Court curbed the expansive scope of Executive Order 10450 in its decision in *Cole v. Young* (1956), which held that authority to dismiss homosexuals from government service could only be rightfully applied if the employee's position actually involved matters of national security.

When Democrats regained control of Congress in 1954, it began to review the security measures that followed from Eisenhower's order. Senator Hubert Humphrey, who chaired the Senate Government Operations subcommittee, characterized the executive order as establishing a "government of men and not of laws," and these men, the nearly nine hundred security officers in the Civil Service Commission charged with investigating and dismissing homosexuals, "represent[ed] one of the most powerful and influential forces within the Government itself and within American life generally" because they threatened the "future economic well-being and personal happiness of millions of Americans."[157]

Even as congressional committees and the Supreme Court exerted pressure to curb the institutionalized excesses of the Cold War antigay witch hunt, the Martin and Mitchell affair of 1960 perpetuated the specter of the homosexual menace and the imagined nexus between homosexuality and espionage. Bernon Mitchell was an analyst for the National Security Agency who defected with his friend, William Martin, to the Soviet Union. Subsequent investigation focused on Mitchell's homosexuality; although Martin appeared to be heterosexual, the same-sex coupling of two single men fostered innuendo in the popular press.[158] In response, the Eisenhower administration stepped up its investigation of homosexuality in government once again. The NSA subsequently fired twenty-six of its own staff for alleged homosexuality in the immediate wake of the defection.[159]

Not until 1969, a few years after gay activist Frank Kammeny, a civil servant fired for homosexuality, established a branch of the Mattachine

Society in Washington, DC, and led the first picket of the White House on behalf of fired gay and lesbian federal workers, did the tide against exclusion begin to turn. In *Norton v. Macy*, in which a NASA budget analyst challenged his dismissal after an arrest for picking up another man in a popular gay cruising area, Judge Bazelon of the DC Circuit Court of Appeals found against the Civil Service Commission's policy of treating immorality, and homosexuality defined as an immoral act, as a rational basis for dismissal.[160] The court required a connection between an employee's private expressions of homosexuality, i.e., his or her off-duty conduct, and the justification for firing. Simply asserting homosexuality as grounds for firing—as the federal government, whether through congressional findings or executive orders, had done for the past twenty years—was not enough. The decision came down on July 1, 1969, and it marked the beginning of the end of the exclusion of gays and lesbians from the federal workforce. While subsequent legal rulings upheld dismissals when a connection between homosexuality and security was sustained, e.g. *Schlegel v. United States* (1969), the Civil Service abandoned the exclusionary policy by 1973. [161] In a December bulletin to all agencies, the service adopted the *Norton* standard; federal agencies could not "find a person unsuitable for Federal employment merely because that person is homosexual," although they could refuse to hire a homosexual when "homosexual conduct affects job fitness—excluding from such considerations, however, unsubstantiated conclusions concerning possible embarrassment to the Federal service."[162] The foundation for barring gays and lesbians from federal employment narrowed considerably. The *Norton* decision, a major turning point in the way the federal government saw its homosexual citizens, is often overshadowed by the Stonewall riots in Greenwich Village, which had occurred only a couple of days prior and are often characterized in the popular imagination as "the emblematic event in modern gay and lesbian history."[163]

Variations in Political Homophobia and the Modalities of Regulatory Recognition

Why did the Lavender Scare occur when it did? The scare and subsequent policies of exclusion such as the Eisenhower executive order constituted what historians Michael Bosia and Meredith Weiss refer to as "political homophobia," or a "state strategy . . . powerful enough to structure the experiences of sexual minorities and expressions of sexuality" and "for building an authoritative notion of national collective identity."[164] Why was there an episode of political homophobia in the 1950s but no episode prior, particularly if a seismic Red Scare also occurred in the wake of the First World War? In answering this question, political scientist Rick Valelly contends that while "straight acceptance of gays and lesbians did not exist in the 1920s, 1930s, and 1940s . . . neither did persecution of gays and lesbians exist in the United States before the 1950s."[165] While Terry's accounts of urban police raids in the 1930s, recounted earlier in this chapter, calls Valelly's description into question, Valelly is right to suggest that the Lavender Scare was a unique and unprecedented episode of targeted political homophobia by the federal government. Explanations of its timing have relied on postwar conservative shifts in political culture that reinforced traditional gender norms and values that the war experience disrupted. For example, D'Emilio contends, "The anti-homosexual campaigns of the 1950s represented but one front in a widespread effort to reconstruct patterns of sexuality and gender relations shaken by depression and war."[166] But, Valelly offers a different answer, which explains this episode as a manifestation of particular institutional developments, electoral incentives, and entrepreneurial actions.

This answer is not incongruous with explanations that emphasize increasing cultural hostility toward gender-role transgression, sexual difference, and political ideologies other than liberalism. Nevertheless, for Valelly, the Lavender Scare served electoral objectives, namely, Republican aims to retake the presidency and Congress after being shut out as a minority party for nearly twenty years. Furthermore, political homophobia acquired its particular partisan and policy traction due to the creation of a new institution: the congressional investigative subcommittee.[167] The Lavender Scare, then, happened at a particular moment because political developments—partisan Republican electoral incentives that compelled minority Republicans to utilize the issue of homosexuality in an entrepreneurial fashion as well as a post–New Deal congressional desire to reign in and investigate executive authority in the wake of dominant Roosevelt years—established a context for deepening the stigma associated with homosexual identity. Valelly contends that the nonoccurrence of a similar scare after World War I indicates how the Lavender Scare served particular electoral imperatives and took shape due to particular institutional developments at midcentury.[168] In illustrating this claim, Valelly brings the institutional dynamics of Congress, presidency, and political party into a deeper connection with sexuality, particularly homosexuality, than before.

Insofar as the Lavender Scare was explicitly targeted against the homosexual—against an individual whose sense of sexual selfhood is predominantly characterized by same-sex desire—it was unique. But, it was not the first manifestation of political homophobia in the United States. Our potential blindness to earlier episodes of political homophobia stems from attempts to find definitive hostilities toward homosexuality and the homosexual when those concepts were neither fully formed nor resonant prior to midcentury. The Lavender Scare was grounded in a fear of individuals who expressed same-sex erotic desire. However, this specific homophobia was very much a midcentury position; it relied on a particular type of regulatory recognition of homosexuality that was not fully developed until midcentury. Therefore, earlier episodes would not necessarily take the shape of the Lavender Scare because the homosexual did not clearly exist in the form in which it had been defined by the mid-twentieth century. If we are to see earlier episodes, the particular modality of regulatory recognition of homosexuality—as an ill-defined combination of various sexual inversions and gender transgressions—needs to be engaged.

The post–World War II Lavender Scare is more readily apparent because of the work done by bureaucrats and military personnel to make the homosexual identity more concrete by the mid-twentieth century. Employing the first modality of regulatory recognition, of seeing not homosexuality and homosexuals but a broad category of sexual and gender transgression, reveals two earlier episodes of political homophobia. The first occurred in the years of the late nineteenth and early twentieth centuries and was made manifest first in attacks on antipartisan mugwump political reformers as effeminate and second in Progressive reformers' attempts to bolster their own manliness, having learned from the failures of their mugwump predecessors. The second was wrapped within the context of the first Red Scare, in which many of the anarchists deported from the United States were also fierce advocates of homosexual decriminalization and other legal reforms and were also attacked by Progressives, notably Theodore Roosevelt, as threatening sexual and gender confusion and disorder that would undermine the Progressive attempts to cultivate a robust democratic national community. In other words, these episodes of political homophobia were not antihomosexual per se (as the Lavender Scare was) because the regulatory recognition of homosexuality had not yet fully developed. Instead, these instances were shaped by the ideas and concepts of sexual inversion, fears of degeneracy, and concerns about the collapse of gender differences that compelled and were maintained by contemporary sexologists.

When Richard Hofstadter commented on the intertwining of anti-homosexual and anticommunist rhetoric that defined midcentury American politics, he noted a historical precedent in the late nineteenth century. According to Hofstadter, "more recent attacks by Senator Mc-Carthy and others upon the Eastern and English-oriented prep-school personnel of the State Department, associated with charges of homo-sexuality, are not an altogether novel element in the history of Ameri-can invective."[169] He was referencing criticism of Liberal Republican reformers, so-called mugwumps, who bolted from their party in 1872 over disgust with corruption in the Grant administration. That act left them vulnerable to charges of not grasping the quid pro quo dynamics endemic to successful party functioning. But, as Hofstadter notes, these criticisms were not limited to the dismissal of these reformers as "hypo-critical and impractical."[170] Instead, they attacked the reformers' mas-culinity. The mugwumps were men of "fastidious manners," denounced as "political hermaphrodites," and members of the "third sex," defined in terms of emergent theories of sexual inversion: "effeminate without being either masculine or feminine; unable either to beget or bear; pos-sessing neither fecundity nor virility; endowed with the contempt of men and the derision of women, and doomed to sterility, isolation, and extinction."[171]

By refusing to commit to the binary party structure of politics, these nineteenth-century reformers were the political manifestation of the newly discovered sexual invert. If sexual inverts were considered a com-bination of both sexes, having "bodies, conduct, attitudes, tastes and personalities characteristic of the 'opposite' sex," then mugwumps em-bodied similar peculiarities and blendings.[172] They not only displayed the effeminacy that challenged contemporary meanings of masculinity, ranging from bookishness to fashion consciousness, but also advocated a politics that disrupted norms of participation so integrally tied to the Jacksonian party politics defining much of the nineteenth century.

In his account of the meanings of political manhood at the turn of the twentieth century, historian Kevin P. Murphy examines the intersections of the contemporaneous medical development of sexual inversion and the critique of mugwump reformers as gender transgressors. By the late 1870s, Murphy argues, politicians who opposed the mugwump characterization of party politics as corrupt began to frame their critique using the emerging discourse on sexual inversion: "They utilized the concept of a third sex to make sense of threats to the political system," and "by linking their critique of reformers to the stigmatization of the sexual invert, party stalwarts discovered a powerful rhetorical weapon with which to oppose reform."[173] Mugwumps articulated an alternative notion of masculinity, one that drew upon traditions of abolitionism and American transcendentalism and that emphasized independence, individualism, and self-restraint; it was thereby fully in line with their aims for civil service reform that might undermine the party capture of governing institutions.[174] But it contradicted extant conceptions of manhood, which were integrally tied to the norms of mass partisan participation and homosocial activity in which "manliness on the urban streets was tied to honor, to one's status among peers."[175]

This older form defined manliness as a matter of group loyalty, and thus, to the extent that mugwump reformers challenged the party system, they challenged the dominant gender norms of the age, and suffered retaliation in kind. The newer sexology rhetoric of gender transgression was mercilessly applied. As Murphy further argues, hostilities toward mugwumps invoked the trope of degeneracy theory that animated the sexology of the studies. Just as same-sex desire and gender transgression were thought to indicate the devolution of civilization and thereby threaten the health of the American nation, the mugwump refusal to abide by the traditional norms of political party networking were critiqued as spelling the doom of political organizing.[176] Success in electoral politics relied upon the lubrication that patronage provided. Remove spoils and the political system becomes unable to reproduce itself.

Responding to this criticism, a second generation of late-nineteenth-and early-twentieth-century reformers, as Murphy points out, attempted to counter the accusations of effeminacy and sexual inversion by embracing this very critique. These newer Progressive reformers accepted the older notion of political manhood as integrally tied to the camaraderie and social setting that were at the heart of political machines at Tammany, but turned that dynamic toward the antithetical end of reform.[177] In so doing, they adopted one of the key practices developmental scholars point to as a mechanism of ideational change: responding to crisis by suggesting that what was thought to be the source of the problem is actually the source of the solution. Of course, Progressives would not rely upon the political party as the appropriate political form; rather, they would establish new organizations and clubs. The party machines were still corrupt, but the underlying masculine social purpose that the party performed was embraced.

These newer reformers, Theodore Roosevelt among them, utilized the traditional party-based notion of manhood, and in attempting to "emulate the 'rough' manly style of Tammany leaders," put that form to the antithetical end of transforming urban politics rather than maintaining the corruption of extant party governance.[178] They sought to redefine the pursuit of urban reform as requiring virility. No longer the aspiration of the effete, bookish, and overeducated upper class who knew not the masculine labors of the working class, urban politics was reconstructed as "a rough homosocial arena" that might be a "crucible in which they [reformers] could test and remake their own masculinity and, at the same time, free themselves from the effeminate stigma that had attached to the mugwumps."[179] Of course, many of these reformers admitted that they indeed had many of the qualities contemporary sexologists associated with sexual inversion, including romantic attraction to members of the same sex, fatigue, poor physical health, underdeveloped musculature, and excessive interest in intellectual, particularly literary, pursuits. Roosevelt himself demonstrated many of these qualities in his youth.[180] Thus, the effort may have been both an effort of rhetorical framing as well as a more deep-seated psychological compensation.

Roosevelt's rhetoric of masculinity, as much as his own self-presentation, particularly the cultivated Rough Rider hero of the Spanish

American War, is evidence of this imperative to embrace a hypermasculinity that might counter the effeminacy crisis that sexology studies identified. For Roosevelt, and many of his peers and supporters, modernization, urbanization, and industrialization were producing a nation of "mollycoddles," men who were "too fastidious, too sensitive to take part in the rough hurly-burly of the actual work of the world."[181] Mollycoddles were the political parallel to the scientific sexual invert: persons who were "a combination of a woman and a man with the weaknesses of each and the strong points of neither."[182] These were, for Roosevelt, the mugwumps, and their gender transgression had undermined their ability to achieve the reforms they sought. If Progressives like Roosevelt were to succeed in their political reforms where the mugwumps had failed, their success would be countering this degenerate tendency toward gender transgression and sexual inversion by embracing traditional notions of masculinity but putting them in the service of antithetical ends.

Elements of robust masculinity needed to be combined with the industrious self-restraint that the original mugwump reformers embraced.[183] The hurly-burly of machine politics was, paradoxically, the necessary ingredient for Progressive reform. By linking Progressive politics and gender presentation in these terms, Roosevelt, the face of the Progressive party and broader movement, turned upon many of his fellow reformers who refused to compromise with the existing party structure, characterizing them as "weak," timid," "vain," and "slightly disordered mentally" with a "twist in mental make-up."[184] In other words, the reformer who held to the mugwump ideal shared the same qualities as the sexual invert. But the central point is that the reformers turned on themselves, utilizing the derogatory terms of sexual inversion to tarnish both the earlier generation of mugwump reformers from whom they were descended as well as their contemporary opponents. Such effeminate individuals were castigated as fundamentally unable to participate in the rough-and-tumble world of politics. As Roosevelt warned Harvard undergraduates in 1907, they should avoid becoming such mollycoddles at all costs, as such men "forfeit the right to be considered one of the governing and . . . become one of the governed."[185] In short, sexual inversion was defined by Progressive reformers as fundamentally counter to robust democracy.

Roosevelt used the gendered discourse of sexual inversion not only to discredit his critics while simultaneously bolstering the masculine credentials of Progressive reform but also to undermine the ideas of anarchists, a set of beliefs gaining an American following by the late nineteenth century. As a result, the hostilities toward anarchism, which defined much of U.S. politics at the turn of the twentieth century and increased exponentially during and in the immediate aftermath of the First World War, were motivated not only by concerns about political ideology that challenged extant power relations and governing institutions but also by the sexual and gender transformations that such ideology espoused.

Roosevelt ascended to the presidency by the anarchist assassin's bullet; Leon Czolgosz shot and killed President McKinley in 1901, and Roosevelt, the vice president, took office. But his criticism of anarchist philosophy did not rely only on manifest themes of violence; it also employed themes of confusion, disorder, chaos, and perversion, all of which were concepts common to the emergent scientific discourse of sexual inversion. Roosevelt characterized the anarchist as "a criminal whose perverted instincts lead him to prefer confusion and chaos to the most beneficent form of social order" and as an "enemy of system and progress."[186] Anarchists, like sexual inverts, were, for Roosevelt, "persons who are of low moral tendency."[187] As much as the sexual invert both seemed to disrupt the natural order and be a harbinger of the devolution of civilization, the anarchist presented the same threat.

However, criticisms of anarchism, often articulated through the discourse of sexual inversion, were not mere logic by analogy; instead, they recognized how the anarchist tradition in the United States from the late nineteenth century through the First World War was a fierce and, in many ways, the only advocate of homosexual rights in the United States. According to Terence Kissack, unlike Europe, which experienced a burgeoning homosexual rights movement during the early twentieth century, the United States saw no corresponding movement. Instead, "the first sustained US-based consideration of the social, ethical, and cultural place of homosexuality took place within the English-language anarchist movement."[188]

Anarchism did not have a consistent rationale for supporting homosexual rights, and its advocacy was not consistent over time. Support for sexual freedom and the decriminalization of same-sex relations increased after the trial of Oscar Wilde in 1895. Convicted to two years' imprisonment and hard labor for committing gross indecency as defined by the 1885 Labouchere Amendment, Wilde's trial and punishment functioned as "a critical turning point in the American anarchists' view of homosexuality. . . . After Wilde's trial . . . the anarchist sex radicals addressed homosexuality with greater frequency and in a more favorable light."[189] Key among these anarchists were Benjamin R. Tucker and Emma Goldman. Each defended Wilde and homosexuality more generally in distinct terms. Tucker conceived of homosexuality as a matter of individual expression and liberty. He criticized the conviction as excessive state intervention into the life of a man "who has done nothing in the least degree invasive of any one," and whose only offense was that "he has done something which most of the rest of us (at least such is the presumption) prefer not to do."[190] Goldman, influenced by the more liberal sexologists, tended to view homosexuals as an unjustly persecuted minority group. Writing to Magnus Hirschfeld, the German sexologist and founder of the first homosexual rights organization, the Scientific-Humanitarian Committee, Goldman proclaimed, "as an anarchist, my place has ever been with the persecuted."[191]

Anarchist views about homosexual rights, especially after the Wilde trial, were embedded within a larger critique of institutionalized power and sexual norms. As Margaret Marsh characterizes the movement, "Commonly calling themselves free lovers, anarchists believed that adults could decide what type of sexual association they desired and were capable of choosing the nature and duration of that association."[192] Therefore, the position on homosexual rights paralleled other radical positions on marriage, birth control, and family structure.

The crackdown on civil liberties that occurred during the First World War in the forms of the Espionage Act of 1917, the Alien Immigrant Act, and the Sedition Act of 1918 essentially wiped out the country's anarchist movement. In October 1918, Congress also passed the Anti-Anarchist Act, which authorized the deportation of immigrant anarchists to their countries of origin. Emma Goldman, who was imprisoned for the duration of the war for her antiwar rhetoric, was deported to the Soviet Union shortly after peace was declared.[193] Goldman did return to the United States in 1934 for a speaking tour. Although the U.S. government censored her topics, limiting them to arts and literature, she continued to advocate for homosexual rights through those themes. She gave addresses on popular literature that featured lesbian characters, such as Radcliffe Hall's novel, *The Well of Loneliness*, and Lillian Hellman's play *The Children's Hour*. However, Goldman could not draw the audiences or have the political impact that she might have had prior to the war.[194] Capturing the collapse of anarchism due to suppression by the U.S. federal and state governments, the liberal magazine the *Nation* wrote, "Today the Anarchists are a scattered handful of survivors, and the extreme left is divided among the various communist groups. . . . Emma Goldman is not a symbol of freedom in a world of tyrants; she is merely a wrong-headed woman."[195] As Kissack documents, the American Left, after the war and the persecution of the anarchist movement, was dominated by the Communist Party, which had little interest in the issues of sexual expression that were woven into the anarchist critique of state authority. Kissack notes that "following Stalin's rise, the sexual politics of the American CP became largely indistinguishable from the mainstream society in which it operated . . . [such that] by the end of the 1920s, the anarchist sexual politics of the pre–World War I era was largely forgotten."[196]

Political homophobia was present in American politics well before the Lavender Scare of the 1950s. It took at least two forms: first, rhetoric that borrowed from the new sexology to delegitimize political opposition, and, second, the active elimination during and after World War I of American anarchism, which was the only political movement that openly advocated for homosexual rights. The first form of political homophobia did not take the same discursive structure as that of the Lavender Scare because the homosexual, as such, did not yet exist. The attacks, first by the party machines against mugwump reformers and then by Progressive pragmatists against idealist reformers, utilized the image of sexual inversion and degeneracy to castigate political enemies. Furthermore, insofar as the first pro–homosexual rights movement was the American anarchist movement, the political suppression and eradication of that movement sufficed to eliminate any emerging pro-homosexual sentiment. The first Red Scare then, did not have a corresponding and separable Lavender Scare, because sexual freedom itself was integrated into anarchist political ideology. Communism, by contrast, eschewed homosexuality and denounced sexual freedom, leaving anarchists like Emma Goldman wholly disheartened and disillusioned with the political ideas animating the newly founded Soviet Union.[197] Communism and homosexuality could be construed as two distinct threats to national security in the 1950s, and, indeed, congressional debate about how to pursue each, as a loyalty threat or as a security threat, indicates as much. But, anarchism and sexual freedom were not so separable. Consequently, the elimination of the anarchists essentially functioned to eliminate the most vocal advocates of homosexual rights in the United States to that point.

Conclusion

George Chauncey points out that "discriminatory measures against homosexuals . . . are in fact not ancient but a unique and relatively short-lived product of the twentieth century.[198] This claim relies on the supposition that the homosexual is also a recent construction. Consequently, if the target of institutionalized fear, hatred, and sanctioning was not recognized to exist, then the regulatory apparatus of that fear, hatred, and sanctioning could also not exist. This chapter has sought to nuance this claim by drawing attention to the way regulatory authorities gradually came to identify the homosexual by the mid-twentieth century. That process of seeing homosexuality required the deliberate building of administrative infrastructure, for sure, but more than that, distinct modalities of regulatory recognition compelled more and diverse layers of that apparatus. And, beyond this claim of state development, this chapter has illustrated that sexuality is institutionally implicated and embedded in multiple orderings of authority in distinct ways over time. To see this idea, different conceptions of what that sexuality is, or distinct modalities of definition and recognition by those authorities, must be engaged.

In more concrete terms, political homophobia did not burst upon the scene with the Lavender Scare, and it is not enough to suggest that there were local urban precursors of such institutionalized homophobia in the 1930s, although there surely were. Rather, this chapter has shown that the earlier episodes of political homophobia may go unrecognized because they took a fundamentally different shape. And, they did so because the regulatory recognition of persons expressing same-sex desire at that time was fundamentally different than it was by midcentury.

Additionally, this chapter highlights various mechanisms that drive political development, including processes of bureaucratic learning that lead to the building and routinization of administrative policy, entrepreneurial actions ranging from ignoring higher authorities to creating rhetorical and ideational transpositions, and the competition to frame policy and political problems. The political learning detailed in this chapter—coming to see what constituted so-called sexual inversion—illustrates what Paul Pierson refers to as "collective learning," or a dynamic whereby "large numbers of people within and across organizations must come to see things in a similar way."[199] While learning may be a reliable dynamic under certain conditions, Pierson posits that it is generally rare in political settings because the high number of actors involved increases the possibility of diverse and divergent interests and objectives.[200] In these situations, learning may not be the most reliable mechanism of institutional change as "outcomes cannot easily be matched rationally to changing environments."[201] The chapter also traces the divergent aims of sexologists. Some sought to identify the sexual invert to promote legal reform such as decriminalization. Others sought to identify the sexual invert to maintain criminal sanctioning via eugenic policies that might further cultivate a particular national community in which the invert would, over time, be eradicated.

Nevertheless, the aim to discover and identify was common, and this commonality suggests the possibility of learning. The project of homosexual identification was part of a much broader Progressive agenda to develop a robust citizenry, which appealed to a range of sectors. And, the circumstances of collective learning could prevail across different orders of authority such as private regimes of medicine and science as much as public regimes of criminal law, immigration policy, military regulation, and political party structure.

Entrepreneurial actions are evident in both policy implementation and in rhetoric and ideas about homosexuality. First, punishment for sexual inversion varied, as is exemplified by variation in access to GI benefits under circumstances of a blue discharge. Whereas the regulatory language was clarified over time, the institutional design of benefit disbursal enabled entrepreneurial acts, some of which benefited homosexuals even as they maintained institutionalized racism. Second, as this chapter detailed, Progressive reformers, such as Roosevelt, turned their opposition's criticism on its head. Aware that the reformers who preceded him were subject to attacks as hermaphrodites, third sexes, and political inverts due to their rejection of norms of political manhood embedded in the dynamics of political party machines, Roosevelt embraced the problem as the solution. By adopting the tactics of camaraderie thought to engender corruption, Roosevelt deflected accusations that reformers lacked sufficient masculinity to engage in politics while also redefining the goal of urban reform as a masculine endeavor.

Finally, in this process of gradual regulatory recognition, first as the identification of a broad category of sexual inversion as a threat to national community and then as the narrower classification of the homosexual as threat to security, competition over defining the nature of the threat is evident. In the first case, some sexologists sought legal reform that might destigmatize sexual inversion and cut the imagined link between inversion and criminality. In the second case, during the early years of the Lavender Scare, members of the Truman administration struggled to define homosexuality as a mental illness but not as a security threat. These attempts were not successful, and homosexuals were targeted as perilous to the nation throughout the twentieth century until a defined gay rights movement, which challenged this conception, began to take shape in the early 1950s.

Explanations for why alternative conceptions of homosexuality as illness but not threat did not take hold stem, in part, from the lack of support for this counternarrative. The only movement that advocated alternative conceptions of homosexuality beyond a minority of scientific and government elites was anarchism. And, this movement was eradicated through a series of congressional and state statutes that enabled imprisonment, silencing, and ultimately deportation of anarchists. Any alternative recognition of homosexuals, not as a threat but as an unjustly discriminated-against minority class, would not be widely articulated until the mid-1950s and would not gain much acknowledgment by public and private regulatory authorities in the United States until at least the 1970s. It would take a social movement to accomplish this.

3

Gay Is Good

Multiple Paths to Recognizing Unjust Discrimination

[T]here are no minority problems. There are only majority problems. There is no Negro problem except that created by whites; and Jewish problem except that created by Gentiles. To which I add and no homosexual problem except that created by the heterosexual society.
—Donald Webster Cory (Edward Sagarin), *The Homosexual in America*, 1951[1]

One century ago, the first Justice Harlan admonished this Court that the Constitution "neither knows nor tolerates classes among citizens." *Plessy v. Ferguson*, 163 U.S. 537, 559 (1896) (dissenting opinion). Unheeded then, those words now are understood to state a commitment to the law's neutrality where the rights of persons are at stake. The Equal Protection Clause enforces this principle and today requires us to hold invalid a provision of Colorado's Constitution.
—Justice Anthony Kennedy, *Romer v. Evans*, 1996[2]

Maybe we have reached a critical historical juncture. Struggles for human rights always begin with brave men and women who stand up, isolated, against the forces of oppression. But, in the United States, victory really arrives on the glorious day when the people with money decide discrimination is bad for business.
—Gail Collins, "The State of Arizona," 2014[3]

When Edward Sagarin, a sociologist at the City University of New York, writing as Donald Webster Cory, penned *The Homosexual in America* in 1951, he framed homosexuality not as a social ill—as the early sexologists had recognized it—or an individual psychological disease—as many medical professionals named it by the middle of the twentieth century—but as a foundation upon which to mobilize for equal rights. Conceptualizing the homosexual as a menacing other only contributed to the manifestation of disorders that psychologists had understood as consequences of homosexuality:

> There would be no need for the invert to feel guilty, to suffer remorse, to be forced to suppress hatred toward his love-object, if society did not condemn so bitterly. He would not be faced with the paradoxical problem of attempting on the one hand to be proud of himself and on the other to deny his temperament, if it were not so difficult to live in a world that demanded such a denial.[4]

Cory sought to remake that identity as the basis for positive acknowledgment and social mobilization. In so doing, he contended that it was the regulatory authorities and not the homosexual that needed to be reformed.

Over the course of the latter half of the twentieth century, while branches of the federal government continued to see the homosexual mostly as a threat to the national community, other authorities at the state and local levels and in private corporations—at different times and at different paces—began to recognize the gay and lesbian citizen not as someone to be excluded in order to protect the polity but as someone unfairly oppressed by the polity. Sometimes this shift was triggered by concerted efforts of social movement actors; at other times it was an externality of a general trend toward liberalization in laws governing sexual acts and expression. This third modality of recognition—in the pattern of five modalities defined in this book—also drew upon contested processes of self-definition that structure the identity politics of the modern postwar gay and lesbian rights movement. Should sexuality be the basis of a collective identity along an ethnic-minority model, or should sexual regulations no longer be considered the state's legitimate concern? Could discrimination be curbed by defining homosexuals as a distinct minority unjustly subject to prejudice and, perhaps, eligible for the active affirmation of and protection by the state? Or would a better strategy be to define sexuality as a private concern not legitimately within the state's purview at all? In short, would equality follow from falling within or from living outside the state's sight?

Framing homosexuals as a discriminated-against group comparable to ethnic, racial, or religious minorities is evident in the mission statement of one of the first post–World War II gay rights organizations, the Mattachine Society. During its early years, the Mattachine Society sought to foster a cognizable homosexual culture, to link with other groups seeking civil rights, and to lead a discursive shift in the way homosexuality was understood, from deviant act to oppressed minority:

> The Mattachine Society holds it possible and desirable that a highly ethical homosexual culture emerge, as a consequence of its work, paralleling the emerging cultures of our fellow minorities . . . the Negro, Mexican, and Jewish peoples. . . . It is necessary that the more far-reaching and socially conscious homosexuals provide leadership to the whole mass of social deviants if the first two missions (the unification and the education of the homosexual minority) are to be accomplished. . . . Only a Society, providing enlightened leadership, can rouse the homosexuals . . . one of the largest minorities in America today . . . to take the actions necessary to elevate themselves from the social ostracism an unsympathetic culture has perpetrated on them.[5]

In the midst of Cold War anxieties about communism, Mattachine's allusions to a Leninist-styled vanguard leading a new homosexual rights movement undermined support for the original leadership.[6] The later, more classically liberal leadership of the Mattachine tactically shifted; rather than emphasize homosexuality as distinct and positive and thereby place the normative critique on the biases and prejudices of the majority, many sought to minimize the difference that homosexuality represented. Marilyn Reiger's statement at the 1953 Mattachine convention is illustrative: "We know we are the same . . . no different than anyone else. Our only difference is an unimportant one to the heterosexual society, unless we make it important. . . . [H]omosexuality is irrelevant to our ideals, our principles, our hopes and aspirations."[7] The juxtaposition of Cory's characterization of homosexuality as the founda-tion on which to build a new culture, ethic, and rights claim and Reiger's minimization of homosexuality as unimportant captures a dynamic trope, one that animated movement organizational strategies and the ways public and private regulatory authorities would see or refuse to see gay and lesbians persons and citizens over the remainder of the twenti-eth century.

As this chapter details, some states and municipalities began to pass nondiscrimination legislation recognizing homosexuality as a person-hood status, marking a shift from conceptualizing homosexuality as a criminal act. These efforts were contentious. Early victories were often reversed, hardly marking the durable shift in authority that constitutes political development.[8] And, rather than seek recognition as a minority class, litigation strategies often called for shielding sexuality from state sight, compelled, in part, by the path-dependent nature of common law constitutionalism and the development of privacy jurisprudence.[9] Those within the lesbian and gay rights movements disagreed about how ho-mosexuality could and should be defined and acknowledged. This lack of consensus was often reflected back in the shifting recognition by state authorities. The century would end with the Supreme Court paradoxi-cally maintaining each position simultaneously: homosexual acts could be criminalized but homosexual persons could not be explicit targets of discrimination.

This chapter addresses these tensions from the mid-twentieth cen-tury onward. It describes how different factions within the homophile movement advocated distinct notions of homosexuality as either collec-tive identity of an oppressed minority that might actively seek state rec-ognition or an individualized sexuality that would gain freedom by not falling within the state's sight. It then delves into the way the Supreme Court viewed these distinct conceptions of homosexuality as conduct or character, as act or status, in three landmark cases: *Boutilier v. Immigra-tion and Naturalization Service* (1967), *Bowers v. Hardwick* (1986), and *Romer v. Evans* (1996).[10] It examines how, unable to secure a national civil rights bill that might establish federal-level recognition of and pro-tection from discrimination on the basis of sexual orientation, rights ad-vocates pursued protections through different avenues: municipal-level passage of statutory protections from discrimination in employment, housing, and accommodations, inclusion of HIV disease in the Americans with Disabilities Act (ADA), and workplace mobilization targeting private human resource policies.[11]

The Homophile Movement and Contested Self-Definitions of Homosexuality

Whether homosexuality defined conduct or character was a central node of tension evident in recognition by governing authorities and disputes within early homophile groups as well as later post-Stonewall gay liberation and gay rights organizations. Some attempted to shift the primary understanding of sexuality from conduct, made manifest as psychological disorder, to a positive trait at the foundation of a common identity. Others sought to minimize the differences between homosexuality and heterosexuality, and in so doing, advocated a more libertarian approach that undermined the rationale for morals legislation and criminalization. The Marxist-influenced homophile activists who established the Mattachine Society in 1951, such as Harry Hay and Chuck Rowland, while not endorsing a biologically essentialist view of homosexuality, did conceptualize their sexuality as the cornerstone upon which a collective identity could be built and through which cultural oppression might be confronted. They challenged antihomosexual attitudes maintained and perpetuated by medical, state, and religious authorities, and they critiqued internalized homophobia as a variation on false consciousness.[12] By working to reframe homosexuality as distinct and valuable, the early Mattachine struggled to change the notion of homosexuality from an act to an unjustly discriminated-against class of persons comparable to religious, racial, or ethnic minorities.

As the Mattachine expanded and Cold War anticommunism heated up, members became uneasy with its secretive cell structure. In response, men frustrated with the communist-influenced organization founded an alternative, ONE, Inc. ONE focused on publishing a national periodical, *ONE* magazine, as that would promote exactly what Mattachine's secret organizational structure precluded: public development and unification of a gay and lesbian minority class.[13] Mattachine members also called for a national convention that might bring the organization into the open. Far from mitigating dissent, the convention brought two clashing perspectives to the fore. Some, like Hay and Rowland, maintained the original ethos of building a distinct ethical homosexual culture. Others, like Marilyn Reiger, Hal Call, and Kenneth Burns, emphasized assimilation. Ultimately, Hay and allies were ousted.

The more liberal second-generation leaders of the Mattachine and, later, the Daughters of Bilitis (DOB), founded in 1955, focused efforts less on reforming institutions and more on assisting homosexuals to live within the parameters of the prejudice they faced. New leadership promoted what D'Emilio referred to as a "retreat into respectability."[14] The DOB Statement of Purpose captures this perspective by defining its aim as "[e]ducation of the variant, with particular emphasis on the psychological, physiological and sociological aspects, to enable her to understand herself and make her adjustment to society in all its social, civic, and economic implications."[15] DOB's mission statement accepted the extant construction of homosexual identity by medical, psychological, and state authorities rather than clearly challenging it, as early Mattachine leaders had done. When the Mattachine membership voted to eliminate any mention of a distinct homosexual culture from its mission statement, it seemed to undercut the potential for mobilization insofar as it refused to acknowledge the commonality that could be a basis for collective identity development.[16]

The ascension of a more assimilationist leadership did not drown out more radical voices that advocated an ethnic-minority model of collective identity development. *ONE* magazine promoted that alternative. Its Statement of Purpose exemplifies this construction of homosexuality:

> ONE does not claim homosexuals are better or worse than anyone else, that they are special in any but one sense. And in that one sense ONE claims positively that homosexuals do not have the civil rights assured all other citizens. ONE is devoted to correcting this. ONE means to stimulate thought, criticism, research, literary and artistic production in an effort to bring the public to understand deviants and deviants to understand themselves as the two sides are brought together as one.[17]

ONE was "undoubtedly the most contentious and radical" of the homophile organizations established during the 1950s.[18] Given that it maintained a national orientation since its primary purpose was to publish a national magazine at the very time when the Mattachine fragmented, ONE was the most stable and visible of the three homophile organizations and, in historian Craig Loftin's estimation, "the most prominent."[19]

Even as the Mattachine and the DOB turned their efforts toward education, accommodation, and assimilation, ONE developed a collective consciousness grounded in difference. Publications served as vehicles for network building and community development since public spaces for that purpose were limited.[20] Mattachine leaders expanded their publication capacities by founding the Pan-Graphic press, which, by 1955, began publishing the *Mattachine Review*. A year later, the DOB started to distribute the *Ladder*. The three magazines—ONE, *Mattachine Review*, and the *Ladder*—had an estimated monthly circulation as high as twenty thousand, but ONE had the broadest reach. In its thirteen-year run from 1953 to 1965, about half a million copies were distributed, and its monthly circulation was nearly double that of the *Mattachine Review* and five times that of the *Ladder*. The magazine's content reflected "a civil rights impulse," offered "explicit rebukes of antigay discrimination," and "argued that homosexuals comprised a distinct minority with a rich history and culture."[21] Even as organizational leadership of homophile organizations turned from the minority model, the primary publication and national network-building vehicle of the movement maintained it; "gay pride [was a] key aspect of the magazine's civil rights impulse."[22]

Although assimilationist voices were ascendant, some of the leadership of various Mattachine societies around the country approached gay and lesbian identity in ways similar to those espoused in the pages of ONE. Frank Kameny, founder of the Mattachine of Washington, DC (MSW), ridiculed other Mattachine groups that seemed preoccupied with uncovering a cure for homosexuality. He maintained at a speech given to the Mattachine Society of New York (MSNY) that there was no reason for a cure because there was no illness. Instead, gays and lesbians should learn from the burgeoning African American civil rights movement:

> I do not see the NAACP or CORE worrying about which chromosome and gene produces black skin or about the possibility of bleaching the Negro. I do not see any great interest on the part of the B'nai B'rith Anti-Defamation League in the possibility of solving the problems of anti-

semitism by converting Jews to Christians. . . . [W]e are interested in obtaining rights for our respective minorities as Negroes, as Jews, and as homosexuals. Why we are Negroes, Jews, or homosexuals is totally irrelevant, and whether we can be changed to white, Christians, or heterosexuals is equally irrelevant.[23]

Kameny promoted this new approach by establishing the East Coast Homophile Organizations, or ECHO, in 1963 as a regional coalition that might coordinate action among MSW, MSNY, the Daughters of Bilitis in New York (DOBNY), and the Janus Society of Philadelphia. Yet, DOBNY soon withdrew due to ideological differences that centered on whether to promote actively the notion of gays and lesbians as a discriminated-against minority.[24] DOBNY criticized Kameny's approach since such "demonstrations which define homosexuality as a unique minority defeat the very cause for which the homosexual strives—TO BE AN INTEGRAL PART OF SOCIETY."[25] This tension was evident in clashes between Kameny and the leader of MSNY, Dick Lietsch. Lietsch saw the Mattachine as a form of collective support for homosexuals that might "help them come to grips with themselves." He critiqued Kameny's mobilization efforts: "We're not interested in 'bringing them out' and encouraging them to give up their heterosexual activities. . . . [We] encourage them to swing both ways and enjoy themselves, and try to help them keep out of trouble."[26] Lietsch's construction of sexuality as sex acts—his advocacy for reform such that the acts would no longer fall within the legitimate purview of state regulation—is readily apparent.

This conception of sexuality stands in stark contrast to Kameny's vision of an empowered gay minority class grounded not in deregulation of a criminal act but in promotion of a positive notion of the individual and his or her community:

> We must instill in the homosexual community a sense of the worth of the individual. . . . We must counteract the inferiority, which ALL society inculcates into him in regard to his homosexuality. . . . Our people need to have their self-esteem bolstered—singly, and as a community. The very idea of changing to heterosexuality . . . is a tacit acknowledgment of inferiority. . . . People who are TRULY equal, and TRULY not inferior, do NOT consider acquiescing to the majority and changing themselves.[27]

Kameny's words reflect the perspective advanced by Cory: discrimination against gays and lesbians reflected not a legitimate assessment of homosexuality as illness or threat but an unreasonable bias and prejudice by majority cultures, perpetuated by majority institutions. Reform would come not by changing the homosexual or accomplishing only statutory reform and decriminalization of private behavior. Social change had to be grounded in understanding the homosexual as facing unjust discrimination and focusing attention on the institutions, laws, and policies that perpetuated this construction. As Elizabeth Armstrong has noted, by the late 1960s many leaders within the homophile movement began to question whether viewing sexuality through the lens of privacy was less a route to reform and more the very form of psychological debilitation that Cory, Hay, and now Kameny considered it to be. Instead, there was a sense of "the possibility that public revelation of sexual identity might have personal psychological rewards."[28] A new ethos considering privacy advocacy as merely perpetuating another form of lying about oneself began to emerge within the latter years of the homophile movement. One essay in the gay and lesbian magazine the *Vector* laments,

> We lie so that we may live. Whether it is to our boss, or the draft board, or the civil service, we rarely can afford to divulge the simple truth of our homosexuality. But this is merely the beginning. Lying begets lying: we have to cover up for so many of our activities and doings that we find ourselves in a mire of untruths.[29]

The regulatory shift that Kameny advocated would come only after gays and lesbians mobilized on that basis, when they came out as a minority demanding the attention of the state for equal rights. It would require, as Kameny would famously declare, that gays and lesbians

> look the world squarely in the eye as the homosexuals that you are, confident in your equality, confident in the knowledge that as objects of prejudice and victims of discrimination you are right and they are wrong, and confident of the rightness of what you are and the goodness of what you do; it is time to live your homosexuality fully, joyously, openly, and proudly, assured that morally, socially, physically, psychologically, emotionally, and in every other way: *Gay is good*. It is.[30]

Act versus Identity in the Making of a Minority: Contested Pathways to Recognition of Discrimination

The year 1952 was pivotal in the development of homosexual identity. During that year the shift from a biological, congenital, or hereditary notion of homosexuality toward a more psychologized one was fully evident. The American Psychological Association released its first *Diagnostic and Statistical Manual* that classified homosexuality as "sociopathic personality disturbance." That same year Congress passed the Immigration and Naturalization Act, which permitted exclusion and deportation of individuals diagnosed with "psychopathic personality," thereby ensuring that openly homosexual persons could be barred from entering or remaining in the United States.

Between 1953 and 1956, forty-seven homosexuals were barred from entry into the United States on the basis of "psychopathic personality" diagnoses as opposed to being classified, as they were in the 1920s, 1930s, and 1940s as "persons of constitutional psychopathic inferiority."[31] And, as Margot Canaday has documented, by midcentury immigration of-ficials moved from not really being able coherently to identify homo-sexuality as a condition and thus to exclude gender-nonconforming individuals as liable to become "public charges" to a more concrete exclu-sion for "psychopathic personality." The regulatory shift from biological to psychological as the defining characteristic of homosexuality as illness was central to the meaning of modern homosexuality at midcentury.[32]

In 1952 the Mattachine Society of Los Angeles was incorporated as a nonprofit organization. Also, during that year, psychologist Evelyn Hooker began working with its members. Her work would ultimately serve as the foundation for removing homosexuality from the *DSM* in 1973.[33] And, that change was crucial to the way homosexuality was presented to the public by news media. According John Zaller, "in the aftermath of the APA vote, the mainstream press began to take a dif-ferent view of their efforts." Consequently, "what changed in the 1970s was that the press was no longer seeing homosexuals as social deviants, but as ordinary citizens suffering the effects of homophobic prejudice."[34] Work begun in 1952 was critical to the process of shifting public dis-course about gays and lesbians toward viewing them as a discriminated-against minority class.

Furthermore, by the mid-1950s, indicators of a new sexual libertarianism were evident. First, the American Law Institute (ALI), an organization of fifteen hundred lawyers and legal scholars, drafted the Model Penal Code in 1955, which decriminalized all private consensual adult sexual behavior.[35] The proposed code, according to William Eskridge, established a more utilitarian notion of common good rather than imposing an outdated "hodgepodge of moral prohibitions."[36] Early adopters of the code's sodomy decriminalization included Illinois in 1961 and Connecticut in 1969. Second, the Supreme Court revised its notion of obscenity, thereby potentially paving the way for freer sexual expression under First Amendment protections, and, by the mid-1960s, began to define a zone of privacy and choice that encompassed consensual heterosexual adult sexual behaviors.

ONE, Inc. v. Oleson marked the first time the Supreme Court ruled that First Amendment guarantees of press and expression protected homosexual content. Despite *ONE's* claim in its mission statement that "this magazine is not and does not wish to be merely an erotic publication," the United States Postal Service refused to distribute one of its issues in 1954.[37] *ONE* brought suit against the Postal Service, and despite losing at lower federal courts, it won on appeal to the Supreme Court. The decision has been called "*the* seminal gay rights case in America."[38] This characterization would suggest that the ruling is a major landmark in the Court's seeming waffling between acknowledging, quite early on and certainly before the Stonewall riots of 1969, the legitimacy of some gay rights claims and yet dismissing others in a way that seems wholly inconsistent. On the one hand, the Court ruled in favor of *ONE*, indicating that publishing on the topic of homosexuality was not per se obscene. Similarly, in 1962, the Court, in *MANuel Enterprises v. Day*, overturned a lower court's holding that the Postal Service legitimately designated a male physique magazine, which included images of nude or mostly nude male models, as obscene.[39] While *ONE* was founded to promote the development of a positive gay collective identity, physique magazines may have also advanced collective identity development as they contributed to a nationwide gay-oriented consumer identity and market.[40] Therefore, these two decisions were critical to the rise of the gay and lesbian rights movements as they maintained some of the primary vehicles through which a positive gay identity was being constructed and promoted at midcentury.

On the other hand, these decisions hardly exemplified a new judicial liberalism that challenged the notion of homosexuality as psychologically pathological. In *ONE v. Olesen,* the Court did not articulate a full rationale. Instead, it reversed the Ninth Circuit's ruling, merely citing its earlier decision in *Roth v. United States.*[41] And, the ruling in *MANuel* only attained majority support as three justices ruled in favor on procedural grounds. Any judicial intent to promote an alternative and more positive notion of homosexuality cannot be inferred from these rulings. Indeed, by 1966, the Court ruled in *Mishkin v. New York* that obscenity standards that had been loosened not even a decade earlier in *Roth* could be revised to exclude protecting materials that catered to homosexuals.[42]

While the Postal Service generally maintained the authority to strike against efforts to promote a positive homosexual identity, the Court also generally upheld immigration regulations that continued to position the homosexual as a threatening alien. One early case suggested possible reform. In *Rosenberg v. Fleuti,* the Court vacated the deportation order of George Fleuti, who was diagnosed as a homosexual.[43] Fleuti returned to the United States after a one-day trip to Mexico in 1956, but the Court did not consider this as reentry. Fleuti entered the United States before the passage of the Immigration and Naturalization Act of 1952 and thus before the psychopathic personality exclusion provision was in effect. As a result, the deportation order was vacated on procedural grounds.

Yet, because of the procedural dismissal, *Fleuti* did not address the constitutionality of the act's exclusion of homosexuals on the basis of "psychopathic personality." Four years later the Court upheld the act in *Boutilier v. Immigration and Naturalization Service.*[44] Justice Tom Clark's ruling for the majority of six justices illustrates how regulatory authorities grappled with and blurred the lines between defining homosexuality as conduct versus defining homosexuality as character. The definition of homosexuality put forward by the Court struggled with similar challenges that divided the homophile movement.

The Court agreed to hear *Boutilier* due to a circuit split. In 1966, the Ninth Circuit overturned the deportation of a U.S. permanent resident from Canada who admitted to homosexual conduct prior to entry on the grounds that the exclusionary law was void for vagueness.[45] The phrase "afflicted with psychopathic personality" was too expansive a category, and it was unclear that homosexuals could be so classified.

However, that same year the Second Circuit ruled that the exclusionary law was constitutional and that Michael Boutilier could be deported.[46]

Justice Clark wrote for a majority of six to uphold the law. He drew in part on the Second Circuit ruling drafted by Judge Irving Kaufman, who had worked for Clark when the latter served as United States attorney general in the Franklin Roosevelt administration.[47] Kaufman maintained that Boutilier was deported on the basis of his pre-entry conduct, i.e., that he had admitted to engaging in homosexual sex acts. In the first sentence of the lower court ruling, Kaufman defines homosexuality as nonconformist behavior:

> Although a relatively young segment of contemporary society prides itself on its readiness to cast off conventional and tested disciplines and to experiment with nonconformance and the unorthodox merely to set out its contempt for traditional values, certain areas of conduct continue to be as controversial in modern and *beau monde* circles as they were in bygone and more staid eras.[48]

Nevertheless, later in the ruling, Kaufman defines homosexuality as an innate characteristic. He understood the law as not targeting behaviors or acts but as intended to exclude certain *persons*: it "was never designed to regulate *conduct*; its function was to exclude aliens possessing certain *characteristics*."[49]

Clark's ruling for the Court majority similarly illustrates this slippage between conduct and character, act and personhood. Michael Boutilier, a Canadian national, entered the United States in 1955, and the Immigration and Naturalization Service (INS) initiated proceedings against him when, during an application for citizenship about eight years later, the Public Health Service diagnosed him as afflicted with psychopathic personality. In describing the facts that precipitated the Court's review, Clark characterized Boutilier as engaging in heterosexual and homosexual sex in Canada prior to entry into the United States, and then living as a homosexual after entry.[50] The affidavit that Boutilier gave to INS officials in 1964 indicated that while he cohabited with a Eugene O'Rourke and engaged in homosexual sex with him, he "abandoned all sexual practices within the past several months because of his annoyance and disgust with the problems that these activities have brought about."[51] The record did not show that Boutilier was asked about any history of homosexual acts at the time of his entry, although he indicated that he was homosexual during a Selective Service examination, and he was subsequently classified as 4-F.[52] Nevertheless, Clark wrote that Boutilier "admitted being a homosexual at the time of entry."[53]

Clark maintained that the law was not vague because it did not, in fact, ban homosexual conduct; it banned homosexual persons. According to Clark, "The petitioner is not being deported for conduct engaged in after his entry into the United States, but rather for characteristics he possessed at the time of his entry."[54] Insofar as that construction was offered, Clark maintained that the act "imposes neither regulation of nor sanction for conduct," and it did not matter whether Boutilier had ceased to engage in any homosexual sex acts after entry into the United States as the exclusion "never applied to petitioner's conduct after entry."[55] Rather, "when the petitioner first presented himself at our border for entrance, he was already afflicted with homosexuality. The pattern was cut, and under it he was not admissible."[56] Clark emphasized that Boutilier's conduct was evidence of a deeper homosexual character in order to counter the claim that the act was vague. Boutilier need not be informed that he could be deported for homosexual behaviors as the law was not aimed at regulating conduct. The law was not vague in that it was never intended to warn individuals to stop their homosexual behaviors; Boutilier ran afoul of the law because he was a homosexual, not because he engaged in same-sex sexual behavior. Whether he had stopped made no difference because the conduct was indicative of the character. The conduct was how the character was made manifest.

Clark's construction of homosexuality as character was exactly the idea that Boutilier's lawyer, Blanch Freedman, had tried to avoid and, indeed, challenge. She contended that the law was vague because it failed to inform Boutilier that homosexual conduct would result in deportation. Second, she maintained that homosexual conduct did not indicate psychopathic personality, and that Congress had not intended to exclude all homosexuals on that basis. Third, she argued that Boutilier's due process rights were violated as he had never been given a medical examination by the Public Health Service to determine his sexuality.[57] But, Clark's conception of homosexuality as character negated these contentions. If homosexuality was an innate condition, then homosexual acts were irrelevant as they were not the law's target. Therefore, Boutilier did not need to be so informed, and his due process rights were not thereby violated. Insofar as Boutilier admitted to being a homosexual at the time of the Selective Service interview and had given sworn affidavits indicating a history of homosexual sex acts, it did not matter for Clark whether medical officers examined Boutilier at time of entry because Boutilier's conduct indicated the excludable condition of character. Clark maintained that Boutilier gave evidence of this condition—that "petitioner's contention must fall by his own admission"—when he acknowledged that "for over six years prior to his entry petitioner admittedly followed a continued course of homosexual conduct."[58] Given this pattern, Clark argued that the condition was evident: "The existence of this condition over a continuous and uninterrupted period prior to and at the time of petitioner's entry clearly supports the ultimate finding."[59]

Boutilier's recognition of homosexuality as a status, condition, or character rather than as a sexual behavior stands in stark contrast to the Court's construction of homosexuality nineteen years later in *Bowers v. Hardwick*. But, since the Court's definition of homosexuality as status was used to negate a gay rights claim—that it, in Marc Stein's words, rendered gays and lesbians "not eligible for U.S. citizenship" and "not welcome on U.S. land"— it is little wonder that homophile activists during the mid-1960s, such as Lietsch and Willer, were gravely troubled by Kameny's calls to define homosexuals as a class of persons, to see homosexuality as "neither an affliction to be cured nor a weakness to be resisted" but to instead recognize "that the homosexual is a first-class human being and first-class citizen, entitled, by right, to all of the privileges and prerogatives of his citizenship, and to all of the God-given dignity of his humanity."[60] Justice Clark recognized the homosexual to be a person and denied that person citizenship status on that basis.

Given the outcome in *Boutilier*, it is hardly surprising that lawyers at Lambda Legal Defense, who represented Michael Hardwick in the *Bowers* litigation, would seek to define homosexuality as private sexual behavior. Personage—regardless of the contemporary notion that gay rights should not be denied since gays are, as Lady Gaga reminds us, "born this way"—offered no refuge for *Boutilier*.[61] Furthermore, homosexuality as private sex act could build on both precedents laid since the 1960s, which carved out a zone of sexual privacy for heterosexuals, and two state-level precedents that spoke directly to homosexuality: *People v. Onofre* out of New York and *Baker v. Wade* out of Texas.[62]

First, a line of Supreme Court precedent, including *Griswold v. Connecticut*, which upheld the right to use contraception within the marital bedroom, *Eisenstadt v. Baird*, which extended legal use of contraception to single individuals, and *Roe v. Wade*, which held that abortion access fell within a zone of sexual privacy, established a trend.[63] The legal doctrine of privacy would seemingly shield consensual same-sex sexual intercourse between adults from criminal sanction. Second, *Onofre* marked the first time that a state court invalidated a sodomy ban in the context of same-sex sex acts. When New York appealed the ruling to the Supreme Court, the latter declined to issue a writ of certiorari.[64] And, in *Baker*, a lower federal court declared that the Texas ban on sodomy violated rights of privacy and equal protection: "The right of two individuals to choose what type of sexual conduct they will enjoy in private is just as personal, just as important, just as sensitive—indeed, even more so—than the decision by the same couple to engage in sex using a contraceptive to prevent unwanted pregnancy."[65] *Baker* was a clear victory in defining homosexuality as a private matter the regulation of which did not fall within the state's legitimate purview.

Nevertheless, that the Court would issue a nationwide invalidation of statutes criminalizing consensual same-sex intimacy was hardly guaranteed. By the tenth anniversary of the Stonewall riots, in 1979, twenty-two states eliminated bans on consensual homosexual sex; however, this was more a consequence of updating legal codes than of early gay rights activism. Only three bans fell as a consequence of advocacy litigation; nineteen were removed via legislative action at a time when there was no cognizable electoral benefit to supporting gay rights. Ellen Andersen has demonstrated that "the major instigator of reform was the Model Penal Code," and "sodomy reform piggybacked on a larger project of penal reform."[66] Between 1984 and 1991, no sodomy laws were repealed. And, in 1985, the Fifth Circuit overruled the lower federal decision in *Baker* and reinstated the Texas sodomy ban, thereby maintaining the criminalization of homosexual sex in half the states.[67]

When upholding the constitutionality of the Georgia ban on sodomy, the ruling by the five-justice majority in *Bowers*, delivered by Justice White, defined homosexuality as nothing more than the act of sodomy:

"[R]espondent [Harwick] would have us announce, as the Court of Appeals did, a fundamental right to engage in homosexual sodomy. This we are quite unwilling to do."[68] Insofar as consensual intimacy might fall within the zone of privacy, the Court made clear that this zone was restricted to heterosexual intimacy and heteronormative contexts:

> [W]e think it evident that none of the rights announced in those cases bears any resemblance to the claimed constitutional right of homosexuals to engage in acts of sodomy that is asserted in this case. No connection between family, marriage, or procreation, on the one hand, and homosexual activity, on the other, has been demonstrated, either by the Court of Appeals or by respondent.[69]

And, when evaluating whether a fundamental right was at issue, the Court, referring to such a right as following from deeply rooted tradition, again framed homosexuality as a sex act that could find no such support: "It is obvious to us that neither of these formulations would extend a fundamental right to homosexuals to engage in acts of consensual sodomy. Proscriptions against that conduct have ancient roots."[70]

Lambda lawyers pursued the conception of homosexuality as conduct inasmuch as they relied on the precedent of *Stanley v. Georgia*, which overturned a conviction for viewing obscene materials in the privacy of one's home.[71] Homosexuality was analogized to viewing pornography; it was an act that resulted in sexual gratification. The Court dismissed this comparison:

> *Stanley* did protect conduct that would not have been protected outside the home, and it partially prevented the enforcement of state obscenity laws; but the decision was firmly grounded in the First Amendment. The right pressed upon us here has no similar support in the text of the Constitution, and it does not qualify for recognition under the prevailing principles for construing the Fourteenth Amendment.[72]

A claim to privacy, grounded in the Fourteenth Amendment's due process clause, could not serve as an impermeable barrier to state action. And, refusal to see gays and lesbians as a class of persons rendered them noncognizable by the structure of the Equal Protection Clause of the Fourteenth Amendment. Those who engaged in homosexuality, according to the Court majority, had no constitutional recourse against state criminalization.

The dissent, authored by Justice Blackmun, did not reframe the question as whether a state law unconstitutionally discriminated against a class. It merely held that homosexual conduct fell within a zone of privacy that followed from the sexual privacy jurisprudence rooted in *Griswold*. Even as the dissent declared, "This case is no more about 'a fundamental right to engage in homosexual sodomy,' as the Court purports to declare, *ante* at 191, than *Stanley v. Georgia*, 394 U.S. 557 (1969), was about a fundamental right to watch obscene movies," it maintained that this case is about "'the most comprehensive of rights and the right most valued by civilized men,' namely, 'the right to be let alone.' *Olmstead v. United States*, 277 U.S. 438, 478 (1928) (Brandeis, J., dissenting)."[73] Thus, homosexual acts—whether approved or not—fell within "a certain private sphere of individual liberty . . . kept largely beyond the reach of government."[74] What was at stake in this case, as was at stake in the contraception cases like *Griswold* and *Eisenstadt*, was "the freedom an individual has to choose the form and nature of these intensely personal bonds."[75] What was at stake was the freedom to engage in a private intimate act.

Neither the majority nor the dissent recognized gays and lesbians as a distinct class of persons facing unjust discrimination. Such recognition was, in part, precluded by the Georgia statute in question, which banned both same-sex and opposite-sex sodomy. As a result, the law did not target a particular class. Nevertheless, Justice Stevens offered a view of sexuality that was neither mere act nor act protected within the private sphere:

> These cases do not deal with the individual's interest in protection from unwarranted public attention, comment, or exploitation. They deal, rather, with the individual's right to make certain unusually important decisions that will affect his own, or his family's, destiny. The Court has referred to such decisions as implicating "basic values," as being "fundamental," and as being dignified by history and tradition. The character of the Court's language in these cases brings to mind the origins of the American heritage of freedom—the abiding interest in individual liberty

that makes certain state intrusions on the citizen's right to decide how he will live his own life intolerable. Guided by history, our tradition of respect for the dignity of individual choice in matters of conscience and the restraints implicit in the federal system, federal judges have accepted the responsibility for recognition and protection of these rights in appropriate cases.[76]

Stevens discussed a distinct conception of sexuality, one that characterized sexuality and the right to express intimacy as constitutive of human dignity. By focusing on dignity, Stevens, if only for himself and Justices Brennan and Marshall, who joined his dissent, moved beyond the limits of the sexual act to a richer conception of the way sexuality defines selfhood. In this way, the Stevens dissent suggested some form of recognition of homosexuals as persons—a recognition denied by the ruling and dissent—even if that recognition did not register the extant doctrine of suspect class and increased scrutiny of laws that affect persons suffering a long history of discrimination and political powerlessness.[77] With equal treatment not even considered, the liberal promise of privacy was hardly sustained. As Deborah Gould poignantly summarizes, "In allowing government intrusion into gay bedrooms, the *Hardwick* ruling, emanating from the highest echelons of the state and offering the final word on gay rights, demolished the logic of the private sphere and forced a recognition of gays' de facto *noncitizenship*."[78] Taken together, *Boutilier* and *Bowers* suggested no clear pathway for gay equality; the Court upheld the constitutionality of state discrimination against homosexual persons in the former and against homosexual acts in the latter.

Boutilier maintained that the state could legitimately exclude homosexual persons from the United States. It implied much more: "If the state could do this, what was to prevent it from doing anything that was viewed as 'legitimate' state action in relation to psychopaths, including disfranchisement and institutionalization?"[79] *Boutilier* opened the door to a broad array of state action against homosexual persons beyond only excluding gay and lesbian aliens; it fundamentally threatened the status of gay U.S. citizens. *Bowers* maintained the state regulatory power to criminalize homosexual conduct. In this context, not only would equality seemingly require that homosexuality be considered a personhood status rather than a conduct, but it would also need to be understood as a status that provoked a long, unwarranted, and irrational history of discrimination. The Court would recognize gays and lesbians as such ten years after *Bowers* in *Romer v. Evans* (1996).[80]

In *Romer*, the Court struck down an amendment to the Colorado constitution that prohibited adoption or enforcement of any statute "whereby homosexual, lesbian or bisexual orientation, conduct, practices or relationships shall constitute or otherwise be the basis of or entitle any persons or class of persons to have or claim any minority status, quota, preferences, protected status or claim of discrimination."[81] In essence, the amendment made it legally impossible for gays, lesbians, or bisexuals to make a cognizable discrimination claim grounded in sexual orientation. It essentially wrote them out of the political community, at least on the basis of their sexuality.[82] Opponents of the amendment argued that nondiscrimination statutes ensured equal access to public accommodation or employment opportunity regardless of sexual orientation. Supporters argued that these ordinances granted lesbians, bisexuals, and gay men special rights.[83]

The Court majority's conception of homosexuality in *Romer* starkly diverged from its statements in *Bowers*. Writing for the *Romer* majority, Justice Anthony Kennedy defined homosexuals as a "named class, a class we shall refer to as homosexual persons or gays and lesbians."[84] The Court maintained that the amendment removed gays, lesbians, and bisexuals from the community, barring them from liberties entitled to all persons: "Homosexuals, by state decree, are put in a solitary class with respect to transactions and relations in both the private and governmental spheres. The amendment withdraws from homosexuals, but no others, specific legal protection from the injuries caused by discrimination, and it forbids reinstatement of those laws and policies."[85] In this last statement the Court alludes to the dialectical relationship of identity construction: while Kennedy acknowledges that homosexuals are a class of persons, he also suggests that this class status is reinforced by the regulatory recognition and fundamental exclusion stipulated in the amendment. The law both recognizes the class and maintains it.

Justice Scalia's dissent, by contrast, harkened back to the Court's earlier construction of homosexuality in *Bowers* as a legitimately criminalized sex act: "If it is constitutionally permissible for a State to make homosexual conduct criminal, surely it is constitutionally permissible for a State to enact other laws merely disfavoring homosexual conduct."[86] *Romer* contradicted *Bowers* in that *Bowers* permits exactly what the Colorado amendment achieves, namely, singling out an individual for unfavorable treatment because the individual violates the majority's social mores. If homosexuals can be imprisoned, then less invidious forms of discrimination are allowable. For Scalia, the homosexual is the sexual act; a distinction between orientation and conduct is "a distinction without a difference."[87]

The majority rejected this claim, holding that while a state may criminalize an act, it may not discriminate against a person or a class of persons without a rational purpose.[88] Kennedy's ruling for the Court named gays and lesbians as a class subject to a history of unjust discrimination. He thereby offered a modality of recognition distinct from earlier ones, which had emphasized homosexual sex acts as manifestations of disease fundamentally threatening to the body politic, a modality reinforced by *Bowers*. Ten years after *Bowers*, the Court took a new position toward homosexuality and, particularly, toward homosexuals by doing exactly what *Bowers* refused to do: it recognized LGB persons as a class of discriminated-against individuals. Kennedy thereby brought the Court in line with the third modality of recognition discussed in this book: seeing the gay, lesbian, or bisexual individual as subject to unjust prejudice.

While this status-conduct distinction permitted *Bowers* and *Romer* to coexist, it created a readily identifiable friction.[89] Homosexuality had been defined for nearly a century of medical science, social movement activism, and state policy as manifest through behavior.[90] But now, the Court embraced the very construction that gay rights advocates avoided in *Boutilier* and could not utilize in *Bowers*. Rather than characterize homosexuality as sexual behavior legitimately shielded from public sanction, the Court instead saw lesbian and gay citizens as unjustly subject to state-sanctioned discrimination for being themselves. Nevertheless, the Court refused to interrogate the basis of that discrimination, namely, the open expression of sexuality. In this way, the Court's action followed the underlying logic of one of the most visible congressional compromises on gay and lesbian rights, the passage of Don't Ask, Don't Tell, discussed in more detail in chapter 4.

The jurisprudential line from *Boutilier* to *Bowers* to *Romer* reveals much about how homosexuality is seen by the Court. The three cases reveal a Court gradually coming to see gays and lesbians as a discriminated-against class; the rulings moved from six justices maintaining the deportation of *Boutilier* for homosexuality to five justices maintaining the criminality of homosexual sexual relations in *Bowers* to only three seeking to maintain state-sponsored discrimination against gay and lesbian persons in *Romer*. From another angle, these cases exemplify a complicated history of both social movement and institutional dissent about how to recognize homosexuality as act, status, or both.[91] As Canaday has argued, the Court's constructing homosexuality as character or status in *Boutilier* in order to maintain the constitutionality of an exclusionary statute creates "an ambivalent legacy of fixing homosexuality as identity." Homosexuality, understood as identity, was hardly a construction that fostered reform in *Boutilier*. Even as it is more presently adopted as a pathway toward equal treatment, Canaday points out that by utilizing it, gays and lesbians open themselves to long histories of "regulation by state authority."[92] This construction has both "emancipatory" and "repressive" effects, and thereby gives credence to the positions that divided the early homophile movement leadership.[93] Homosexuality as identity or personhood status, in other words, in no way assured equality, which, at the very least, calls into question whether that construction is necessary to promote equal treatment and/or the successful recognition of rights claims.

Municipal and State-Level Recognition of Discrimination

Romer was triggered by an amendment to the Colorado constitution, which itself was triggered by municipal regulations that protected against discrimination on the basis of sexual orientation. While many repeals of sodomy bans occurred as part of a broader revision of the general criminal code, the same characterization cannot be made of the passage of statutes that guarded against discrimination on the basis of sexual orientation in housing, employment, and public accommodations. Many of these resulted from the clear work of gay rights activists.

One organization working toward this goal was the Gay Activist Alliance (GAA). The GAA was a post-Stonewall organization that was established when former Gay Liberation Front (GLF) members, including Jim Owles, Marty Robinson, Arthur Evans, and Arthur Bell, grew increasingly frustrated by the GLF's New Left radicalism, which tended to focus on connections among marginalized groups to target structural oppression rather than target gay and lesbian concerns and which embraced a nonhierarchical structure that often made concerted action difficult to organize. The GLF's statement of purpose captures both the more rebellious and the more inclusive perspective: "We are a revolutionary homosexual group of men and women formed with the realization that complete sexual liberation for all people cannot come about unless existing social institutions are abolished."[94] By contrast, the GAA emphasized working within existing political structures to seek statutory reform. The GAA was focused less on a broader ethos of sexual liberation and more on defining gays and lesbians as a minority group that legitimately sought legal protection from discrimination.[95] To that end, by 1970, the GAA of New York persuaded the representatives from New York, Bella Abzug and Ed Koch, to denounce publicly police practices targeted against gay men and lesbians, including bar raids and entrapment. That year, the GAA of New York also began a campaign for a citywide ban on discrimination based on sexual orientation in employment. After repeated demonstrations at City Hall, the GAA secured a mayoral endorsement of the proposal in 1971 and an executive order that banned city agencies from discriminating against gays, lesbians, and bisexuals in their hiring. But, the broader city council did not pass the legislation, leaving the protections unstable and dependent upon subsequent mayoral actions.[96]

Other GAAs pursued similar strategies for nondiscrimination regulations at the municipal level. Failures in Boulder, Chicago, Minneapolis, and Philadelphia outnumbered the successes. In 1972, the first municipal protections against employment discrimination based on sexual orientation were passed in Ann Arbor and East Lansing, Michigan. San Francisco adopted a similar law that year. In 1973, the District of Columbia pioneered a ban on sexual-orientation discrimination in all employment. In 1975, Pennsylvania banned such discrimination, but only in state employment. California did so in 1979.[97]

Challenging the criminalization of same-sex intimacy and promoting nondiscrimination statutes occurred simultaneously, but they often drew on distinct if not openly contradictory conceptions of homosexuality and of how and whether it should be recognized by the state. Sodomy reform not only often rested on constructing homosexuality as an act but also drew on liberal and libertarian arguments against state oversight of private behaviors and personal choice. Nondiscrimination statutes, far from arguing against state interference, *required* state action to protect gays and lesbians from discrimination. Nevertheless, while sodomy reform might have seemed initially easier to achieve both because the sought-after outcome did not require positive action on the part of the state and because it could and was folded into a broader portfolio of criminal reforms, often gay and lesbian advocates had more success securing nondiscrimination statutes. This may have been due to the fact that sodomy reform had to occur at the level of the state, while federalism created many more venues for nondiscrimination statutes in the form of city-wide and county-wide ordinances. It may also reflect that sodomy reform halted, as Ellen Ann Andersen has aptly demonstrated, due, in part, to the AIDS crisis.[98]

By 1981, protections against discrimination on the basis of sexual orientation in employment, housing, and/or public accommodations were in place in large cities such as Detroit, Los Angeles, Seattle, and Washington, DC, as well as college towns like Urbana, Illinois. These municipal-level successes suggest, as Marc Stein has contended, that when promoting nondiscrimination legislation, "the movement was most effective when it presented gays and lesbians as a minority group made up of individuals with fixed and innate sexual orientations."[99] This construction clearly drew on the cultural frames of difference, unjust oppression, and immutable characteristics promoted by the African American civil rights movement and second-wave feminism.[100]

In 1982, Wisconsin became the first state to ban all such employment discrimination. Massachusetts did so in 1989. Between these years, New York, Ohio, New Mexico, Rhode Island, Washington, and Oregon took the more limited action of banning sexual-orientation discrimination in state employment (Oregon's law was repealed by popular referendum in 1988, a year after its passage). Not until 1991 did Connecticut and Hawaii follow Wisconsin's and Massachusetts's lead and ban such discrimination in all employment. A year later, California, New Jersey, and Vermont followed, while Oregon reinstated its ban on discrimination in state employment. In 1993, Minnesota pioneered a ban on discrimination based on sexual orientation and gender identity in all employment.

Since then, other states have followed, while still more have implemented bans against discrimination based on sexual orientation only.[101] During these years, various municipalities acted to pass nondiscrimination statutes either when their states would not or in addition to the state action.[102] As of 2015, a gay, lesbian, or bisexual can be legally fired for his or her sexual orientation in twenty-eight states; a transgender person can be legally fired in thirty-one states.[103]

Once instituted, these bans have not been stable. They have been repealed, reinstated, and repealed again. Popular referenda overturned city council actions against discrimination in Boulder, Colorado, in 1974. And, through the advocacy of Christian and New Right activists, led in part by former Florida orange juice spokeswoman Anita Bryant and her "Save the Children" campaign, antidiscrimination ordinances were repealed in Dade County, Florida, in 1977, in Eugene, Oregon, Saint Paul, Minnesota, and Wichita, Kansas, in 1978, and in San Jose, California, in 1980.[104] In addition, early victories for local-level nondiscrimination statutes may have worked against state-wide expansions insofar as early successes created a new popular awareness and widened the scope of conflict, mobilizing previously unaware opponents. Increased public salience of these proposed statutes often worked against their adoption or in favor of their repeal during the 1970s through the 1990s.[105]

Louisiana's 1992 ban on discrimination in state employment was eliminated in 1996, reinstated by executive order in 2004, and allowed to expire in 2008.[106] An Ohio ban on sexual-orientation discrimination in state employment went into effect via executive order in 1983, but Republican Governor Kasich let it expire in 1999; protections to both sexual orientation and gender identity were renewed via executive order under a Democratic governor in 2007. The protection for gender identity was allowed to expire via a 2011 executive order by reelected Governor Kasich, which only banned sexual-orientation discrimination.[107] Thus, while employment nondiscrimination policy may be passed via legislative statute, it may be implemented through the less stable mechanism of executive orders, which expire at the end of each gubernatorial term. While federalism and separation of powers do offer, in theory, more opportunity structures for activists to seek their policy aims, the achievements secured may be more or less stable depending on the branch of government through which they are obtained.

That Kasich maintained the nondiscrimination principle for sexual orientation in 2011 (even as he eliminated the protection for transgender individuals) whereas he killed it in 1999 suggests a durable shift in authority that deserves examination. How and why did a governor from a political party that has been consistently hostile to a range of gay rights claims support a nondiscrimination principle for gays and lesbians? Did the action reflect trends in public opinion and thus a calculus of electoral cost and benefit? What role did media, movement actors, and countermovement mobilization play? How had the issue agenda shifted by 2011, perhaps away from the less contentious issue of employment protections and toward the more controversial question of recognizing same-sex relationships, and how might that shift have affected the perceived legitimacy of some claims? And, finally, how might the distinction between sexual orientation and gender identity be considered? Had, by 2011, the construction of gays, lesbians, and bisexuals as an unjustly discriminated-against class taken hold whereas public understanding and acceptance of transgender identities remained shallow?

The pattern of municipal and state-level nondiscrimination statutes suggests that institutional design can encourage policy variation. While separation of powers affords federal branches some measure of independence, federalism provides distinct venues the opportunity to experiment. Thus, the structure of American governance goes some way toward explaining variations in laws affecting LGBT rights. And, yet, there is no definitive evidence that these policy moves are the consequence of any systemic process of policy diffusion, whereby certain states may innovate as "policy laboratories," and then other, particularly geographically nearby or culturally similar states, may soon follow.[108] In evaluating the adoption of nondiscrimination statutes applied to private employers, for example, Klawitter and Hammer uncovered regional variation, which might not be unexpected: "Pacific . . . New England, and East North Central cities and counties have been most likely to adopt. Local governments in the Mountain and Southern regions have been least likely to adopt."[109] Ultimately, as this pattern could be a consequence of cultural and demographic factors, such as higher income, higher education level, or more urban concentration, which are highly correlated with public acceptance of gays and lesbians serving equally and openly in the workplace, these scholars could point to "only mixed support for the application of patterns of spatial and temporal diffusion developed for state-level policies."[110] Rather than enabling some states to become policy laboratories for others to watch and model downstream, federalism has promoted policy variation that maps onto cultural and demographic difference, leaving gay and lesbian citizens more or less recognized by accident of their location.

The push for antidiscrimination law, the parallel discursive shift to reframe homosexuality from act to personhood, and the attempts to analogize prejudice against gays and lesbians as similar to race-based and gender-based bias did not only occur at the municipal and state levels. In 1974, the newly formed National Gay Task Force successfully lobbied Representative Bella Abzug of New York to introduce an amendment to the Civil Rights Act of 1964, which would have restricted discrimination on the basis of "sexual preference" in employment, housing, and public accommodation. While it had garnered twenty-five cosponsors by 1975, the effort began to languish. By 1981, the bill had only fifty-nine cosponsors in the House and a few in the Senate. Nevertheless, the national gay civil rights bill was introduced and reintroduced every year after 1974, garnering additional cosponsors until the late 1980s, when focus shifted to antidiscrimination legislation for people with HIV/AIDS. By 1993, the gay civil rights bill was scaled back and reintroduced as the Employment Non-Discrimination Act (ENDA), discussed further in chapter 4.[111]

HIV Disease, Disability Status, and the ADA: The Unstable Recognition of Discrimination

That the proposed gay civil rights bill was, in part, displaced by the AIDS crisis represents a larger pattern of the public health crisis reshaping the gay and lesbian rights movement over the course of the 1980s and 1990s. Gay rights advocates increasingly gained access to Congress during the 1980s and 1990s, but hearings on AIDS-related issues dramatically outpaced those on other gay rights concerns.[112] And, while AIDS was used as a weapon by the New Right to halt if not roll back significant movements toward rights recognition made during the 1970s, it also fundamentally reoriented the scale, organizational structure, and organizational orientation of the gay rights movement.[113]

The onset of the AIDS crisis compelled a dramatic increase in the number of people coming out of the closet, in part because institutional response to the crisis by the Reagan administration proved lackluster. An early executive director of the Gay Men's Health Crisis (GMHC) aptly stated, "for a white man with a graduate degree and a good job who can pass, [discrimination was] not an issue. Never was. Until [AIDS] really got down to it and you realized they want you to die. . . . You are literally left to die."[114] The crisis also brought new visibility to gay and lesbian concerns, although the value of this visibility has been hotly debated. Queer theorist Leo Bersani referred to it as "the visibility of imminent death, of promised invisibility . . . [and] the pathos and impotence of a doomed species."[115] The Helms Amendment, with its requirement that AIDS funding not acknowledge homosexual sex acts, rendered homosexuality invisible as a policy matter. Yet, ironically, the debate over the Helms Amendment brought gay rights and related AIDS concerns much more visibly into public discourse. In so doing, it bore out what legal theorist Carl Stychin sees as "the paradox . . . that in seeking to silence an identity and deny a right of sexual citizenship, the prohibition of expression creates discursive space for the identity to be excluded. A prohibition must acknowledge the existence of the prohibited and thus brings the prohibited practices into the public domain of discourse."[116] In short, AIDS brought acknowledgment of homosexuality in new ways, opening up opportunities that had not existed before, even if much of the visibility was negative.

The intransigence of the Reagan administration, coupled with the lack of visibility given to the crisis in the mainstream press, prompted the formation of the AIDS Coalition to Unleash Power in 1987. In part developed to promote attention to the crisis, ACT UP ignited enthusiasm for direct-action protest more reminiscent of the liberationist strand of the early 1970s than of the national-level interest-group politics that had emerged since the mid-1970s.[117] At the same time, however, AIDS mobilization did attract wider participation from gay and straight communities and brought into movement politics a large influx of white male conservative and wealthy individuals who had little connection to the liberationist ideals of the 1970s, and consequently, AIDS mobilization steered the broader movement away from its leftist orientation.[118] Capturing the shift, former National Gay and Lesbian Task Force executive director Urvashi Vaid wrote, "in place of liberation, the AIDS movement substituted nondiscrimination; instead of building a movement, it built agencies and bureaucracies; instead of placing its political faith in training and organizing gay and lesbian people, and our allies, into an electoral coalition, it placed faith in friends in high places."[119] The AIDS movement did undermine the liberationist tendencies and aspirations of the 1970s. First, the public health crisis created calls to shut down some of the institutions central to sexual liberation and gay identity: bathhouses. Second, it required government recognition—often federal action—and action on a scale never sought before and fundamentally at odds with the libertarian angle that motivated some aspects of sexual liberation: "The spread of the AIDS epidemic also drew more and more gays and lesbians to the view that federal intervention on gay-related issues was essential."[120] Nevertheless, as discussed above, the roots of the more reformist position have always been evident in the gay rights movement; defining gays and lesbians as a minority suffering unjust discrimination and seeking government recognition of this status has been an aim of at least one faction within the broader movement since midcentury.

Federal intervention was codified when individuals with HIV disease were included in the Americans with Disabilities Act (ADA), which made discrimination in employment, housing, and public accommodations against people with AIDS illegal. As Chai Feldblum, who lobbied tirelessly for ADA coverage for people with HIV disease, explained shortly after the law's passage, "a person with AIDS, as well as a person with asymptomatic HIV infection, would be covered under the first prong of the definition [of disability, i.e., 'has a physical or mental impairment that substantially limits that person in one or more major life activities']."[121] ADA inclusion had profound effects for gay and bisexual men not only because the law impedes discrimination against those with HIV but also because it protects people from discrimination based on *perceived* HIV status. In other words, the ADA prevented a landlord from denying an individual housing because of concerns that gay tenants might contract HIV.[122] ADA inclusion thereby functioned as an alternative route for gay men to receive some protection from discrimination inasmuch as gay male sexuality was linked to HIV infection during the first years of the crisis.

If Congress did not recognize gays, lesbians, or bisexuals as a discriminated-against class, inclusion in the ADA meant that it at least recognized a subset of this population as such. But closer analysis of the law's development, the way it has been judicially interpreted over time, and the way it might be utilized going forward—particularly as the social understanding of HIV shifts from terminal illness to a manageable if chronic disease—indicates that ADA inclusion does not guarantee equal rights recognition.

During the early years of the AIDS crisis, the virus was most associated with homosexuality in the public imagination and public health discourse.[123] HIV was framed as a plague, which affected socially stigmatized groups like homosexuals, heroin and other intravenous drug users, and Haitians, as well as so-called innocents like children afflicted with hemophilia.[124] These constructions of who was the most likely to be afflicted with HIV disease meant that the possibility of targeted discrimination against these groups, including preventing access to housing and education as well as employment, was very real. The likelihood of discrimination—and the lack of any statutory defense against it or legal framework to understand and combat it—potentially exacerbated the difficulties with promoting testing and awareness. The 1988 report by the Presidential Commission on the Human Immunodeficiency Virus Epidemic, unequivocally expressed this concern:

> HIV-related discrimination is impairing this nation's ability to limit the spread of the epidemic. . . . Public health officials will not be able to gain the confidence and cooperation of infected individuals or those at high risk for infection if such individuals fear that they will be unable to retain their jobs and their housing, and that they will be unable to obtain the medical and support services they need because of discrimination based on a positive HIV antibody test.[125]

It also reaffirmed that the fear of contagion, which motivated this discrimination, was baseless: "discrimination against persons with HIV infection in the workplace setting, or in the areas of housing, schools, and public accommodations, is unwarranted because it has no public health basis. Nor is there any basis to discriminate against those who care for or associate with such individuals."[126] Some legal infrastructure was in place to combat the discrimination at the local and state level: "it is illegal to discriminate against persons with AIDS in those local jurisdictions with AIDS-specific anti-discrimination statutes, in those states which include AIDS as a protected handicap under their disability anti-discrimination laws, and in programs which receive federal funds."[127] And, yet, the *Report* made clear that this was hardly sufficient:

> Nevertheless, complaints of HIV-related discrimination persist and their number is increasing. . . . Just as our society has taken a definitive stand on discrimination against persons with other handicapping conditions and illnesses—such as cerebral palsy, mental retardation, and cancer— society must take a stand on discrimination against persons with HIV infection. . . . Persons with HIV infection must be clearly and definitively guaranteed their civil rights and be protected against discrimination just as persons with other disabilities are. Such protection enables the HIV-infected person to become a partner with social institutions in limiting further spread of the infection and supporting effective care-giving systems.[128]

Banning discrimination would serve clear public health objectives, according to the *Report*, and was in keeping with strides made toward equality as part of the broader "rights revolution" after midcentury. Nevertheless, no clear legal framework was in place at the federal level to understand bias against people with HIV as systematic discrimination or to combat it.

Frameworks against discrimination had taken shape through the development of scrutiny doctrine, discussed in much more detail in chapter 6. However, extant definitions of suspect or protected classes did not neatly fit the circumstances of HIV infection. Since the *Bowers* Court refused to recognize gays and lesbians as a discriminated-against class, thereby perhaps triggering more scrutiny of laws and actions affecting this group, there was no clear juridical route to prevent HIV discrimination through its constructed connection to gay sexuality.[129]

Arthur Leonard, professor of law at New York Law School, broke new ground when he utilized the definition of disability as articulated in section 504 of the Rehabilitation Act of 1973 as the tool to guard against discrimination based on actual or perceived HIV status.[130] The law prohibited any entity receiving federal financial assistance from discrimi-

nating against a "qualified individual with a disability," and it defined
the disabled as "any person who (i) has a physical or mental impairment
which substantially limits one or more of such person's major life activities, (ii) has a record of such an impairment, or (iii) is regarded as having
such an impairment."[131] Leonard argued that individuals with HIV disease qualified as disabled as their immune systems were compromised
and the "ability to fight infection and preserve health is logically a major
life function."[132] Furthermore, disability law could be an alternate route
to guarding against discrimination on the basis of homosexuality insofar
as the act protected from discrimination anyone "regarded as" having
an impairment. In other words, while sexuality is not considered an impairment, the link between HIV and gay sexuality in the public imagination provided protection for asymptomatic HIV-positive individuals as
well as, potentially, for gay and bisexual men generally. In other words,
the law protected more than just symptomatic HIV-positive individuals
from discrimination in hiring, firing, or promotion "because the motivation of the employer is the same unlawful motivation as that expressly
condemned by the statute: animus against a class of individuals which
unfairly ignores their individual qualifications and is based on prejudi-
cial beliefs about the class."[133]

Within two years of Leonard publishing his theory of HIV status as a
protected disability class, the Supreme Court plugged one of the holes in
the theory. Leonard had not addressed the possibility of whether someone with HIV might be dismissed from work or banned from school
because of fear of contagion, a dismissal possibly motivated more by a
concern for public health than by discriminatory intent. In *School Board
of Nassau County v. Arline* (1987), involving a woman with tuberculosis,
the Court ruled that infectious disease could qualify as a handicap under
section 504 of the Rehabilitation Act because the "impairment was se-
rious enough to require hospitalization, a fact more than sufficient to
establish that one or more of her major life activities were substantially
limited by her impairment."[134] In the wake of the *Arline* ruling, the Office of Legal Counsel in the Reagan administration Justice Department
issued a memo in 1988 that HIV qualified as a disability by the terms of
the act, and that even asymptomatic HIV, given its physiological impact,
also qualified: "from a purely scientific perspective, persons with HIV
infection are clearly impaired."[135]

Courts treated HIV as a disability within the meaning of the Rehabilitation Act or similar state laws.[136] This judicial consensus was solidified by congressional statute with the passage of the Americans with Disabilities Act in 1990. Congress utilized explicit phraseology, adapted from the judicial scrutiny doctrine, to recognize persons with disabilities as a suspect class and thus to establish that actions against them should be treated with higher scrutiny than mere rational basis review. The ADA recognized that disabled individuals

> are a discrete and insular minority who have been faced with restrictions and limitations, subjected to a history of purposeful unequal treatment, and relegated to a position of political powerlessness in our society, based on characteristics that are beyond the control of such individuals and resulting from stereotypic assumptions not truly indicative of the individual ability of such individuals to participate in, and contribute to, society.[137]

The framing of disability as the marker of a suspect class drew on the logics of strict scrutiny as applied to race discrimination and intermediate scrutiny as applied to sex and gender discrimination. The qualities of political powerlessness, immutable characteristic, and negative stereotype, all developed in those doctrinal lines, were applied to new effect. In this way, the ADA essentially "extends the scope of coverage of the 1964 Civil Rights Act to persons with disabilities," as well as to the subsequent judicial interpretations of that statute and corresponding doctrinal development.[138] Insofar as the ADA covered HIV and those "regarded as" having HIV, and inasmuch as gay sexuality was linked— rightly or wrongly—with the social stigma of homosexuality, then the ADA provided some avenue for protection against discrimination when a national gay civil rights bill appeared all but dead.

Challenges to utilizing the ADA to protect against discrimination of persons with HIV disease come from at least two sources. First, the ADA recycles the definition of disability from the 1973 Rehabilitation Act, which obviously went into effect before the initial discovery of HIV in 1981. As a result, the ADA has been somewhat of an awkward fit.[139] The legislative history of the ADA reveals congressional intent to include those infected with HIV within the definition of a disabled class.[140] Responding to this legislative history, the Court fitted HIV infection within the first prong of the ADA's definition of disability, sometimes stretching its parameters. This is most evident in the federal court decision in *Doe v. Kohn Nast & Graf, P.C.*, which addressed whether an attorney, fired from his firm, was disabled by HIV and thus protected from such action by the ADA.[141] In rendering its judgment, the Court maintained that the ADA was hardly explicit as to whether and how HIV disease fell within its orbit; the law "provides no express guidance as to whether an IIIV-infected person comes within the ambit of the Act."[142] The Court grounded its consideration of HIV as disabling on the basis of the physiological symptoms of the disease, including rash, fever, weight loss, and swollen lymph glands.[143] The Court was compelled to link HIV to clear manifestations of physical illness. Doing so undermined the aim to include asymptomatic HIV-positive individuals as covered by the ADA. To avoid this outcome, the Court stretched the definition of "major life activity" beyond work and employment to include sexual reproduction as asymptomatic HIV-status individuals were so impaired because they risked transmission to a partner or offspring.[144]

Second, courts have resisted stretching concepts, and instead, have relied on jamming circumstances into narrow renderings of law, which potentially has devastating effects for the inclusivity of disability status as originally imagined by Leonard. In *Abbott v. Bragdon*, the federal court for the First Circuit considered whether an HIV-positive woman was illegally denied dental care by the terms of the ADA.[145] While the court accepted that HIV-positive status constituted a disability, it questioned whether the disability substantially impaired a major life activity. Ultimately, it considered the individual in question to be impaired because the disease is "a substantial restriction on reproductive activity."[146] Limitations of this analysis are apparent. As Wendy Parmet and Daniel Jackson contend,

> the court's conclusion that Ms. Abbott was disabled was based in large part on the fortuity of her own fertility. Should other courts adopt this analysis requiring an individualized demonstration of how HIV status affects an individual's own reproductive intentions, the fate of many individuals who cannot show that their HIV status has caused them to alter their childbearing plans will be uncertain. For example, a woman who

has become HIV-positive after menopause could not satisfy the court as to her "fecundity." . . . And, of course, many gay men might find it difficult to explain how they have altered their reproductive plans because of their infection. Thus, the protection of asymptomatic HIV-positive individuals might be quite haphazard at best and depends on a circumstance—the plaintiff's fertility and reproductive intentions—that really has nothing to do with the discrimination at issue.[147]

Abbot demonstrates that the ADA has become an unstable basis for protection against discrimination as medical technology has advanced and as protease inhibitors have increased the potential for asymptomatic HIV and undetectable viral loads.

Inasmuch as disability depends on demonstrating individualized impairment of a major life activity and not on the social perception and potential stigma of HIV as itself disabling—a concept once pursued by Justice Brennan but only in dicta and never elaborated—the ADA's protections would seem to cover less and less.[148] And, inasmuch as the ADA provided an alternative route for some protections against discrimination on the basis of sexuality, the stringent requirement and individualized requirement of impairment of a major life activity proves a potential challenge. Without an explicit federal nondiscrimination law, gains in equal recognition for gays and lesbians remain, as the case of the Ohio executive nondiscrimination orders discussed in the previous section and as the *Abbot* and *Kohn* rulings on the scope of ADA protections suggest, "incomplete, conditional, and ultimately revocable."[149]

Regulatory Recognition in the Private Sector: Human Resource Policies as Pathways to Equal Treatment

Other arenas for social change in the recognition of gays and lesbians as a discriminated-against class have been private corporate human resource policies, both in terms of the inclusion of sexual orientation (and to a lesser extent gender identity) in nondiscrimination policies and in terms of the extension of equitable partner benefits to gay- and lesbian-identified employees. Benefits can be "hard benefits," which include medical, dental, and vision insurance, or "soft benefits," which include family leave, life insurance, bereavement leave, health coverage that includes one's partner if the worker leaves a job, such as COBRA, pension or retirement savings plans such as a 401(k), adoption assistance, childcare services, discounts on company goods or services, and long-term care insurance. Companies often extended soft benefits to the partners of gays and lesbians before providing them with hard benefits, an incremental process that only further illustrated the excluded and fragmented status of gay and lesbian employees.[150]

Equitable benefits means that lesbian, gay, and bisexual employees receive the same benefits already offered to heterosexual employees and their spouses. Prior to same-sex-marriage recognition at the state level, this extension required the establishment of domestic partner benefits. The Human Rights Campaign (HRC), the national LGBT-rights interest group that has tracked the development of corporate human resource benefits for LGBT employees, first used the provision of healthcare benefits as an indicator of equitable benefits in the 1990s.[151] Since 2002, the HRC has published an annual Corporate Equality Index (CEI), which evaluates companies by six criteria: (1) inclusion of sexual orientation in nondiscrimination policy, (2) inclusion of gender identity in nondiscrimination policy, (3) provision of domestic-partner health benefits, (4) provision of transgender-inclusive benefits, (5) organizational competency practices or commitment to LGBT-inclusive diversity training, and (6) a stated public commitment to the LGBT community. The pool of firms evaluated by the CEI includes the Fortune 1000 companies and the top two hundred revenue-grossing law firms as ranked by the magazine *American Lawyer*. In addition, any private for-profit employer with at least five hundred employees can participate in the ranking. The first CEI in 2002 ranked 381 companies; the most recent 2015 CEI ranked 781.[152]

Attending to this dimension of private regulatory recognition is important for at least two reasons. First, many of the benefits associated with welfare in developed countries, including healthcare, family leave, and access to life insurance, are, in the United States, provided through private employers as part of a broad compensation package that includes salary. Second, corporate recognition of gays and lesbians as entitled to equal rights has complex and nuanced effects on public policy development, potentially spurring but also potentially diminishing the prospects for broader state-level change.

Whether or not the United States is exceptional for its political development has long been a debate among American political development scholars.[153] Much less debated is that U.S. welfare policy has taken a distinctly more privatized path than other Western democracies with advanced economies. The U.S. Constitution contains no explicit language affirming welfare rights; insofar as they have developed, either rooted in maternalist practices of widow pensions in the late nineteenth century, Progressive Era statutes for workers' compensation, or New Deal policies for Social Security and unemployment insurance, these laws have only been adjudicated as constitutionally permissible, not constitutionally required as a matter of state or federal obligation to citizens.[154] Capturing this distinction, Mary Ann Glendon contended that the U.S. Constitution embraced rights before welfare while European democracies did the reverse.[155] Accordingly, much of the U.S. system of welfare provision flows not from the state but from the private sector. Consequently, Jacob Hacker has argued for greater attention to private-sector developments in explanations of policy outcomes: "institutionalist analyses must examine the evolution and effects of private as well as government institutions. . . . [I]nstitutionalists need to become even more self-consciously historical in their analyses of politics, and to broaden their inquiries to consider the constraints that the development of private market institutions creates for public policy making."[156]

Broadening the field of inquiry beyond state institutions also responds to recent scholarship in the sociological literature on social movements, which has been critical of excessive reliance on the state as the primary target of social change. Josh Gamson has highlighted, for example, how ACT UP activists targeted the "invisible enemy," such as pharmaceutical companies.[157] Steven Epstein has evaluated how ACT UP targeted specific practices, such as drug-testing protocols and pricing policies, in their efforts to increase access to anti-HIV therapies.[158] Indeed, as reviewed in chapter 1, substantial criticism has been leveled at political-opportunity and political-process theories of social-movement mobilization to the extent that they maintain a structural bias toward the state and do not explore other institutional arenas that may be relevant both to the construction of social-movement actors and as targets of social reform.[159] Corporate human resource policies are one such arena. Nicole Raeburn, for example, noted that while much scholarly attention has, since the 1990s, been directed toward gay and lesbian political mobilization, "scholars have yet to direct their attention to a significant development in the struggle for equal rights: the rise of a lesbian, gay, and bisexual workplace movement."[160] Insofar as that movement has, in the last two decades, achieved the successes of nearly all Fortune 500 companies issuing nondiscrimination statements including sexual orientation by 2014 and nearly two-thirds providing health coverage for same-sex partners, corporate recognition of gay and lesbian personhood and equality has significant ramifications.[161]

Homophile and post-Stonewall gay rights activists targeted private-sector job discrimination as a priority for reform. By 1965 the Mattachine Society of Washington, DC, was organizing picket lines outside the White House where gay men in suits and lesbians in dresses carried placards calling to "[e]nd employment policies against homosexuals."[162] In 1971, when Pacific Telephone & Telegraph announced that it would "not knowingly hire a homosexual," the Gay Activist Alliance picketed PT&T and its parent company, Atlantic Telephone & Telegraph (AT&T). The action was unsuccessful, and advocates were unable to get the company to comply with the San Francisco city ordinance banning discrimination on the basis of sexual orientation by any city contractor, which passed in 1972. In 1973, protestors mobilized outside of Northwestern Bell of Minnesota, an AT&T subsidiary, when it announced that it would not hire "admitted homosexuals." But, a year later, facing a lawsuit by the American Civil Liberties Union, and in the context of a newly passed Minneapolis antidiscrimination ordinance that included sexual orientation, Northwestern Bell dropped its antigay policy.[163]

Raeburn's analysis of the rise of gay and lesbian employee groups and the subsequent adoption of equitable benefits within the Fortune 1000 reveals low-level mobilization in the 1980s followed by a significant rise in the early 1990s, and then a denouement in the mid- to late 1990s.[164] The first period is hardly surprising in the context of the New Right and the successful backlash against the gay rights policy victories of the mid-1970s. Furthermore, given the rise of AIDS and the conservative movement, "gay and lesbian activists did not concentrate on gaining advances in the workplace or any other arena; instead, they focused by necessity on preventing further assaults on gay rights."[165]

The increase in gay and lesbian employee mobilization and subsequent inclusion within benefits packages during the 1990s and early 2000s had multiple influences. First, in 1991, Cracker Barrel, which operated restaurants mostly in the South and Midwest, after announcing that it would fire any employee "whose sexual preferences fail to demonstrate normal heterosexual values," dismissed eleven employees.[166] In response, gay rights advocates staged sit-ins at the restaurants and called for boycotts, and the National Gay and Lesbian Task Force launched a publicity campaign against the corporation.[167] The actions drew attention in the mainstream media, and the shareholders called for a resolution to institute human resource policies with protections against antigay discrimination.[168] Second, when Bill Clinton, campaigning for president in 1992, stated his intention to lift the ban on gays, lesbians, and bisexuals from serving in the military, he triggered a larger conversation about fairness in the workplace.[169] Third, the successful passage of Colorado's Amendment 2, which made it "legally impossible for gay rights laws to ever be established," created awareness of a tangible and motivating grievance. It created an opportunity, if properly framed, to mobilize employees to secure recognition through their firms since the state was opposed.[170] More broadly, the realization that public policy arenas were becoming a hostile venue to gay rights advocates by the early 1990s may have triggered some to look inward, to secure recognition and protections from discrimination directly from their employers. Finally, employee advocacy could utilize the new, more direct protest tactics of ACT UP and Queer Nation, which were overtly hostile to corporate America in many instances, as a useful foil; gay and lesbian employees asking only for nondiscrimination policies and equitable benefits were far more moderate.[171] In her interviews of gay and lesbian employee groups, Raeburn found that "many employee activists reasoned that their 'professional' requests for equality at work seemed far less threatening to corporate elites than did the militant stances of queer activists."[172]

Fortune magazine took note of these opportunities for mobilization within the workplace when it ran a cover story, "Gay in Corporate America," in its December 16, 1991, issue.[173] Journalist Thomas Stewart described the rise of gay and lesbian employee groups and how they are welcomed yet also held at bay in corporate communities:

Anxious and alienated, but unwilling to remain so, gay men and lesbians are rapidly forming employee groups like the one whose huge banner greeted all those on their way to the elevators at Levi Strauss's San Francisco headquarters in June: lesbian and gay employee association celebrates pride week. Similar groups, many blessed by management, exist at companies ranging from AT&T to Xerox.[174]

He described how gay-identified employees coordinated to lobby for policy changes:

[H]omosexual employees at AT&T, Boeing, Coors, Du Pont, Hewlett-Packard, Lockheed, Sun Microsystems, US West, and many other corporations have joined together for fellowship or to lobby top management on issues that are important to them. These include attacking overt workplace hostility, extending employee benefits to domestic partners, not just to spouses, and even little things like making sure that partners are welcome at company social events whenever husbands or wives are.[175]

Stewart was cautious about whether equality in the workplace could be achieved. He noted the fairly limited inroads made thus far: "Hundreds of employers, including dozens of FORTUNE 500 companies, have pledged not to discriminate on the basis of sexual orientation, but gay and lesbian executives are under no illusion that they will soon win mainstream acceptance in corporate America." And yet, twenty years after the publication of the piece, by 2012, all one hundred companies on *Fortune* magazine's list of best places to work include sexual orientation in their nondiscrimination and harassment policies.[176] As of 2014, 89 percent of all Fortune 500 companies include sexual orientation in their nondiscrimination policies, while 66 percent include gender identity. Sixty-six percent also provided domestic partner health benefits and 34 percent provide transgender-inclusive benefits. Nearly half provided diversity training, which includes content on LGBT concerns.[177]

This dramatic change in the span of about twenty-five years would not have been possible without the concerted efforts of mobilized employees within firms as well as the development of LGBT professional associations that shared best practices across fields. As Raeburn notes, "the majority of equitable-benefits adopters instituted this policy change only after facing internal pressure from mobilizing groups of lesbian, gay, and bisexual employees."[178] Nevertheless, some scholars give explanatory weight to other mechanisms. Some suggest that expansion of benefits exemplifies "mimetic isomorphism" or that once a leading organization adopts a policy, similar firms will follow so as to recruit and retain talent as well as maintain and attract customer bases.[179] This domino effect would indicate that employee politicization and mobilization may be far less important to a firm than whether and how establishment of nondiscrimination policies and provision of equitable benefits affects its market share and profit motive.[180]

Gay and lesbian interest groups such as the Human Rights Campaign emphasize how equal treatment in the workplace was hardly political and more a matter of good business sense. When the HRC issued its 2001 *State of the Workplace Report*, it contended that the trend toward equal treatment "seems to be attributable to sheer market forces."[181] The "good for business" model has deep roots in gay rights organizing. When the gay liberationist student organization from the University of Minnesota, FREE (Fight Repression of Erotic Expression), surveyed companies' position on gay and lesbian employees in 1970, it included with the survey a cover letter that argued that forcing these employees to stay in the closet had negative effects on productivity and profit.[182]

Policy adoptions are not simply a way to recruit and retain talent; they signal corporate values to potential customers and market to the niche of the gay consumer, the so-called pink dollar, as well as other customers who value nondiscrimination.[183] The responses from Angie's List and Apple, among other companies, to the passage of an Indiana statute that may have permitted discrimination against LGBT individuals under the claim of religious expression—discussed in this book's introduction—exemplify this kind of signaling. When Raeburn and others conducted analyses of firm concerns about openly supporting LGBT persons or appealing to an LGBT market niche in the early 2000s, it was far more plausible to contend that political stances might undercut the bottom line. Maintaining the separation between business and politics may reflect strategic ignorance insofar as admitting political motivations potentially alienates customers.[184] Emphasizing market forces is "an intentional discursive strategy to allow potential adopters, who often fear right-wing backlash, to rationalize benefits adoption."[185]

By 2013 only two Fortune 100 companies—Walmart and Exxon—did not grant benefits to gay or lesbian employees, and their reconsideration of this policy illustrated the strategic rhetoric that emphasizes external, often market, pressures as justification. In late September 2013, following pressure from gay rights advocates and its own shareholders, Exxon announced that it would extend health insurance and other benefits to the spouses of gay and lesbian employees starting October 1.[186] The move followed the publication of a cover article in the gay and lesbian news weekly the *Advocate*, which asked, "What's Wrong with Exxon?" and noted that since 2012, the firm had received "a negative 25 out of 100 possible points on its [HRC] Corporate Equality Index."[187] It further noted that Exxon had worked for the past fifteen years to squash annual shareholder resolutions to adopt equitable benefits. The company rolled back nondiscrimination policies and benefits inclusion as it merged with other oil firms in the 1990s and 2000s. It eliminated policies that were already in place at Mobil and XTO Energy: "It is the only company known to have ever permanently done so."[188]

When Exxon made its announcement, it rationalized the decision without any reference to equal treatment or response to employee, customer, or shareholder demand. It did not reference profit motive or other best business practice aims, as had become the norm. Rather, it innovated by holding the Supreme Court and other arms of the federal government responsible. Exxon asserted that its hand was forced by the Supreme Court's ruling in *United States v. Windsor*, which compelled the federal government to recognize same-sex marriages and thereby offer same-sex couples similar rights and benefits where they were already recognized by state governments.[189] By claiming that "spousal eligibility in our U.S. benefit plans has been and continues to be governed by the federal definition of marriage and spouse," the corporation placed all responsibility for its move on the liberal move by the Court and the executive branch.[190] The Labor Department, which regulates employee-based retirement and health insurance plans, interpreted *Windsor* as requiring that "all legally recognized same-sex couples were entitled to the same protections as opposite-sex couples."[191] The department was clarifying how *Windsor* affected ERISA, or the Employment Retirement Security Act, which regulates employee benefits. Of course, the federal government does not mandate that employers offer health coverage to employee spouses. Therefore, Exxon's hand was hardly forced by the Court or the Obama administration. Rather, when Exxon announced that it would "recognize all legal marriages for the purposes of eligibility in U.S. benefit plans to ensure consistency for employees across the country," it revealed its motivation.[192] Having a singular policy was far more economically rational than maintaining distinct policy regulations for different employees.

Walmart, like Exxon, announced in the fall of 2013, months after the *Windsor* ruling, that it would offer partner benefits to same-sex employees. Like Exxon, it contended that the motivation came from the Supreme Court. Walmart's senior vice president, Sally Welborn, explained,

> It's a business decision, not a moral or political one. We operate in 50 states, hundreds of municipalities and Puerto Rico, and as clarified under the Supreme Court's decision to strike down section 3 of the Defense of Marriage Act (DOMA), each of these states are developing different definitions of marriage, domestic partner, civil union, etc. By developing a single definition for all Walmart associates in the U.S. and Puerto Rico, we are able to ensure consistency for associates across our markets.[193]

Walmart recognized how *Windsor* served only to fragment the nature of gay and lesbian citizenship even further. Compelling the federal government to recognize marriage where it was already recognized by the states and not compelling other states to so recognize the *Windsor* ruling reinforced a regime of varying status over space. And, to the extent that the Obama administration announced that the federal government would not recognize civil unions, the human resource regulation of employees became increasingly complicated for firms that had multiple outlets across the country. This situation was particularly onerous for firms where there existed extreme diversity within a specific region; for example, a firm based in metropolitan Chicago, which might have employees living in nearby states, faced the problem that same-sex couples could be married in Minnesota but could acquire only a civil union in Illinois and a limited domestic partnership in Wisconsin.

An amicus brief submitted by 278 employers prior to Supreme Court oral argument in *Windsor* emphasized the hardship that this variation imposed:

We are located in or operate in states that recognize marriages of certain of our employees and colleagues to spouses of the same sex. At the same time, we are subject to section 3 of the federal Defense of Marriage Act ("DOMA"), which precludes federal recognition of these marriages. This dual regime uniquely burdens amici. It puts us, as employers, to unnecessary cost and administrative complexity.[194]

Expanding on this argument, the brief's first point was that "DOMA Imposes Compliance Burdens upon Employers" in the realm of benefits and prevents "a Workplace Ethos of Transparent Fairness."[195] The problem with DOMA was, in part, that it was costly for corporations to maintain distinct categories of employees in terms of their access to human resource benefits and the differential tax regulations that applied to benefits packages. This cost came from at least two sources: administrative costs and compensatory costs. Administrative costs followed from federal law compelling employers to see their employees differently in terms of eligibility for benefits and treatment by the tax code. The amicus brief stipulates,

In states recognizing marriage between two people of the same sex, DOMA requires amici simultaneously to treat employees with same-sex spouses as (1) single for the purposes of federal tax withholding, payroll taxes, and workplace benefits that turn, as most do, on marital status, and (2) married for all other purposes under state law, including state community property laws. This requires amici in effect to maintain two sets of books—one for married employees with same-sex spouses, and another for married employees with different-sex spouses. The double entries ripple through human resources, payroll, and benefits administration.[196]

In addition, the firms attempt to compensate gay and lesbian employees for the way the lack of federal recognition of their marriages affects their income. "DOMA enforces discriminatory treatment of spousal retirement and healthcare benefits. In many other benefit-related matters, amici may incur the cost and administrative burden of 'workarounds' (employer-created benefit structures attempting to compensate for the discriminatory effects of DOMA), or leave the married workforce in separate castes."[197] In essence, for a federally recognized married straight couple, spousal benefits are not considered taxable income. However, given DOMA, those same benefit packages for same-sex partners were taxed, essentially leaving gay and lesbian employees with less income for the same work. Many firms tried to compensate this loss in order to equalize treatment and thereby retain and attract talent; this practice was most evident at technology firms, law firms, and universities.[198] Even this practice seemed to follow a pattern of competitive pressures yielding mimetic isomorphism: "A small number of organizations, including Kimpton Hotels and Cisco, have had the policy in place for several years. But it wasn't until Google started compensating its employees last June that the movement really began to take off. Apple, Facebook, Barclays, McKinsey, and Bain & Company are some of the prominent names that followed suit."[199] By 2011 Yale and Columbia University announced similar programs.[200]

Beyond the frame of administrative cost burden, the amicus brief also laid out a number of other arguments about why DOMA harmed firms. But, again, these held to a general frame of discrimination as a bad business model, not to the position that these firms were taking any definitely political stance in favor of equal rights. For example, the brief contended, "[t]he capital of modern enterprises is in many ways a human capital. Success depends on the talent, morale and motivation of the workforce for private and public employers alike. To attract the best employees and colleagues, amici must offer robust workplace benefits and a workplace ethos of transparent fairness."[201] Its opening argument was that DOMA impairs the ability of firms to recruit and retain talent. It goes on to argue that benefits packages inspire employee loyalty to the firm and increase productivity and performance because they foster worker satisfaction.[202]

The brief's arguments are not inaccurate, but they do emphasize the market rationale for equal treatment rather than a political or moral rationale for equality. As Raeburn has pointed out, framing the adoption of equal benefits policies as solely good business practice—or, as the amicus brief makes clear, fighting against a federal policy that blocks such adoption—and viewing this process as a rational market process that all businesses will eventually come to adopt erases the agency and concerted efforts of employee advocates.[203] Furthermore, this framing may actually demobilize gay and lesbian employees who might come to see these policies as inevitable.[204] Or, taking the issue from the realm of firm-based micro-economies to policy-based macro-economies, given the spread of these policies over the last twenty-five years, the motivation for a federal Employee Non-Discrimination Act (ENDA) may be undercut by the success of these policy implementations at the firm level. Put differently, we might ask, has the creation of nondiscrimination policies over the previous two decades inclusive of sexual orientation at many Fortune 500 companies undermined or crowded out efforts to achieve federal and state legal workplace protection? Have these policies worked against efforts to pass a federal ENDA since they potentially lessen the perception of discrimination?

Indeed, the misperception of equality in the workplace that follows from the expansion of these firm-based benefits policies may explain why ENDA has stalled while same-sex marriage recognition has advanced. Same-sex marriage only achieved majority support in 2011. By contrast, a majority of Americans have supported equal employment opportunities regardless of sexual orientation since the mid-1970s.[205] Nevertheless, employment nondiscrimination legislation covering sexual orientation and gender identity lies dormant if not dead in Congress. Why has marriage recognition gained more traction than employment nondiscrimination despite the patterns in public support? This phenomenon may follow from the public perception that workplace discrimination is not real or that protections are already in place. Recognizing this possibility, the Human Rights Campaign created a commercial to air during the groundbreaking coming-out episode of the ABC sitcom *Ellen* in 1997. HRC commissioned a nationwide survey where over 40 percent of respondents incorrectly indicated that federal protections against discrimination on the basis of sexual orientation were already in place. The commercial showed a lesbian fired as her coworkers wondered how that action was legal. ABC, however, did not sell HRC national airtime, so the ad was only viewed in select cities, many of which had nondiscrimination ordinances already in place.[206]

Media portrayals, public misperceptions, and policies at individual private firms may foster what Urvashi Vaid coined "virtual equality," whereby equality is seen where it does not exist as a matter of statutory enforcement. This circumstance undermines the awareness and motivation necessary for political mobilization.[207] Nevertheless, these firm-based human resource policy adoptions since the 1990s reveal a significant and durable shift in the way private employers recognized gay, lesbian, and bisexual employees. Corporate reaction to the Indiana law in 2015—as discussed in the introduction—illustrates the durability of this shift insofar as corporations could essentially coerce state government to respond. Folding these identities within a broader discursive structure of "good business sense" and diversity awareness and thus framing them in ways parallel to racial, religious, and ethnic minorities, human resource officers came to embrace and companies to defend recognition of gays and lesbians as an unjustly persecuted minority.[208]

Conclusion

The dynamic tensions displayed since midcentury regarding how to frame homosexuality to secure nondiscrimination—as a private act beyond the legitimate sight of the state or as a minority personhood status that required state intervention—illustrate a variety of the mechanisms often at play in tracking American political development. Movement actors, lawyers, lobbyists, and others demonstrated high levels of entrepreneurship and political creativity. More often than not, the frames pursued were evidence of strategic attempts to "fit" within the broader political contexts, i.e., to draw parallels to race, gender, and ethnic civil rights movements or to exploit the new libertarian liberalism of the 1950s and 1960s that removed morals legislation as a broader legal reform.[209]

More than showcasing episodes of creativity and strategy, this chapter revealed how regulatory institutions and ideas interacted in the reshaping of homosexuality from a source of national threat to a marker of discriminated-against minority class. While lawyers for *Boutilier* emphasized that homosexuality was a private sexual behavior that could be stopped, the Supreme Court saw things differently; it understood homosexuality as a deeply entrenched status. As Margot Canaday has argued, when constructing homosexuals as the threat to nation, as the personification of the anticitizen, "in using the law to constitute status, in the way they did, in using legal words to designate the people, Congress and the INS probably had little idea that they were lending authority to a burgeoning gay rights movement that continues to this day to base its claim on a legal-political conception of homosexuals as potentially good citizens."[210] The construction of sexuality as a status—as an innate characteristic—was clearly in place by *Boutilier*. In this way, the Court's ruling embraced the recognition that bureaucrats had developed and members of Congress had already statutorily embraced.

Of course, the Court redeployed the status-based conception of homosexuality in *Romer* to antithetical ends, to serve the cause of equal protection, not discrimination. In so doing, the Court was hardly activist; it still followed democratic trends. By *Romer*, some state and municipal governments had already recognized gays and lesbians as an unjustly discriminated-against minority. Congress and the president had already done so by including HIV disease in the ADA and, as discussed in the next two chapters, by passing Don't Ask Don't Tell, the policy that permitted gays, lesbians, and bisexuals to serve in the military so long as their sexuality went unexpressed.

Judicial constructions of homosexuality—and efforts by lawyers to convey particular constructions—as status in *Boutilier*, as act in *Bowers*, and as minority class in *Romer*—illustrate how ideas and institutions interact in making and stabilizing gay identity. In this way, greater attention to sexual identities bridges two schools of thought that have defined the study of American political development: one that has focused on ideas and culture and another that has focused on institutions.[211] The branch that emphasizes ideas sees "development as occurring at the time a new idea springs forth that eventually shapes the final outcome" whereas the branch that focuses on changes in institutional configurations stresses that development is reflected in the outcomes, not the origins.[212] This chapter has aimed to trace the development of the idea—the idea of gays and lesbians as a discriminated-against minority class—from its midcentury origins to its institutionalized entrenchment in state recognition through state and municipal statutes and in *Romer* as well as in the private sector through corporate human resource policies. Indeed, as Exxon is the only Fortune 100 to have ever rescinded nondiscrimination and equitable-benefits policies and ultimately put them in place in late 2013, the recognition of gays and lesbians as a discriminated-against class entitled to equal treatment is a durable shift in private governing authorities of human resource management.

The chapter has sought to reveal further how ideas move from contestation to stabilization. A particular modality of recognition of homosexuality only endures insofar as it can present itself as natural or commonsensical. And, the chapter has traced the way movement and regulatory actors gradually trended toward the modality of discriminated-against class, even as, at the state level, antidiscrimination ordinances were passed, then repealed, and then passed again, only highlighting how no one idea about the meaning of sexuality had become entrenched. Partly this occurred through the concerted efforts of homophile and gay rights leadership, who established and maintained networks, newsletters, and other publications, such as *ONE*, that put forward a stable viewpoint of homosexuality as a minority status and foundation for identity-based political organizing. Intellectual and network entrepreneurs are identifiable.[213] Partly this occurred because regulatory authorities responded by passing antidiscrimination ordinances. Consequently, over time, older modalities were at least partially "denaturalized" and a newer one was able to take hold.

This process did not occur through one institutional venue. Activists pursued change through legislatures, courts, and executive officials at city, county, state, and federal levels. They pursued reform in the public sector as well as in the private workplace. The variety of tactics adopted and the fact that gay rights advocates pursued legislative reform as a conscious movement strategy (as opposed to legal challenges instigated by individuals who may or may not be affiliated with a broader movement organization) prior to pursuing litigation call into question some of the normative warnings against litigation as a mechanism for social change.[214] While litigation may provoke backlash, legislative change does as well. Anita Bryant's Save Our Children campaign and Colorado's Amendment 2 are cases in point. Taking a longer and more expansive view—what APD scholars refer to as "fullness of time"—of the movement and its dynamic relationship to regulatory institutions that exert distinct forms of power over citizens allows for more ready assessment of the halting and fractious adoption of a new form of regulatory recognition and avoidance of poorly evidenced normative judgments in favor of or against particular movement strategies.[215]

This newer modality—of gays and lesbians as a recognized discriminated-against minority—never reached a status of complete universality. To understand that, one need only witness the failure to pass a comprehensive gay civil rights bill, see that protections from discrimination in the workplace are wholly contingent on where one lives and for what firm one works, or consider that the Supreme Court has not defined gays and lesbians to be a suspect class or laws that affect them to be subject to higher judicial scrutiny.

Finally, to bear out the durable shift in private-sector human resource policies, one need only consider how Tim Cook, chief executive officer of Apple, framed his sexuality when he publicly came out in an essay in *Bloomberg Businessweek* in October 2014.[216] Cook disavowed the notion that sexuality was a matter of privacy. In expounding upon why he considered "being gay among the greatest gifts God has given me," Cook detailed how it affected his understanding of the world around him. His sexuality helped him understand "what it means to be in the minority and provided a window into the challenges that people in other minority groups deal with every day."[217] This characterization of sexuality as not only a minority status but also a lens through which we see the world is profoundly different from understanding sexuality as a bedroom act. As pointed out in an essay by Daniel D'Addario in *Time*, Cook's announcement strikes a far different tenor than when CNN anchor Anderson Cooper came out in 2012 by stating, "In a perfect world, I don't think it's anyone else's business, but I do think there is value in standing up and being counted."[218] In the corporate world, there is a durable frame shift: from sexuality as a private matter that really shouldn't matter at all—an idea that would resonate with the liberal homophiles—to sexuality as mattering a great deal in that it positively affects one's performance and outlook—an idea that would clearly resonate with some of the original claims of the earliest founders of Mattachine, such as Harry Hay.

While such framings represent a positive move for many gay rights advocates, that they are occurring within the order of the workplace and only within certain employment sectors highlights the fragmented nature of gay and lesbian citizenship. Access and recognition is context dependent, and market mechanisms hardly substitute for definitive statements and statutes from the state that would give recourse against discrimination. While the corporate protests against the proposed 2014 Arizona law and the 2015 Indiana law that would have permitted religious belief as a rationale to discriminate against LGBT persons were heartening, the pressure they exerted did not alter the status quo.[219] It remains perfectly legal to discriminate against LGBT-identified persons in both of those states since no nondiscrimination statute that includes sexual orientation or gender identity is in force in those states or in the majority of the others. If there is a durable shift in the way gays and lesbians are recognized, the shift is limited to certain states, certain industries, and certain companies. Those limitations reinforce fragmented citizenship; they hardly overcome it.

4

Recognizing Ourselves

Gay and Lesbian Interest Groups and the Consequences of Self-Definition

> We are gay in many different ways, but we are all subject to homophobia, and we have always depended on the hatred of strangers to keep us together. So it's no surprise that our battles with each other reflect the structure of our oppression. . . . [T]his conflict is ultimately about control. Behind the sound and fury lies a perennial question: Who owns gay liberation?
> —Richard Goldstein, "Cease Fire!" 2000[1]

In the year 2000, writer and activist Richard Goldstein pleaded for a cease fire among three national gay, lesbian, bisexual, and transgender advocacy groups—the Human Rights Campaign (HRC), the Metropolitan Community Church, and the National Gay and Lesbian Task Force (now the National LGBTQ Task Force)—that disputed the strategy, design, and need for a national march in Washington to bring attention to LGBT discrimination.[2] While all three organizations agreed that unjust discrimination must be challenged, they disagreed on how best to promote social change. This conflict was well documented in the press, and it brings to the fore a distinct form of recognition not yet addressed: organizational identity.[3]

In this book's introduction, recognition was defined as a form of power, and as explored there and in other chapters, that recognition is not only externally imposed. Self-definition may clash with extant regulatory recognitions, provide conceptions of collective identity that are a necessary ingredient to promote social change, and function as a form of self-empowerment. This chapter explores how two national interest groups—the National LGBTQ Task Force (hereafter the Task Force) and the Human Rights Campaign (HRC)—adopted the third modality of recognition, i.e., gays and lesbians as an unjustly discriminated-against minority, to promote three policy objectives that defined much of the national public discourse about gay and lesbian rights in the 1990s: access to open service in the military, protection from discrimination in the workplace, and access to civil marriage. And, it illustrates how these two interest groups were able to develop their own organizational identity or reputation to align with this modality.

Organizational identity refers to the way an interest group defines itself as unique or the way it differentiates itself from allied and competitor groups.[4] It is multifaceted and includes membership demographics, internal perception of the group measured by organization leaders' public statements and official mission statements, and reputation or public perception of the group by officials with whom they seek to work, such as members of Congress, presidential administration, or other interest groups. It is observable through rhetoric, public organizational histories, press releases, and mission statements, and it is developed, reinforced, or undermined over time as different strategic actions amass and maintain constituencies. It may function as a constraint or resource for strategic action since "strategic choices are not simply neutral decisions about what will be most effective. . . . They are statements about identity."[5] Insofar as organizational action is a manifestation of organizational identity, over time, that identity may be refined, narrowed, and solidified. Pursuing new directions may be quite difficult without incurring potential losses, ranging from offending constituents to confusing possible partners and allied organizations or officials.[6]

The 1990s heralded unprecedented national focus on lesbian and gay rights concerns. Gay and lesbian characters were prominent on the small and large screen; celebrities were coming out of the closet by choice.[7] Visibility was evident across a wide range of policies and political domains: the inclusion of sexual orientation in the 1990 hate crimes legislation, the lifting of antigay restrictions in the 1991 Immigration Act,[8] the expanding roster of out gay and lesbian public servants,[9] the rise in local ordinances prohibiting discrimination on the basis of sexual orientation,[10] and the increase in congressional hearings and votes on LGBT concerns.[11] Nevertheless, basic civil rights claims first articulated at the 1979 National March on Washington for Lesbian and Gay Rights had not yet been secured. As veteran activist Robin Tyler summed up the moment, "We've got visibility. We've developed a GLBT industry. But we don't have one basic thing that we asked for in 1979. . . . We've got to go back to Washington."[12]

With Bill Clinton's election to the presidency, interest groups representing sexual-minorities communities seized an unprecedented political opportunity to press a multifaceted rights agenda.[13] Three aims that defined that national discourse—equal and open access to military service, federal employment nondiscrimination legislation, and freedom to marry—were not the only ones that comprised a multifaceted rights agenda. Their prominence reveals an important dynamic of interest-group action: the issues pursued by an organization are not solely determined by that organization. External imposition can carry significant consequences for whether and how the organization responds. Given this lack of control over an issue agenda, an organization may be well or poorly positioned to respond. How the interest organization is recognized, or what its reputation is, and whether that reputation is congruent with the issue at stake and the institutional venue through which the issue is pursued will all play a significant role in the organization's ability to harness the opportunity.[14]

Interest groups can seek reform through municipal, state, and federal legislatures by lobbying mayors, governors, or presidents for direct executive action; by supporting litigation in federal and state judiciaries; or by mobilizing grassroots support for popular referenda and ballot initiatives. This variety of institutional venues can foster a range of advocacy strategies. This chapter assesses the way organizational reputation influences strategies and tactics. It evaluates how different organizational identities influence the aims and strategies pursued by the Task Force and HRC. It examines the role played by material resources as well as the importance of carving out a unique niche to maintain organizational longevity. It then integrates identity into an account of action by expanding on political scientist Theda Skocpol's concept of "fit."[15] After describing the distinct organizational identities of the Task Force and the HRC, the chapter applies this theory of fit to make sense of the distinct organizational actions taken with regard to military access, employment nondiscrimination, and same-sex marriage. Finally, the chapter considers the theory of fit after a spate of same-sex marriage bans passed in 2004, and argues that the "radicalness" of marriage—made radical by the fact that it had been so roundly rejected at the voting booth in 2004—opened an opportunity window for the Task Force to reengage the issue.

Interest-Group Strategic Action

Explanations of interest-group tactics and strategies have focused on an array of variables, including leadership skills, resource availability, political opportunities, and organizational niche. Congressional testimony from 1973 to 1999 reveals the Task Force's absence as a witness for hearings on the Employment Non-Discrimination Act (ENDA) and the Defense of Marriage Act (DOMA), which is reinforced by a general assessment in the secondary literature of the Task Force's inability or refusal to devote significant resources to these matters.[16] Since the political opportunity existed during the early 1990s for the Task Force and the HRC to become substantial players in the pursuit of a wide range of yet-unmet gay and lesbian rights claims, why did the HRC emerge as the more prominent organization at the federal level on these issues?

One explanation points to organizational leadership decisions. But this only begs the question of why the leaders made these decisions. Another explanation suggests that limited resources may drive interest-group decision making.[17] The Task Force may have been materially spent after its campaign to lift the military ban on gays and lesbians. Task Force leadership may also have been ideologically disgusted with the compromise of Don't Ask, Don't Tell. Furthermore, limited resources may force groups in the same issue space to specialize into certain niches; some will focus on litigation strategies, others on lobbying; some will focus on national issues, others will focus on local and grassroots initiatives. This niche theory tends to have a functionalist conception of organizational identity that narrows identity to an organization's purpose.[18] It observes the outcome—the actions pursued— and often considers them the result of rational actions grounded in the interests of organizational leadership.[19] Niche theory predicts that groups "lock" into particular areas and tactics. Yet, if interest groups can identify a niche and build and sustain its membership on that basis, how does a group develop new strategies over time? Niche theorists tend to assert that some organizations respond more effectively to usually externally imposed changes; they are able to adapt while others may die off. Christopher Bosso's erudite study of environmental advocacy groups is illustrative: "organizations were forced to transform themselves over time from relative amateur outfits, often supported by a few elite patrons, into today's mass-based professional advocacy organizations. . . . [T]hey responded to internal organizational stresses and external political pressures."[20] Bosso asserts that adaptation may be possible, and points to the crucial, often entrepreneurial, role of leadership in this process.[21] But what of those factors that might constrain adaptation, particularly a well-developed organizational reputation? The identity so carefully created as a means to promote organizational sustainability may be the very factor that inhibits the organization from thriving over time.

Identity refers to different, albeit related, concepts in the social movement literature, and its many meanings make the concept challenging to employ. It has been used to account for the way LGBT movements maintain themselves through the development of identity-based autonomous subcultures replete with institutions such as bookstores, bars, choirs, medical clinics, and symbols like the rainbow flag, pink triangle, or red ribbon.[22] It is conceptualized not only as a foundation for mobilization but also a consequence of that mobilization.[23] And, identity has been utilized to explain shifts in movement aims as people with distinct identities and political aspirations join and alter the aims of a movement.[24]

Most recently, and as explored in this chapter, identity has been defined as a tool that can be strategically deployed. Identity as a strategy assumes that it can be refashioned so that it may be fitted to whatever tactic may achieve a particular goal: "Activists may define their identities in different ways depending on the strategic situation. If they are representing their group in a public audience, they may cast themselves as more unified and more homogenous than they would in a setting of fellow activists."[25] Mary Bernstein has fruitfully pushed identity from a static outcome or input variable in movement development to a more analytically compelling notion of identity as dynamic and tactical.[26] She argues that LGBT activists may deploy identity through at least two framing strategies: a more radical identity as critique and a more moderate identity as education.[27] The first strategy presents gay and lesbian identity as a path to cultural change and a politics of recognizing differences. The second strategy is less confrontational, primarily focused on challenging negative stereotypes by deemphasizing differences; this strategy aims to garner allies outside the LGBT communities.[28] Bernstein suggests that LGBT organizations can use either strategy depending on various circumstances, which include the group's political access, its organizational structure, and the type and extent of the opposition.[29]

One possible challenge to Bernstein's theory is based on the cases she selects. She focuses on state-level organizations, many of which are established to challenge antigay ballot initiatives. These organizations may have little prior history and thus not much preexisting reputation that might inhibit their ability to represent themselves in different ways to different audiences. These campaigns may develop into more sustained organizations after the vote on the initiative (or they may not) and attract additional resources to LGBT concerns, but their inception in the context of the initiative may free them to be more instrumental to achieve that initial goal of defeating an antigay initiative.[30] They may employ whatever tactic might achieve that goal even if it might undermine longer-term aims of movement development.[31] Because they often did not exist or existed only on a much smaller scale prior to the episode of political organizing, their organizational identities are potentially more fluid and can be deployed more strategically than the historically entrenched multi-issue national organizations under study here.

By the mid-1990s, the Task Force had existed for two decades and HRC had existed for a decade and a half, accumulating resources, members, and reputations all grounded in their actions, statements, and aims accrued over that time. Given the length of time the national interest groups had existed and given that they had developed reputations and catered to particular constituencies for that period, these groups' identities might not be as flexible. Connections to particular constituencies and the organization's previous political actions can make its identity sticky, and that stickiness may influence an organization's observable actions or statements.

Linking Organizational Identity, Issue, and Institutional Venue into a Theory of Fit

If movement organizations are concerned with developing and maintaining coherent identity—especially as they build alliances and represent themselves as responsible sources of information for legislators—it does not follow that they can easily reformulate their identity. Doing so carries risks of alienating their constituents as well as confusing potential allies. It therefore behooves interest groups to maintain relative stability of their reputational identity in order for them to maintain or gain deeper access to legislators.[32] Consequently, options for viable tactics may be limited insofar as they cannot challenge that reputation. The ability to exploit a political opportunity will depend on how the organizational identity *fits* with the issue that has emerged at the forefront of an organization's agenda, regardless of whether the organization brought it there, and with the institutional venue through which that issue is being primarily pursued. Leadership's attempts to pursue actions that seem incongruent with organizational identity can only occur if a plausible argument can be put forth that the actions are indeed congruent with identity despite initial appearances.

Organizational identity fit with issue and institutional venue can be observed over the lobbying histories of the Task Force and HRC. Critical opportunity existed, and yet one or both organizations may have been unable to seize it due to a misfit among these three variables. For this claim to be verifiable, the organizational identities of these two interest groups must be sufficiently distinct prior to any political opportunity for social change coming into play. Second, the issues that defined much of the agenda of national LGBT political action—military access, employment nondiscrimination, and marriage—would have to be exogenously induced. The groups could be working already on these issues, but what matters is timing. Did these issues enter the national discourse when these interest groups were best prepared to advocate for their position? Greater fit is expected, obviously, when an interest group selects the timing and the issue on which to lobby, but there may be clear potential for misfit when the issue is imposed by events beyond the organization's control. Third, the possibility of misfit between identity and institutional venue follows from the idea that institutional venues have distinct reputations regarding accessibility. There can exist certain "ascriptive barriers" to participation, such that groups might work less or communicate less with institutions in which their own demographics are underrepresented.[33] And, because "at the local level, of course, leaders mirror their constituents more closely," those groups who do not see their reflection in a certain venue or level of governance may seek out and interact with one where it is mirrored.[34] In short, the organizational identities of the Task Force and HRC must be clearly distinct, agenda issues must be exogenously induced, and institutions must carry distinct reputations and histories of access for a theory of fit among identity, issue, and institutional venue to be testable.

Organizational Reputations of the Task Force and the Human Rights Campaign

Do the Human Rights Campaign and the Task Force maintain distinguishable identities and reputations? The organizations' respective websites indicate that they share several concerns, including same-sex marriage, employment nondiscrimination, hate crimes legislation, equal access to military service, adoption and parenting matters, and HIV/ AIDS, among others.[35] It would follow, therefore, that if identity is determined in functionalist terms by the construction of an issue niche, then repeated calls for the two groups to merge should probably have been heeded.[36] Yet, while both organizations operated at the national level and were preoccupied by many of the same concerns, they employed different strategies to achieve social reform, and their leadership maintained that they appealed to distinctive membership bases given their organizational philosophies, which embrace fundamentally different interpretations of a politically gay identity.

Despite their lobbying on a similar array of issues, their respective mission statements, for example, suggest that the Task Force and HRC have distinct identities and target a different range of venues to achieve their similar aims. In its mission statements from the mid-1990s, the Task Force has described itself as committed "to build the political power of the lesbian, gay, bisexual and transgender community from the ground up." It achieves these objectives by "training activists, organizing broad-based campaigns to defeat anti-LGBT referenda and advance pro-LGBT legislation, and by building the organizational capacity of our movement." And, it explicitly positions itself "as part of a broader social justice movement," which works "to create a nation that respects the diversity of human expression and identity and creates opportunity for all."[37] In 2014, the Task Force appended different mission descriptions at the bottom of its press releases. Some noted, "The National Gay and

Lesbian Task Force Action Fund builds the grassroots political power of the lesbian, gay, bisexual and transgender community. The Task Force Action Fund does this through direct and grassroots lobbying to defeat anti-LGBT ballot initiatives and legislation, and works to pass pro-LGBT legislation and other progressive initiatives."[38] Others contained this text but also added the sentence: "The Task Force is the country's premier social justice organization fighting to improve the lives of LGBT people and working to create positive, lasting change and opportunity for all."[39]

This explicit identification of a broader social justice movement of which LGBT rights are a part and to which the Task Force contributes distinguishes the organization from HRC. HRC has described itself as "the largest national lesbian, gay, bisexual, and transgender civil rights organization" and as envisioning "an America where LGBT people are ensured of their basic equal rights, and can be open, honest and safe at home, at work and in the community."[40] The 1999 mission statement described it "as the nation's largest lesbian and gay political organization" but included the terms "bisexual" and "transgendered" by acknowledging that its then 360,000 members were "gay, lesbian, bisexual, transgendered, and straight."[41] By 2003, the mission statement was revised to indicate that HRC "provides a national voice on gay and lesbian issues" and that it "effectively lobbies Congress; mobilizes grassroots action in diverse communities; invests strategically to elect a fair-minded Congress; and increases public understanding through innovative education and communication strategies." Furthermore, HRC indicated that it "is a bipartisan organization," which distinguishes it from the Task Force's clear reference to being part of a progressive social justice movement.[42] While both groups are often lumped together as within-system organizations on a reform-revolutionary spectrum that organizes much gay and lesbian movement scholarship, their mission statements reveal key differences in identity and organizational culture.[43]

The distinct organizational identities are made manifest in clashes regarding preparation for and support of the Millennium March on Washington for Equality. No single issue such as AIDS, the Supreme Court's upholding of state sodomy bans, or the military debate galvanized the movement as had occurred in 1987 and 1993, the years of previous marches. The pressing issues were wide and diverse, and the most prominent ones by late 1999 seemed to center at the state level, including recent passage of an anti–gay marriage initiative in California and the legislative approval of civil unions in Vermont.[44] The Task Force lent its support to another national march to take place in 2000 only after reaching a compromise with HRC that the latter organization would also endorse a state-by-state initiative called "Equality Begins at Home," spearheaded by the Task Force, to be timed concurrently with the Millennium March.[45] The dispute was an expression of different strategies grounded in distinct organizational identities. Although they lobbied on similar issues, these groups embodied distinct notions of a politically gay identity, advocating strategies at different institutional venues and employing distinct tactics in those venues.

Interviews with staff members from each organization highlight key differences in organizational identity. To describe their own organization, HRC personnel used phrases such as "the premiere national and sometimes the only national GLBT organization," "the hub" of LGBT organizing, and "an advocacy group advocating on behalf of the GLBT community at the federal, state, and the local level" that "focuses like a laser beam on GLBT rights." Staffers identified as working with the "largest," the "most well known," and the "most respected" LGBT organization with the "most clout on Capitol Hill" because it had "been at it the longest" and thus had earned a reputation of being "at the forefront" as "the leaders in the movement." HRC staffers claimed to be "the first to get a press call" on any and all issues of concern to the LGBT community.[46] As one high-ranking staffer from HRC noted, the model of organizational success for HRC is the National Rifle Association: "If we could be as effective as the NRA with their PAC, with their influence, with their ability to get legislation passed and block it, and we applied that model to GLBT civil rights, we would be a phenomenal success."[47]

When HRC staffers characterized the Task Force, their descriptions included remarks such as the following: "the Task Force has never had an identity that it was at the center of the GLBT movement"; "a lot of the Task Force's identity is based on whoever is leading it at the time. . . . [I]t's much more fluid as to its leadership than HRC is"; "they are a little more edgy"; "they appeal a little bit more to the leftist, sort of grassroot-y sort of folks. . . . They have more 'street cred' with the leftists, with college-age kids, with the 'rally people'"; "they are a little bit smaller than us. . . . But just as passionate"; "they take positions on other issues that HRC has not on things not necessarily related to gay rights"; "they have a broader and some might say a more partisan agenda"; and, "the Task Force is more progressive than the Human Rights Campaign. . . . [T]he Task Force will take a position on the war, or on economic justice issues, or on environmental issues, or on the death penalty that we [at HRC] won't wade into."[48]

All of these descriptions suggest not only that the Task Force is perceived as more embedded in a broader social justice movement of the Left and that it is understood to pursue different tactics to mobilize for LGBT rights—and thus that its mission statement is understood by the other primary national LGBT organization—but also that HRC staffers, in making the implicit comparisons between their organization and the Task Force, seek to position their organization as the one that operates through established channels and networks of national politics in a bipartisan manner. HRC staff members mention their size and perceived clout to pursue national-level reform and attract large donors, often admitting that their tactics and identity may not resonate with progressive activists. The statements seek to establish a clear difference in mission and membership that might allow for, if not collaboration, at least coexistence and not direct competition, each organization pursuing LGBT rights by distinct strategies.

When Task Force staffers were asked to define their organization's identity, one described it as "progressive more than just being LGBT specific. . . . [I]t's a progressive organization that happens to be LGBT rather than an LGBT organization with a progressive focus." It was also described as "definitely grassroots focused; it's not about federal, it's more about national, state, and local level organizing."[49] Another staff member characterized the Task Force as charged with "building grassroots political power of our movement," which views "LGBT rights as embedded within a broader social justice movement" and which focuses on "the intersection of racism, classism, and homophobia."[50] Another characterized the organization as having

> [a] consistent focus on the movement. . . . [T]he Task Force has consistently interacted with activists and organizers on the ground where on the ground has meant local issues, local projects, local campaigns, or at the state level, or for that matter, even at the federal level. The focus of the

work has been to generate activity that emanates from the group up as opposed to from a top-down strategy. . . . The National Gay and Lesbian Task Force puts the "move" in "the movement."[51]

Task Force staff labeled HRC a more politically mainstream organization. They emphasized that HRC was "limited on how far out on a limb they are willing to go on issues of race, economics, and gender" and that its organization was "top-down" and "hierarchical."[52] One former staff member analogized HRC's approach to membership recruitment and tactics to those employed by the American Association of Retired Persons (AARP):

> HRC has sought to position itself similarly to AARP. You turn fifty-five or fifty, and you pay your ten dollars, and you get your AARP card, and you get your discount. So now you decide that you are gay and you pay your thirty-five dollars, or you pay your 150 dollars and you rent your tux, and you go to your HRC dinner. They have really sought to brand themselves as "if you are gay, then this is where you are." And it seems like there is more of a test to part of the Task Force. We make it hard. You have to *believe* in things. You have to understand some more complex things about politics. The Task Force makes it hard to be a generic person and buy in. . . . I don't know if that is good or bad. I think the Task Force requires that you know a little bit more about things. I don't think people come out and join the Task Force, but HRC has really sought to brand itself as that kind of a popular thing. . . . It's the perception of marketing. Be part of this. It's fun. It's cool. It's hip. This is who we are. We even have a store in Dupont Circle. Wear our shirts. Buy our soap. Wash your hair with our shampoo. Buy our dog collars, versus you're not antiracist enough to be a member of the Task Force. You're not going to pass the test to be a member of the Task Force. The Task Force makes it hard. . . . The Task Force wants to be accessible, but in the past it hasn't done that. . . . It would never occur to the Task Force to open a store.[53]

In this characterization, the Task Force is distinguished by having a higher threshold, a deeper commitment to and awareness of critical issues and the integrated nature of social justice activism that crosses and links notions of class, nationality, race, gender, and sexuality. HRC, by contrast, is characterized as aiming for sheer numbers, as oriented toward amassing a large membership base and focusing on brand development. Indeed, HRC's ubiquitous logo—a yellow equal sign on a blue square background—brands items for sale at the organization's retail establishments in Provincetown, Massachusetts, and the Dupont neighborhood of Washington, DC. HRC describes the store as

> [a] premier destination for lesbian, gay, bisexual, and transgender travelers—the DC Store is the best place for individuals touring or attending annual conferences in Washington, DC who would like to take home the perfect souvenir. The DC Store has a wide spectrum of merchandise featuring the signature Human Rights Campaign's equality logo. Our apparel selection includes t-shirts, sweatshirts, jackets and caps. We offer a wide variety of merchandise including key chains, lapel pins, bracelets, necklaces and sterling silver jewelry.[54]

Despite its broader and more progressive concerns for social justice and grassroots mobilization, as the characterization by staffers indicated, in much literature that evaluates these two organizations, the Task Force is considered a reform-oriented "within-system" group in part because, when it was founded (as the National Gay Task Force, NGTF) in New York City in 1973, its premise was a direct refutation of the nonhierarchical structure and revolutionary ideologies embraced by the Gay Liberation Front (GLF) and the Gay Activist Alliance (GAA). The NGTF was established by former members of the GAA who had grown weary of the GAA's unruly lack of structure and who envisioned an organization with a dues-paying membership and a full-time paid staff to lobby on a broad swath of issues ranging from removing homosexuality from the American Psychological Association's register of mental illness to seeking the introduction of a federal gay civil rights bill.[55] Early NGTF codirectors, such as longtime gay and lesbian activists Jean O'Leary and Bruce Voeller, were accused of elitism for adopting a model of social change that embraced "the liberal reform mode" of "letting us in" and a top-down rather than a more open and participatory democratic structure.[56] Despite NGTF's success in lobbying Congresswoman Bella Abzug (D-NY) to introduce a federal gay civil rights bill initially in 1974 and to garner twenty-four cosponsors by 1975, the organization was unable to draw a membership base from "an indifferent community that, barely five years after Stonewall, was not feeling particularly threatened."[57] By 1979, the NGTF was languishing with an annual budget of barely two hundred thousand dollars.[58]

NGTF's inability to achieve its legislative aims during the first few years of its existence motivated the establishment of the Gay Rights National Lobby (GRNL), the precursor to the Human Rights Campaign, in 1976.[59] GRNL was directed by longtime Minnesotan gay activist Steve Endean, and initial relations between GRNL and NGTF were cordial; the groups had interlocking boards of directors.[60]

GRNL lobbied for the federal gay civil rights bill. It defined itself solely as a national lobby organization in contrast to NGTF's intention to be an informational clearinghouse for grassroots organizations as well as to support pro-gay and lesbian efforts at all levels of government.[61] In the late 1970s and early 1980s, when the advocacy community focused on this gay civil rights bill, GRNL thrived while the NGTF decayed. When Charles Brydon and Lucia Valeska replaced O'Leary and Voeller as codirectors in 1979, Valeska dismissed GRNL as nothing more than a "one-person operation with a board of directors that hasn't met in two years and an annual budget of $50,000."[62] Indeed, by 1981 the organizations appeared to be working at cross-purposes. The directors at the NGTF began to lobby on federal issues, thereby negating an earlier turf-division agreement between the two organizations and confusing sympathetic members of Congress.[63] For example, GRNL had negotiated with Representative Pete McCloskey (D-CA) to introduce legislation ending the ban on gay men and lesbians serving in the military. However, Valeska, on behalf of the NGTF, wrote to McCloskey urging him to shelve the bill.[64]

In the wake of Republican national electoral victories in 1980, GRNL's Steve Endean established the Human Rights Campaign Fund (HRCF) as a political action committee to allocate funds to sympathetic congressional candidates.[65] The HRCF (renamed HRC in 1996) was based on seed money from James Hormel, the heir to the processed ham fortune; David Coors, scion of the American brewing family; and David Goodstein, editor of the gay and lesbian news magazine the *Advocate*.[66] In 1982, HRCF began hosting its primary fundraising event, a series of annual black-tie dinners that would attract nationally prominent keynote speakers. For example, former vice president and future presidential candidate Walter Mondale spoke at the 1982 dinner in New York City, which raised fifty thousand dollars—this at a time when NGTF's budget was shrinking.[67] Yet this fundraising strategy of relying on $150-per-plate dinners had drawn much criticism as it attracted a primarily white, male, upper-class constituency, thereby affecting both the organizational identity and the political strategy to follow. Contrasting the diversity of the Task Force's membership with the homogeneity of HRC's base, political scientist David Rayside explicitly connected organizational identity to organizational strategy:

> The task of forging links between national political groups and the grass roots of the social movement is made more difficult by the fact that many of those who engage in mainstream politics are not representative of the "average person." . . . Those who are most involved in lobbying and campaign fund-raising inevitably replicate some of the inequalities embedded in the political institutions they are seeking to enter or challenge. . . . HRC fund-raising dinners, at $150 or $175 a plate, produce an entirely predictable demographic: mostly men, mostly white, most wearing tuxedos. Even the ticketholders who break gender and race lines are usually similar in educational level and occupational standing.[68]

Attempting to dismiss this characterization of their organization's membership, HRC staffers pointed to a wider array of fundraising and outreach techniques developed and adopted since the late 1990s. While conceding that originally the organization had predominantly attracted and catered to wealthy white gay men, a senior staffer pointed to more recent internal studies revealing a more diverse membership base. Indeed, the comments attest to the stickiness of organizational identity even after demonstrable facts of membership demographics have changed:

> They used to call us the Human Rights Champagne Fund, and that still sticks. . . . But that's not who we are. . . . In response to the contention that our main membership is dinners and I actually don't think that's true. . . . [W]e have a very aggressive direct mail program. . . . [W]e have a very aggressive canvassing program where literally we send people out and they door knock and they bring people in. We bring people in at Pride over

the summer. So we bring in a lot of twenty and thirty-five dollar members through that stream, and probably much more so than bringing them in through dinners. . . . And the dinner component of our fundraising is only probably about 20 percent of our overall fundraising. . . . I think there is a reputation deficit there. I think we have changed. I think we have diversified. I think we have grown. And I think you see that in the staff too. People think from the outside that you are an all-male white organization, and then they come in, they work with us, and they are shocked. We have women, we have parents, we have older people, we have minorities, we have transgender people, we have straight people. We have a very diverse staff here, people from different political backgrounds, from different regional backgrounds.[69]

Yet, even as HRC has diversified, its perceived lack of diversity stands in sharp contrast to the early emphasis placed on racial and gender diversity at the Task Force. Until Matt Foreman's appointment as executive director of the Task Force in 2003, women had held that position continuously since 1987. And the Task Force's board of directors reached gender parity in the early 1990s.[70]

AIDS reshaped these organizations as well as relations between them. By August 1982, in an effort to halt NGTF's financial decline and end what some considered Valeska's mismanagement, the organization's board of directors replaced Valeska with Virginia Apuzzo, a well-known activist who had recently served as assistant commissioner of operations in the New York City Health Department. Her knowledge of public health was critical as she reengineered NGTF's mission to address AIDS prevention, education, and funding.[71] By contrast, Steve Endean's inability to shift GRNL's focus to AIDS issues as well as his increasingly confrontational relationship with the NGTF leadership hastened GRNL's demise.[72] In a stark reversal of circumstances just two years prior, by 1984, GRNL and HRCF faced financial ruin while NGTF was establishing itself as a national voice on HIV/AIDS prevention, education, and related discrimination concerns. In 1985, HRCF absorbed GRNL as its lobbying arm and began an earnest campaign on various AIDS-related issues, particularly fighting passage of the Helms Amendment.[73]

By the late 1980s, the Task Force occupied a strong position in national politics while seeking to maintain the grassroots orientation that defined it at its founding. This duality, which is less evident in HRC's history and self-presentation, bears out how founding conditions continue to impress themselves upon organizational identity. Commitment to grassroots mobilization took form in the Task Force's annual "Creating Change" conferences, first hosted in 1988, which sought to energize local activism.[74] As John D'Emilio notes, the Task Force employed a hybrid strategy, targeting multiple levels of government and attempting to remain connected with grassroots protest:

> It was combining outsider and insider sources into an elegantly choreographed—and compellingly innovative—strategy for change. Not content with the constraints that the unwritten rules of inside-the-beltway politics impose, and unwilling to accept the marginality that often came with grassroots protest, the Task Force tried to play with both. It lobbied and it agitated. It negotiated and it mobilized. It supported breaking the law and challenging the law. It tinkered with the system to effect small immediate changes, and it expressed a commitment to a more expansive vision of social justice.[75]

The Task Force's organizational identity as not quite within-the-beltway fostered a strategy that was more open to critiquing political institutions than compromising with them and to endorsing more direct actions. This identity encouraged the group to devote more attention to state-level organization than HRC did and, critically, to be more open early on in its existence to recruiting staff and members from communities of color.

In short, while HRC's organizational identity conforms to that of a national lobby organization focused on the implementation of well-defined political and policy aims, the Task Force's identity remains more fluid. This positioned the Task Force to participate in national-level politics, when new political opportunities arose with the election of Bill Clinton to the presidency. Yet, with the disappointing outcome on lifting the ban on openly gay men and lesbians in the military, which was the reinforcement of silence through the Don't Ask, Don't Tell compromise, the Task Force was able, given its organizational identity as still wedded to local and state organizing, to retreat from the federal sphere, which it did for much of the remainder of the decade. By seeking to engage that aspect of its organizational identity, the Task Force was both unwilling and unable to work with federal-level institutional political opportunities newly available to LGBT advocates, particularly the passage of an Employment Non-Discrimination Act.

Fit and Misfit of Identity, Issue, and Institutional Venue in the 1990s: Military Service, ENDA, and DOMA

As detailed above, HRC embodies an organizational identity embracing incremental change through working with legislative and executive branch officers, primarily at the national level, to achieve social reform. By contrast, the Task Force has, at some points, focused on federal-level policy making and, at others, sought meaningful and participatory connection to the grassroots of the gay and lesbian movements. During the 1990s, the Task Force shifted toward a more local and grassroots position, bringing it out of line with two of the three national-level issues that dominated gay and lesbian political concerns: the passage of the Employment Non-Discrimination Act and the attempts to defeat passage of the Defense of Marriage Act. Indeed, a Task Force staffer observed the organization's refusal to lobby on behalf of ENDA or fight against DOMA:

> The Task Force was not as active on DOMA and ENDA, but rather focused on other projects. I think the reason is a very basic one of the organization's philosophy. The Task Force was most heavily involved in working at the state and local level and did not dedicate vast resources to federal legislation. For example, we were not the lead organization fighting the federal DOMA bill, but we were working with state organizations trying to hold off bills at the state level across the country. Likewise, while we supported ENDA at its introduction, we withdrew later because of its lack of transgender inclusion after working closely with state and local organizations who passed transgender-inclusive state and local laws.[76]

The more fluid organizational identity of the Task Force enabled the organization to shift its focus away from federal legislation after the Don't Ask, Don't Tell debacle, but it also constrained it from actively participating at the federal level to secure the passage of ENDA. Its newly revitalized focus on grassroots and state-level reform did not conform to the institutional venue, namely, Congress, in which this legislation was being debated. And, given its more progressive identity that emphasized and recognized diversity within sexual-minority communities, ENDA, as constructed by 1996 without the inclusion of protections based on gender identity, did not conform to the Task Force's stated political identity.

The Task Force's programmatic agenda, coined "Fight the Right," began in earnest during the 1992 election cycle and continued through most of the 1990s. It lacked a specific proactive policy goal and revealed the organization's traditional ambivalence about whether to work through established political channels or across partisan identities, something to which HRC specifically states its commitment. One staffer at the Task Force characterized this "Fight the Right" agenda as the first step in the organization's downward slide in the 1990s, as it became increasingly locked out of national-level political discussion. This new campaign represented

> [t]he dissolution of issue specific projects like the Privacy Project and the Anti-Violence Project. . . . [I]t was one of the dynamics that led to the collapse. . . . Not only did people outside of the organization not understand what we did, we no longer understood what we did. . . . Fight the Right was too much and not enough. The right wing was literally everywhere. . . . No gain we made went uncontested. So when we say, fight the right, we were talking about literally the right wing anywhere it raised its head. . . . It was not enough in the sense that there were only two-and-a-half staff people assigned to the Fight the Right project. . . . To say that we were fighting the right was just kind of ludicrous. Better we should have been called the movement building department, something a little bit more real.[77]

David Rayside describes the Task Force's strategic shift as "distanc[ing] itself from the traditional rule of lobbying, perhaps more so than at the end of the 1980s [since] most of the staff had experience in direct action and supported its use."[78] Ultimately this strategy did little to promote the organization's ability to participate in the issues that dominated the national focus of the gay and lesbian rights movement in the mid-1990s.

The Task Force strategy after the establishment of Don't Ask, Don't Tell drew on the organization's credibility as a grassroots organization. As one former staff member recalled,

> After Clinton's inauguration in 1993, following the Reagan and Bush years, there was a great sense of optimism about Washington being the place where we were going to finally win something . . . hence the omnibus gay civil rights bill being abandoned and the more winnable ENDA. Then with 1993 Don't Ask, Don't Tell, the 1995 state level DOMA explosion, and the 1995 [sic] mid-term congressional elections that brought Newt's "Contract on [sic] America," it became clearer that Washington wasn't the answer.[79]

Misfits between identity and issue are possible because the organization does not define the content and parameters of its agenda. The debate over lifting the ban on openly gay men and lesbians in the military and same-sex marriage recognition were not at the forefront of either the Task Force's or HRC's agendas when they burst upon the national political stage by the early 1990s. This exogenous imposition of freedom to serve and freedom to marry provides cases to assess fit and misfit among identity, issue, and institutional venue. They offer the possibility of verifying the implications of the theory presented in this chapter.

The immense attention focused on the military ban during the 1992 presidential campaign season and the resulting compromise policy Don't Ask, Don't Tell, which President Clinton authorized as an executive order in 1993 and which Congress passed as law in 1994, has been called "a fluke." And, the effort spent during the first months of the new Clinton administration on the matter was critiqued as "only consum[ing] time and resources that would otherwise have been devoted to work on the gay civil rights bill."[80] However, both litigation and legislative lobbying on this matter were hardly new by the early 1990s. Overturning the ban was a goal that dates back to the years immediately following the end of the Second World War.[81] Numerous lawsuits seeking to overturn the military's ban—most notably *Matlovich v. Secretary of the Air Force* (1978) and *Berg v. Claytor* (1978)—were attempted.[82]

Equal access to military service had been a common goal of the NGTF and the GRNL. Former Task Force executive director Urvashi Vaid notes that her organization viewed the ban on gay service members as "one of the top three problems facing gay America, the other two being national AIDS policy and a federal gay civil rights bill."[83] However, there is little question that AIDS funding for research, education, and prevention remained the unparalleled top priority of the movement throughout the 1980s and into the 1990s.[84] In his analysis of the political machinations involved in lifting the ban, Rayside notes that this issue was "not a priority in most activist agendas. For most of the 1980s, the spreading AIDS epidemic and the surge of anti-gay measures at state and local levels preoccupied the movement. But the sheer number of discharges, averaging 1,800 per year in the first half of the 1980s, and 1,000 per year from 1988 to 1991, maintained the issue's visibility."[85] Gary Lehring reaffirms this assessment in his study documenting the attempts to lift the ban during the first months of the Clinton presidency:

> Clearly, a place in the military is not at the top of the wish list for most people in the gay community. Greater funding and awareness of AIDS; the Employment Non-Discrimination Act; and a federal civil rights law for lesbians, gay men, and other sexual minorities are all issues with the potential to generate more excitement among the movement's grass roots. Although "a military project" has for years been part of the organizational structure of the National Gay and Lesbian Task Force, the decision to make the issue part of Clinton's compensation for the gay community's support in the 1992 election was not made by the gay community. Indeed, it was not even made by the leaders of the nation's lesbian and gay political organizations, most of whom realized that the community's support for lifting the ban might be a mile wide but was only an inch deep.[86]

Vaid recognized that AIDS remained at the top of the national gay and lesbian rights agenda as defined by that advocacy community: "Until AIDS hit our people, most of us never paid attention to national politics, and when the movement finally did develop a legislative presence in Washington, in the 1980s, its agenda was consumed by the problems presented by AIDS."[87] Furthermore, many within the post-Stonewall generation viewed the armed forces as patriarchal and homophobic and did not seek inclusion within it.[88] Although lobbyists pursued equal service in the military, especially after the Task Force convened the Military

Freedom Project (MFP) in 1988, it was catapulted to its national prominence on the LGBT agenda by circumstances external to any intentions
by interest-group leadership.[89]

The military ban did not receive much media attention until Department of Defense spokesperson Pete Williams was outed in 1991 in
the national gay and lesbian news magazine the *Advocate*.[90] This event
prompted then–secretary of defense Richard Cheney to suggest that the
military ban was potentially outdated and that its repeal should be considered.[91] Bill Clinton, as a Democratic candidate for president in 1992,
brightened the spotlight when, in an attempt to win over gay and lesbian
voters despite his poor record as governor of Arkansas on gay and lesbian rights, he announced an intent to lift the ban via executive order.[92]
Clinton's focus on the military-access issue dismayed many LGBT activists who were concerned that attention to the ban, which affected only a
small subset of the community, would displace the more pressing needs
of the AIDS epidemic.[93]

Despite having risen to the top of the issue agenda as a result of these
exogenous forces, the military issue fit within the strategic aims of the
Task Force. Lobbying on the issue to various degrees since the late 1970s,
the Task Force stepped up its commitment by spearheading the Military
Freedom Project (MFP) in the late 1980s. HRC organized its own initiative, "Operation Lift the Ban," in March 1993, only after it had become
clear that lifting the ban was the new Clinton administration's priority.[94]
The MFP (which had, by April 1993, included representatives from the
Task Force, HRC, the American Civil Liberties Union, and the National
Organization for Women), the Ad Hoc Military Group, the Gay, Lesbian, and Bisexual Veterans Association, the Joint Chiefs of Staff, and
the staffs of Representative Gerry Studds and Representative Barney
Frank failed to coordinate any of their efforts to seek policy reform on
the ban over the objections of Senator Sam Nunn, chair of the Senate
Armed Services Committee.[95] While HRC and the Task Force clung to
Clinton's promise for an executive order lifting the ban, both groups
underestimated the grassroots capabilities of an evangelical Right to
mobilize to maintain the ban.[96] Following the failure to lift the ban, the
Task Force retreated from congressional and presidential lobbying, leaving the field open for HRC to claim its turn, exploit opportunities, and
garner resources.[97] The Task Force reached back to its identity roots,

removing itself from the federal level and returning to promoting state- and local-level activism. Organizational identity played out as abandoning the venue, not the issue, as military service equality remained on the roster of issues for the Task Force to advocate.

As attention was drawn to the federal level for other issues of the mid-1990s, namely, the Defense of Marriage Act and the Employment Non-Discrimination Act, the Task Force's renewed focus on grassroots and state-level politics correlated with significant financial strain.[98] Between 1993 and 1996, when the Task Force consciously shifted focus from the federal arena, both its staff and its budget diminished by half.[99] By the end of 1996, the Task Force's twenty-two professional staffers oversaw an operating budget of $2.4 million and served about forty thousand members. The Task Force's organizational history indicates that the group took no action on ENDA. Instead, between 1993 and 1996, the organization invested its resources in other areas, including its annual "Creating Change" conference and its Policy Institute, which deepened connections between the movement and the academy.[100]

By contrast, HRC's organizational history refers predominantly to the interest group's actions supporting ENDA and opposing ENDA during these same years.[101] HRC had mobilized a membership base of at least 135,000, maintained a professional staff of sixty, and operated with an annual budget of ten million dollars.[102] HRC's identity congruence with the issues defining the national movement during the mid-1990s and the institutional venues within which these issues were being debated correlated with its greater resource mobilization and staff expansion.

Given that LGBT interest groups were unable to mount an effective effort to lift the military ban, the prospects for congressional approval of a federal gay civil rights bill appeared slim. Following the approval of Don't Ask, Don't Tell, the federal gay civil rights bill, introduced annually since 1974, was scaled down. Excised were all protections except those relating to employment, and the bill was renamed the Employment Non-Discrimination Act. ENDA was introduced in June 1994 by Senators Edward Kennedy (D-MA) and Lincoln Chaffee (R-RI) with 28 senatorial cosponsors and by Representatives Barney Frank (D-MA), Gerry Studds (D-MA), and Connie Morella (R-MD) with 107 House cosponsors.[103] The bill sought only to prevent discrimination in the workplace on the basis of sexual orientation (not gender identity). It included broad religious and military exemptions. It also prohibited the use of "disparate impact" as evidence of discrimination.[104] Kennedy organized hearings on ENDA in July 1994. The Task Force did not participate, but HRCF did serve as witness. Early momentum on the bill stalled when, following the 1994 midterm congressional elections, a Republican majority assumed control of both chambers of Congress. Furthermore, HRCF encountered LGBT movement opposition to ENDA due to its failure to include expressions of gender identity among its protections. At this time, this constituency had little to no voice inside HRCF, but it had a small but growing voice inside the Task Force. HRCF, which was heavily invested in securing passage of ENDA, convened a summit with representatives of the transgender community to manage the emerging rift; however, the organization refused to lobby on behalf of altering the language of ENDA to include sexual orientation.[105]

ENDA came to a vote in September 1996 as part of a compromise that included a vote on DOMA. Republican leadership offered Senator Kennedy an opportunity for a vote on ENDA (with no amendments) in exchange for a vote on DOMA (with no amendments).[106] ENDA failed in the Senate by a vote of 50 to 49. DOMA passed by a vote of 85 to 14.[107] The pairing of the two bills enabled numerous senators to appear to oppose discrimination, by voting for ENDA, while protecting themselves from criticism of undermining traditional marriage, by voting for DOMA.

Although the question of same-sex marriage reached Congress by 1996 and the timing of DOMA was not opportune for lesbian and gay advocates, it, like the lifting of the military ban, was not an entirely new issue for the LGBT movements. That the issue was imposed exogenously at this level means that it was not intentionally brought by national gay rights organizations, not that it was not taken up by the broader advocacy community. Nor should it be taken to mean that gay men and lesbians did not want some form of state-sanctioned union. Indeed, when the Task Force hosted its annual Creating Change Conference in 1990, agenda items included repealing sodomy laws, advocating for civil rights legislation, and increasing protection and reporting of hate crimes; same-sex marriage was not on the agenda, but advocating for domestic-partnership benefits was.[108] That relationship recognition was not articulated as marriage reveals the extent to which the LGBT communities remain divided on whether they should seek marriage as one of their policy goals, even as the pro-marriage movement has become a clearly dominant voice, at least by the mid-2000s.[109] Furthermore, cases litigated on the question of same-sex marriage date at least to *Baker v. Nelson* (1971), in which the plaintiffs, two men, sought the right to marry in Minnesota, citing their fundamental right to marry under the Ninth Amendment and analogizing restrictions on same-sex marriage to antimiscegenation laws struck down by the Supreme Court in *Loving v. Virginia* (1967).[110] Public interest law organizations, such as Lambda Legal Defense and Gay and Lesbian Advocates and Defenders (GLAD), assisted in marriage-related cases at the state level throughout the 1990s, particularly in Hawaii and Vermont.[111] However, the issue remained primarily in the legal rather than the legislative domain until state-level and congressional-level DOMAs were proposed in the mid-1990s.

Nevertheless, marriage was not a high priority of the Task Force or the HRC until the Hawaii Supreme Court ruled in *Baehr v. Lewin* in 1993 that refusal to recognize same-sex marriage violated the state constitution's guarantee of equal protection. According to historian George Chauncey, neither organization pursued the issue with great intensity until this case positioned LGBT rights advocates on the defensive, fighting statutory and constitutional bans at the state and federal level that came in the wake of *Baehr*. Both organizations "mostly ignored the issue, either because they were critical of marriage, saw it as a hopeless cause, or, most commonly, simply had other priorities."[112]

And yet, within the gay and lesbian communities, some form of state-recognized unions became a more prominent cause for a variety of reasons in the late 1980s and early 1990s. First, the AIDS crisis highlighted how gay men, without marriage, were restricted from caring for their partners. Without marriage, hospital visitation was restricted, lines of responsibility for decisions about care were confused, and inheritance rights went unacknowledged.[113] This obstacle was not confined to the context of the HIV/AIDS crisis. As the Sharon Kowalski case demonstrated, without some form of state recognition, gay and lesbian couples had no claim to one another. Kowalski, who was in a relationship with Karen Thompson and with whom she jointly owned a home, was injured in an automobile accident. As Thompson was not recognized as Kowalski's wife, she was denied access to her partner at the hospital,

Kowalski's parents denied their daughter's lesbian relationship, and Kowalski's father was appointed guardian over Kowalski, a power he used to deny Thompson any visitation. Thompson sued, and after several years of litigation and eight years after the automobile accident, the Minnesota court of appeals ruled Kowalski capable of appointing her own guardian, whereupon she selected Thompson. Notably, however, the court had to make up its own phraseology to describe the couple's relationship since it was, in fact, accorded no formal state recognition. The court called it "a family of affinity, which ought to be accorded respect."[114]

The second imperative for marriage stemmed from a demand for familial stability and security related to parental rights. As Chauncey has argued, the 1980s brought improvements in reproductive technology leading to a "lesbian baby boom."[115] In addition, by the mid-1980s, the paradigm of second-parent adoption, which established relations of step-children and step-parents, was extended to include same-sex partners. Nevertheless, without marriage, the children of same-sex couples were left materially and legally vulnerable in a variety of ways, a circumstance only recently recognized as harmful by the Supreme Court in its 2013 *United States v. Windsor* ruling.

However, the battle for marital recognition primarily took place within the courtroom. While same-sex marriage may have been at the forefront of the litigation-focused advocacy organizations, it does not appear to have been at the top of the agendas of either the Task Force or HRC. On this question, these groups were involved not so much to promote pro-same-sex-marriage legislation as to fight legislation that would ban such marriages. In the wake of *Baehr*, states moved to ban recognition of same-sex marriage by defining marriage by statute as a union between a man and a woman; thirteen states did so in 1996; nine followed in 1997. Five more states followed in 1998 while Alaska became the first state to ban same-sex marriage by constitutional amendment that year. Two more states banned same-sex marriage by statute in 1999, and three more did so in 2000. Also, in 2000 Nebraska became the second state to ban same-sex marriage by constitutional amendment.[116] To guard against federal recognition of same-sex marriage, Congress passed and President Clinton signed DOMA in 1996. In other words, litigation for same-sex marriage, often brought by plaintiffs with little to no direct connection to gay and lesbian interest groups, forced the issue onto the agendas of HRC and the Task Force, and these groups were forced to respond in the legislative arena from a defensive posture.

Interviews with HRC and Task Force staff members confirm the impact of same-sex marriage as an exogenous issue, one for which these organizations were not fully prepared. One HRC staffer discussed the national debate on same-sex marriage as it had taken shape by the mid-2000s this way:

> The agenda is defined both by us in the movement and by exogenous factors. . . . Would we have chosen in this moment to have marriage front and center? Probably not. Is the Congress ready for it? Is the American public ready for it? Probably not yet. . . . In this last election [of 2004] Karl Rove gave the final exam on the first day of class. We didn't have an opportunity to educate on the issue before he came out with eleven ballot measures, and we lost on every single one. And the issue was forced by the *Goodridge* decision [in Massachusetts, ruling that the state constitution did not preclude recognition of same-sex marriage] that came out in November of the prior year and then landed on the ballot.[117]

Much like the debate over service in the military, marriage was similarly viewed as a controversial goal within movement communities. While working for the Task Force Policy Institute, legal scholar Paula Ettelbrick debated with the then-director of Lambda Legal Defense, Thomas Stoddard, about whether marriage should be a movement priority. Ettelbrick considered marriage as contradicting the ideological foundations of the movement:

> Marriage runs contrary to two of the primary goals of the lesbian and gay movement: the affirmation of gay identity and the validation of many forms of relationships. . . . Being queer means pushing the parameters of sex, sexuality, and family, and in the process transforming the very fabric of society. . . . The moment we argue, as some amongst us insist on doing, that we should be treated as equals because we are just like married couples and hold the same values to be true, we undermine the very purpose of our movement and begin the dangerous process of silencing our voices.[118]

Stoddard, despite acknowledging that the legal possibility of state-recognized same-sex marriage was slim from the vantage point of when he was writing in 1989, claimed it as a worthy objective for the movements. For Stoddard, marriage recognition was the cultural and legal barrier that distinguished gay from straight relationships, enabling the disparagement and denigration of the former. Lack of access to marriage was the basis for belittling and discriminating against same-sex relationships. Stoddard considered marriage to be "the political issue that most fully tests the dedication of people who are not gay to full equality for gay people, and it is also the issue most likely to lead ultimately to a world free from discrimination against lesbians and gay men."[119] Marriage's newly prominent position during the early and mid-1990s did not result from any deliberate moves or consensus on the issue among the gay and lesbian lobbyists at either the Task Force or HRC. HRC's organizational identity as first and foremost a congressional lobby group and its more conservative and bipartisan identity and membership enabled it, unlike the Task Force, to mount a fight against DOMA's passage.

HRC's inability to defeat DOMA can be explained, at least in part, by the political machinations that brought ENDA and DOMA to a vote on the same day as well as the lack of political opportunity by 1996, and the division within movement communities about whether marriage recognition was even worth pursuing or whether it ran fundamentally counter to the ideas of gay liberation. Craig Rimmerman highlights the lack of opportunity, the interest groups' lack of control over its own agenda, and the debate that marriage inspired within the movement communities in the mid- to late 1990s:

> Same-sex marriage is not a crucial issue for many movement members. Those who think it should be a key goal—individuals such as Andrew Sullivan and Bruce Bawer—generally represent the movement's more moderate to conservative element. But as we have already learned from the military debate, the movements cannot control when specific issues will come to the fore. And in many ways the issue of same-sex marriage could not have come up at a worse time. The Republicans now controlled both houses of Congress, it was a presidential election year, and the movements simply did not have the time, organizational skills, or resources to mount an effective organizing educational campaign on an

issue that appeared to be unpopular with the American public—certainly not a campaign equal to challenging the Christian Right's vast organizational resources.[120]

This passage highlights the contention that marriage, at least in the mid-1990s, was promoted by and appealed to a more politically moderate and assimilationist understanding of what it means to be politically gay, an understanding that defines the organizational identity of HRC but that has not always corresponded to the identity of the Task Force. Especially during these years when the Task Force was pursuing more grassroots and local means to "Fight the Right," lobbying against federal legislation banning state-sanctioned same-sex marriage, an issue that did not even fit within the objectives of the Task Force at the time, was a complete misfit of identity, issue, and institutional venue.

The Task Force Embraces Marriage as HRC Steps Back: Pushing an Alternative Modality of Recognition

Stephen Skowronek and Karen Orren critique Theda Skocpol's theory of fit as creating challenges similar to niche theory: interests may lock into certain tactics, strategies, and rationales, which are more likely to produce political stasis than political change. According to Orren and Skowronek,

> [S]ocial interests that thrive by filling a niche within established institutional forms or by discovering a channel for action made available by them have little interest in seeking major changes in governing arrangements that favor them; on the contrary, they can be expected to hold politics to the present path, pressing only for those adaptations that promise to maintain the current relationship between institutional politics and public policy.[121]

This is a trenchant assessment, particularly in uncovering the theory's limits in assessing groups whose issues and identities do not fit with institutional design. Orren and Skowronek contend instead that the groups that do *not* fit within extant institutional and ideational configurations may drive political change because "they are also the interests most likely to elaborate programmatic interests in substantial institutional change, to hammer at established forms of government, and to throw their support to those who promise to alter them."[122] Those interests whose identities do not align with issues that dominate popular conceptions of a movement's agenda may be more articulate and more engaged in promoting alternatives and pushing for different regulatory recognitions than the ones bounding the meaning of gay and lesbian citizenship.

The misfit of the Task Force's identity with the issues defining many elements of the gay and lesbian rights agenda and with the institutional venues through which these were being pursued should then hardly be dismissed as unproductive.[123] Its ideational commitments to more progressive constructions of LGBT rights, which drew attention to diversity within the sexual-minorities communities and reached across identities to link LGBT rights with other progressive causes, remained a powerful alternative to the positions taken by the HRC. And, crucially, neither organization was making significant headway by the early 2000s on the three issues covered in this chapter.

This circumstance of policy failure enables a consideration of Orren and Skowronek's critique. The HRC was neither winning nor maintaining policies that secured LGBT equality in the workplace; nor was it successfully defending against the backlash hostile to same-sex marriage. Despite being positioned to act on all three issues—despite its organizational reputation's fit with issue and institutional venue—HRC failed to secure its ideal outcome on any of them. This lack of success created discursive and strategic space for the Task Force to reengage with these issues, particularly employment nondiscrimination and same-sex marriage, as they continued to define interest-group priorities and remained a topic within national discourse on LGBT rights. But, crucially, the issues were redefined, through circumstances often, but not exclusively, external to organizational action, in ways that aligned with the organizational identity of the Task Force.

As state legislators responded to the *Baehr, Baker v. Vermont,* and *Goodridge* rulings by proposing and passing state DOMAs and constitutional bans on same-sex marriage, and as that issue continued to be characterized in national political discourse as a matter of state's rights, the Task Force's organizational identity as focused on state-level matters brought it in line with the issue. The organizational identity of the Task Force positioned the interest group as a potentially better fit in terms of the institutional-venue level at which the matter was increasingly debated. Indeed, the Task Force's increasing advocacy for same-sex marriage is no more clearly apparent than in the clash on strategy between HRC and the Task Force following the 2004 election.

In the months following the Supreme Court's ruling in *Lawrence v. Texas* and *Goodridge*, then-executive director of the Task Force, Matt Foreman, issued a statement, "The Promise and the Peril," which warned "LGBT people and their friends to prepare for a backlash against recent legal victories."[124] Three weeks later, the Task Force declared its support for a new political initiative, DontAmend.com, a website devoted to opposing the federal constitutional marriage amendment that would ban same-sex marriage.[125] In other words, as marriage was repeatedly framed by politicians and gay rights advocates as a matter best left for the states to decide, the Task Force was increasingly positioned to engage it without undermining or confusing its organizational identity. And, it sought ways, through intermediaries like DontAmend.com, to challenge federal antigay initiatives without undermining its identity or historic focus on state and local politics and movement building. As President George W. Bush pushed the federal marriage amendment as a 2004 election issue, the Task Force responded:

> No set of circumstances can justify the support of the President of the United States for amending the Constitution to endorse discrimination against a group of Americans. We cannot and will not be silent in the face of even considering enshrining our second class citizenship in this nation's most sacred document. We consider this a declaration of war on lesbian, gay, bisexual and transgender America. The President is clearly using our lives and families to pander to the political and religious extremists that comprise his base. We did not ask for this fight, but if the President wants one, he will have one. And that fight will involve civil disobedience across this country.[126]

Foreman could position the Task Force as compelled by circumstances to fight the initiative, thereby again not undermining its organizational identity even as it engaged in federal-level politics.

Same-sex marriage was put to a vote in the 2004 election. Numerous journalistic and scholarly accounts have argued that putting forward ballot initiatives proposing state constitutional bans on same-sex marriage was a successful get-out-the-vote mechanism for the Republican Party.[127] And, all eleven ballot initiatives succeeded.[128] While HRC was considered instrumental in the defeat of the Federal Marriage Amendment, it did not devote a similar level of resources to state ballot initiatives.[129] In the wake of these defeats, HRC called for adopting a "new, more moderate strategy with less emphasis on legalizing same-sex marriages and more on strengthening personal relations."[130] To demonstrate its willingness to work within the political system and grapple with the realities of compromise, HRC indicated that it might support the Bush administration's initiative to privatize Social Security in return for the extension of federal partner benefits to gay senior citizens, recognition that did not require marriage, but might have required congressional statutory approval of a civil union.[131] The day following HRC's announcement of this new strategy, the Task Force and nearly ninety other gay rights leaders sent a letter, titled "Where We Stand," to every member of Congress, in which they flatly rejected HRC's approach:

> We specifically reject any attempts to trade equal rights for lesbian, gay, bisexual and transgender people, a group that includes many elders, for the rights of senior citizens under Social Security or, for that matter, the rights of any other group of Americans. . . . [A]lthough the struggle for freedom can be difficult and painful for those without full equality, it would be an historic mistake to grow tired of the battle or surrender basic rights and equality in order to make the road easier. . . . We will not sacrifice our rights—or the rights of others like senior citizens—on the altar of political expediency.[132]

When defending the letter's criticism of HRC's new tactic, the Task Force's Foreman contended that HRC's position "really represented a sharp change in what has always been a united voice in our community—that we don't negotiate our rights."[133] While HRC's strategy implied an unprecedented bargaining for rights, which was deemed offensive, inappropriate, and counterproductive by other leading members of the

LGBT-rights activist communities, philosophical and strategic clashing between HRC and the Task Force, as this chapter has illustrated, was hardly a new phenomenon.

Following the passage of eleven state ballot initiatives constitutionally to ban same-sex marriage, the Task Force took the lead between the two organizations in expressing its intention to continue to support same-sex marriage campaigns without compromise. While HRC turned away from same-sex marriage in the wake of defeat, the Task Force doubled down. HRC decided to moderate its aims. Instead of pursuing marriage equality directly, HRC decided to articulate other ways that might "re-introduce ourselves to America with the stories of our lives"[134] by "communicating the struggles of gays in their families, workplaces, churches and synagogues."[135] Responding to this shift, Foreman admitted, "The legal strategy to win marriage rights is a decade ahead of the political strategies to educate the public and the legislatures," thereby agreeing that there had to be more focus on public education, as HRC insisted. He nevertheless maintained that reframing the issue away from a clear demand for marriage recognition was the wrong tactic. He contended that HRC's strategy was preemptive capitulation that would do more long-term harm than good: "A lot of gay people understand the concept of bullies. The worst thing you can do with a bully is not fight back because you'll only get hit harder the next day."[136]

Marriage, long criticized as a goal antithetical to the meaning of gay liberation, could, because of the now-bipartisan opposition to it, as well its striking defeat at the ballot box in 2004, be reframed as a radical objective. Such radical valence was reinforced by HRC's decision to retreat from the issue and pursue an alternative and more incremental course. The issue now potentially more easily aligned with the more radical and progressive identity of the Task Force. Furthermore, the reframing of marriage after DOMA and especially after the defeat of a federal marriage amendment in 2004 as a matter best decided at the state level, positioned the Task Force as able to engage the issue without sacrificing its organizational identity as a group focused on state-level rights advocacy. In other words, marriage presented an identity-institutional fit as well. The structural alignment was in place if the Task Force was willing to articulate it, and Foreman's criticism of HRC's move suggested that organizational leadership would seize the opportunity.

As Foreman's comments about the marriage-recognition movement after 2004 suggest, interest groups can take on a new tactical approach so long as that approach is framed as consistent with its organizational identity. Strategies can shift so long as the move remains rhetorically congruent with the way the organization is recognized by its membership, its partners, and its own staffers and leadership. New tactics can be pursued so long as they are justified in terms of long-standing commitments embedded in and made manifest through organizational identity. Even if an organization seeks to go so far as to repudiate its prior commitments, it can only do so if it persuasively constructs such repudiation as in line with the organization's first principles. In a different context, Stephen Skowronek describes the action as requiring that leaders "set out to retrieve from a far distant, even mythic, past fundamental values that they claimed had been lost in the indulgencies of the received order."[137] To reconstruct political action, the new action must always be framed as realizing and not replacing fundamental principles.

This dynamic became increasingly evident in 2005, as interviews suggested that HRC and the Task Force were considering new initiatives that would seem to violate the presumptions of niche theory. They appeared to pursue objectives that were wholly beyond the parameters of their past experience and that would trample on the turf of the other. HRC sought to lobby "downward" to state and local levels while Task Force staffers discussed new objectives to focus "upward" to lobby the federal government, thereby confounding the functionalist expectations of niche theory. The Task Force's proposed federal-level agenda had two components. First, it aimed to leverage federal dollars for health and human services downward to local community centers. Thus, the group's aim was still distinct from that of the HRC insofar as the former group conceived of targeting various branches of the federal bureaucracy to fund local-level service organizations. As one Task Force staffer indicated by commenting on the lack of clear political opportunities by the mid-2000s,

> It would seem to be that the water is full of sharks, and why would we throw our tender selves into that pool right now. . . . ENDA is dead, ENDA is not going anywhere. It's just not happening for ENDA. . . . Given that

that is true, there is time, even if it is not successful right away, there is the opportunity to rethink the concept of a larger piece of legislation. . . . And then there is this whole [executive-branch] agency piece, which is really the connection to the grassroots because Matt's [Foreman] idea is to shake the federal tree so that some of the resources filter back down to our community organizations out in the country. It is not about inside-the-beltway stuff. It's about trying to get federal money to Milwaukee.[138]

This strategy, while federally focused, conforms to an identity emphasizing local organizing as critical to gaining equal rights. Additionally, the Task Force maintained an aim of reintroducing some broadly based nondiscrimination legislation. It sought to shelve ENDA and redesign legislation similar to ENDA's predecessor, a gay civil rights bill. The objective was to reaffirm the Task Force's leading role, relative to HRC, as a more progressive organization focused on embracing diversity within the movement.[139]

By 2007, while no gay civil rights bill took shape, the Task Force ultimately praised a redesigned ENDA introduced by Representative Barney Frank, which included protections for gender identity, thereby bringing transgender individuals within its scope.[140] Holding fast to its organizational identity committed to trans inclusion, the Task Force strongly protested when House sponsors split the bill in two, offering one bill that included sexual orientation only and one that included gender identity only in an attempt to secure passage of the one protecting sexual orientation.[141] The organization stated, "it is unconscionable that congressional leaders would rush to a decision to strip protections for transgender people at the same time as states across the nation are adding these protections at an unprecedented pace."[142] It further argued against the notion that members of Congress did not understand or were so uncomfortable with transgenders that trans inclusivity would mean that ENDA protections for sexual orientation would fail:

Gender identity language has twice passed through the House in the hate crimes bill, and earlier this year there were similar last-minute concerns among new members. We were able to overcome them then, and should be given the chance to do so now. It is incredibly ironic that today, the same day news is breaking about the House removing gender identity protections from ENDA, the Senate just voted 60–39 to allow a voice vote on a transgender-inclusive hate crimes bill. The bill then immediately passed.[143]

Reaffirming the Task Force's commitment to inclusion, Foreman argued for more time to garner support for the trans-inclusive ENDA and against splitting the bill in two.[144] Ultimately, House mark-up on the noninclusive ENDA was postponed.[145] And, in October 2007, the Task Force announced a campaign for a unified ENDA, in which it joined a coalition of over 150 organizations writing a joint letter to Congress to support trans inclusivity; HRC did not join this coalition or sign this letter.[146] But, this move eventually meant that no ENDA passed, due to the end of the legislative session.[147] Nevertheless, the Task Force's organizational identity as committed to representing the full LGBT community was preserved even as the more instrumental goal of achieving an admittedly narrower ENDA was lost.

While the Task Force expanded its focus on federal issues, HRC moved toward more state-focused lobbying in response to the rash of anti–gay marriage initiatives. As one staffer explained,

> The mission and the identity have become much more congruent over the years. I felt there was a disjuncture when the focus was strictly on federal Congressional kinds of things because we know that this is one part of securing equality . . . and while it is important, we have finally realized that state work, local work, and policy kinds of work are just as integral to executing our mission of equality.[148]

The statement suggests that HRC was moving toward the direction that the Task Force was already pursuing, particularly with its focus on policy development through its think tank, the Policy Institute, and its focus on supporting state and local organizing. But, the staffer was also very clear that these moves were in addition to, not exclusive of, congressional lobbying.

The Task Force's moves into the federal marriage debate in 2004 and HRC's moves toward the state level demonstrated that tactics can shift so long as rationales continue to be framed in terms consistent with the well-understood, well-recognized, and ultimately sticky organizational identity. HRC remains a mainstream organization fighting for rights-based equality for LGBT-identified individuals. The Task Force remains a more progressive organization targeting local-level activism and supporting a perspective on LGBT rights as a component of a broader social justice movement that embraces racial, sexual, and economic equality. In both cases of new tactics, the shift in venue must still be framed to fit with the organization's identity as it has taken shape over the years. Far from reshaping the organizational identity, these moves to diversify tactics continue to be discussed in the same ways despite their exploration of new strategic possibilities. Thus, organizational identity remains a rhetorical constraint on strategic action.

Conclusion

This chapter has explored organizational identity as a contributing factor influencing actions of two national LGBT interest groups: the National LGBTQ Task Force and the Human Rights Campaign. Both organizations premise their work on defining gays and lesbians as an unjustly discriminated-against minority; they have pursued social change in distinct ways, appealing to distinct constituencies, and building distinct organizational identities. This identity is path dependent; it becomes more entrenched over time and can constrain a group's ability to seize an opportunity if that opportunity develops on an issue or through an institutional venue that does not align with it. Over the course of the 1990s, as opportunities developed to secure employment-nondiscrimination legislation and to fight federal legislation banning same-sex marriage, the Task Force's identity seemed to limit the organization's engagement with these issues, yielding advocacy space at the national level to HRC. However, by the mid-2000s, political opportunities regarding same-sex marriage and ENDA took new form. And, the entrepreneurial Task Force executive director seized these opportunities to reframe the new ENDA and marriage discussion as congruent with the Task Force's organizational identity.

Same-sex marriage changed in two ways. First, as litigation persisted in the state courts, and with the Massachusetts Supreme Court becoming the first to rule that the state constitution required same-sex marriage recognition, the issue became defined rhetorically and institutionally as a state matter. Second, after eleven states banned same-sex marriage by ballot measures in the 2004 election, both political parties came out in opposition to it, and the HRC decided that same-sex marriage was too extreme an issue to pursue in the short term, the issue took on a new, more progressive valence by dint of it being rejected so widely at a popular level. This new "radical" conception of marriage could challenge the more historical progressive critique of the institution as patriarchal, heteronormative, and generally out of step with the gay liberationist and queer philosophies that had, in part, animated the Task Force from its earliest years. Task Force executive director Matt Foreman rhetorically reconstructed the struggle for marriage equality as aligned with the Task Force's organizational identity as state-focused, progressive, and refusing to engage in inside-the-beltway politics.

ENDA was reintroduced in 2007 to include protections based on sexual orientation *and* gender identity. The trans-inclusive ENDA resonated with the Task Force's organizational commitment to the diversity of the entire LGBT communities. When House sponsors decided to split the bill in two, with one focused on sexual orientation and the other focused on gender identity, the Task Force balked and organized pressure to unify the bills. Never fully retreating from congressional lobbying—particularly as the Task Force remained involved in lobbying throughout the 1990s and early 2000s for congressional hate crimes legislation to include sexual orientation—once the issue of employment nondiscrimination was congruent with the organization's commitment to trans inclusivity, the Task Force took a leadership position.

Both of these examples suggest that organizational identity constrains strategic action. As Darren Halpin and Carsten Daugbjerg argue, "founding identity (inclusive of history, ideology and mission) is not simply (or only) a force of constraint, it is also a force for enablement (both for organizational change and reproduction)."[149] They contend, "it is precisely the power of identity that makes it an asset for potential agents of radical change. If they [organizational leaders] can frame the case for change in broad organizational form . . . as consistent with founding 'ideology and principles' then they can take advantage of focusing events to effect radical change."[150] Thus, identity is still a constraint. Actions must always be framed as congruent with first principles even if initial appearances suggest they may be otherwise. Foreman's actions and rhetoric in 2004 on marriage and in 2007 on ENDA bear out this claim.

This chapter has relied on concepts of historical institutionalism critical to the study of American political development. In particular, it has utilized path dependency to explain how organizational identity operates upon strategic action. To study organizational change as path dependent is hardly to break new ground.[151] Nevertheless, few have applied the insights of path dependency to LGBT organizational identity.[152] Path dependence would indicate that interest-group organizations either "persist and become increasingly entrenched or are abandoned."[153] Yet, the existence of the Task Force for over forty years and the continued strength of the Human Rights Campaign after nearly thirty-five years would suggest something else. There must be some way in which organizations are not wholly path dependent, but can adapt over time.

While organizational identity exhibits qualities of path-dependent constraint, an entrepreneurial leader can rhetorically shape opportunity for acting on an issue and within an institutional venue so that it resonates with the organization's reputation. In the case of the Task Force, Foreman rhetorically linked organizational identity to the new forms that older issues now took. Furthermore, he could do so because his stewardship had maintained the organization's investment—even if limited—in operating at the national level.[154] Leadership plays a critical role in whether organizational change over time exhibits qualities associated with "lock-in" or whether the organization can be nimble enough to exploit opportunities without damaging its reputation, alienating its membership, befuddling its allies, or confusing potential legislative or executive partners in government.

Finally, entrepreneurial leadership played a critical role in creating the discursive space for another modality of regulatory recognition. By the late 1990s, gays and lesbians secured limited municipal recognition of their relationships as well as human resource policies that provided some benefits on par with those available to straight colleagues. Local governance authorities and private firms began to recognize that gays and lesbians constituted a minority suffering an unjust history of discrimination. Nevertheless, this shift was hardly secure or consistent across regulatory authorities; local ordinances were repealed and corporate policies were incremental and partial. Indeed, the votes on ENDA and DOMA, held on the same day, showcased that modality; members of Congress were able to embrace that regulatory recognition by voting for ENDA even as they rejected an alternative recognition increasingly on the horizon, namely, the gay or lesbian person not as a solitary individual but as constituted by a relationship. Marriage challenged that modality of the discriminated-against individual by highlighting that gay men and women were not just individuals and that sexuality was not only a private matter. Marriage, unlike the other issues, required that regulatory authorities see sexuality as both public and relational. While military access and employment nondiscrimination required that the gay, lesbian, bisexual (and in the case of the later ENDA, transgender) individual be viewed as subject to unjust discrimination, the recognition was only of an individual. And, the defining quality of that individual could be hidden from view; the sex in which those individuals engaged could be kept behind closed doors. Marriage, by contrast, required a different kind of recognition. It required seeing a relationship and seeing it publicly.

HRC retreated from advocating this modality of recognition after the blow of losing eleven state ballot measures in 2004. The Task Force and other LGBT-rights organizations, particularly legal organizations such as Lambda Legal Defense and Gay and Lesbian Advocates and Defenders, seized upon this opportunity as the courtroom was the primary venue in which attempts to force the state to recognize LGBT peoples in this new way were being fought. Nevertheless, wider embrace of this modality was years away. Instead, a different modality—one that constructed LGBT individuals as discriminated against and recognized their sexuality, but held that sexuality from public view, shunting it to the private sphere—became far more prevalent over the 1990s and early 2000s. This modality was evident among all three federal branches and in public opinion, and it is discussed further in chapter 5.

5

Respect for Private Lives

Closeting Same-Sex Sexuality in Public Opinion, Policy, and Law

It is the promise of the Constitution that there is a realm of
personal liberty which the government may not enter. . . .
Had those who drew and ratified the Due Process Clauses of
the Fifth Amendment or the Fourteenth Amendment known
the components of liberty in its manifold possibilities, they
might have been more specific. They did not presume to have
this insight. They knew times can blind us to certain truths
and later generations can see that laws once thought necessary and proper in fact serve only to oppress. As the Constitution endures, persons in every generation can invoke its
principles in their own search for greater freedom.
—Justice Anthony Kennedy, *Lawrence et al. v. Texas*, 2003[1]

Thursday, June 26, 2003, a day before annual gay pride events commem-
orating the Stonewall Riots of 1969 in New York City, was the last day
of the Supreme Court's 2002–2003 session. It was also the day when the
Court announced its ruling in *Lawrence v. Texas*.[2]

Lawrence involved the constitutionality of a Texas law that criminalized same-sex sexual acts but did not criminalize similar different-sex
behavior. The decision could have reinforced the Supreme Court's five-
to-four ruling seventeen years earlier in *Bowers v. Hardwick*, which upheld a Georgia ban on both same-sex and different-sex sodomy.[3] Or,
given the factual differences between the laws, the ruling could also have
found the Texas law unconstitutional as a matter of equal protection
(as it treated straight sex differently than gay sex) while leaving *Bowers*
intact.[4] Instead, the Court reevaluated *Bowers* and ruled that the Texas
statute violated a fundamental right of privacy, which follows from the
Fourteenth Amendment's due process clause. *Bowers* was overturned not

because social mores had changed and gays and lesbians had achieved a level of social acceptance but because, in the words of Justice Anthony Kennedy, "*Bowers* was not correct when it was decided, and it is not correct today. It ought not to remain binding precedent. *Bowers v. Hardwick* should be and now is overruled."[5]

By wiping away *Bowers*, the Court "changed forever Americans' sense of constitutional law."[6] It not only applied the oft-controversial doctrinal right of privacy, but it also fundamentally reimagined gay and lesbian identity.[7] As discussed in chapter 3, the Court had articulated a cleaved notion of sexuality in its 1996 ruling in *Romer v. Evans* by distinguishing sexual behavior from identity. Kennedy's ruling in *Lawrence* exploded this distinction by positing conduct as constitutive of status, and furthermore, intimate conduct as constitutive of human dignity. By taking responsibility for *Bowers*' misunderstanding of the liberty at stake, Kennedy offered "as close as the Court would ever get to an apology to gay and lesbian Americans for the wrong, and for the harm, it had done them."[8]

By 2003, only Texas and thirteen other states maintained criminal sodomy bans.[9] Decriminalization remained a primary aim of the gay rights movement because criminal status touched on nearly every other claim that gays and lesbians pursued. Insofar as the state brands an individual a criminal, that recognition affects one's ability to secure a job, maintain custody of or adopt children, serve in the military, or receive security clearance.[10] Consequently, upon hearing the *Lawrence* ruling, Ruth Harlow, legal director of Lambda Legal Defense and Education Fund, which represented John Lawrence and Tyron Garner in the litigation process, declared, "For decades, these laws have been a major roadblock to equality. They've labeled the entire gay community as criminals and second-class citizens. Today, the Supreme Court ended that once and for all."[11] And, Suzanne Goldberg, an attorney for Lambda who represented Lawrence and Garner from the beginning of the litigation, said that the ruling "removes the reflexive assumption of gay people's inferiority. *Bowers* took away the humanity of gay people, and this decision gives it back."[12]

Lawrence also gave judicial imprimatur to another form of regulatory recognition of gay and lesbian citizenship. In Kennedy's words, the state could no longer "demean their existence or control their destiny by making their private sexual conduct a crime."[13] Yet did *Lawrence* really establish a principle of equality for gays and lesbians? While Kennedy pointed rhetorically to equality, *Lawrence* did not consider whether same-sex relationships were equal to different-sex relationships. At stake was whether private consensual sexual relations could be entered into without fear of criminal sanction. What was at stake was personal liberty or autonomy, not necessarily equality. What was at stake was not how the state would see a same-sex relationship, but whether it would see same-sex sex at all.

Consequently, this chapter reevaluates *Lawrence*. It explores the ruling as embedded within a broader dynamic in which all three federal branches, over the course of a decade, adopted a fourth modality of regulatory recognition: decriminalizing homosexuality but privatizing the same-sex relationship. This modality rests on the idea that sexuality is a private matter, the *public* expression of which the state may be free to sanction. The Court adopted this modality in its *Lawrence* ruling, but in so doing, it *followed* trends evident in public opinion and actions taken by other federal branches.

To support this interpretation of the *Lawrence* Court as hardly activist, the chapter reviews trends in public opinion, public policy, and jurisprudential development that support privatizing sexuality and that endorse a liberty claim but not an equality claim. Political rhetoric draws on both values, often refusing to acknowledge how they may be in tension. And, recognition of this tension between liberty and equality has fostered debates on how the constitutional basis of LGBT rights claims should be framed.[14] By evaluating policies such as Don't Ask, Don't Tell and the Defense of Marriage Act, and Supreme Court rulings, including *Hurley v. Irish-American Gay, Lesbian & Bisexual Group of Boston* (1995), *Romer v. Evans* (1996), *Boy Scouts of America v. Dale* (2000), and *Lawrence v. Texas* (2003), this chapter illuminates the state's refusal to see gay and lesbian citizens at all.[15] While no longer criminalized, they were left beyond the boundaries of federal recognition. They could exist free from explicit sanction so long as they did not publicly express their sexual identities.

Furthermore, Justice Anthony Scalia's claims, offered in dissent, that *Lawrence* cut a path directly to same-sex marriage triggered news media to frame the ruling in that context. While Kennedy structured the ruling as a private liberty concern, the dissent brought to the fore a public equality framing, upon which media seized and through which a distinct modality of regulatory recognition could occupy public discourse and the public imagination. This chapter explores whether this subsequent focus on the equality of publicly sanctioned same-sex marriage explains a noticeable if short-lived drop in popular support on a variety of gay rights issues in the immediate wake of the *Lawrence* ruling. It provides evidence of this shift in public opinion and offers various hypotheses, relying on the literature of framing effects, as to why it may have occurred. It then offers evidence of a shift in televised news media discourse about *Lawrence*; earlier coverage emphasized that private personal liberty was at stake, while after the ruling was announced, media framing shifted to the decision's implications for public equal marriage recognition. The chapter then turns to the policy domain to demonstrate how the *Lawrence* ruling aligned with a pattern of regulatory recognition already established by the Clinton administration and Congress. And, it shows how this pattern of higher public support for liberty claims relative to equality claims is mirrored in the Supreme Court's own jurisprudence on homosexuality by reviewing four cases involving gay rights claims between 1995 and 2003. It thereby reveals synchronicity among the Court, the elected branches, and public opinion and challenges the characterization of *Lawrence* as a judicially activist ruling.

Opinion Shift Immediately after the *Lawrence* Ruling

Between May and July 2003, Americans' expressed opinion on the legality of consensual homosexual sex sharply shifted direction. In May, the largest percentage of survey respondents to date—about 60 percent—supported decriminalizing this sexual activity. As shown in figure 5.1, two months later, only 49 percent opposed criminalization while support jumped from 35 to 46 percent. Since question wording was consistent, the possibility that the swing was an artifact of the survey is low.

One intervening event that might explain this swing was the *Lawrence* ruling. Yet, if, before the Court announced its decision, a majority of the public favored decriminalizing homosexual sex and the Court

Do you think homosexual relations between consenting adults should or should not be legal?

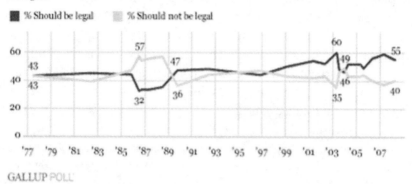

Figure 5.1. Opinion Change on the Legality of Homosexual Sex
Source: Lydia Saad, "Americans Evenly Divided on Morality of Homosexuality," Gallup, 18 June 2008.

ruled in accordance with these preferences, why would the public oppose decriminalization only weeks later?

Television news coverage of *Lawrence* may hold an answer. The coverage was not wholly negative; it did not clearly suggest that the ruling was flawed. Instead, news media tended to focus on the implications of *Lawrence.* Consequently, the downward trend might reflect public support of other gay rights claims to which *Lawrence* may have opened the door, particularly same-sex marriage. Although the ruling dealt primarily with one gay rights claim—one that majorities supported, namely, decriminalization—media discourse may have framed the ruling in terms of its implications, focusing on one implication that majorities at the time opposed, namely, same-sex marriage.[16] As legal historian Michael Klarman suggests in his account of backlash against gay rights litigation victories, given patterns of public support for homosexual decriminalization, "*Lawrence* probably would have been an uncontroversial ruling were it not for the extent to which gay marriage was emerging as a salient issue by 2003."[17] This chapter provides evidence that *Lawrence* was read through the lens of same-sex marriage, a more radical modality of regulatory recognition, rather than being read in terms of what the case was about, namely, the decriminalization and privatization of consensual sex, a modality of recognition well in place by 2003.[18]

Ben Page and Robert Shapiro contend that "short-term movements in public opinion, in fact, can largely be accounted for (and predicted) by quantitative analysis of what news, from what sources, appears in the mass media."[19] This claim may be particularly true for opinion on judicial rulings because the public's connection with courts is often indirect and mediated through news coverage, rendering its opinion highly susceptible to media influence.[20] Therefore, variation in public understanding of a judicial ruling can be gauged by identifying variation in the way news media discussed the ruling.[21]

One expectation might be that media discourse about *Lawrence* was negative or that it claimed that the Court's constitutional interpretation was faulty, that the Court's opinion illustrated liberal judicial activism, or that gays and lesbians were not entitled to an already contested privacy right. This could be assessed by evaluating whether media gave more attention to Justice Scalia's dissent, which highlighted how allegedly disruptive the ruling was: "What a massive disruption to the current social order, therefore, the overruling of *Bowers* entails" precisely because it "effectively decrees the end of all morals legislation."[22] Such coverage would focus people's attention on why the ruling was incorrect, thereby depressing popular support for decriminalization. Some scholars have characterized discourse around *Lawrence* in just this way: "the decision in *Lawrence* had a negative influence on support for same-sex relations because media coverage of the decision turned negative and provided mixed signals about the Court's position by highlighting Justice Scalia's dissenting opinion."[23]

While content analysis demonstrates that media coverage was, at times, negative in this sense, the more prominent frame had very little to do with constitutional interpretation of a privacy right per se. Rather, the majority of television media discussing *Lawrence*, as detailed below, focused on the ruling's implications for same-sex marriage. In dissent, Scalia repeatedly drew attention to the ruling's implications for public relationship recognition in the form of same-sex marriage: "The Court today pretends that . . . we need not fear judicial imposition of homosexual marriage" and "This case 'does not involve' the issue of homosexual marriage only if one entertains the belief that principle and logic have nothing to do with the decisions of this Court."[24]

Given the institutional design of federalism and possibilities for state experimentation, same-sex marriage was already at the forefront of political imagination by June 2003, thereby opening the possibility that it could be an implication of *Lawrence*. In 1993, the Hawaii Supreme Court, in *Baehr v. Lewin*, ruled that such marriages were constitutionally required.[25] This decision sparked a federal response in the 1996 Defense of Marriage Act (DOMA) as well as a rash of state DOMAs or constitutional amendments to ban same-sex marriage.[26] In 1999, in *Baker v. Vermont*, the Vermont Supreme Court ruled that public recognition equal to cross-sex marriage was required by that state's constitution, resulting in legislative establishment a year later of "civil unions," which afforded the same state rights and benefits as cross-sex marriage did.[27] By June 2003, same-sex marriage was considered constitutionally required in Canada, and another case, *Goodridge v. Department of Public Health*,[28] which would result in the first state establishing same-sex marriage, was proceeding in Massachusetts.[29]

At the time of the *Lawrence* ruling, public opinion shows support for gay rights when they are framed as a matter of private liberty rather than as a matter of publicly recognized equality. By the early 2000s, Americans were more supportive of the autonomy of gays, lesbians, and bisexuals to live free from persecution—to not be fired or barred from military service because they are gay—than they were of claims seeking public recognition of homosexuality as equal to heterosexuality.[30] Personal autonomy claims such as the right to live protected from physical violence or the right to pursue a job or career without threat of being fired translate into policies such as employment nondiscrimination statutes and hate crimes laws. Because they reflect consideration for the *individual* to thrive regardless of sexual orientation, they do not necessarily invoke comparison to heterosexual *relationships* and consequently, they do not call into question the validity of heterosexuality as the preferred norm. As Gary Mucciaroni argues,

> The lack of threat that Americans perceive from protecting gays and lesbians against hate crimes and discrimination in employment and housing is critical for understanding the gay rights movement's relative success on these issues. The public overwhelmingly supports the principles that individuals should be judged solely on their performance on the job and that they should be secure from physical harm. The impersonal nature of marketplace and public safety issues raises none of the concerns that

some heterosexuals have about homosexual conduct and relationship issues. These issues are the easiest for people to bracket the question of the morality of homosexuality.[31]

By contrast, support for same-sex marriage and adoption rights has lagged behind.[32] Americans in the early 2000s were ambivalent toward LGBT-identified persons; they supported gays and lesbians as autonomous individuals having a fundamental right to live free from harm. However, when pressed on whether the state should publicly recognize homosexuals not just as individuals but also as having equal access to sanctioned relationships, Americans, until quite recently, have been unsupportive.[33]

Legal scholar Kenji Yoshino has characterized this sentiment as "gay individuals are more palatable than gay couples."[34] Same-sex-marriage and parental-rights claims are construed as gays and lesbians "flaunting their belief in their own equality."[35] Ian Ayres and Jennifer Brown have found that "public support for non-discrimination in employment is much stronger than support for non-discrimination in marriage."[36] If a gay rights claim is defined via media framing as being about equality, public support for that right could plausibly decrease.

Television Media Frames, Public Opinion, and the *Lawrence* Ruling

Government officials, legal experts, policy advocates, and media commentators engage in a continuous struggle to define a given issue through their particular frame.[37] Some versions of media framing effects theory assume that the public has limited capacity to process information and is unaware that it holds conflicting ideas on the same subject because it does not often reflect on those ideas.[38] Media report stories in ways that may prime certain considerations to be more salient and may help us to side with a particular view.[39] Nelson and Kinder suggest, "carried by mass media, frames influence public opinion by circumscribing the considerations citizens take seriously."[40] Consequently, public opinion may be an expression of those ideas brought to "the top of the head" by the way media outlets frame the news.[41]

The *Lawrence* ruling and dissent offered competing characterizations of what the decision was about. Kennedy's ruling for the majority focused on the liberty that all individuals have to choose to engage in a loving relationship free of state and cultural stigmatization. Scalia's dissent emphasized how decriminalization opens the door to state recognition of same-sex marriage as equal to cross-sex marriage. Media focus on Scalia's dissent could prime the public to think more about an issue that it mostly opposed. Furthermore, media stories highlighting the implications of *Lawrence* in terms of publicly sanctioned same-sex marriage or civil union may have triggered ideas about equality. The alternative frame, namely, that consensual homosexual sex acts should not be criminal because they are acts of personal liberty occurring in private, may also have been evident in media discourse. But, what was the balance between the two, and was there any evident change in the dominant frame over time?

To build the database of television news coverage described in table 5.1, I conducted a search for any story utilizing the word "gay" or "homosexual" between December 2002 and December 2003 on four networks: ABC, CBS, NBC, and CNN.[42] This search yielded 107 televised news reports. The year 2003 was full of news on gay-related subjects that were not directly connected to the *Lawrence* ruling, including stories on Canada's adoption of same-sex marriage, Wal-Mart's inclusion of sexual orientation in its nondiscriminatory employment policy, and the elevation of a gay New Hampshire bishop in the Episcopal Church. Stories about Wal-Mart and the Episcopal Church were removed from the database. Three stories on the legalization of same-sex marriage in Canada were included because they all aired in June, just a few days before the *Lawrence* ruling was announced and because subsequent coverage of the implications of *Lawrence* explicitly suggested that Canadian-style same-sex marriage might follow from the ruling. The remaining database of fifty-three television news clips was coded twice. The first coding tested for tone, and identified whether the coverage utilized a frame that was negative, positive, or balanced toward gay rights and/or endorsed or criticized the ruling. The second coding identified whether the coverage emphasized the ruling as reflecting privacy concerns or focused on implications for relationship recognition.

With regard to the first coding, when no obvious opinion was voiced, a positive coding was assigned when the report included more interviews of individuals applauding the *Lawrence* decision. A negative coding was assigned when the report included more interviews of people critical of the ruling, regardless of rationale, as well as when the ruling was criticized as "activist." When the coverage was about equal in terms of representing each perspective, the balanced coding was assigned, as a potential viewer would have been equally exposed to different viewpoints, and, therefore, no obvious direction in opinion formation would follow.

For example, Bob McNamara's report on public reactions to *Lawrence*, aired on CBS on June 26, 2003, was coded as negative since it concentrated more heavily on opposition to the ruling, highlighting opinions such as, "It really sickens me that this could happen," "I'm afraid that the Supreme Court Justices, like most of America, are ignorant of the homosexual lifestyle," and "It [the *Lawrence* ruling] is going to put the gay lifestyle into a better light, and this is something that most families across America are fighting." And, while the piece profiled the ecstatic reaction of the lawyer for the petitioners, Mitchell Katine, it devoted most of the segment to a southern Baptist minister, Reverend Bob Smith of the Carroll Baptist Church of Southlake, Texas, who maintained that homosexuality was a sin and that he would work with homosexual congregants who wished to, in McNamara's words, "leave the lifestyle." The minister stated, "Coming out of this [homosexual lifestyle] is a process. This is not an event. It is not a magic thing, and . . . it will be difficult." A negative coding was also given to Ted Koppel's July 2, 2003, *Nightline* interview of law professor and then-editor of the *New Republic*, Jeffrey Rosen, for the latter's framing of the *Lawrence* ruling as "unnecessarily broad," which then led to his endorsement of O'Connor's more limited concurrence. By contrast, Jeff Greenfield's analysis for CNN on June 26, 2003, was coded as positive because it concentrated exclusively on explaining the privacy jurisprudence endorsed in the Kennedy majority opinion, and it gave no analysis of the counterclaims made by Scalia. And, a CBS report on August 2, 2003, was coded as positive because its coverage of same-sex marriage focused exclusively on the endorsements of same-sex marriage by parents of gay children.

The second coding was more difficult to assign, in part because sometimes the frame shifted over the course of the report. Most of the coverage following the ruling (coverage on June 26 and after) began by stating that the question was about whether consensual homosexual sex in the privacy of one's own home could be criminalized, but it often concluded by highlighting and, indeed, emphasizing that the real question now was whether and how the ruling could jeopardize the legality of bans on same-sex marriage. Therefore, coverage that ended by discussing same-sex marriage and suggesting that that issue was really what was at stake in the *Lawrence* decision was assigned a same-sex marriage implications coding.

Some frames were clearly discernable. For example, when, on April 23, 2003, NBC reported Rick Santorum's remarks on homosexuality in the context of the Supreme Court's review of the Texas statute, it highlighted the issue of homosexual sex in the privacy of one's own home. Similarly, when on June 22, 2003, CBS reported on the upcoming ruling, the case was defined as "involving two gay men arrested for violating sodomy laws in a private home." These reports were coded as a privacy frame. When Bryan Williams introduced NBC's coverage on June 26, 2003, he noted, "Until today it was legal for individual states to at least try to legislate what went on in the bedroom. Not anymore. Homosexual conduct is no longer a crime." Also, because the segment's title graphic was "IN THE BEDROOM," this clip was coded as having a privacy frame. Finally, Koppel's interview of Rosen was assigned the privacy code, given the latter's focus on the history of privacy jurisprudence, with Rosen at one point saying,

> But as a constitutional matter, it is hard to see in the Constitution, a single right, not of privacy, but we are talking here of sexual autonomy broad enough to cover all the things that Justice Scalia is afraid of. The Constitution protects different aspects of privacy. It protects the privacy of the home against unreasonable searches and seizures. It protects conscience against false incrimination in court, but it doesn't say anything about sexual autonomy. So when—it's not just conservatives, liberals as well, and I'm part of this group—who were skeptical of cases like *Roe v. Wade*, not because—I'm enthusiastically pro-choice—but because the Court never explained very clearly where this broad right of sexual autonomy came from. It's not rooted in tradition. It's not rooted in the text. And, in this case they didn't really give an explanation, they just expanded it, and, you know made conservatives very afraid.

Other clips were assigned a marriage/public-implications frame. Jackie Judd's report for ABC on June 26, 2003, highlighted that "what really alarms conservatives is how this ruling will be interpreted in years to come and whether it opens the door to such things as legally recognized gay marriages." Cynthia McFadden's report for that same network and on that same broadcast filmed legal scholar Cass Sunstein commenting on the ruling's implications: "Obviously the decision raises questions about custody for gay couples and about marriage for gay couples, and about employment discrimination by the government against gay people, so this is a very big deal." That same report also showed the director of the ACLU's gay and lesbian rights project, Matt Coles, stating, "This case takes away one of the principle justifications for not letting same-sex couples marry." Similarly, CBS's report by Rick Schlesinger on June 26, 2003, ended with this statement: "That 1986 [*Bowers v. Hardwick*] ruling was used to prop up many laws that gay rights activists have fought against bitterly. Now they may try to use this decision as powerful ammunition possibly starting tomorrow when arguments are scheduled in New Jersey in the continuing dispute over gay marriages."

And, on June 29, a CBS report noted of *Lawrence*, "That ruling . . . knocked down one of the chief objections to same-sex marriage, that homosexual conduct is illegal. . . . Challenges to state laws barring gay marriages are already in the works and more are in the works." On the July 2, 2003, ABC *Nightline*, Ted Koppel framed the import of *Lawrence* in the following terms:

> But where the Supreme Court's decision is likely to have the greatest continuing impact is in the area of same-sex marriage. That is one of the few points of agreement between those who celebrate the Court's six to three ruling and those who denounce it. Both sides are convinced that the effect of the Court's ruling—intended or not—will be to hasten the day when same-sex marriages are legalized nationwide.

Ultimately, Koppel asked, "Will last week's landmark Supreme Court decision lead to legal gay marriages in this country?"

In short, much of the coverage skimmed over the ruling itself as a privacy decision grounded in the due process clause of the Fourteenth Amendment and, instead, asked about the implications for civil-relationship recognition. This framing reflects the way the *Lawrence* decision was embedded in a range of other gay rights concerns due to the federalist system: state courts in New Jersey and Massachusetts were already actively reviewing same-sex marriage cases when the *Lawrence* decision was handed down. Similarly, only days before *Lawrence* was handed down, Canadian courts ruled that denial of same-sex marriage violated the Canadian constitution.

Of the fifty-three coded television clips, ten were coded as positive, ten were coded as negative, and the remaining thirty-three were considered balanced. Only six mentioned the case prior to the ruling. Of these six, five were coded as neutral and one was considered positive. All negative media framing of the *Lawrence* decision occurred *after* the ruling was handed down. This finding offers some explanation for the corresponding downturn in public support for the decriminalization of homosexuality and for the lower levels of acceptance of homosexuality. On the other hand, of the total coverage of *Lawrence*, only 19 percent clearly emphasized a negative perspective, while 19 percent was positive, and the remaining 62 percent presented both perspectives in equal measure.

A more striking pattern emerged when the news clips were coded for whether the ruling was framed as a matter of individual autonomy and privacy or as having implications for relationship recognition in the form of same-sex marriage or civil union. Of the fifty-three clips, sixteen were assigned a privacy code, while thirty-three were assigned a marriage code. One discussed the implications of the ruling in terms of the status of the Don't Ask, Don't Tell policy, and three discussed the implications solely for creating a mobilization issue that might benefit Republican candidates in the 2004 election season. Thus, the majority of reports discussed the ruling in terms of whether it leads to marriage, a topic that was deeply unpopular among the American public prior to the ruling.

Of the six reports that covered the *Lawrence* case prior to the ruling, five discussed the matter solely in terms of privacy. One, which covered the Canadian court ruling requiring same-sex marriage, was coded as a marriage frame insofar as it asked whether states would be required to recognize the marriages as valid should gay Americans choose to travel to Canada to wed and then return home. Of the remaining forty-seven reports after the ruling was delivered, thirty-two of them, or 68 percent,

TABLE 5.1. Coded Television News Clips about *Lawrence v. Texas*

Network	Day	Date	Title	Code 1	Code 2
1. NBC	Mon.	Dec. 2, 2002	Supreme Court / Affirmative Action / Gay Rights	Balanced	Privacy
2. CBS	Tues.	Apr. 22, 2003	Santorum / Anti-Gay Remarks	Balanced	Privacy
3. NBC	Wed.	Apr. 23, 2003	In Depth (Santorum's Anti-Gay Remarks)	Balanced	Privacy
4. CNN	Sun.	Jun. 15, 2003	SC / Sodomy Laws / Adams, Sprigg Interviews	Balanced	Privacy
5. NBC	Thurs.	Jun. 19, 2003	Canada / Gay Marriages	Positive	SSM
6. CBS	Sun.	Jun. 22, 2003	Supreme Court / Expected Rulings	Balanced	Privacy
7. ABC	Thurs.	Jun. 26, 2003	Supreme Court / Sodomy Laws / Reaction		
A. Peter Jennings Introduction				Balanced	Privacy
B. Jackie Judd Report				Balanced	SSM
C. Cynthia McFadden Report				Balanced	SSM
8. CBS	Thurs.	Jun. 26, 2003	Supreme Court / Sodomy Laws / Reaction		
A. Dan Rather Introduction				Balanced	Privacy
B. Richard Schlessinger Report				Balanced	SSM
C. Bob McNamara Report				Negative	Privacy
9. NBC	Thurs.	Jun. 26, 2003	Supreme Court / Sodomy Laws / Reaction		
A. Bryan Williams Introduction				Balanced	Privacy
B. Pete Williams Report				Balanced	SSM
10. CNN	Thurs.	Jun. 26, 2003	Supreme Court / Sodomy Laws / Privacy		
A. Aaron Brown Introduction				Positive	Privacy
B. Bob Franken Report				Balanced	Privacy
C. Jeff Greenfield Report				Positive	Privacy
11. CNN	Fri.	Jun. 27, 2003	Segment 7 (Bad Week for Conservatives)	Negative	Privacy
12. CNN	Sat.	Jun. 28, 2003	Headlines Tonight & Tomorrow	Positive	Privacy
13. CBS	Sun.	Jun. 29, 2003	Gay Pride / Marriage	Balanced	SSM
14. ABC	Wed.	Jul. 2, 2003	Nightline: Same-Sex Marriage		
A. Ted Koppel Introduction				Balanced	SSM
B. Michel Martin Report				Positive	Privacy
C. Robert Krulwich Report				Positive	SSM
D. Koppel Interview of Jeffrey Rosen of Geo. Washington Univ. Law School				Negative	Privacy

TABLE 5.1. (*cont.*)

Network	Day	Date	Title	Code 1	Code 2
15. NBC	Wed.	Jul. 2, 2003	Bush: Iraq, Gay Marriage	Balanced	SSM
16. CNN	Sun.	Jul. 13, 2003	Massachusetts / Same-Sex Marriages	Balanced	SSM
17. CNN	Sun.	Jul. 13, 2003	Legal Roundup / Bloom, Tacopina Interviews	Positive	SSM
18. CNN	Sat.	Jul. 19, 2003	Gays in the Military / Donnelly, Greer Interviews	Balanced	DADT
19. CBS	Wed.	Jul. 30, 2003	Same-Sex Marriage / Law	Positive	SSM
20. ABC	Wed.	Jul. 30, 2003	Same-Sex Marriage	Negative	SSM
21. CNN	Wed.	Jul. 30, 2003	Bush Press Conference	Balanced	SSM
22. ABC	Thurs.	Jul. 31, 2003	A Closer Look (Disputed Union)	Negative	SSM
23. NBC	Thurs.	Jul. 31, 2003	Gay Rights / Catholic Church	Negative	SSM
24. CNN	Thurs.	Jul. 31, 2003	Segment 7 (Gays in America)	Balanced	SSM
25. CBS	Sat.	Aug. 2, 2003	Weekend Journal (Gays' Parents)	Positive	SSM
26. CBS	Tues.	Nov. 18, 2003	Massachusetts / Same-Sex Marriage		
A. Dan Rather Introduction				Balanced	SSM
B. Mika Brzezinski Report				Balanced	SSM
C. Wyatt Andrews Report				Balanced	Elec.
27. NBC	Tues.	Nov. 18, 2003	Massachusetts / Same-Sex Marriage		
A. Tom Brokaw Introduction				Balanced	SSM
B. Pete Williams Report				Balanced	SSM
C. Jim Avila Report				Balanced	SSM
28. ABC	Tues.	Nov. 18, 2003	Massachusetts / Gay Marriage / Political Fallout		
A. Ron Claiborne Report				Balanced	SSM
B. Peter Jennings Comment				Negative	SSM
C. Jake Tapper Report				Balanced	Elec.
29. CNN	Tues.	Nov. 18, 2003	Massachusetts / Gay Marriage / Political Fallout		
A. Aaron Brown Introduction				Balanced	SSM
B. Dan Lothian Report				Balanced	SSM
C. Jeff Greenfield Report				Balanced	Elec.
30. CNN	Tues.	Nov. 18, 2003	Gay Marriage / Bennett, Garry Interviews	Balanced	SSM
31. NBC	Wed.	Nov. 19, 2003	Same-Sex Marriage / Politics	Negative	SSM

TABLE 5.1. (*cont.*)

Network	Day	Date	Title	Code 1	Code 2
32. CNN	Wed.	Nov. 19, 2003	Massachusetts / Gay Marriage / Reaction	Balanced	SSM
33. CNN	Sun.	Nov. 23, 2003	National Roundup	Positive	SSM
34. NBC	Sun.	Nov. 30, 2003	Gay Marriage / Massachusetts	Negative	SSM
35. CNN	Sun.	Nov. 30, 2003	National Roundup	Negative	SSM

framed the issue around implications for same-sex marriage, while only 23 percent discussed the ruling as a matter of individual privacy. In other words, reporting shifted over time from frames emphasizing privacy to frames drawing attention to possibilities of public recognition of same-sex marriage and thus of homosexuality as a relational status equal to heterosexual coupling. Coverage after the ruling did not simply emphasize disagreement with the ruling, i.e., characterizing it as negative, but did focus on how *Lawrence* could compel public acknowledgment of homosexual relations through civil-relationship recognition.

Institutionalized Closeting: Regulatory Refusal to See Same-Sex Relationships in Policy

Federal action at the turn of the twenty-first century reflected public opinion that homosexuality was a private activity and that gay men and lesbians as individuals should not be criminalized. During the decade between 1993—when Don't Ask, Don't Tell took effect—and 2003—when the Court decriminalized consensual homosexual relations in *Lawrence*—federal authorities, through separate actions by each branch, embraced this common conception of sexuality as noncriminal but essentially private. Taken together, Don't Ask, Don't Tell (DADT), the Defense of Marriage Act (DOMA), and the Supreme Court's ruling in *Lawrence v. Texas* reveal and reinforce the government's refusal to see the gay, lesbian, or bisexual citizen. The lesbian, gay, and bisexual citizen was no longer seen as a criminal, but neither was he or she seen by the terms of the very characteristic that established the collective identity on which the post-Stonewall rights movement had been based.

As discussed in chapter 4, military service and same-sex marriage were not at the top of movement demands when debates about them became nationally prominent. The compromise policy short-handed as Don't Ask, Don't Tell began as a campaign promise from Bill Clinton in 1992 to lift the ban on gays, lesbians, and bisexuals in the military.[43] Clinton took up the repeal banner to gain credibility with gay and lesbian communities against his primary rivals, Paul Tsongas of Massachusetts and Jerry Brown of California, who both maintained stronger records of supporting LGBT rights.[44]

Clinton executed a compromise policy, originally known as "Don't Ask, Don't Tell, Don't Pursue, Don't Harass," in 1993, and Congress passed it into law in 1994. Under the policy, service members could not be asked about their sexuality, they were not to disclose it, their superiors could not investigate it without credible grounds, and they were prohibited from harassing one another about it.[45] Service members violated the statute by "telling" their homosexuality in any of three ways. First, the member would be discharged if, in the absence of mitigating circumstance, "the member has engaged in, attempted to engage in, or solicited another to engage in a homosexual act or acts."[46] Second, a soldier would be discharged if he or she "has stated that he or she is a homosexual or bisexual." However, this statement could be overruled if there were additional findings "that the member has demonstrated that he or she is not a person who engages in, attempts to engage in, has a propensity to engage in, or intends to engage in homosexual acts."[47] Finally, if the service member "has married or attempted to marry a person known to be of the same biological sex," then he or she would be discharged.[48] The "don't ask" part of the policy is not part of the statute, but follows from a Department of Defense regulatory directive, which states, "Applicants for enlistment, appointment, or induction shall not be asked or required to reveal whether they are heterosexual, homosexual, or bisexual."[49]

Don't Ask, Don't Tell continued the military ban on homosexual conduct. Yet, since the being of sexuality is expressed through the conduct of sexuality, or since identity exists through its recognition by self and other, this status-conduct distinction required hiding the conduct and thus a refusal to acknowledge the status. The homosexual person was compelled to go unseen and unheard. Consequently, Chai Feldblum criticized DADT as nothing but "a reaffirmation of the current ban."[50] Carrying this claim further, Tobias Wolff contended that DADT employed "the denial of the homosexual possibility" or the refusal to acknowledge that the soldier's sexual orientation might not be heterosexual:

> This active refusal is inscribed, explicitly, into the Don't Ask, Don't Tell policy, which contemplates the presence of gay, lesbian, and bisexual soldiers in the military and yet relies for its operation upon the widespread, consensual hallucination that these soldiers will simply disappear when they are compelled to silence. A policy that counts upon straight soldiers to deny the possibility that their fellow soldiers might be gay, despite the fact that the policy itself expressly permits gay soldiers to serve, would seem to embody "denial" in its most literal form.[51]

And, Kenji Yoshino suggested that by seeming to lift the outright ban on gays, lesbians, and bisexuals in the military, and thus appearing to liberalize the existing policy, the new DADT policy continued to do harm to gays, lesbians, and bisexuals because it "simultaneously dampens the empowering aspects and amplifies the disempowering aspects of gay invisibility."[52] If sociopolitical reform for equal rights requires the visibility of the minority making the rights claim, then Don't Ask, Don't Tell denied LGB soldiers that possibility. It shoved them into the closet, behind closed doors, expecting them to go unseen and unheard. And, if they were seen or heard in any way, then they would have violated law. Consequently, homosexuality remained incompatible with military service, and a tactic for reform, namely, visibility, was seemingly shut down.

In 1996, two years after Congress passed DADT into law, the Supreme Court evaluated the constitutionality of an amendment to the Colorado Constitution in *Romer v. Evans*. As discussed in chapter 3, Kennedy's ruling for the Court named gays and lesbians as a class as subject to a history of unjust discrimination, thereby shifting the way the Court recognized and defined homosexuality. Yet, this seemingly new move by the judiciary was already congruent and perhaps surpassed by the president and Congress when they adopted DADT.

In *Romer*, the Court declared a Colorado amendment unconstitutional because it singled out a class of people and held them outside the community, unable to access the liberties and rights granted all others: "Homosexuals, by state decree, are put in a solitary class with respect to transactions and relations in both the private and governmental spheres.

The amendment withdraws from homosexuals, but no others, specific legal protection from the injuries caused by discrimination, and it forbids reinstatement of those laws and policies."[53] In naming homosexuals as a class, "a class we shall refer to as homosexual persons or gays and lesbians," the Colorado constitution and Justice Kennedy, for the majority, redefined what homosexuality was.[54] It was not merely a sex act, but an identity of a person or group of persons. And, while a state may criminalize an act, it may not discriminate against a person or a class of persons without a rational purpose.[55] A century after *Plessy v. Ferguson*, which maintained state segregation laws based on race, the *Romer* Court refused to commit the same error now with sexual orientation.[56] For the *Romer* majority, a person could not be legitimately discriminated against on the basis of who he or she was, but could be sanctioned for what he or she did.[57] Indeed, that action could be public (as in a soldier disclosing or performing his or homosexuality or bisexuality) or private (insofar as *Romer* did not strike down state laws criminalizing private consensual same-sex intercourse). This status-conduct distinction enabled *Bowers* and *Romers* to coexist even as it created a readily identifiable friction: homosexuality had been defined for nearly a century of medical science, social movement activism, and state policy as manifest through behavior.[58] The *Romer* ruling maintained a status-conduct distinction at the foundation of DADT as well as hewed closely to the private-public distinction of sexuality also evident in DADT enforcement. It was thus fully in line with the logic of DADT, and it was reinforced by congressional action to pass the Defense of Marriage Act (DOMA) later in 1996.

DADT and *Romer* can be and have been construed as gay rights victories; DADT represented at least a rhetorical shift on equality of access for LGB service members—the official ban on gay, lesbian, and bisexual persons was, after all, officially no longer in existence—and *Romer* stood as a clear declaration that discrimination against LGB individuals as a class of persons was unconstitutional. Therefore, 1996 appears an oddly schizophrenic year, in which the Court handed gay rights advocates a victory and the elected branches handed them a striking defeat in the form of DOMA, which, for purposes of federal recognition, defined marriage as a union of one man and one woman. Michael Klarman sums up the conventional wisdom: "At almost precisely the same time that Congress debated DOMA in response to the *Baehr* backlash, the

U.S. Supreme Court struck a blow in favor of gay rights in a narrowly reasoned decision that ruffled few feathers."[59]

The distinct issues that each branch confronted might explain these divergent moves. While Congress and the executive branch dealt with the then-unpopular specter of same-sex marriage, the Court's *Romer* ruling confronted the possibility of gays, lesbians, and bisexuals being discriminated against in employment, housing, and public accommodations. While the elected branches faced down same-sex sexual relationships, the Court was viewing LGB persons not in a relational context but as individuals. And, as public opinion largely supported gays and lesbians having the autonomy and personal freedom to lead productive lives without fear of employment discrimination, Klarman's account of why little public backlash erupted in the wake of the *Romer* ruling is readily understandable.[60]

From another perspective, *Romer*, DADT, and DOMA are hardly out of alignment. Indeed, DADT and *Romer*'s common relegation of homosexuality to the private sphere and the state's refusal to recognize gay, lesbian, or bisexual sexuality was employed once more when Congress passed DOMA. DOMA was initially introduced in May 1996, the same month when the Supreme Court announced its holding in *Romer*. The legislation was passed and sent to the president for his signature in September. The process through which DOMA was passed indicates the kinds of recognitions the state was willing to grant gay and lesbian citizens. DOMA and the Employment Non-Discrimination Act (ENDA) were brought to a vote on the same day in September 1996.[61] ENDA, as discussed in chapter 4, banned employment discrimination on the basis of sexual orientation. That ENDA lost by only one vote but that DOMA suffered a resounding defeat was not only a political ploy by which members of Congress might avoid the accusation of being antigay and the accusation of undermining traditional marriage. It also reflected the emerging decade's theme with regard to the way the state was willing to see gay and lesbian citizens. The state was willing to see them as autonomous individuals entitled to protections to pursue lives and careers that accorded with personal autonomy. In this way, Senate votes for ENDA accorded with patterns in public opinion, which tended to increasingly support nondiscrimination in employment, in military service, and in decriminalization.

Nevertheless, the end result—the failure of ENDA and the passage of DOMA—also revealed that the state closed its eyes to the very quality that defined identity as gay and lesbian, namely, relational sexuality. DOMA refused to see the relationship at the core of sexual identity, that the identity is expressed through connection with another. While DOMA construed the possibility of relational sexuality through marriage, the refusal to see any relational same-sex sexuality—whether it be a one-night stand or a monogamous, committed, long-term relationship—was reflected by the resounding support for DOMA, which paralleled the public's sustained view in the mid-1990s that same-sex sexual acts were immoral, that same-sex relationships should not be state sanctioned, and that same-sex sexual relations were generally "icky."[62]

In short, the DOMA-ENDA pairing rested on the same logic as DADT: the state would not officially criminalize the identity, but it would also not recognize much less sanction the relational activities that give that identity meaning. Furthermore, that ENDA failed is further evidence that *public* expressions of sexuality were not permitted. Employment protections against firing or refusing to hire on the basis of sexual orientation require that sexual orientation be seen and acknowledged. That no such protection passed, even if that law was meant to protect the *individual* and not even recognize a homosexual *relationship*, indicated the extent of the state's refusal to see sexuality at all. Public expressions of sexuality, whether through the individual or relational, were not permissible. Both the status-conduct distinction and the private/public boundaries of sexuality, articulated in the DADT policy and reiterated by the *Romer* majority, were expressed once more in the congressional vote coupling of ENDA and DOMA.

Institutionalized Closeting: Regulatory Refusal to See Same-Sex Relationships in Law

This compulsion to privatize same-sex sexuality such that it was not in and of itself a rationale for discrimination but public expression of it may be (whether publicly expressed in the military or in the workplace) was evident in two Supreme Court rulings in the 1990s besides *Romer*. First, in 1995, the Court ruled unanimously in *Hurley v. Irish-American*

Gay, Lesbian, and Bisexual Group of Boston (GLIB) that a gay rights
organization could be banned from the annual St. Patrick's Day Parade
even though the parade was supported by the city of Boston. Because the
parade was funded through taxes and utilized police services, it potentially fit the definition of public accommodation, and Massachusetts
banned discrimination based on sexual orientation in public accommodations.[63] The ruling overturned decisions by the lower state trial court
and the Supreme Court of Massachusetts.

The Court viewed the parade as an expressive activity and not a public accommodation. Writing for the unanimous Court, Justice Souter
noted that "'[p]arades are public dramas of social relations, and in them
performers define who can be a social actor and what subjects and ideas
are available for communication and consideration.'"[64] Parades depend,
by definition, on being seen such that, as Souter noted, "if a parade or
demonstration receives no media coverage, it may as well not have happened."[65] Furthermore, GLIB was formed to be expressive; its purpose
was to be seen:

> In 1992, a number of gay, lesbian, and bisexual descendants of the Irish
> immigrants joined together with other supporters to form the respondent
> organization, GLIB, to march in the parade as a way to express pride in
> their Irish heritage as openly gay, lesbian, and bisexual individuals, to
> demonstrate that there are such men and women among those so de-
> scended, and to express their solidarity with like individuals who sought
> to march in New York's St. Patrick's Day Parade.[66]

GLIB was not a gay rights organization operating with a broad agenda
of political and social goals like the Human Rights Campaign, Gay
and Lesbian Allies and Defenders, or the National Gay and Lesbian
Task Force. It "was formed for the very purpose of marching in" the
St. Patrick's Day parade.[67] For the Court, this conflict was between two
identifiable speech positions: the organizers' aim not to endorse the gay
organization versus the gay organization's aim to be visible. Requiring
GLIB's inclusion would alter the message of the parade:

> The message it disfavored is not difficult to identify. Although GLIB's
> point (like the Council's) is not wholly articulate, a contingent march-

ing behind the organization's banner would at least bear witness to the fact that some Irish are gay, lesbian, or bisexual, and the presence of the organized marchers would suggest their view that people of their sexual orientations have as much claim to unqualified social acceptance as heterosexuals and indeed as members of parade units organized around other identifying characteristics. The parade's organizers may not believe these facts about Irish sexuality to be so, or they may object to unqualified social acceptance of gays and lesbians or have some other reason for wishing to keep GLIB's message out of the parade. But whatever the reason, it boils down to the choice of a speaker not to propound a particular point of view, and that choice is presumed to lie beyond the government's power to control.[68]

The recognition sought by GLIB was denied. Souter's ruling established that sexual orientation is, indeed, expressive and that its content and meaning relies upon recognition. But, it contended that this recognition need not be granted, at least insofar as the state cannot require private entities to grant recognition.[69]

Five years later, in *Boy Scouts of America v. Dale*, a closely divided Court ruled that the Boy Scouts could expel James Dale for his expressed homosexuality.[70] Like Massachusetts, New Jersey public accommodations law bans discrimination based on sexual orientation, and Dale maintained that the Boy Scouts of America (BSA) qualified as a public accommodation.[71] Also, like Massachusetts, state courts found for Dale.[72] The Supreme Court reversed, with five justices finding that the BSA was a private expressive association, the identity of which was premised on the exclusion of homosexuals.[73]

The majority contended that "to determine whether a group is protected by the First Amendment's expressive associational right, we must determine whether the group engages in 'expressive association.' . . . [T]o come within its ambit, a group must engage in some form of expression, whether it be public or private." [74] The Scouts were expressive because the organization was animated by a mission to "instill values in young people."[75] The audience is comprised of these young people, and that mission is premised on the Scout Oath, which requires these young people to be "morally straight," and the Scout Law, which requires that they be "clean."[76]

It is not at all clear that homosexuality violates these mandates. As Justice Stevens noted in his dissent, "It is plain as the light of day that neither one of these principles—'morally straight' and 'clean'—says the slightest thing about homosexuality. Indeed, neither term in the Boy Scout's Law and Oath expresses any position whatsoever on sexual matters."[77] To meet this criticism, the Court majority asserted that the Scouts had to have articulated clear guidelines against homosexuality. It cited the 1978 position statement of the Boy Scouts' Executive Committee as a statement against homosexuality:

Q. May an individual who openly declares himself to be a homosexual be a volunteer Scout leader?

A. No. The Boy Scouts of America is a private, membership organization and leadership therein is a privilege and not a right. We do not believe that homosexuality and leadership in Scouting are appropriate. We will continue to select only those who in our judgment meet our standards and qualifications for leadership.[78]

The Court also pointed to the BSA's 1991 position statement: "We believe that homosexual conduct is inconsistent with the requirement in the Scout Oath that a Scout be morally straight and in the Scout Law that a Scout be clean in word and deed, and that homosexuals do not provide a desirable role model for Scouts."[79] And, it relied on a 1993 statement: "We do not believe that homosexuals provide a role model consistent with these expectations. Accordingly, we do not allow for the registration of avowed homosexuals as members or as leaders of the BSA."[80] The majority posited that these statements comprised a coherent position on the incompatibility of homosexuality with Scouting values. Having demonstrated the BSA to be an expressive association, the identity of which was premised upon excluding homosexuality, the Court majority indicated that including Dale within its ranks would undermine the expression and thus alter the identity:

[W]e must also give deference to an association's view of what would impair its expression. . . . That is not to say that an expressive association can erect a shield against antidiscrimination laws simply by asserting that mere acceptance of a member from a particular group would impair its message. But here Dale, by his own admission, is one of a group of gay Scouts who have "become leaders in their community and are open and honest about their sexual orientation."[81]

The majority relied on the position in *Hurley* that including a speaker whose speech is antithetical to organizational identity undermines First Amendment freedoms of expression and association: "The presence of an avowed homosexual and gay rights activist in an assistant scoutmaster's uniform sends a distinctly different message from the presence of a heterosexual assistant scoutmaster who is on record disagreeing with Boy Scouts policy. The Boy Scouts has a First Amendment right to choose to send one message but not the other."[82]

Justice Stevens, writing the dissent in which three other justices joined, challenged that the ban on homosexuality was integral to BSA identity. If it were not, then the organization could be held accountable to the New Jersey public accommodation law. The Boy Scouts' mission made no mention of its professed antihomosexuality, and the organization was hostile to the very exclusion that it now sought to permit: "Neither the charter nor the bylaws of the Boy Scouts of America permits the exclusion of any boy."[83] And, Souter pointed to how the Scout Handbook indicated that the BSA was the last place a scout should turn for sexual education.[84] All this, coupled with BSA's openness to people of various faiths, led Stevens to conclude, "it is even more difficult to discern any shared or common moral stance on homosexuality."[85] Then, the dissent evaluated the same documents upon which the majority relied to establish its claim that the BSA was premised on its antihomosexuality.

First, the 1978 memo indicated that a scout leader should be terminated if he openly declared his homosexuality, as Dale had done, but it also indicated this could be done *only* "in the absence of any law to the contrary. . . . In the event that such a law was applicable, it would be necessary for the Boy Scouts of America to obey it."[86] New Jersey's public accommodations statute was a law to the contrary, which would seem to override the Scout's lawsuit by its own admission.

Second, documents from the 1990s were irrelevant as they were issued *after* Dale's expulsion and therefore constituted post hoc justification. The first statement tied the exclusionary policy to the Scout Oath and the Scout Law in much the same way that the majority opinion did. But the latter rested on a different rationale for exclusion; expulsion followed from "the expectatio[n] that [the BSA's] members preferred to exclude homosexuals."[87] This shift was important for Stevens because it demonstrated that the ban did not constitute "any expressive activity or any moral view about homosexuality. It was simply an exclusionary membership policy similar to those we have held insufficient in the past."[88] The BSA never took a definitive stance on homosexuality and the handbook definitions of "morally straight" and "clean" bear little resemblance to the 1991 and 1993 statements. The failure to reconcile them suggests no coherent expressive meaning, and the dissent maintained, "At a minimum, a group seeking to prevail over an antidiscrimination law must adhere to a clear and unequivocal view."[89] Dissenters rejected the notion that the BSA was an expressive association whose identity was integrally tied to a coherent and consistent position against homosexuality: "To prevail in asserting a right of expressive association as a defense to a charge of violating an antidiscrimination law, the organization must at least show it has adopted and advocated an unequivocal position inconsistent with a position advocated or epitomized by the person whom the organization seeks to exclude."[90] The BSA, according to the four dissenters, had not done so.

Even if the Court followed the dissenters' position, that possible ruling would still have relied on the same distinction of private status versus public conduct that coursed through DADT, the ENDA-DOMA pairing, *Hurley*, and *Romer*. Stevens maintained that the BSA could be against homosexuality, but the 1990s statements, if they meant anything, were only addressing codes of conduct, not orientation. The BSA outlawed conduct, not status or orientation. But, now, according to Stevens, it sought to exclude Dale on the basis of status or orientation rather than conduct. The dissent maintained that there was no reason to suggest that Dale's conduct was in any way contrary to the Oath or Scout Law.

However, if *Hurley* holds, then Dale's First Amendment right to advocate for gay rights does not extend to his role as a scoutmaster. If Dale, in Scout uniform, advocated for gay rights, then he could plausibly be undermining the BSA's expressive identity, if it is conceded that the BSA's organizational identity was premised on banning homosexuality (which is extraordinarily difficult to concede, especially since the BSA has since relaxed its restrictions to permit the participation of out gay scouts).[91] But, no evidence was presented that Dale engaged in such advocacy while in uniform. And, the BSA did not claim that it excluded Dale for advocating gay rights as a scoutmaster. Nevertheless, the majority contended that Dale's merely being an openly gay man carried a political message contrary to the identity of the BSA. Dale's presence as an out gay man, according to the majority, contradicted and undermined the identity of Scouting.

And, so, with a bare majority, the Court maintained its requirement that homosexuality be closeted, shielded from view, and compelled into silence. While the Court, in *Hurley* and *Dale*, continued to express the notion, laid out most clearly in *Romer*, that homosexuality was a status and not merely a sexual act, it placed clear limits on whether and how that status could be publicly expressed and acknowledged. As legal scholar Jason Pierceson has summarized these rulings' implications, "When you speak out, your right to antidiscrimination protection ends."[92]

This desire to keep homosexual conduct and expression private even if homosexual status or identity was no longer clear grounds for state-sanctioned discrimination reached its apotheosis in *Lawrence v. Texas*. *Lawrence* has been called the *Brown v. Board of Education* and the *Loving v. Virginia* moment of the LGBT-rights movement.[93] However, unlike *Brown* and *Loving*, *Lawrence* was not decided as a matter of equal protection.[94] Rather, Justice Kennedy subsumed an equal protection claim under fundamental rights as protected by due process: "As an alternative argument in this case, counsel for the petitioners and some amici contend that *Romer* provides the basis for declaring the Texas statute invalid under the Equal Protection Clause. That is a tenable argument, but we conclude the instant case requires us to address whether *Bowers* itself has continuing validity."[95] Kennedy sought to reverse *Bowers* fully. To do so, he had to engage *Bowers* on its own assumptions. By directly engaging the fundamental right claim, he linked conduct and identity in precisely the opposite way in which *Romer* (and DADT, *Hurley*, *Dale*, and ENDA-DOMA) had decoupled them:

> Equality of treatment and the due process right to demand respect for
> conduct protected by the substantive guarantee of liberty are linked in

important respects, and a decision on the latter point advances both in-terests. If protected conduct is made criminal and the law which does so remains unexamined for its substantive validity, its stigma might remain even if it were not enforceable as drawn for equal protection reasons. When homosexual conduct is made criminal by the law of the State, that declaration in and of itself is an invitation to subject homosexual persons to discrimination in both the public and in the private spheres. The cen-tral holding of *Bowers* has been brought in question by this case, and it should be addressed. Its continuance as precedent demeans the lives of homosexual persons.[96]

Criminalizing conduct stigmatizes status insofar as the status gains meaning and is only cognizable to self and other through conduct. To say that a homosexual person is not criminal and is thus entitled to pro-tections against discrimination, yet to maintain criminal sanction of the homosexual act makes no sense as the act constitutes and expresses the identity. This was indeed Justice Scalia's claim in his dissent in *Romer*, when he defended the constitutionality of Colorado's Amendment 2:

> If it is constitutionally permissible for a State to make homosexual con-duct criminal, surely it is constitutionally permissible for a State to en-act other laws merely disfavoring homosexual conduct. (As the Court of Appeals for the District of Columbia Circuit has aptly put it: "If the Court [in Bowers] was unwilling to object to state laws that criminalize behavior that defines the class, it is hardly open . . . to conclude that state sponsored discrimination against the class is invidious. After all, there can be no more palpable discrimination against a class than making the conduct that defines the class criminal." *Padula v. Webster*, 822 F. 2d 97, 103 (1987).)[97]

If the Court permitted the criminalization of the homosexual act, surely it must permit the exclusion of those who engage in the act from the political community. What is criminalization if not a form of exclusion? In *Romer*, Scalia calls the distinction between sexual orientation and sex-ual conduct "a distinction without a difference."[98] In *Lawrence*, Kennedy responds to Scalia's claims in *Romer* by agreeing that the status-conduct distinction indeed makes no sense. Status and conduct are linked: the criminalization of one leads to the inevitable and unjust stigmatization of the other in violation of an equality principle. To render the choice to engage in homosexual intimacy a fundamental right of privacy, according to Kennedy, is to remove a primary and institutionally reinforced rationale for stigma.

But in subsuming a claim of discrimination as unequal under due process liberty or privacy concern, *Lawrence* stands primarily as a ruling about individual autonomy rather than a ruling about equality. This distinction is heightened by the fact that *Lawrence* did not engage whether gays and lesbians constituted a suspect class such that any equal protection claim they might make would be potentially reviewed under a higher scrutiny threshold. Kennedy's ruling makes no mention of scrutiny levels or even equal protection more broadly construed. By avoiding an equal protection argument, the Court sidestepped the question of whether sexuality was a suspect classification or whether gays, lesbians, or bisexuals constituted a suspect class.[99]

Lawrence illustrated the Court's propensity to favor arguments highlighting liberty claims or asserting that individuals, as befits human dignity, should be entitled to respect for their autonomous choices. As legal scholar Kenji Yoshino summarizes this trend,

> In an era when the Supreme Court has closed many civil rights doors, it has left this one wide open. It is much more sympathetic to "liberty" claims about freedoms we all hold than to "equality" claims asserted by a subset of the population. It is easy to see why. Equality claims—such as group-based accommodation claims—inevitably involve the Court in picking favorites among groups. In an increasingly pluralistic society, the Court understandably wishes to steer clear of that enterprise. Liberty claims, on the other hand, emphasize what all Americans (or more precisely, all persons within the jurisdiction of the United States) have in common. The claim that we all have a right to sexual intimacy . . . will hold no matter how many new groups proliferate in this country.[100]

Even the stunning judicial victory for gay and lesbian rights, which *Lawrence* was, not only maintained the closet but kept within a trajectory of jurisprudence evident in *Romer*, *Hurley*, and *Dale*. Although gay rights advocates lost in *Hurley* and *Dale*, the Court's rationale from

Romer through *Lawrence* is consistent: permit the identity, but shield the act, conduct, or expression of that identity from the state's sight. *Lawrence* decriminalized the sexual activity but relegated it to the closet, or at least behind the bedroom door, out of the state's sight. The gay, lesbian, or bisexual citizen is not seen. Indeed, the majority in *Lawrence* defined the issue as deserving constitutional respect due to its deeply private nature. As a matter of ideational development, *Lawrence*, even as it upsets the tradition of *stare decisis*, follows the same logic of privatization already endorsed by both elected branches by the mid-1990s and maintains the same privatization rationale relied upon in *Hurley*, *Romer*, and *Dale*.

Kennedy's ruling blurred the privatization impulse evident in DADT and DOMA by drawing explicit analogies between private consensual same-sex intimacy and state-sanctioned civil marriage: "To say that the issue in *Bowers* was simply the right to engage in certain sexual conduct demeans the claim the married individual put forward, just as it would demean a married couple were it to be said marriage is simply about the right to have sexual intercourse."[101] Relying on this analogy, David Eng contends that the Court made a significant move toward liberal inclusion:

> In conferring on gays and lesbians the Constitutional right to "intimate sexual conduct" as couples ("two persons"), and by describing this right to privacy "as an integral part of human freedom," the majority opinion in *Lawrence* constituted gay and lesbian recognition, enfranchisement, and inclusion among "We the People" as a privileged relationship between freedom and intimacy, domesticity and couplehood.[102]

Yet, Kennedy explicitly denied such formal public sanction: "The statutes [under review] do seek to control a personal relationship that, whether or not entitled to formal recognition in the law, is within the liberty of persons to choose without being punished as criminals."[103] At the end of his ruling, he rejected recognition outright: "The present case . . . does not involve whether the government must give formal recognition to any relationship that homosexual persons seek to enter."[104]

While the intimate association is no longer criminal, the Court afforded *no* recognition of a relationship of which such intimacy is constitutive. Homosexual intimacy was held beyond the state's view; neither was it criminal nor was it given the public recognition of heterosexual intimacy through marriage. Although the Court now admitted that intimacy and sexual activity were expressive and constitutive of gay, lesbian, and bisexual identity, and the landmark nature of that claim should not be minimized, *Lawrence* maintained the requirement of keeping that identity shielded away just as *Hurley*, *Dale*, and DADT, DOMA, and ENDA's failure all refused to permit state sanctioning of the public expression of that identity.

By drawing attention to the way Kennedy *preserved* the federal government's ongoing blindness to the sexuality of its gay and lesbian citizens, the *Lawrence* ruling can be seen in a new light. Focusing on modalities of changing conceptions of homosexuality and the consequent scope and dimension of regulatory power involved brings into clearer relief, in ways counter to conventional wisdom, the actions of different federal branches. Uncovering this modality of privatization of same-sex relationships repositions the Court as the last mover in its *Romer* and *Lawrence* rulings. *Hurley*, *Romer*, *Dale*, and *Lawrence* are all of a piece in that each defined homosexuality as an individual identity or status and none sanctioned the public acknowledgment of that status. The Court is the *last* governing institution to take this stance. The military first adopted this position of privatization through the executive order of Don't Ask, Don't Tell, which was later reconfigured as congressional statute. The executive and legislative branches reinforced this modality of privatization by passing DOMA and by failing to pass ENDA. The Court perpetuated this privatization of homosexual identity and same-sex relations after that modality gained traction through executive and legislative action.

That the Court's rulings in *Hurley*, *Romer*, *Dale*, and *Lawrence* reflect an underlying logic of closeting same-sex relations, already embodied in actions taken and policies supported by the elected federal branches, further calls into doubt the characterization of the Court as a counter-majoritarian institution.[105] This criticism, which relies on the Court's unelected status, was articulated and dismissed by Alexander Hamilton in *Federalist 78*,[106] and it became a prominent model by which to understand popular backlash and elected-branch hostilities toward the Court for much of the twentieth century.[107] More recently, this view has been critiqued.[108] Scholars have argued that the Court is part of a political regime that is often ideologically aligned with the elected branches[109] and have described how the elected branches can utilize the Court as a tool to achieve their own ends.[110]

Many scholars have begun referring to a majoritarian Court, by which they mean that the Court's rulings are often aligned with and reflect public opinion, particularly to maintain public support for institutional legitimacy.[111] And, the Court has articulated various positions to demonstrate that even when overturning precedent, it is hardly acting in a way that is countermajoritarian. For example, in *Lawrence*, Kennedy pointed to how a minority of states maintain statutory bans on sodomy and that the United States, in permitting these laws, was out of step with developments in other Western democracies. The Court has sought to position its rulings, at least rhetorically, as reflecting democratic trends, in part to maintain its institutional legitimacy.[112]

This chapter adds to that notion of the Court's majoritarianism by showing how that majoritarian impulse was also evident in its position as a last mover to adopt a regulatory recognition already operating in policies authorized by the legislative and executive branches. Thus, majoritarianism was not only demonstrated via alignment with public opinion or through a strategic imperative to maintain institutional legitimacy and not incur the wrath of the elected branches. It has also been manifest in the congruence of ideas and assumptions that underlie the actions taken by each branch. The Court accepted that gays, lesbians, and bisexuals constituted an oppressed minority in *Romer*, and it ruled to eliminate this oppression while also shunting the oppressed out of sight. In this way, the Court's rulings in *Romer* and *Lawrence* mimic the logics that underscored the elected branches' actions of developing and implementing Don't Ask, Don't Tell. The compromise policy officially lifted the military ban on gays, lesbians, and bisexuals in the armed forces, but their service was conditioned on their silence and invisibility. If Congress had wanted to acknowledge and remedy institutionalized prejudice against gay, lesbian, and bisexual individuals, it could have passed the ENDA. Similarly, if the Court had wanted to acknowledge the institutionalized prejudice, it could have raised the scrutiny level applied to statutes that classify on the basis of sexual orientation. Neither branch did so. ENDA remains only a possibility, continuously introduced but not yet passed. The Supreme Court has not used higher scrutiny for laws that discriminate on the basis of sexual orientation.[113] These parallel logics and their consequences not only indicate judicial congruence with the federal branches, which illustrates how the Court is hardly out of step with the other branches, but they also highlight how the federal form of regulatory recognition of LGB citizens was limited to maintaining their noncriminality and invisibility.

Conclusion

This chapter has highlighted two conceptions of homosexuality evident in the 1990s and early 2000s in public opinion, federal policy, and law: as a private behavior in which people have an individual liberty to engage without fear of persecution and criminalization and as an identity that gains expression in an intimate relational status, which should be respected as a legitimate private choice but which may or may not be entitled to formal public recognition from the state. Justice Kennedy's ruling for the majority in *Lawrence v. Texas* walked the line between these conceptions. While he maintained that the ruling to decriminalize consensual homosexual sex did not extend to state recognition of the relationship in which the sexual act occurs, he nevertheless contended that to understand the decision as solely about behavior was to reduce opposite-sex marriage to the heterosexual sex act. Antonin Scalia, in dissent, saw no limits to Kennedy's ruling; instead, *Lawrence* represented judicial nullification of all morals legislation.

These two conceptions of homosexuality provide a way to explain why public opinion on a range of matters related to gay rights— acceptance of homosexuality, support for decriminalization, and a trend of increasing support for relationship recognition—dramatically shifted in the immediate wake of the *Lawrence* decision. Televised news media coverage of *Lawrence* throughout 2003 indicated that the shift in public opinion corresponds to media focus on gay and lesbian equality as it manifests in the claim of public relationship recognition. The frame that focused attention on same-sex marriage created a depressive effect.

The effect did not last. The resurgence of public support for gay and lesbian rights claims to pre-*Lawrence* levels raises questions about the media's influence on public opinion. The pattern may indicate that the media's effect degrades over time, suggesting either that people do hold something akin to true beliefs about a given issue, which may be disrupted when there is a tremendous amount of coverage on that issue but, after the media frenzy fades, may settle back to their initial "true" position. Indeed, social values issues, which may more readily be understood and categorized in terms of absolutes, may be less susceptible to media effects than beliefs about more nuanced policy matters, such as fiscal or monetary policy, which tend to be more complex and not invoke "primordial loyalties."[114]

But, as this chapter has also sought to illustrate, media effects could be considered in more institutional than psychological terms. The media's effect may not only be on people's decision about what or how to think. In addition, media frames function as empirically observable data about ideas and about how discourse takes new form over time. Media framing of *Lawrence* may have begun a process whereby LGBT communities and the broader public came to understand the primary issue of the LGBT rights movements to be first and foremost about equality and less about sexual privacy and autonomy. News media may have functioned as a primary agent in fostering a shift toward an alternative modality of regulatory recognition—same-sex marriage—as a possibility in the public imagination. If that is the case, then the media's effect on structuring the agenda of the movement and the public's perception of it may be substantial indeed, just in a way distinct from the "direct effects" conceptualization reviewed above.

This possibility points back to the institutionalist perspective on prejudice and homophobia raised by American political development scholars such as Paul Frymer, introduced in chapter 1. Prejudice is not only an individual psychological trait but is also a social phenomenon empirically traceable through policy and discourse, reinforced and validated by institutions. News media is one institution that plays a key role in the dynamic of ideational change over time. As Frymer argues, reliance on individual psychology and the irrationality of prejudice promotes a shallow accounting of how prejudice shapes and is shaped by our political and cultural institutions: "By treating race and racism merely as an evil deriving from individual sickness, it makes it difficult if not impossible, for politics to regulate race and racism, and denies the ways that our political institutions are active in not just enabling but creating racist thought and behavior."[115] An account of sexuality politics oriented toward the institutional and ideational context, such as that offered in this book, does not stop at individual psychology as the source of the explanatory mechanisms for political, social, or legal change. Rather, it considers homophobia as "embedded in and produced by institutions."[116] Media construction of homosexuality as a private intimate "bedroom" matter or as a matter of publicly recognized equality is part of a deep pattern of "political reasoning," which "is always conducted as part of a struggle to control which images of the world govern policy."[117]

Finally, APD scholars have defined political development to connote "a durable shift in authority . . . [or] a change in the locus or direction of control, resulting in a new distribution of authority among persons or organizations within the polity at large or between them and their counterparts outside."[118] Conventional wisdom tends to review the 1990s as a decade marked by various wins and losses for LGBT-rights advocates, suggesting no consistency or durability. While full repeal of the military ban did not materialize, DADT was secured. While DOMA passed, ENDA received the most senatorial support to date, coming just one vote shy of passage. While gay rights advocates were handed a unanimous loss by the Supreme Court in the *Hurley* case, a year later they secured a major victory in *Romer*, only to lose once more in *Dale*, and then secure a spectacular victory in *Lawrence*, one sought for decades. But, against this narrative of mixed results that might indicate the inconsistency of public opinion about gay and lesbian rights, as gays and lesbians themselves became more visible and inched toward public acceptance, this chapter has brought to light a consistent frame of recognition in the executive, congressional, and judicial actions between 1993 and 2003. All were manifestations of a modality of privatization, of permitting the lesbian, gay, or bisexual person to exist free from criminal sanction so long as he or she remained beyond public view. DADT, the failure of ENDA, DOMA, *Hurley*, *Romer*, *Dale*, and *Lawrence*—all are animated by that principle.

That all federal authorities—Congress, the president, and the Supreme Court—passed and implemented policies or wrote decisions that adopted the same logic of recognizing homosexuality as noncriminal but also privatizing same-sex relationships is evidence that a fourth modality of regulatory recognition—privatization—was a comprehensive and durable ideational, policy, and legal shift. But, by the time the Court fully endorsed it with the *Lawrence* ruling, this durability was already giving way. That Scalia could raise the specter of same-sex marriage to delegitimize the majority's holding and that this dissent would resonate so intensely as to dominate the coverage of the ruling testifies to how the modality of regulatory recognition of gay and lesbian citizenship was already changing.

When developmental scholars have discussed durable shifts in governing authorities, they have tended to focus on institutional change, paying separate and perhaps even less attention to the roles played by cultural and ideational change.[119] By drawing attention to media frames and highlighting a particular moment in the shift in public discourse about same-sex relations—by pinpointing a clear pivot from private sexual conduct to publicly recognized relationship—this chapter highlights how ideas are important to the process of durable shifts. Media frames and discourse are an empirically identifiable source of those ideas. In this chapter, they enable the identification and tracking of ideas about gay and lesbian rights claims even when institutional change has lagged. In short, a developmental perspective focused on media framing as one of many possible processes within the struggle to define political ideas may help us to understand the dynamics of ideational development so necessary for institutional change to proceed.

6

A History of Discrimination

Gays and Lesbians as a Suspect Class

The Supreme Court has yet to rule on the appropriate level of scrutiny for classifications based on sexual orientation. It has, however, rendered a number of decisions that set forth the criteria that should inform this and any other judgment as to whether heightened scrutiny applies: (1) whether the group in question has suffered a history of discrimination; (2) whether individuals "exhibit obvious, immutable, or distinguishing characteristics that define them as a discrete group"; (3) whether the group is a minority or is politically powerless; and (4) whether the characteristics distinguishing the group have little relation to legitimate policy objectives or to an individual's "ability to perform or contribute to society" [citations omitted].
—Attorney General Eric Holder, 2011[1]

Windsor, of course, did not expressly announce the level of scrutiny it applied to the equal protection claim at issue in the case, but an express declaration is not necessary. . . . *Windsor* review is not rational basis review. In its words and its deed, *Windsor* established a level of scrutiny for classifications based on sexual orientation that is unquestionably higher than rational basis review. In other words, *Windsor* requires that heightened scrutiny be applied to equal protection claims involving sexual orientation.
—Judge Stephen Reinhardt, *SmithKline Beecham Corporation v. Abbott Laboratories*, 2014[2]

On February 10, 2014, the attorney general of Nevada, Catherine Cortez Masto, announced that she would withdraw the state's brief, submitted in January, defending its constitutional amendment banning same-sex marriage. The amendment's constitutionality was pending before the U.S. Court of Appeals for the Ninth Circuit.[3] Three weeks earlier, in *SmithKline Beecham Corporation v. Abbott Laboratories*, Judge Stephen Reinhardt ruled for a unanimous Ninth Circuit that gays and lesbians constituted a suspect class and that laws classifying on the basis of sexual orientation were subject to heightened scrutiny.[4] Reinhardt invoked the jurisprudential doctrines of tiered scrutiny and suspect class, developed over the latter half of the twentieth century, whereby judges are more skeptical of laws that target a particular class of people, especially if that class has suffered an identifiable history of discrimination or is considered politically powerless. Heightened scrutiny holds that unless these laws are substantially related to an important government aim, they run afoul of the Fourteenth Amendment's guarantee of equal protection. Masto contended that Nevada's constitutional ban on same-sex marriage would not withstand this higher standard of judicial review.

As Attorney General Eric Holder's 2011 letter—quoted at the opening of this chapter—indicates, a suspect or protected class is a legal designation granted to classes of individuals that have endured a history of discrimination where that discrimination is based on a distinguishable or immutable characteristic and the group has been rendered politically powerless by that discrimination.[5] If suspect-class status is granted, then judges scrutinize laws that classify by that identity more closely than the lowest threshold of rational basis review requires. The rational basis standard is most deferential to the legislature; it stipulates only that laws must be rationally related to a legitimate government purpose.[6] The highest level of scrutiny tends to be most fatal to a statute. Even so, laws have survived strict scrutiny and failed rational basis review.[7] Nevertheless, lawyers seeking to have an antigay law overturned have generally tried to convince a judge that gays and lesbians constitute a suspect class and that sexual orientation is a suspect classification so that laws that affect this class or invoke this classification are reviewed with higher scrutiny.[8]

The Ninth Circuit's designation of gays and lesbians as a suspect class and sexual orientation as a suspect classification was based on the Supreme Court's ruling in *United States v. Windsor*, issued months earlier.[9] According to Reinhardt, *Windsor* indicated that classifications based on sexual orientation should be treated more skeptically than rational basis review permits. Yet, when the Supreme Court struck down DOMA's section 3 in *Windsor*, it did so without expressly recognizing gays, lesbians, or bisexuals as a suspect class or subjecting sexual-orientation classifications to higher scrutiny. Instead, it maintained its nearly two-decade tradition of acknowledging how gays and lesbians exhibit some qualities of suspect-class status, but then holding that the law in question does not even survive rational basis review.[10] As Justice Scalia contended in his dissent, it is not at all clear what level of scrutiny the Court applied in *Windsor*.[11] The ruling never indicated. Insofar as the Court held that Section 3 of DOMA caused harm, as it was motivated only by congressional animus toward gays and lesbians, and maintained that animus is not a basis for law, then the majority's rationale seemed to invoke standards of rational basis review. The Court has ignored arguments to raise the scrutiny standard put forward by litigants; it has ignored findings of state and lower federal courts to this effect; and, it has ignored the Obama administration, which endorsed application of suspect-class status for gays and lesbians. The Court's refusal to recognize gays and lesbians as a suspect class is evaluated in the next chapter, particularly as it represents a sustained shift from an increasingly muddied doctrine of tiered scrutiny.

This chapter focuses on how other officials—state and lower federal judges and executive officials—have recognized gays and lesbians as a suspect class, deliberately invoking that jurisprudential designation, when contending that gays and lesbians should be able to access civil marriage. Marriage has never been only a fundamental right. Civil marriage has functioned also as a classificatory tool through which state regulatory authorities define the boundaries and parameters of citizenship. Through civil marriage, individuals become legible to the state for purposes of policy, economic, and legal stability.[12] Consequently, the battle over same-sex-marriage recognition is, as Amy Brandzel suggests, one of the many "struggles over citizenship in the United States."[13] Marriages produce "order, stability, and a means of identifying and recognizing individuals. That is, they will make gays and lesbians intelligible and acceptable to the state as citizens."[14] More critically, queer theorist Michael Warner contends that state-sanctioned marriage for gays and lesbians is not only a granting of rights but also an expansion of state power, the power to recognize, construct, define, and limit its citizenry in ever-changing ways.[15]

Executive branch officials and state and lower federal judges have utilized the explicit implications of suspect-class designation—that gays and lesbians are officially recognized as a discriminated-against and politically powerless class—to promote a new recognition of gay and lesbian status: full capability to enter into the rights and responsibilities of marriage. The first part of this chapter discusses executive officials and their controversial assertions of independent constitutional interpretation on the question of marriage recognition. Even as the Supreme Court developed scrutiny doctrine, focusing only on Supreme Court justices discounts the roles played by other actors in shaping constitutional meanings even if those other actors explicitly rely on the interpretive tools developed by the Court.[16] As William Novak contends, focusing only on Court recognition "fetishiz[es] courts and judges and radically understat[es] the role of other creative lawmakers in the American tradition."[17] The second part of the chapter surveys characterizations of gays, lesbians, and bisexuals as a suspect class through close readings of state judicial rulings and concurrences in same-sex-marriage rulings from Hawaii, Vermont, Massachusetts, New Jersey, New York, California, Connecticut, and Iowa. The third part evaluates the lower federal litigation of California's Propostion 8 and summarizes some trends in federal court rulings or marriage in the year after *Windsor*. Taken together, these sections demonstrate the lasting impact of scrutiny doctrine. They point to the incredible power of the Court to define the discursive, ideational, and strategic terrain of pluralism and identity politics. As examined in the next chapter, however, the Supreme Court has not applied this doctrine to evaluate gay and lesbian rights claims, and its resistance to expanding suspect-class and scrutiny doctrine may indicate judicial attempts to innovate while other federal and state actors hold to the durable ideational shift—the concepts of suspect class and suspect classification—that defined so much of civil rights strategy and litigation in the twentieth century.

Executive Authority and Same-Sex Marriage: Conflicting Responsibilities to Interpret and to Enforce the Law in Historical Context

If the Supreme Court has resisted declaring gays and lesbians a suspect class, some executive officials have not, often relying on the Court's scrutiny doctrine to make seemingly independent decisions about whether to recognize same-sex marriage. In May 2014, in the context of Pennsylvania's federal lawsuit to uphold its statutory ban on same-sex marriage, the state's auditor general, Eugene DePasquale, advocated that the lawsuit be abandoned.[18] The litigation's cost to taxpayers, DePasquale contended, should be reconsidered because it was exacerbating the one-billion-dollar budget shortfall: "We can't afford legal bills like this when the administration is looking at making additional budget cuts."[19] But, furthermore, he maintained that the litigation was unwise since not only was it likely to fail but also the current ban on recognizing same-sex marriage was unjust: "We cannot afford to pay $300–$400 per hour to fight for an *unfair* law that denies recognition of, and penalizes, legally married same-sex couples."[20] The statement's substantive claim, namely, that the current ban is "unfair," triggers the question of who has authority to interpret the constitutionality of a law.

Separation of power doctrine often assigns each branch a particular responsibility with regard to the law: the legislature creates it, the executive enforces it, and the judiciary interprets and either upholds it or strikes it down. The judiciary has constitutional interpretive authority. And yet, each branch appears to share this responsibility. In drafting law, Congress makes a judgment as to whether the law it writes, debates, and passes for the president's signature is within constitutional limits. When signing or vetoing legislation, the president makes an independent claim that the legislation has constitutional foundation. Constitutional interpretation is an iterative and dynamic process, a dialogue among the three branches in which no one branch can claim full responsibility or ultimate authority.[21]

To defend the claim that the Court has primacy over determining the Constitution's meaning, Chief Justice Marshall's claim in *Marbury v. Madison* that "[i]t is emphatically the duty of the Judicial Department to say what the law is" is often invoked.[22] The Supreme Court did so in

Cooper v. Aaron when it declared its own interpretive supremacy as integral to the balance of powers: "the basic principle that the federal judiciary is supreme in the exposition of the law of the Constitution . . . has ever since been respected by this Court and the Country as a permanent and indispensable feature of our constitutional system."[23] Nevertheless, a recurring history of popular antijudicial protest and independent constitutional interpretation by executive and congressional officials suggests that such a principle has not been wholly conceded or universally respected.[24]

Judicial supremacy considers the Court's rulings to be synonymous with constitutional meaning and all governing actors to be bound to take them as such. Departmentalism considers the other federal branches as capable of making or even required to make their own independent judgments of constitutional meaning.[25] Departmentalism has enjoyed sporadic and recurring prominence; it has characterized some presidents' actions and been used to justify antagonisms with the federal judiciary. Jefferson, Jackson, Lincoln, and Franklin Roosevelt stand out as presidents who asserted the legitimacy of independent executive interpretation.[26] It experienced a resurgence during the Reagan administration when Attorney General Edwin Meese III contended that political officials could resist Supreme Court rulings.[27]

Over time, however, executive assertions have not been fully independent of judicial actions; while the earliest invocations of executive authority may have rested on the president's claim of having an independent responsibility to adopt a distinct understanding of the Constitution's meaning, later invocations seem more tempered, often harnessing judicial authority to executive ends or limiting the scope of the executive's own claims rather than offering a full-throated position contrary to the Court's stance.[28] While Keith Whittington has argued that "judges, lawyers, politicians, and the general public today accept the principle of judicial supremacy—indeed they assume it as a matter of course," the scope of presidential claims to interpret constitutional authority often appears more restrained and to have narrowed over time.[29]

The Obama administration's position on the federal Defense of Marriage Act recalls, to a limited extent, departmentalist theory. The president concluded that Section 3 of the law, which defined marriage as a union between one man and one woman, was unconstitutional. According to Attorney General Eric Holder, the president determined that gays and lesbians constituted a suspect class, that laws affecting that class should be held to heightened judicial scrutiny, and that DOMA would not survive that level of scrutiny: "given a number of factors, including a documented history of discrimination, classifications based on sexual orientation should be subject to a more heightened standard of scrutiny."[30] Holder also stipulated that the president's position had no clear federal judicial precedent:

> Section 3 of DOMA has now been challenged in the Second Circuit, however, which has *no established or binding standard for how laws concerning sexual orientation should be treated.* In these cases, the Administration faces for the *first time* the question of whether laws regarding sexual orientation are subject to the more permissive standard of review or whether a more rigorous standard, under which laws targeting minority groups with a history of discrimination are viewed with suspicion by the courts, should apply.[31]

Even as the administration's decision not to defend DOMA raises questions about the scope of executive power and which branch holds responsibility for constitutional interpretation, the decision's reliance upon the judicially created scrutiny doctrine embeds it within an expression of judicial authority.[32] In other words, the executive branch *relies* upon judicial reasoning and precedent rather than articulating a fully independent conclusion. Similarly, earlier actions by mayors to grant same-sex marriage licenses in 2004 rely on judicial claims to bolster their positions. Most recently, state attorneys general have asserted authority to not enforce state bans on same-sex marriage. These positions also do not resist judicial interpretations so much as utilize or harness them for justification. When asserting that bans on same-sex marriage are unconstitutional, these executive officials, whether mayors, state attorneys general, or President Obama, do not offer a full-throated departmentalism; by invoking and relying upon judicial doctrine, their independent authority is cabined and, to a degree, respectful of judicial authority.

In February 2004, months after the U.S. Supreme Court decriminalized consensual homosexual sex and the Massachusetts Supreme Court declared that refusal to recognize same-sex marriage violated the state's constitution, Gavin Newsom, mayor of San Francisco, ordered city clerks to grant marriage licenses to same-sex couples.[33] About two weeks later Jason West, mayor of New Paltz, New York, officiated at numerous same-sex weddings.[34] And, in March 2004, the county commissioners of Multnomah County in Oregon instructed its marriage clerks to grant licenses to same-sex couples.[35] By mid-March, all of these executive actions were stopped by judicial rulings, but in the intervening weeks, over seven thousand marriage licenses were granted.[36]

When justifying his action, Mayor Newsom referenced the oath he took upon his installation as mayor "to uphold the constitution of the State of California."[37] By invoking the oath as justification for an assertion of independent interpretative authority, Newsom adopted a common rationale among departmentalist executives. For example, Andrew Jackson similarly defended his veto of the legislation to reauthorize the charter of the second Bank of the United States:

> If the opinion of the Supreme Court covered the whole ground of this act, it ought not to control the coordinate authorities of this Government. The Congress, the Executive, and the Court must each for itself be guided by its own opinion of the Constitution. Each public officer who takes an oath to support the Constitution swears that he will support it as he understands it, and not as it is understood by others. It is as much the duty of the House of Representatives, of the Senate, and of the President to decide upon the constitutionality of any bill or resolution which may be presented to them for passage or approval as it is of the supreme judges when it may be brought before them for judicial decision. The opinion of the judges has no more authority over Congress than the opinion of Congress has over the judges, and on that point the President is independent of both. The authority of the Supreme Court must not, therefore, be permitted to control the Congress or the Executive when acting in their legislative capacities, but to have only such influence as the force of their reasoning may deserve.[38]

Yet whereas Jackson claimed that he had undertaken his own separate assessment of the constitutional legitimacy of the bank legislation, "having considered it with that solemn regard to the principles of the

Constitution which the day was calculated to inspire, and come to the conclusion that it ought not to become a law," Newsom explained his constitutional assessment by relying on judicial pronouncements.[39] In the letter to the county clerks issued February 10, 2004, instructing that they issue marriage licenses, Newsom noted how his decision followed from prior California court rulings:

> The California courts have interpreted the equal protection clause of the California Constitution to apply to lesbians and gay men and have suggested that laws that treat homosexuals differently from heterosexuals are suspect. The California courts have also stated that discrimination against gay men and lesbians is invidious. The California courts have held that gender discrimination is suspect and invidious as well. The Supreme Courts in other states have held that equal protection provisions in their state constitutions prohibit discrimination against gay men and lesbians with respect to the rights and obligations flowing from marriage.[40]

By repeatedly invoking judicial principles, Newsom carefully constructed his position as flowing from judicial authority, not as antithetical to or independent of it. In this way, it is not wholly departmentalist even as it grates against a principle of judicial supremacy. By contrast, Mayor Jason West of New Paltz did not justify his actions by referencing any judicial authority. While he sought counsel from the attorney for New Paltz and was advised against performing the marriages, he did so anyway.[41] And, he did not notify or consult with the town's board before action. Instead, "he moved ahead quickly with the marriages in part because he feared that he would be arrested before the ceremonies could be performed."[42]

The actions taken by the Multnomah County Board of Commissioners in Portland, Oregon, are more similar to those of Newsom, particularly in their reliance on their oath to uphold the state constitution and their reliance on judicial precedent as justification for their actions. In January, the board voted to seek counsel from the county attorney on whether it could require the issuance of marriage licenses to same-sex couples.[43] The attorney issued a confidential opinion on March 2, 2004, which authorized the action by referencing the oath of office: "[Each] Multnomah County Commissioner is required by state law to take an oath to support both the federal and state constitutions. The County's duty to act in compliance with the constitution applies even when a court has not yet found a particular statute or government action unconstitutional."[44] Although no Oregon court had found that the refusal to recognize same-sex marriages amounted to a constitutional violation, the executive branch could independently so find and then act accordingly by virtue of the oath to uphold the constitution. Yet, this departmentalist claim was tempered by the county attorney's reliance upon a 1998 Oregon Court of Appeals decision that held that a policy that permitted providing health benefits to the spouses of cross-sex married couples but denied them to the domestic partners of gay and lesbian couples violated the state constitution's ban prohibiting any kind of favoritism of particular state citizens.[45] In other words, like Newsom's justification, the Multnomah position relied on judicial precedent as much as on the oath of office.

Dawn Johnsen, a scholar of executive assertions of constitutional interpretation, developed a set of standards that might justify executive legitimacy in constitutional interpretation when she served in the Office of Legal Counsel during the Clinton presidency. She contends that presidents may decline to enforce a statute in certain contexts. For Johnsen, the "President does not most faithfully execute the laws, either by invariably refusing to enforce statutes based solely on his independent views of what the Constitution means or by enforcing all statutes regardless of their constitutional infirmities."[46] Rather, she suggests that legitimate refusal to execute and enforce a statute can occur when (1) accurate and honest appraisal of the law by the executive's legal counsel has been undertaken, (2) the executive is duly respectful of the constitutional authority of the coequal legislative and judicial branches, (3) disagreements among the three branches as to the law's constitutionality are rare and when they occur are disclosed in a timely fashion, and (4) the executive has consulted with any other affected administrative agencies before his or her final determination is rendered.[47] In applying these standards to the mayoral actions, legal scholar Sylvia Law contends that they "came close to meeting the standards articulated by the OLC to define the President's authority to interpret the constitution."[48]

While Johnsen disagreed with Law's assessment, finding that the mayor's actions could not be justified by the OLC standards she helped develop, she did defend Obama's decision not to defend the constitutionality of DOMA by these standards.[49] The decision is hardly unprecedented. For example, when current Chief Justice John Roberts was solicitor general during the George W. Bush administration, he refused to defend federal statutes that permitted race to be a consideration when encouraging underrepresented minorities to seek broadcasting licenses.[50] While staking out an independent position, the Roberts memo wholly relied on the implications of the judicially constructed scrutiny doctrine. The decision to enforce but not defend DOMA was a more assertive strategy than the one by which Obama approached a repeal of Don't Ask, Don't Tell. With regard to DADT, the administration continued to enforce and defend the law even as it had voiced objections and worked with Congress to repeal it. Johnsen refers to this kind of action as "the constitutionally superior course of persuading Congress to repeal laws the Presidents had determined were unconstitutional."[51]

With regard to DOMA, the decision to enforce but not defend the law potentially left the law without an advocate before the bar, as such responsibility usually falls to the solicitor general, an agent of the executive. The law was defended by the Bipartisan Legal Advisory Group of the House of Representatives (BLAG) in the *Windsor* case, indicating that Congress or its agent can defend laws duly passed.[52] But, the administration's action also *maintained* the separation of powers by permitting the ultimate constitutionality of DOMA to be determined by the judiciary. In this regard, Obama's actions were even more limited than those taken by the mayors. As Johnsen has argued, "President Obama chose to enforce the law and present his constitutional views in litigation, which allows the courts, not the President, to decide DOMA's fate."[53] The president was not undermining judicial authority and articulating a different vision of constitutional meaning as coequal; rather, he was acting in a rare instance to harness that authority to his preferred constitutional interpretation. In this way, he avoided the potential chaos of constitutional indeterminacy that follows from a more robust departmentalism.

Within the year since the *Windsor* ruling, seven state attorneys general have refused to defend their state constitutional or statutory bans on same-sex marriage.[54] And, Attorney General Eric Holder supported these refusals even as he cautioned that they should be rare. Holder contended that state AGs should subject such laws to the highest level of scrutiny and that "engaging in that process and making that determination is something that's appropriate for an attorney general to do."[55] To defend these refusals, each attorney general invoked the scrutiny doctrine as developed by the Court. The Nevada attorney general, as discussed in the opening of this chapter, contended that as the Ninth Circuit had elevated gays and lesbians to suspect-class status, the state's ban could not withstand that threshold. The Virginia attorney general took the position articulated most prominently by the California Supreme Court in 2008, discussed further below: "Virginia's ban on marriage between same sex couples violates the Fourteenth Amendment of the U.S. Constitution on two grounds: marriage is a fundamental right being denied to some Virginians, and the ban unlawfully discriminates on the basis of both sexual orientation and gender."[56] Thus, his position follows the same logic as Newsom's 2004 letter citing the positions of other state judicial rulings.

California's attorney general declined to defend Proposition 8, which had overturned a state Supreme Court ruling that the Constitution required recognition of same-sex marriage. The attorney general's statement is brief: "I declined to defend Proposition 8 because it violates the Constitution. The Supreme Court has described marriage as a fundamental right 14 times since 1888. The time has come for this right to be afforded to every citizen."[57] Nevertheless, the statement invokes the position taken by the state supreme court in 2008 that marriage, regardless of the sexual orientation of those who seek to enter the union, is a fundamental right and relies on the Supreme Court's ruling in *Loving* that marriage is a fundamental right. In Illinois, the attorney general went further, not only declining to defend the ban but also seeking permission to argue against it, requesting "the right to intervene in this case to present the Court with arguments that explain why the challenged statutory provisions do not satisfy the guarantee of equality under the Illinois Constitution."[58] And, the Pennsylvania attorney general not only alluded to how a ban may violate one or more constitutional principles but also said that defending the law violated legal ethics: "I cannot ethically defend the constitutionality of Pennsylvania's version of DOMA where I believe it to be wholly unconstitutional. . . . It is a lawyer's ethical obligation under Pennsylvania's Rules of Professional Conduct to withdraw from a case in which the lawyer has a fundamental disagreement with the client."[59]

These actions are not without controversy. Colorado's attorney general, for example, opposed the nondefense rationale:

> Depending on one's view of the laws in question, such a "litigation veto" may, in the short term, be a terrific thing; an unpopular law is defended and the attorney general can take credit. . . . But in the longer term, this practice corrodes our system of checks and balances, public belief in the power of democracy and ultimately the moral and legal authority on which attorneys general must depend.[60]

Yet, whether by making an independent judgment that a law is unconstitutional or by basing a refusal to defend it on an ethical code of responsibility, these attorneys generals did not undermine judicial authority when voicing their claim about a ban's constitutionality. Since the judiciary still must render judgment, the balance of powers was maintained. Since executive interpretation of the marriage bans was grounded in entrenched judicial doctrine, judicial power to set the parameters of constitutional interpretation was preserved. And, even if attorneys general refused to defend a ban, the *Windsor* ruling indicated that the standing to defend a law could be pursued by state agents outside the executive branch. Ultimately, in all cases of executive claims not to enforce bans on same-sex-marriage recognition, their constitutionality remained for the judiciary to decide. The action taken by these executives did not so much undermine the courts as the ultimate interpreters of constitutional meanings as they enlivened public discourse by contributing to the possible meanings from which a court may ultimately select its own.

Gays, Lesbians, and Bisexuals as a Suspect Class and Sexual Orientation as a Suspect Classification: Changing Recognitions by State Courts

Whereas the Supreme Court has repeatedly resisted applying suspect-class status to gays and lesbians or subjecting laws that classify by sexual orientation to heightened scrutiny, even as it has struck down such laws, state and lower federal courts have applied these doctrines. While state-level same-sex-marriage rulings indicate early refusal to designate gays and lesbians as a suspect class, the California Supreme Court's 2008 ruling in *In re Marriage Cases* marks a turning point.[61] State supreme courts did not consistently consider exclusionary marriage laws as sexual-orientation discrimination, nor did they identify sexual orientation as a suspect classification and gay persons as a suspect class until this ruling in 2008. This shift was paired with an explicit framing of marriage as a fundamental due process right regardless of the gender of individuals seeking to access that right. Consequently, state and lower federal courts have built a foundation for marriage equality that can rest not on equal protection jurisprudence but instead (or also) on the due process liberty tradition, which emphasizes intimate association, and which the Supreme Court embraced in *Lawrence* and *Windsor*.

In 1993, the Hawaii Supreme Court issued its three-to-one ruling in *Baehr v. Lewin* declaring that the state must demonstrate a compelling interest if it is to deny marriage recognition to same-sex couples.[62] While this court was not the first to consider same-sex marriage, it was the first to do so when same-sex marriage had become a stated goal of national gay and lesbian interest groups.[63] Marriage, or some form of recognized partnership, was increasingly called for as HIV/AIDS, the Sharon Kowalski case, and parenting concerns brought about by higher rates of joint adoption by same-sex couples and the lesbian baby boom all exposed the instability that relationships endure when not recognized by state regulatory authorities.

The Hawaii court called for the application of the highest possible judicial scrutiny, but it did so without acknowledging the sexual orientation of the individuals who sought to marry.[64] That the sexual orientation was highlighted neither by the Hawaii Supreme Court nor by the plaintiffs themselves is evidence of the strategic imperative to compel the highest level of scrutiny possible. The denial of same-sex marriage was considered as a matter of sex discrimination.

The plaintiffs in this case, three same-sex couples—Ninia Baehr, Genora Dancel, Tammy Rodrigues, Antoinette Pregil, Pat Lagon, and Joseph Melilio—alleged that Hawaii's refusal to grant them marriage licenses violated their right to privacy and their right to equal protection under the state's constitution. The Hawaii court dismissed the privacy claim by determining that same-sex marriage did not fall within the scope of a fundamental right, but it also held that the state's refusal to recognize same-sex marriage constituted sex discrimination, which could only be overcome by the government showing that such refusal was narrowly tailored to meet a compelling government interest. Why did same-sex marriage not meet the standard of a fundamental right, why was refusal to recognize same-sex marriage a matter of sex and not sexual-orientation discrimination, and why was sex discrimination held to strict scrutiny instead of heightened or intermediate scrutiny?

The court traced the doctrinal determination of marriage as a fundamental right. The United States first declared the importance of marriage in *Maynard v. Hill* (1888), when it referred to marriage as "the most important relation in life" and as "the foundation of the family and of society, without which there would neither be civilization nor progress."[65] It then, in *Meyer v. Nebraska* (1923), characterized the "right to marry, establish a home, and bring up children" as a liberty protected by the due process clause of the Fourteenth Amendment.[66] It referred to marriage as a fundamental right in *Skinner v. Oklahoma ex rel. Williamson* (1942) when it linked marriage and procreation to strike down a state law that permitted sterilization of "habitual criminals" without their consent.[67] The court indicated that the state law "involves one of the basic rights of man. Marriage and procreation are fundamental to the very existence and survival of the race."[68] The court then moved to decouple marriage from procreation by turning to the Supreme Court's ruling in *Zablocki v. Redhail* (1978), which struck down a Wisconsin statute that prohibited a state resident from obtaining a marriage license unless he was in compliance with child support obligations.[69] But, even if the Supreme Court's jurisprudence had turned from considering marriage as inextricably linked to procreation, the Hawaii court determined that the federal case law "demonstrates that the federal construction of the right to marry . . . presently contemplates unions between a man and woman."[70] If the court were then to extend the fundamental marital right to include same-sex couples, it would have to determine that this right was deeply rooted in history and tradition and central to the maintenance of ordered liberty. The court was unwilling to do so; the due process claim was not sustained.[71]

The court did maintain the equal protection claim. It considered marriage "a state-conferred legal status, the existence of which gives rise to rights and benefits reserved exclusively to that particular relationship," and it held that the state maintained a monopoly on conferring this status "for more than a century."[72] The plaintiffs contended that state authorities refused to grant a marriage license "on the *sole* basis that the applicant couple is of the same sex."[73] And, the plaintiffs never identified as homosexual. Thus, while the state maintained that it viewed these couples as homosexual—it stipulated that "the state is under no obligation 'to take affirmative steps to provide homosexual unions with its official approval' . . . [and that homosexuals] are neither a suspect nor a quasi-suspect class and do not require heightened judicial solicitude"—the plaintiffs never self-identified nor did the court recognize the couples as gay or lesbian for purposes of evaluating the classificatory exclusion.[74] Indeed, the court argued that for the state's claim against heightened scrutiny to make sense, it would have to assume that the couples in question were, in fact, homosexual, but this was "a fact not pleaded in the plaintiffs' complaint."[75] The court reviewed the matter as sex discrimination.

The Hawaii Constitution has a more explicit ban on sex discrimination than the U.S. Constitution. Article I, Section 5 of the Hawaii Constitution indicates that no person "shall be denied of equal protection of the laws, nor be denied the enjoyment of civil rights or be discriminated against in the exercise thereof because of race, religion, sex, or ancestry."[76] Article I, Section 3 of the state constitution declares, "Equality of rights under the law shall not be denied or abridged by the State on account of sex."[77] To determine the level of scrutiny applied to a statute impinging upon this equal rights amendment, the Hawaii court turned to the Supreme Court's ruling in *Frontiero v. Richardson*.[78] While the law in question in that case was struck down, the justices split on whether the law should be subject to strict scrutiny and sex viewed as a suspect classification or whether the law failed rational basis review. The Hawaii court highlighted Justice Powell's explicit reference to the national Equal Rights Amendment (ERA) and the fact that it was, at the time of the *Frontiero* ruling, under consideration by state legislatures. If it were ratified, then sex classifications would be subject to strict scrutiny; therefore, Powell contended, the court should exhibit prudence and not resolve the question before the democratic process had been worked through. In light of Powell's statement, the Hawaii court determined that the sex classification that limited marriage licenses only to cross-sex couples would be held to strict scrutiny since Hawaii had its own explicit sex-equality provision.[79]

This first victory for same-sex marriage was ironically achieved by blocking the gay and lesbian identities of these couples from view. They did not expressly so identify nor did the Court see them as such. Same-sex marriage was made possible only by the court *not* seeing sexuality and instead determining this case on the basis of sex discrimination. Legal scholar Andrew Koppelman contends that the sex-classification rationale accepted by the Hawaii court was hardly only a strategic sleight-of-hand to achieve the highest level of scrutiny possible. Instead, it represented a philosophical commitment to exposing how discrimination against gays and lesbians was deeply rooted in sex discrimination, in assumptions about gender roles, and in discriminatory traditions of sexual hierarchy. To challenge bans on same-sex marriage as discrimination only against gays and lesbians is, by this argument, to miss larger dynamics of patriarchal oppression: "the notion that discrimination against gays involves only the rights of gays is similarly shallow. It fails to recognize that the stigmatization of gays in contemporary American society functions as part of a larger system of social control based on gender."[80] The plaintiff's strategy in *Baehr*, then, was logically confronting the root cause of the state's discriminatory practice.

Nevertheless, sexism and heterosexism, while having common roots in male supremacy, are distinguishable constructs. As Cheshire Calhoun contends, "patriarchy and heterosexual dominance are two, in principle, separable systems. . . . [E]ven if empirically and historically heterosexual dominance and patriarchy are completely intertwined, it does not follow from this fact that the collapse of patriarchy will bring about the collapse of heterosexual dominance."[81] Legal scholar Edward Stein reveals substantial differences between the two oppressive dynamics and asserts that, in his estimation, institutional supports for sexism, particularly within the family, had been weakening while institutional supports for heterosexism, particularly within the family, had been strengthening since at least the 1990s. For Stein, writing after the passage of DOMA whereas Koppelman's assessment came two years before DOMA, "homophobia, though it has gradually become disentangled from sexism, remains entrenched in our society."[82] While Stein conceded Koppelman's point that "many laws that discriminate on the basis of sexual orientation have their origins in sexism," he illustrated how "these laws are maintained because of homophobia and despite the repeal of many sexist laws."[83] Same-sex marriage needed to be challenged in precisely the way that the *Baehr* case had not done, as a matter of sexual-orientation discrimination directly.

The Vermont Supreme Court, when it ruled in 1999 that the state must devise a means to grant the rights and benefits of civil marriage to same-sex couples in *Baker v. Vermont*, addressed whether denial of marriage to same-sex couples constituted sexual-orientation discrimination.[84] However, it did so only in a concurrence with the court's ruling. The majority decision, announced by Chief Justice Amestoy, held that Vermont's denial of civil marriage recognition to same-sex couples violated the state constitution's unique Common Benefits Clause. The Common Benefits Clause states

> [t]hat government is, or ought to be, instituted for the common benefit, protection, and security of the people, nation or community; and not for the particular emolument or advantage of any single man, family, or set of men, who are a part only of that community; and that the community hath an indubitable, unalienable, and indefeasible right, to reform, alter or abolish government, in such manner as shall be, by that community, judged most conducive to the public weal.

The Vermont court maintained that these words do not indicate a standard for how they might be interpreted, but they did set forth a "principle of inclusion," which "underscores the framers' resentment of political preference of any kind."[85] Although this principle of inclusion is similar to the Fourteenth Amendment's guarantee of equal protection, the court also made clear that it was more extensive than the federal clause: "the Common Benefits Clause of the Vermont Constitution differs markedly from the federal Equal Protection Clause in its language, historical origins, purpose, and development. While the federal clause may thus supplement the protections afforded by the Common Benefits Clause, it does not supplant it as the first and primary safeguard of the rights and liberties of all Vermonters."[86] Accordingly, the court set out to establish an interpretive test that emphasized inclusion and explicitly refrained from applying "the rigid, multi-tiered analysis evolved by the federal courts under the Fourteenth Amendment."[87] The court was not interested in labeling gays and lesbians a suspect class. Indeed, the court posited that doing so would violate the spirit of the Common Benefits Clause, whose inclusive imperative compels the court to avoid "labeling the excluded class as 'suspect,' 'quasi-suspect,' or 'non-suspect' for purposes of determining different levels of judicial scrutiny."[88] Rather, the court was only concerned with whether a group of people is excluded from access to benefits and rights afforded all Vermonters.

The Vermont court examined whether the government's purpose for excluding same-sex couples from marriage "bears a reasonable and just relation to the governmental purpose."[89] That phrasing was similar to the rational basis standard; however, the court stipulated that in balancing the weight given to the government's rationale for the classificatory exclusion versus the challenging party's claim to inclusion, it "must look to the history and 'traditions from which [the State] developed' as well as 'those from which it broke.'"[90] Pointing to history and tradition would seem to invoke an examination of fundamental rights, which might imply the application of strict scrutiny. And, the court contended that it must "examine the nature of the classification to determine whether it is reasonably necessary to accomplish the State's claimed objectives."[91] But this language again confused the distinct phraseology of scrutiny tiers. "Reasonable" would indicate rational basis review whereas "necessary" would imply the application of strict scrutiny.

In concurrence, Justice Dooley criticized the interpretative test put forth by the majority as unnecessarily vague. The court's refusal to adhere to tiered-scrutiny doctrine left it unable to determine whether gays and lesbians were a suspect class. The court erred when it proclaimed, "most decisions have concluded that lesbians and gay men are not a suspect classification, inferring that any conclusion to the contrary is wrong."[92] While he wrote, "In this concurrence, I do not detail a suspect-classification analysis," he did come fairly close to doing so.[93] He argued that the refusal to find gays and lesbians to be a suspect class was grounded in the state court's reliance on *Bowers v. Hardwick*, which permitted the criminalization of consensual same-sex sexual activity. However, *Bowers*, according to Dooley, was "not applicable in Vermont today," as the state repealed its antisodomy law in 1977 and had prohibited discrimination on the basis of sexual orientation since 1992.[94] Such actions would seem to indicate that gays and lesbians have endured an unjust history of discrimination; otherwise, why would discrimination based on sexual orientation be expressly banned?

While Dooley contended that sexual orientation could probably be considered a suspect classification, he refrained from making this claim the centerpiece of his disagreement with the ruling. Instead, he focused on the court's loose analytical framework and its refusal to apply established scrutiny doctrine. He argued that the court's standard, which "relies wholly on factors and balancing, with no mooring in any criteria or guidelines, however imperfect they may be," was unacceptable.[95] He questioned whether this standard was even "ascertainable," and asserted, "the strength of the federal approach is that it disciplines judicial discretion and promotes predictability."[96] Scrutiny doctrine established guidelines whereas the state court's balancing principle based upon a requirement of inclusion did not.

Justice Johnson concurred in part and dissented in part. The majority sought to return the issue to the legislature to devise a remedy. Johnson saw no reason to do so; she would "simply enjoin the State from denying marriage licenses to the plaintiffs based on sex or sexual orientation."[97] The reference to classification by sex made up the second part of the dissent, where Johnson described the existing restriction to be "a straightforward case of sex discrimination."[98] She restated the position of the Hawaii court: The marriage statute is a sex-based classification, and Vermont jurisprudence held that sex-based classifications that run against the Common Benefits Clause must be "narrowly tailored to further important, if not compelling, interests."[99] Marriage as a sex classification would subject the law to strict scrutiny. While Johnson conceded that the marriage restriction had "its most direct impact . . . on lesbians and gay men, the class of individuals most likely to seek same-sex marriage," she, like Koppelman, rooted the law in "sex-role stereotyping," which is unconstitutional, as the Supreme Court ruled in *Craig v. Boren*.[100]

In *Baker*, the Vermont court ruled that gays and lesbians could not be excluded from access to the rights and benefits that followed from civil marriage. Yet, this determination, like that made by the Hawaii court six years earlier, did not require the court to see the plaintiffs as gays and lesbians. The court was explicit that it would not engage in any suspect-class analysis. In concurrence, Justice Johnson did apply suspect-class analysis, but refused to see the plaintiffs in terms of their sexual orientation and their primary identity as being at stake in this context. While the justice acknowledged that the restriction most likely affected gays and lesbians, she held that the law should be reviewed and found to be an unsupportable sex classification. And, even Justice Dooley, who did discuss whether sexual orientation could be a suspect classification, undermined his determination to that effect by indicating that this finding was not the primary aim of his concurrence. Ironically, two judicial victories for same-sex-marriage advocates were grounded in the court's refusal to recognize explicitly the plaintiffs as gay, lesbian, or bisexual.

When the Supreme Court of Massachusetts considered the question of marriage equality in 2004 in *Goodridge v. Department of Public Health*, it did so in a new legal context: The Supreme Court invalidated any criminality of private consensual same-sex relations between adults months earlier in *Lawrence v. Texas*.[101] Massachusetts was not under the constraint that the Vermont court stipulated when it suggested that the *Bowers* ruling limited it from considering gays and lesbians to be a suspect class. Nevertheless, as with the other state courts, the Massachusetts decision did not treat gays and lesbians as a suspect class either. Instead, it invoked the threshold that Justice Kennedy articulated in *Lawrence*, namely, "that the core concept of common human dignity protected by the Fourteenth Amendment of the United States Constitution precludes government intrusion into the deeply personal realms of consensual adult expressions of intimacy and one's choice of an intimate partner."[102] However, the Massachusetts court did recognize the sexual orientation of the plaintiffs by framing the question before it as whether "homosexual persons should be treated no differently than their heterosexual neighbors."[103] Yet, despite this recognition, the court did not consider whether this class of persons was suspect or whether the classificatory exclusion in the law amounted to a suspect classification. Instead, the court followed the lead of Justice Kennedy to hold the law to the most deferential standard of review, rational basis.

The fourteen couples who brought suit in *Goodridge* claimed that denial of a marriage license violated a fundamental right to marry as a matter of due process and a right to equal protection under the law. In determining how to review each claim, the court stipulated that rational basis review of a due process claim required only "that statutes 'bear a real and substantial relation to the public health, safety, morals, or some other phase of the general welfare.'"[104] And, for an equal protection challenge, the lowest tier of review required only that "an impartial lawmaker could logically believe that the classification would serve a legitimate public purpose that transcends the harm to the members of the disadvantaged class."[105] Since the Department of Public Health contended that there was not a fundamental right to same-sex marriage and that gays, lesbians, and bisexuals did not constitute a recognized class, it recommended that the extant refusal to recognize same-sex marriage be held only to rational basis review. The court agreed that no fundamental rights claim was cognizable since it determined that while access to marriage was a fundamental right, same-sex marriage was not deeply rooted in history nor was it essential to ordered liberty.[106] But the court also held that the statute "does not survive rational basis review" as a matter of equal protection. The state could offer no rational reasons as to why access to marriage should be restricted. So, the court did "not consider the plaintiff's arguments that this case merits strict judicial scrutiny."[107] If the statute cannot even pass the lowest threshold of constitutional review, then there is no reason to evaluate whether suspect-class designation should be applied.

In concurrence, Justice Greaney recycled opinions in *Baehr* and *Baker* when claiming that the law should be subject to strict scrutiny as it was a sex-based classification. Greaney would have struck down the law under "traditional equal protection analysis," which would determine that the marriage statutes, since they only recognize a union of a man and a woman, necessarily "create a statutory classification based on the sex of the two people who wish to marry."[108] Furthermore, Greaney pointed to how existing marriage statutes relied on gender stereotyping, which had not been appropriate foundations for legislation at least since *Frontiero*:

> This case calls for a higher level of legal analysis. Precisely, the case requires that we confront the ingrained assumptions with respect to historically accepted roles of men and women within the institution of marriage and requires that we reexamine these assumptions . . . in order to ensure that the governmental conduct challenged here conforms to the supreme charter of our Commonwealth. . . . I do not doubt the sincerity of deeply

held moral or religious beliefs that make inconceivable to some the notion that any change in the common-law definition of what constitutes a
legal civil marriage is now, or ever would be, warranted. But, as a matter of constitutional law, neither the mantra of tradition, nor individual
conviction, can justify the perpetuation of a hierarchy in which couples
of the same sex and their families are deemed less worthy of social and
legal recognition than couples of the opposite sex and their families.[109]

In short, Greaney's concurrence offered the evaluation for which some
legal advocates had aimed: holding the law to a higher level of scrutiny because of the nature of the discrimination the law enacts and
perpetuates. But even Greaney's analysis did *not* recognize the law as
discriminatory on the basis of sexual orientation. And, the Court's ruling, as written by Chief Justice Marshall, did *not* engage in any analysis
of sexual orientation or gays and lesbians as a suspect class. Once again,
judicial authority refused to recognize and deliberate about what sexual
orientation is and whether gays and lesbians could be recognized by the
suspect-class doctrine.

In 2006, the New Jersey Supreme Court was the first to directly
and *only* frame the denial of same-sex-marriage recognition as sexual-
orientation discrimination in its ruling in *Lewis v. Harris*.[110] The court
begins its ruling with the explicit statement,

> The statutory and decisional laws of this State protect *individuals* from
> discrimination on the basis of sexual orientation. When those individuals
> are gays and lesbians who follow the inclination of their sexual orienta-
> tion and enter into a committed relationship with someone of the same
> sex, our laws treat them, as *couples*, differently than heterosexual couples.
> As committed same-sex partners, they are not permitted to marry or to
> enjoy the multitude of social and financial benefits and privileges con-
> ferred on opposite-sex married couples.[111]

The New Jersey Supreme Court did not consider the marriage law as
a sex-based statute. The refusal to recognize same-sex marriage was
discrimination against gays and lesbians. Nevertheless, the court, like
its counterpart in Massachusetts, refused to engage the question of
whether gays, lesbians, and bisexuals were a suspect class. And, this is

perhaps even more surprising since so much of the rationale for the court's determination that the state must provide some form of recognition of same-sex couples equivalent to cross-sex marriage was premised on a prior legislative action that protected individuals from discrimination on the basis of their sexual orientation. These acts would seem to presume that gays, lesbians, and bisexuals were subject to a history of discrimination and were politically powerless against that discrimination, two qualities of a protected class.

Instead, in evaluating the claims of the seven same-sex couples that New Jersey law violated the due process liberty and the equal protection guarantees of the state constitution, the court, like its Massachusetts counterpart, applied rational basis review. First, it dismissed—as had Hawaii, Vermont, and Massachusetts—that there existed any fundamental right protected by due process to same-sex marriage:

> [W]e cannot find that a right to same-sex marriage is so deeply rooted in the traditions, history, and conscience of the people of this State that it ranks as a fundamental right. . . . [W]e do take note that no jurisdiction, not even Massachusetts, has declared that there is a fundamental right to same-sex marriage under the federal or its own constitution.[112]

And, also like Massachusetts' court, the New Jersey court evaluated the equal protection claim by the rational basis standard. While the Massachusetts Department of Public Health put forth three rationales for refusing to recognize same-sex marriage—"(1) providing a 'favorable setting for procreation'; (2) ensuring the optimal setting for child rearing, which the department defines as 'a two-parent family with one parent of each sex'; and (3) preserving scarce State and private financial resources"—New Jersey only maintained that it did so to sustain the traditional definition of marriage.[113] The state's rationale may have been so limited because it had a strong record of antidiscrimination law, including sexual-orientation antidiscrimination law. The state was a pioneer when it included sexual orientation in its nondiscrimination in employment and public accommodations statutes in 1992, and a New Jersey court ruled against considering a parent's sexual orientation as a legitimate bar to custodial rights of a child in 1974. And, in 2004, when eleven states passed constitutional bans on same-sex marriage, the New

Jersey legislature passed the Domestic Partnership Act, conferring some rights and benefits of civil marriage to same-sex couples.[114]

All of this legislative context indicating a consistent attempt by the state to protect gays and lesbians from various forms of discrimination compelled the court to find that "there is no rational basis for, on the one hand, giving gays and lesbians full civil rights in their status as individuals, and on the other, giving them an incomplete set of rights when they follow the inclination of their sexual orientation and enter into committed same-sex relationships."[115] The state's rationale did not pass rational basis review.

Even as the New Jersey court continued the trend of subjecting state laws discriminating against gays and lesbians to rational basis review, the ruling in *Lewis v. Harris* did make at least three significant moves that would lay foundations for differently recognizing the status of gays and lesbians. First, the question at stake was viewed as a matter of sexual-orientation discrimination first and foremost. As such, the primary identities as put forth by the plaintiffs were plainly recognized. Second, the ruling sought to connect the individual and the same-sex relationship. In so doing, it undermined as irrational the differentiation in public opinion and Supreme Court rulings since *Romer* whereby individual and private rights were far more supported than relationships and public recognition—as discussed in chapter 5. To support the one but not the other was unsustainable insofar as gay and lesbian people follow "the inclination of their sexual orientation" when entering into a same-sex relationship. Third, as Chief Justice Poritz contended in concurrence, there does exist a fundamental right to marriage such that "the plaintiffs' due process rights are violated when the State so burdens their liberty interests."[116] By drawing a distinction between cross-sex and same-sex marriage, as the majority opinion did (and the courts in Hawaii, Vermont, and Massachusetts had already done), the court avoided "the more difficult questions of personal dignity and autonomy raised by this case."[117] In this concurrence, Poritz's discussion of dignity was a clear reference to Justice Kennedy's reliance upon the concept in *Lawrence*.

But, Poritz further contended that emphasizing dignity also undermined, made redundant, or even outright negated any labeling of suspect class. Poritz discussed labels in the context of whether it was appropriate to leave open to the legislature—as the majority ruling had done—the question of whether some designation other than civil marriage, such as civil unions, could be granted in lieu of the title of marriage. Poritz quoted research by legal scholar Martha Minow to highlight his criticism: "The particular labels often chosen in American culture can carry social and moral consequences while burying the choices and responsibility for those consequences. . . . Language and labels play a special role in the perpetuation of prejudice about differences."[118] Poritz laid out how a civil union, even if it conferred exactly the same material rights, benefits, and responsibilities as civil marriage, was, in fact, not civil marriage because it was explicitly called something else. Difference, and thus a basis for ongoing cultural discrimination, remained in place even if formal equality was established.[119]

Across the Hudson River, the New York court, in *Hernandez v. Robles*, ruled that the state constitution did not, at that time, compel marital recognition for same-sex couples but that the legislature was free to extend such recognition if it so chose.[120] It held the state's rationale against recognition to rational basis review. This loss for same-sex marriage advocates seemed to support the traditional claim that discriminatory laws would need to be evaluated at a higher threshold if they were to be overturned. The case presented a cautionary tale as to why so many gay rights advocates sought to have gays, lesbians, and bisexuals recognized as a suspect class and sexual orientation considered a suspect classification.

The court stipulated two grounds on which the legislature could legitimately restrict marriage to cross-sex couples, and each rationale was grounded in a concern for child welfare. First, the court contended, "the Legislature could rationally decide that, for the welfare of children, it is more important to promote stability, and to avoid instability, in opposite-sex than in same-sex relationships. Heterosexual intercourse has a natural tendency to lead to the birth of children; homosexual intercourse does not."[121] The obvious rejoinder to this position is that same-sex couples do, in fact, have children, through adoption, relations with prior opposite-sex partners, reproductive technologies, or surrogacy, and that, as the New Jersey court found, the denial of marriage recognition harms these children by providing fewer protections than the children of straight parents enjoyed: "Significantly, the economic and financial inequities that are borne by same-sex domestic partners are borne by their children, too. With fewer financial benefits and protections available, those children are disadvantaged in a way that children in married households are not."[122] Therefore, if the state's intention was the protection of child welfare, then marriage recognition should be expanded, not constricted. The New York court only stipulated as a possible response to this argument that "the vast majority of children are born as a result of a sexual relationship between a man and a woman, and the Legislature could find that this will continue to be true."[123]

Second, the New York court stated, "The Legislature could rationally believe that it is better, other things being equal, for children to grow up with both a mother and a father."[124] The court did acknowledge that a variety of amicus briefs contested this proposition, and it posited that these briefs could be correct. It nevertheless maintained that "the Legislature could rationally think otherwise."[125] The court's phrasing illustrated how rational basis review is most deferential to the legislature and rarely fatal to the law under consideration. Repeatedly the court used the term "could," which indicates that unlike under higher levels of scrutiny, under the rational basis standard, the state need not prove that its law was definitively rationally related to a legitimate purpose. It needed only to demonstrate that such a link is plausible. As the U.S. Supreme Court contended, when outlining the parameters of this least searching form of legal analysis, "the law need not be in every respect logically consistent with its aims to be constitutional. It is enough that there is an evil at hand for correction, and that it *might be thought* that the particular legislative measure was a rational way to correct it."[126]

The *Hernandez* ruling showcased the challenges faced when existing restrictions on same-sex marriage were not subject to higher scrutiny. Even when the court admitted that a rational basis for the law was questionable, that finding was not enough to challenge a discriminatory action against a class that had not been recognized as protected. Thus, when, two years later, in 2008, the Supreme Court of California ruled that the state constitution compelled same-sex-marriage recognition, and did so by finding gays, lesbians, and bisexuals to constitute a suspect class, the ruling was heralded as a far-reaching advance.[127] California already had established a domestic partnership status for same-sex couples, which conferred identical rights and benefits to those that cross-sex married couples received from the state. Consequently, the court addressed whether not recognizing the same-sex unions as marriages violated the state constitution.[128]

As with all other state rulings surveyed thus far, the plaintiffs in *In re Marriage Cases* made a due process claim of a fundamental liberty interest in marriage and a claim to equal protection before the law. The California court addressed each and held that the refusal of the state to designate same-sex couples as married (as opposed to domestically partnered) violated a fundamental right to marry and that the current law also violated equal protection. On the fundamental right claim, while the court recognized that marriage rights had been traditionally associated with opposite-sex couples, it reflected on its own reversal of the state's prior ban on interracial marriage in *Perez v. Sharp* to illustrate how history was not dispositive.[129] The court maintained that the substantive rights that flow from marriage are "so integral to an individual's liberty and personal autonomy that they may not be eliminated or abrogated by the Legislature or by the electorate through the statutory initiative process."[130] Furthermore, the court contended that the state erred when it distinguished between marriage and same-sex marriage just as it would err when distinguishing between marriage and interracial marriage. At stake was not the form of marriage, but its substance. Focusing on form—same-sex or interracial—erred by "narrowly characterizing the constitutional right sought to be invoked," thereby not allowing the right to be properly "understood in a broader and more neutral fashion so as to focus upon the substance of the interests that the constitutional right is intended to protect."[131] In other words, marriage provided a range of substantive protections, and access to it was fundamental as a matter of personal autonomy and liberty as protected by the California Constitution.[132]

Second, the California court considered and rejected the sex-discrimination claim and explicitly designated sexual orientation as a suspect classification. The marriage statutes classify "on the basis of sexual orientation, a characteristic that we conclude represents—like gender, race, and religion—a constitutionally suspect basis upon which to impose differential treatment."[133] The court determined that such treatment "impinges upon a same-sex couple's fundamental interest in having their family relationship accorded the same respect and dignity enjoyed by an opposite-sex couple."[134] The state's interest in distinguishing marriages from same-sex domestic partnerships, so as to maintain "the traditional and well-established definition of marriage," was not considered compelling, nor was the existing exclusion considered necessary to achieve this interest.[135]

A few months later, the Supreme Court of Connecticut faced a question similar to that before the California court. Both states provided same-sex-relationship recognition. Connecticut recognized civil unions, and California recognized domestic partnerships. Whether this separate determination amounted to an equal protection violation was at issue in *Kerrigan et al. v. Commissioner of Public Health et al.*[136] The Connecticut court reached the same determination as the California court: civil unions are not separate but equal. Instead, as Chief Justice Poritz of New Jersey claimed, they send the message "that what same-sex couples have is not as important or as significant as 'real' marriage, that such lesser relationships cannot have the name of marriage."[137] To reach this conclusion, the court engaged in a systematic analysis evaluating whether gays and lesbians qualified as a quasi-suspect class and thus whether laws classifying by sexual orientation were subject to heightened scrutiny. The court found that gay persons endured a history of discrimination, that sexual orientation was unrelated to a person's ability to participate in or contribute to society, that the distinguishing characteristic of the class, while not immutable, was also not easily changed, and that the class had a history of political powerlessness.[138]

Since the immutability of sexual orientation is subject to debate, the court's rumination on this point requires some detailing. The court did not declare sexual orientation to be immutable; however, it did find that "it is not necessary for us to decide whether sexual orientation is immutable in the same way and to the same extent that race, national origin, and gender are immutable."[139] Instead, the court declared that, as stipulated in *Lawrence*, sexual intimacy is integral to personal identity and sexual orientation plays a "central role . . . in a person's fundamental right to self-determination."[140] Therefore, it operates as "the kind of distinguishing characteristic that defines them as a discrete group for purposes of determining whether that group should be afforded heightened protection under the equal protection provisions of the state constitution."[141]

A year later, the Supreme Court of Iowa conducted a similar analysis as the Connecticut Supreme Court.[142] Utilizing the four-pronged test to determine suspect-class status, the court recognized gay persons as a suspect class and sexual orientation as a suspect classification. In applying the intermediate scrutiny standard such that the statutory classification excluding gays and lesbians from marriage recognition must be substantially related to an important government interest, the court determined that none of the five interests put forward by the state rose to that level.[143]

Before *In re Marriage Cases*, state courts evaluated the exclusionary statutory classifications either by rational basis review or by a higher standard by determining the statute to be a sex-based classification. No court recognized gays, lesbians, and bisexuals as a suspect class or sexual orientation as a suspect classification. Indeed, *Lewis v. Harris* in New Jersey was the first case to explicitly recognize these cases as dealing first and foremost with a matter of sexual-orientation discrimination even as it held that discrimination to rational basis review; *Goodridge* nodded in that direction, but *Harris* was far more explicit and detailed in this regard, stating the sexual-orientation discrimination in its first sentence. By the standards of rational basis review, marriage-equality advocates won their cases in Massachusetts, Vermont, and New Jersey. Yet, the loss in New York illustrated the importance of the traditional legal strategy to raise the level of scrutiny as high as possible so that the deference to the legislative rationales for any exclusionary classification is as low as possible.

Indeed, the strategy was pursued in the California litigation, and following the pattern of concurrences in Massachusetts and Vermont as well as the ruling in Hawaii, plaintiffs in *In re Marriage Cases* contended that the state law constituted an unjust sex-based classification. However, the court rejected this claim and following the lead of the New Jersey court, the California court viewed the marriage restriction for what it was, discrimination on the basis of sexual orientation. However, unlike New Jersey, California engaged in an explicit evaluation of whether sexual-orientation classifications should be subject to more searching scrutiny and found that it should. That same year, the Connecticut Supreme Court applied the four-pronged test of suspect-class designation and ruled that gay persons should be recognized as a quasi-suspect class and that laws affecting that class should be subject to intermediate scrutiny. The Iowa Supreme Court conducted the same analysis and reached the same conclusion a year later, again clearly striking *against* the argument that marriage bans were sex-based classifications:

> It is true the marriage statute does not expressly prohibit gay and lesbian persons from marrying; it does, however, require that if they marry, it must be to someone of the opposite sex. . . . [C]ivil marriage with a person of the opposite sex is unappealing to a gay or lesbian person as civil marriage with a person of the same sex is to a heterosexual. Thus, the right of a gay or lesbian person under the marriage statute to enter into a civil marriage only with a person of the opposite sex is no right at all. . . . [A] gay or lesbian person can only gain the same rights under the statute as a heterosexual person by *negating the very trait that defines gay and lesbian people as a class—their sexual orientation*.[144]

The Iowa Supreme Court described the statute for what it was: a discrimination against gays and lesbians. It fully recognized those individuals as suffering under the established marital regime. Viewing the classification as sex based may have more easily rendered it subject to higher scrutiny under established precedent, but doing so ignored the substantive harm created, and it erased the primary identities of couples appearing before the courts. By directly engaging whether gay persons were a suspect class, California, Connecticut, and Iowa granted a dignity of recognition.

Gays, Lesbians, and Bisexuals as a Suspect Class and Sexual Orientation as a Suspect Classification: Changing Recognitions by Federal Courts before and after *Windsor*

The California court's ruling in *In re Marriage Cases* was overturned by the citizen referendum of Proposition 8. The constitutionality of this proposition was then challenged in federal court. In his ruling in *Perry v. Schwarzenegger*, federal district judge Vaugn Walker spoke to nearly every rationale advanced in the history of contemporary same-sex marriage litigation, addressing whether same-sex marriage was a fundamental right, whether existing statutory exclusions constituted sex discrimination or sexual-orientation discrimination, whether such statutes survived or failed rational basis review, whether gay persons were a suspect class, and, if suspect class status were granted, whether the statutory exclusion would survive higher scrutiny.[145] Walker concluded that the proposition infringed on a fundamental right and that that fundamental right could not be gendered as evidence at trial demonstrated that "states have never required spouses to have an ability or willingness to procreate in order to marry." Therefore, while "race and gender restrictions shaped marriage during eras of race and gender inequality . . . such restrictions were never part of the historical core of the institution of marriage."[146] Walker's historical claim is conceptually distinct from the California Supreme Court's contention (and the position taken first by Chief Justice Poritz of New Jersey) that marriage could not be gendered because the fundamental right to marry inhered in the individual and was a manifestation of personal autonomy. Walker's interpretation was grounded in history whereas the California court's positions were grounded in a philosophical claim about levels of abstraction. Nevertheless, both reached the same conclusion.

Second, Walker contended that Proposition 8 did not even pass muster by the rational basis threshold. The proposition only succeeds in "disadvantag[ing] or otherwise harm[ing] a particular group."[147] It did not do so, Walker maintained, with the intent to achieve any legitimate purpose. Walker could have stopped there, as the New Jersey court had done, but he went further to evaluate whether the law was discriminatory against sex or sexual orientation. Plaintiffs claimed both as part of a strategy to achieve the highest level of scrutiny possible, but Walker did not force a choice. Instead, he argued that the one is implicated in the other; the law represented both forms of discrimination:

> Proposition 8 targets gays and lesbians in a manner specific to their sexual orientation and, because of their relationship to one another, Proposition 8 targets them specifically due to sex. Having considered the evidence, the relationship between sex and sexual orientation and the fact that Proposition 8 eliminates a right only a gay man or a lesbian would exercise, the court determines that plaintiffs' equal protection claim is based on sexual orientation, but this claim is equivalent to a claim of discrimination based on sex.[148]

While the theoretical linkage between sex discrimination and sexual-orientation discrimination was conceded, Walker's reasoning comports with the Iowa court that, in practice, the law burdened gays and lesbians as gays and lesbians, by definition, are the only individuals who would seek to marry someone of the same sex. In so doing, he extended the dignity of recognition to the plaintiffs as gays and lesbians, evaluating the proposition in terms of whom it targeted. Insofar as the law discriminated as a matter of both sex and sexual orientation, Walker held it to higher scrutiny, but to the extent that the practical discrimination was grounded in sexual orientation, he further recognized gays as a suspect class: "evidence at trial shows that gays and lesbians are the type of minority strict scrutiny was designed to protect."[149]

Walker's ruling was appealed to the Ninth Circuit, but in ruling for a unanimous court in *Perry v. Brown*, Judge Stephen Reinhardt narrowed the question before the court.[150] The case was not about whether the state of California could be or is compelled to recognize same-sex marriage. Indeed, that question was decided by the state's supreme court, and consequently, when Proposition 8 was passed on November 4, 2008, the state of California had already recognized same-sex and cross-sex marriages. The effect of the proposition, then, according to Reinhardt, was to "to take away from same-sex couples the right to be granted marriage licenses and thus legally use the designation of 'marriage.'"[151] The court was concerned only with evaluating "the validity of Proposition 8's *elimination* of the rights of same-sex couples to marry."[152]

By framing the question that way, Reinhardt did not evaluate Walker's ruling. He did not assess whether (1) the proposition trampled a fundamental right to marry as follows from the Fourteenth Amendment's due process clause or (2) whether the proposition by excluding same-sex couples from marriage violated the Fourteenth Amendment's equal protection clause. Instead, because the right to marry existed for a few months in 2008 and the proposition eliminated that right, the Ninth Circuit held that the proposition violated the equal protection clause by singling out one group and depriving that group of a right without a legitimate reason.[153]

At least two aspects of that holding should be emphasized. First, the rational basis standard is utilized. Second, Reinhardt's construction of circumstances of the case analogized Proposition 8 to Colorado's

Amendment 2 as evaluated in *Romer v. Evans*: "Proposition 8 is remarkably similar to Amendment 2."[154] Just as the amendment singled out gays, lesbians, and bisexuals, and deprived them of any access to any legal protections on that basis and thereby violated the equal protection clause, so too did Proposition 8. And, similarly, in *Perry v. Brown*, Reinhardt made no determination of suspect-class status because *Romer* indicated that none was necessary. If the Colorado amendment was unconstitutional because it isolated a particular class of people and essentially excluded them from legal and political rights, rendering them unrecognizable before the law, then Proposition 8 essentially did the same thing: "Like Amendment 2, Proposition 8 denies 'equal protection of the laws in the most literal sense' [*Romer* at 633], because it 'carves out' an 'exception' to California's equal protection clause, by removing equal access to marriage, which gays and lesbians previously enjoyed, from the scope of that constitutional guarantee [*Strauss*, 207 P.3d at 61]."[155] Although the scope of Amendment 2 was far larger than Proposition 8's narrow focus on eliminating one right rather than on cutting gays, lesbians, and bisexuals out of the realm of legal and political recognition of the polity, as the amendment would have done, "these differences . . . do not render *Romer* less applicable."[156] Thus, the Ninth Circuit Court upheld Walker's holding: "Proposition 8 serves no purpose, and has no effect, other than to lessen the status and human dignity of gays and lesbians in California, and to officially reclassify their relationships and families as inferior to those of opposite-sex couples."[157]

According to Reinhardt, evaluating the underlying due process claim or the scrutiny level as applied to gay persons, as Walker had done, was unnecessary because evaluating the constitutionality of purposively eliminating a right of a targeted group "is the narrowest ground for adjudicating the constitutional questions before us. . . . Because courts generally decide constitutional questions on the narrowest ground available, we consider [this] argument first."[158] Nevertheless, many commentators noted the strategy inherent in writing a decision so grounded in *Romer v. Evans* when, since *Goodridge,* so many state courts had not only relied on *Lawrence* but had engaged the question of suspect-class status for gays, lesbians, and bisexuals.[159] Reinhardt's ruling indicated that to maintain both the district and the circuit holdings against Proposition 8 required that the Supreme Court break no new doctrinal ground. It merely had to rely on a fifteen-year-old precedent, one that did not engage suspect-class status or even question whether states could legitimately criminalize consensual same-sex sexual activity.

The Supreme Court never evaluated the substance of the district or circuit court holdings when it ruled in *Hollingsworth v. Perry* in June of 2013.[160] It did not engage whether Proposition 8 was constitutional.[161] It ruled that supporters of Proposition 8 did not have standing. Nevertheless, as its denial of standing sustained lower court decisions, the decision was a watershed moment in gay and lesbian legal history. Hardly a decade had passed since the Supreme Court acknowledged homosexuals to be persons subject to a history of discrimination instead of defining homosexuality as a sex act subject to possible criminalization. In 2003, in *Lawrence*, the Court ruled that viewing homosexuality as an act misapprehended its importance to establishing, maintaining, and dignifying personhood. Now, ten years later, the Court, in *Hollingsworth*, and even more so in *United States v. Windsor*, delivered the same day and discussed in more detail below, declared that gays and lesbians should not only be recognized as *persons* entitled to the constitutional dignity that follows from that status but also be recognized as entitled to certain rights of *citizens*, namely, civil marriage[162]—or, at least, that the federal government could not deny states the choice to so recognize gays and lesbians as citizens capable of entering into a marriage contract. Thus, in the span of a decade, the Court's recognition of what it means to be a gay and lesbian person under the Constitution had drastically changed— from criminal act to dignified person to capable citizen.

The Court did engage the question of marriage recognition in *United States v. Windsor*, which it issued the same day as *Hollingsworth*. But in so doing it did *not* apply traditional tiered scrutiny status, did *not* evaluate whether gay persons constituted a suspect class, and instead grounded its rationale in an argument about human dignity as follows from the due process clause of the Fourteenth Amendment. The ruling discussed the sovereign right of states to regulate marriage, thereby invoking the federalism principle, but it stipulated that DOMA violated equal protection and due process liberty as protected under the Fourteenth Amendment. Yet, in so claiming, Justice Kennedy, who wrote for the majority, appeared only to hold both claims to rational basis review, arguing that "the principal purpose [of DOMA] is to impose inequality."[163] Put differently, the law seeks to differentiate for no other reason than animus, and therefore the law fails rational basis review.

In the two years between *Windsor* and *Obergefell*, at least sixteen state courts, twenty-nine federal district courts, and five federal appellate courts struck down state bans on same-sex-marriage recognition.[164] In that same period only one state court (Tennessee), two federal district courts (Louisiana and Puerto Rico), and one federal appellate court (Sixth Circuit) have upheld the state bans.[165] All but two state rulings

TABLE 6.1. State Court Rulings Striking Same-Sex Marriage Bans since *Windsor* (detailing whether and how state bans violate the Fourteenth Amendment's Equal Protection Clause and whether the court finds a fundamental right to marry regardless of sex under the Fourteenth Amendment's Due Process Clause)

Date	Case Name	Court	Suspect Class (EPC)	Fund. Right (DPC)
9/27/2013	*Garden State Equality v. Dow*	New Jersey*		
12/9/2013	*Griego v. Oliver*	New Mexico**	Yes (Intermediate/SO)	No
5/9/2014	*Wright v. Arkansas*	Arkansas	No (Rational Basis)	Yes
7/9/2014	*Brinkman v. Long & McDaniel-Miccio v. Colorado*	Colorado	No (Rational Basis)	Yes
7/17/2014	*Huntsman v. Heavlin*	Florida	No (Rational Basis)	Yes
7/25/2014	*Pareto v. Ruvin*	Florida	No (Rational Basis)	Yes
8/5/2014	*In Re Estate of Bangor*	Florida	No (Rational Basis)	Yes
9/22/2014	*Costanza and Brewer v. Caldwell*	Louisiana	No (Rational Basis)	Yes
10/3/2014	*Barrier v. Vasterling*	Missouri	No (Rational Basis)	No
11/5/2014	*Missouri v. Jennifer Florida*	Missouri	No (Rational Basis)	Yes
11/7/2014	*Lawson v. Jackson County Dept. of Recorder of Deeds*	Missouri	Yes (Intermediate/ Sex)	Yes

*No federal Fourteenth Amendment claim was made. This case dealt with whether the designation of civil union created a material harm for same-sex couples since *Windsor* since the federal government does not recognize them. The Court determined that "[s]ame-sex couples must be allowed to marry in order to obtain equal protection of the law under the New Jersey Constitution" (Docket No. L-1729-11, page 53).
**Earlier rulings in New Mexico that dealt with recognition of same-sex marriage within particular counties include *Hanna v. Salazar* (8/22/2013), *Griego v. Oliver* (8/26/2013), *Stark v. Martinez* (8/27/2013), *Newton v. Stover* (8/29/2013), and *Katz v. Kamarripa* (9/5/2013). All of these cases were won by the same-sex-marriage proponents. They are not included as these cases were appealed, consolidated, and the state supreme court ruled in *Griego*.

deemed same-sex marriage to be a fundamental right protected by the due process clause of the Fourteenth Amendment, and only two subjected the ban to intermediate scrutiny, one court considering it to be a sex-based classification and one considering gays and lesbians to constitute a suspect class (see table 6.1).

Of the federal rulings, all but five considered same-sex-marriage recognition to be a fundamental right protected under the Fourteenth Amendment's due process clause. All but six rulings considered the ban to fall under rational basis review. The others held gays and lesbians to constitute a suspect class and laws classifying by sexual orientation to be subject to intermediate scrutiny. The Ninth Circuit did so following the standard as previously established by that court in *SmithKline*. The Fourth Circuit, in affirming the district court ruling in *Wolf v. Walker*, at least tacitly did so insofar as *Walker* announced that sexual-orientation classifications should be subject to intermediate scrutiny (see tables 6.2 and 6.3.) The clearest point to take away is that federal and state courts considering the marriage bans were more likely to rule the bans unconstitutional because (1) they infringed upon a fundamental right to marry as protected by the Fourteenth Amendment's due process clause and state justification for such imposition does not survive strict scrutiny and/or because (2) they infringed upon the Fourteenth Amendment's guarantee of equal protection of gay and lesbian citizens, and state justification for the laws had no rational basis. In far fewer cases did judges hold the bans unconstitutional by deeming gays and lesbians a suspect class and thus raising the threshold of scrutiny.

The decision of the federal district court of Utah in *Kitchen v. Herbert* is illustrative.[166] First, the court assessed the potential impact of the *Windsor* ruling on the question before it, and held that "the Constitution's protection of individual rights of gay and lesbian citizens" outweighs the state's claim to its sovereign police power to regulate marriage. Citing Justice Scalia's dissent, the federal district judge ruled "that the important federalism concerns at issue here are nevertheless insufficient to save a state-law prohibition that denies the Plaintiffs their rights to due process and equal protection under the law."[167] Then, the judge turned to the due process claim of whether same-sex marriage was a fundamental right and unequivocally stated that the right to marriage cannot turn on the sex of those who seek to access it:

TABLE 6.2. Federal District Court Rulings Striking Same-Sex Marriage Bans since *Windsor* (detailing whether and how state bans violate the Fourteenth Amendment's equal protection clause and whether the court finds a fundamental right to marry regardless of sex under the Fourteenth Amendment's due process clause)

Date	Case Name	Court	Suspect Class (EPC)	Fund. Right (DPC)
12/5/2013	*Gray v. Orr*	Illinois (a)		
12/20/2013	*Kitchen v. Herbert*	Utah	No (Rational Basis)	Yes
12/23/2013	*Obergefell v. Wymyslo*	Ohio	No (Rational Basis)	Yes
1/4/2014	*Bishop v. United States*	Oklahoma	No (Rational Basis)	No
2/12/2014	*Bourke v. Beshear*	Kentucky	No (Rational Basis)	Yes
2/13/2014	*Bostic v. Rainey*	Virginia	No (Rational Basis)	Yes
2/21/2014	*Lee v. Orr*	Illinois	No (Rational Basis)	Yes
2/26/2014	*DeLeon v. Perry*	Texas	No (Rational Basis)	Yes
3/14/2014	*Tanco v. Haslam*	Tennessee	No (Rational Basis)	No
3/21/2014	*DeBoer v. Snyder*	Michigan	No (Rational Basis)	Yes
4/10/2014	*Baskin v. Bogan*	Indiana (b)		
4/14/2014	*Henry v. Himes*	Ohio	No (Rational Basis)	Yes
5/13/2014	*Latta v. Otter*	Idaho	Yes (Intermediate/SO)	Yes
5/19/2014	*Geiger v. Kitzhaber*	Oregon	No (Rational Basis)	No
5/19/2014	*Evans v. Utah*	Utah (c)		
5/20/2014	*Whitewood v. Wolf*	Pennsylvania	Yes (Intermediate/SO)	Yes
6/6/2014	*Wolf v. Walker*	Wisconsin	Yes (Intermediate/SO)	Yes
6/25/2014	*Baskin v. Bogan*	Indiana	No (Rational Basis)	Yes
7/1/2014	*Love v. Beshear*	Kentucky	Yes (Intermediate/SO)	No
7/9/2014	*Burns v. Hickenlooper*	Colorado (d)		
8/19/2014	*Bowling v. Pence*	Indiana	No (Rational Basis)	No
8/21/2014	*Brenner v. Scott Sandoval*	Florida	Not reviewed given DPC	Yes
10/10/2014	*Fisher-Borne v. Smith*	North Carolina (f)		
10/10/2014	*Gerber v. Berlin and Cooper*	North Carolina (f)		
10/10/2014	*General Synod of the United Church of Christ v. Cooper*	North Carolina (f)		

Table 6.2 (*cont.*)

Date	Case Name	Court	Suspect Class (EPC)	Fund. Right (DPC)
10/12/2014	Hamby v. Parnell	Alaska (g)		
10/17/2014	*Majors v. Horne*	Arizona (h)		
10/17/2014	*Connolly v. Roche*	Arizona (h)		
10/17/2014	*Guzzo v. Mead*	Wyoming (i)		
11/4/2014	*Marie v. Moser*	Kansas (j)		

TABLE 6.3. Federal Appellate Court Rulings Striking Same-Sex Marriage Bans since *Windsor*

Date	Case Name	Court	Suspect Class (EPC)	Fund. Right (DPC)
6/25/2014	*Kitchen v. Herbert*	Tenth Circuit	Not reviewed given DPC	Yes
6/25/2014	*Bishop v. Smith*	Tenth Circuit	Not reviewed given DPC	Yes
7/28/2014	*Bostic v. Shaefer*	Fourth Circuit	Not reviewed given DPC	Yes
9/4/2014	*Baskin v. Bogan* and *Wolf v. Walker*	Seventh Circuit (e)	Yes (Intermediate/SO)	Yes
10/7/2014	*Latta v. Otter* and *Sevcik v. Sandoval*	Ninth Circuit	Yes (Intermediate/SO)	Yes

(a) Did not engage the broader equal protection or due process claims but granted a temporary injunction against the state ban on same-sex marriage in the context of one couple given one member's medical condition and imminent death.

(b) Granted a temporary restraining order against enforcing the same-sex marriage ban in Indiana in the context of the imminent death of one member of a same-sex couple.

(c) Granted injunction against the Utah ban on same-sex marriage and stayed this ruling for twenty-one days pending ruling by the Tenth Circuit.

(d) Ruled that the Colorado ban on same-sex marriage and distinction of civil union cannot be maintained given the Tenth Circuit (of which Colorado is part) ruling in *Kitchen* and *Bishop*. Did not directly address equal protection or due process claim.

(e) Affirmed both district court rulings.

(f) Ruled that the North Carolina ban on same-sex marriage cannot be enforced given the Fourth Circuit (of which North Carolina is part) ruling in *Bostic*. Did not directly address equal protection or due process claim.

(g) Ruled that the Alaska ban on same-sex marriage cannot be enforced given the Ninth Circuit (of which Arizona is part) ruling in *Latta*. Did not directly address equal protection or due process claim.

(h) Ruled that the Arizona ban on same-sex marriage cannot be enforced given the Ninth Circuit (of which Arizona is part) ruling in *Latta*. Did not directly address equal protection or due process claim.

(i) Ruled that the Wyoming ban on same-sex marriage cannot be enforced given the Tenth Circuit (of which Missouri is part) ruling in *Kitchen* and *Bishop*. Did not directly address equal protection or due process claim.

(j) Ruled that Kansas ban on same-sex marriage cannot be enforced given ruling by the Tenth Circuit (of which Kansas is part) ruling in *Kitchen* and *Bishop*. Did not directly address equal protection or due process claim.

The Fourteenth Amendment protects the liberty rights of all citizens, and none of the State's arguments presents a compelling reason why the scope of that right should be greater for heterosexual individuals than it is for gay and lesbian individuals. If, as is clear from the Supreme Court cases discussing the right to marry, a heterosexual person's choices about intimate association and family life are protected from unreasonable government interference in the marital context, then a gay or lesbian person also enjoys these same protections.[168]

This conclusion, the judge maintained, is "supported, even required" by the Supreme Court's discussion of a fundamental right of personal autonomy in *Lawrence*. If state action against gays and lesbians cannot be grounded in moral opprobrium, as *Lawrence* declared, and if marriage restrictions cannot be reasonably maintained on procreative grounds, then "[a]ll citizens, regardless of their sexual identity, have a fundamental right to liberty, and this right protects an individual's ability to marry and the intimate choices a person makes about marriage and family."[169] By articulating a fundamental right to marry regardless of the sex and sexual orientation of those individuals who seek to access that right, this court raised the scrutiny level of a law seeking to infringe upon that right to strict scrutiny. The court found that Utah's constitutional ban on same-sex marriage served no compelling government interest.[170]

Furthermore, in *Kitchen*, the federal district court retained the practice of holding laws that classify by sexual orientation only to rational basis review; gays and lesbians were not considered a suspect class. As summarized by the Tenth Circuit Court of Appeals, which upheld the district court's ruling on June 25, 2014, the lower court ruled that the state ban on same-sex-marriage recognition "denied plaintiffs equal protection because it classified based on sex and sexual orientation without a rational basis."[171]

Like the lower court decision, the Tenth Circuit's ruling did not evaluate whether gays and lesbians constitute a suspect class or sexual orientation a suspect classification. Although plaintiffs maintained that the Utah ban constituted sex and sexual-orientation discrimination, the court's ruling and a judicial concurrence did not engage this claim.[172] Instead, the Tenth Circuit grounded its decision on the declaration that marriage, regardless of the sex of those individuals seeking to enter it, is a due process fundamental right, and that infringements of such rights are only upheld if they are narrowly tailored to meet a compelling government interest. Citing that "all fundamental rights comprised within the term liberty are protected by the Federal Constitution from invasion by the States," the court held that Utah's denial of recognition to same-sex couples violated this principle.[173] According to this court, not only is there "little doubt that the right to marry is a fundamental liberty," but the claim that only opposite-sex marriage is fundamental or that "the term 'marriage' by its nature excludes same-sex couples" is flawed.[174] Same-sex marriage does not redefine the meaning of marriage; rather, it opens up an institution to individuals who were previously denied access to it, and such exclusion, according to this court, denied gays and lesbians "equal dignity for their marital aspirations." Reasoning from *Lawrence*, the Court concluded that just because there was no long history of a protected right to homosexual intercourse and no long history of same-sex marriage per se, this history does not thereby prevent the state either from recognizing gays and lesbians as noncriminals, as *Lawrence* did, or from recognizing their potential for marriage. *Lawrence* redefined the issue at stake; at issue was not a right to engage in a particular sexual act but a right to live with basic human dignity. Similarly, the Tenth Circuit reasoned, "Just as it was improper to ask whether there is a right to engage in homosexual sex, we do not ask whether there is a right to participate in same-sex marriage."[175] Access to marriage, and the rights, responsibilities, and stability that union affords, engenders and maintains human dignity. In other words, whether there is "traditional" marriage or same-sex marriage is irrelevant; there is only marriage and the access to it is a marker of basic human dignity. Insofar as the Utah law maintained a distinction between cross-sex and same-sex marriage, it created a sex-based classification that did meet the threshold for any infringement on a fundamental right as guaranteed by due process liberty, i.e., a narrowly tailored means to achieve a compelling end.

Although *Windsor* makes no such explicit claims (1) that same-sex marriage is a fundamental right demanding strict scrutiny, (2) that gay persons constitute a suspect class and laws affecting them should be subject to higher scrutiny, or (3) that sexual orientation is a suspect classification and laws so classifying should be subject to higher scrutiny, some federal judges read that ruling as having some if not all of those implications. Even more telling, while the Tenth Circuit refused to engage *Windsor* as compelling higher scrutiny for laws affecting gays and lesbians determined to be a suspect class, as the Ninth Circuit did in *Smith-Kline*, it nevertheless embraced Justice Kennedy's alternative notion that laws stripping individuals of human dignity are unconstitutional. Even as the Tenth Circuit did not read the review used in *Windsor* as heightened scrutiny while the Ninth Circuit did, the Tenth Circuit did interpret *Windsor* as standing for the proposition that marriage provides certain rights and responsibilities that "support the dignity of each person" and did argue that "a great deal of the dignity of same-sex relationships inheres in the loving bonds between those who seek to marry and the personal autonomy of making such choices."[176] In short, the Tenth Circuit affirmed a right to marry as flowing primarily, if not singularly, from a due process liberty, which guards against state debasement of human dignity, a definition of liberty elaborated by Justice Kennedy in *Lawrence* and *Windsor*. If *Loving v. Virginia* stood both for the proposition that marriage, regardless of race, was a fundamental right protected by the due process clause and for the proposition that the state ban on interracial marriage constituted an overbroad racial classification that served no compelling purpose, the *Kitchen* ruling only embraced the former principle. No equal protection/suspect class analysis was offered. In this way, the Tenth Circuit embraced a pattern of Supreme Court jurisprudence on gay rights claims discussed in far more detail in the next chapter: a pattern of forgoing any recognition of gays and lesbians as a suspect class and of abandoning that doctrine for a newer claim grounded in a seemingly universal claim to human dignity.

Conclusion

By the turn of the twenty-first century, state courts, lower federal courts, and executive branch officials began to recognize gays and lesbians as a discriminated-against minority—at least insofar as it was one of the crucial qualities of a judicially identified suspect class—to serve the development of the fifth modality of recognition discussed in this book: gays and lesbians as eligible for and capable of marriage. Executive officials began to invoke and rely upon the judiciary's scrutiny doctrine to assert independent authority to recognize same-sex marriage shortly after Massachusetts became the first state to recognize same-sex marriage. Mayors were the first to experiment with such recognition. After *Windsor*, state attorneys general assumed independent authority to not defend existing state bans on same-sex marriage, and such refusal has been defended by the Obama administration. This chapter situated this phenomenon within a longer history of executive assertions of independent authority to interpret law. While these assertions pushed the bounds of executive power against a norm of judicial supremacy in determining constitutional meaning, they tended more to *rely* on that judicial authority and, indeed, supremacy, than to undermine it. This reliance was evident insofar as the early mayoral claims, the Obama administration's refusal to defend DOMA, and more recent positions of state attorneys general often explicitly adopted judicially developed scrutiny doctrine even as the Supreme Court has not explicitly applied it to same-sex-marriage litigation.

Judicial recognition of the meaning of gay and lesbian citizenship—at least insofar as that citizenship entails a determination of the capability to enter into civil marriage—has taken divergent paths. State and lower federal courts have invoked the established scrutiny doctrine to recognize gays and lesbians as a suspect class and to declare that denial of marital recognition violates equal protection when that denial is subject to heightened scrutiny. More recently, they have held marriage, regardless of the gender of those seeking to enter into it, to be a fundamental right flowing from due process liberty. Laws violating such rights are subject to strict scrutiny.

Many state rulings before *Windsor* indicated an early and repeated unwillingness to consider statutory refusal to classify same-sex marriage as sexual-orientation discrimination as well as a refusal to apply any higher scrutiny to these laws. If higher scrutiny was considered applicable—and this was most often only considered in concurrences—then it was considered applicable by means of construing the discrimination against same-sex marriage as *sex* discrimination rather than *sexual-orientation* discrimination. This pattern shifted in 2008 when the California Supreme Court was the first to consider sexual orientation as a suspect classification and gays, lesbians, and bisexuals as a suspect class. Furthermore, whereas prior to the California decision, courts refused to consider same-sex marriage a fundamental right following from the Fourteenth Amendment's due process clause, construing instead that marriage's fundamental status was restricted to its cross-sex version, after the California case, state supreme courts consistently named all marriage a fundamental right.

In the wake of *Windsor*, federal courts considering same-sex marriage mostly agreed that same-sex marriage fell within the scope of access to marriage as a fundamental right, as follows from due process. They also stipulated that bans on same-sex-marriage recognition constituted violations of equal protection. Consequently, after *Windsor*, access to same-sex marriage could, as a doctrinal matter, if it came before the Supreme Court, rest simply on a due process liberty claim. The Court would not need to invoke an equal protection claim, and thus, it could avoid the question of gay, lesbian, and bisexual suspect-class status altogether. Indeed, as discussed in the next chapter, on June 26, 2015, in *Obergefell v. Hodges*, the Court did just that.[177]

As was argued in this book's introduction, a developmental approach considers how attention to sexuality as an ordering concern of governance and regulation enriches explanations of a range of concerns of interest to political scientists. In this chapter, attention to sexuality reveals institutional and ideational shifts in the separation of powers, particularly executive branch claims to constitutional interpretation. And, it nuances the blunt dichotomy of departmentalism versus judicial supremacy by demonstrating how executive officials rely on judicial authority to make their own constitutional claims. Similarly, attention to whether and how state governing authorities recognize sexuality reveals insights into the relationship between lower courts and the Supreme Court. These lower courts have innovated in recognizing the constitutional supports for marriage equality by relying heavily upon the established doctrine of suspect-class status and tiered scrutiny. The irony, of course, as explored in the next chapter, is that the Supreme Court has avoided this doctrine when carving its own path to recognizing the constitutionality of gay and lesbian rights generally and marriage equality specifically.

7

A Jurisprudence of Blindness

Same-Sex Marriage, Human Dignity, and the Erosion of Scrutiny Doctrine

Moreover, if this is meant to be an equal-protection opinion, it is a confusing one. The opinion does not resolve and indeed does not even mention what had been the central question in this litigation: whether, under the Equal Protection Clause, laws restricting marriage to a man and a woman are reviewed for more than mere rationality. In accord with my previously expressed skepticism about the Court's "tiers of scrutiny" approach, I would review this classification only for its rationality. As nearly as I can tell, the Court agrees with that. . . . The sum of all the Court's nonspecific hand-waving is that this law is invalid (maybe on equal-protection grounds, maybe on substantive-due process grounds, and perhaps with some amorphous federalism component playing a role) because it is motivated by a "bare . . . desire to harm" couples in same-sex marriages.
—Justice Antonin Scalia, *United States v. Windsor*, dissenting, 2013[1]

Attempting to find a legal label for what transpired in *Windsor* is difficult.
—Judge Christopher Charles Piazza, *Wright v. State of Arkansas*, 2014[2]

[P]etitioners contend that the Equal Protection Clause requires their States to license and recognize same-sex marriages. The majority does not seriously engage with this claim. Its discussion is, quite frankly, difficult to follow. The central point seems to be that there is a "synergy between" the Equal Protection Clause and the Due Process Clause,

and that some precedents relying on one Clause have also relied on the other. Absent from this portion of the opinion, however, is anything resembling our usual framework for deciding equal protection cases.
—Chief Justice John Roberts, *Obergefell v. Hodges*, dissenting, 2015[3]

Supreme Court rulings evaluating laws that classify by sexual orientation include *Bowers v. Hardwick, Romer v. Evans, Lawrence v. Texas,* and *United States v. Windsor.* These have applied rational basis explicitly (*Bowers*) or have not clearly articulated what scrutiny level is applied (rulings since *Bowers*).[4] Each decision does differently define and recognize the meaning and content of gay and lesbian sexuality. Whereas *Bowers* understood homosexuality as conduct, *Romer* conceptualized it as a status separable from conduct. *Lawrence* differently recognized it as a status constituted by and thus inseparable from and nonreducible to conduct. And both *Windsor* and *Obergefell* offered judicial recognition of a new modality of same-sex sexuality, namely, a relationship through which individual dignity is made manifest whereby if such recognition is withheld, unjustifiable material harm is likely to follow.[5] Nevertheless, even as the Court has recognized gays, lesbians, and bisexuals as a discriminated-against class since *Romer*, it has not specified gays, lesbians, and bisexuals as a suspect class subject to higher scrutiny.[6]

The Supreme Court's refusal to recognize gays and lesbians as a suspect class in its string of rulings since *Romer* is interesting as a developmental matter for at least two reasons. First, it marks a clear and sustained, and perhaps even durable, shift from what this chapter will show is an increasingly muddied twentieth-century doctrine of tiered scrutiny. Second, it highlights how, in its gay rights jurisprudence, the Court has embraced what might be called a jurisprudence of blindness. As detailed in chapter 5, while *Lawrence* achieved the long-sought objective of decriminalization, it rendered the state blind to sexuality, a dynamic similar to the way the Rehnquist Court—and to a greater extent the Roberts Court—has pursued color-blindness. Similar to what David

Eng has called "queer liberalism"—or the idea that gay rights are made manifest primarily or even only in the inclusion of LGBT peoples into the dominant modes of relationship recognition already established by heteronormative policy paradigms—this jurisprudence "relies upon the logic of racial colorblindness in its assertion that racial difference has given way to an abstract U.S. community of individualism and merit." Color-blindness and queer liberalism are wedded to a refusal to see differences and a commitment to be "post-identity."[7]

This chapter shows how this jurisprudence of blindness has been built on the eroding foundations of scrutiny doctrine, on the refusal to translate histories of discrimination and powerlessness into the judicially cognizable suspect-class status. This chapter explores its erosion as an empirical matter. It draws attention to the transformations and alterations in the doctrine over time that have made it increasingly muddled, and it highlights how, in its gay rights jurisprudence, the Supreme Court may be shifting to a new doctrine, grounded not in equal protection but foremost in liberty and dignity.[8]

Understanding how scrutiny doctrine eroded over time requires that it be viewed as more than a constitutional interpretative tool. While suspect class and scrutiny is a particular approach used to evaluate laws that impinge on equal protection and fundamental rights, it is also a particular historical construction that was developed over the middle and late twentieth century to legitimate judicial authority after the Court's institutional legitimacy was dealt repeated blows during the late nineteenth and early twentieth centuries. This authority has always been somewhat suspect in a democracy, both because federal judges are unelected and because their decisions may negate majoritarian interests.

This chapter evaluates suspect class and tiered scrutiny as a legitimation theory, rooted in the Court's 1938 ruling in *United States v. Carolene Products*, which drew on early judicial interpretations of the Fourteenth Amendment as intended to end laws and cultures of identity-based subordination.[9] A legitimation theory refers to "the Court's institutional habits in the endeavor to maintain its own legitimacy. It is the Court's institutional perspective on what makes judicial power legitimate."[10] Evidence of such a theory can be assessed through the implications and consistency of the Court's rulings.[11] The reigning judicial legitimation theory prior to the Progressive Era (1890s–1930s) was text-based formalism, or the idea that judges maintained particular legal expertise in interpreting constitutional and statutory text to render neutral rulings. So long as judges adhered to principles and guidelines of legal doctrine and the deduction of original meaning, their institutional legitimacy was generally stable. But, as the formal "science" of legal interpretation was increasingly questioned in the late nineteenth and early twentieth century by Progressive legal realists and as the legal academy and the general public increasingly characterized judicial rulings as mere imposition of personal values and partisan preferences, the judiciary's institutional legitimacy fell into crisis.[12]

The development of suspect class analysis was a response to that crisis, one that reasserted the legitimacy of the Court by reimaging the role of the judge in a democracy. No longer was a judge (only) an expert in doctrine or textual analysis, or at least judicial legitimacy did not rest on that basis. Rather, a judge was an expert in democratic process. Suspect-class analysis offered federal judges a clear role in a democracy when the rationale for their authority was increasingly questioned. When determining the constitutionality of law, judges were to assess the context in which the legislation was considered and whether that process had malfunctioned by excluding interests of classes subject to the law. Judges did not counter democracy's majoritarianism; instead, they ensured that it functioned properly. Tiered-scrutiny and suspect-class doctrine ensured a role for the unelected judge in an otherwise pluralist democracy.

This chapter describes suspect-class analysis and tiered scrutiny as solutions to a crisis of institutional legitimacy. It then reviews particular Supreme Court rulings to illustrate how, over time, the Court altered the scrutiny and suspect-class doctrines. Examination of decisions about racial and sex/gender discrimination reveal two gradual transformations. First, in the context of racial affirmative action rulings in employment and education, the Court conflated difference between suspect class and suspect classification, thereby undermining its initial intention to scrutinize laws affecting "discrete and insular minorities" or classes, and refocusing its attention to laws that classify by race or other classifications more generally and without regard to historical context. Thus, a scrutiny originally developed to monitor the context in which law was crafted in order that undemocratic subordination may be detected and countered was transformed into a decontextualized doctrine of abstract

principle to guard against any classification that might indicate difference. In so doing, the Court exemplified a key dynamic of ideational development: manipulating an idea to serve antithetical ends from those
that it was originally intended to produce.[13] Second, the Court muddled
the boundaries between scrutiny tiers either by altering the language of
threshold tests or by invoking elements that would compel suspect-class
application but not applying the higher scrutiny that would thereby follow. Recognizing these shifts, scholars have suggested new categories of
scrutiny that fall between the three traditional tiers, such as intermediate
scrutiny with teeth or rational basis with bite. Yet, their existence would
suggest that the doctrine has become increasingly unstable. The chapter continues the examination of muddled scrutiny by evaluating *Romer*,
Lawrence, *Windsor*, and *Obergefell*. It highlights, first, that all four rulings
adhere to rational basis review, despite no explicit indication by Justice
Kennedy, who wrote all four, that this threshold was used, and, second,
that Kennedy invents and then continues to apply—since *Lawrence*—a
capacious justificatory constraint by invoking human dignity. Some gay
rights—those that would establish gays and lesbians on more equal footing with straight majorities in terms of noncriminality and access to
formal institutions of recognition such as marriage—*may* follow from
this dignity-inspired jurisprudence of blindness. Other protections from
discrimination—particularly those that position gay and lesbian identity
as an expressive right—may not follow from this jurisprudential logic.

It All Began with "Filled Milk": Judicial Legitimacy and the Development of Higher Scrutiny

By the mid-1930s the Court had endured decades of criticism from the
public and politicians alike for invalidating laws intended to secure public welfare, whether through minimum wages, maximum hours, or tax
regulations.[14] This hostility ebbed and flowed but grew louder as the
Court struck down New Deal policy attempts to mitigate the effects
of the Great Depression as beyond what the text of the Constitution
permits.[15] Since at least the 1890s, this formal textualism had been
challenged by an alternative compulsion that the Constitution adapt
to changing times and new exigencies that the Framers could not have
foreseen. And, the economic crisis and the Court's blocking of policy

responses advanced the critique. The father of the revolt against textualism was the legal realist Oliver Wendell Holmes, who maintained that legal disputes represented "a conflict between two social desires" and that when the text was unclear as to how that conflict would be remedied, which was more often than not, "judges are called upon to exercise the sovereign prerogative of choice."[16] Legal realism accepted that the Constitution's terminology was vague, hardly comprehensive, and subject to interpretation. According to one Progressive Era historian, "Since most of the words and phrases dealing with the powers and the limits of government are vague and must in practice be interpreted by human beings, it follows that the Constitution as practice is a living thing."[17] And, to fill in the gaps of a vague and often silent Constitution, realists embraced the newly emerging social sciences and the evidence they offered in place of formal principles for deducing the meaning of constitutional phrases.[18] Realists maintained that deduction from text was just as flexible and value-laden as their own turn to external factors. In the end, perhaps legal realism served more to debunk claims that textualism was neutral than it did to bolster its own position as a more legitimate alternative to textualism.[19]

Legal realism undermined the authority on which judicial power was originally founded. If, as living constitutionalism granted, "judges are men . . . made of human stuff like the rest and sharing with us the common limitations and frailties of human nature," then legal interpretation was hardly a neutral rendering of legal meaning through constitutional principle.[20] Indeed, legal realism suggested, "the distinction between a government of laws and a government of men is absurd."[21] This clash between the older paradigm of textualism and a newer pragmatic imperative to meet crises without the Constitution as a hindrance was on full display at the Supreme Court through the 1930s.

Differences of interpretation and radical shifts in what the Constitution permitted characterized the Court's jurisprudence of the middle and late 1930s. In the context of sustained popular criticism and under threat of Franklin Roosevelt's judicial reorganization plan, which would have stacked the Supreme Court with as many as six new justices, the Court articulated one of its most dramatic switches in 1937, suddenly upholding a state minimum-wage law that it had seemingly struck down only months earlier and holding New Deal regulations as valid under the commerce clause. The switch served to illustrate how the Court could render the Constitution's text to mean anything it wanted it to mean. It exemplified the precepts of legal realism, that law was political decision making by other means. And, if this was so, then the entire foundation of judicial legitimacy crumbled.

The Court needed a new basis of institutional legitimacy, which it articulated in *United States v. Carolene Products*. At issue in *Carolene* was a federal statute banning interstate shipment of filled milk, or skimmed milk reconstituted with vegetable oil.[22] The statute was based on congressional findings that filled milk was contrary to public health. Congress maintained authority to regulate the substance under the commerce clause. *Carolene* continued the post-1937 pattern of judicial deference in matters of economic regulation. However, in the decision, Justice Stone articulated a new rationale for judicial purpose in a democracy, detailed in the ruling's famous fourth footnote.

The Carolene company had claimed that it had been unfairly targeted by the law and denied of its due process rights. Justice Stone, however, wrote that the statute's characterization of filled milk as a public health hazard was "a declaration of the legislative findings deemed to support and justify the action taken as a constitutional exertion of the legislative power, aiding informed judicial review, as do the reports of legislative committees, by revealing the rationale of the legislation."[23] Carolene had been fully able to represent its interests in the legislature, and the legislature voted against those interests in an open process. That was the nature of representative pluralist democracy. But, in footnote 4, Stone recognized that this interest-based and conflict-ridden democratic process might malfunction. Stone ruminated on circumstances when such a claim might be valid and how the Court would act, drawing attention to the possibility that

> [t]here may be narrower scope for operation of the presumption of constitutionality when legislation appears on its face to be within a specific prohibition of the Constitution . . . [or when] prejudice against discrete and insular minorities may be a special condition, which tends seriously to curtail the operation of those political processes ordinarily to be relied upon to protect minorities, and which may call for a correspondingly more searching judicial inquiry.[24]

Stone's clerk, Louis Lusky, who drafted the footnote, contended that the intent was not to offer a new strict standard for interpreting the commands of the Fourteenth Amendment but rather to point to some salient possibilities that would distinguish between social and economic rights, and thereby help to clarify the territory to which the Court laid claim, thereby carving out its legitimacy.[25] The footnote was a foundation on which the Court's new institutional legitimacy could be constructed over time.[26]

The footnote captured a basic precept of democratic theory, namely, that individuals affected by a law should have some voice in whether the law is adopted.[27] If a law were adopted that affected a class of people and that class were excluded from the deliberative process, the Court would consider the law more suspect. Stone laid out a rationale for the unelected judiciary's legitimacy in a democracy not based on a particular expertise in formally deducing constitutional meaning through text, but grounded in a different kind of expertise, an expertise in democratic process. The Court could stand as guardian of that process and intervene when it malfunctioned. The footnote's guidelines are a vehicle, gradually developed over the latter half of the twentieth century, to justify judicial authority after the Court's institutional legitimacy was dealt repeated blows during the late nineteenth and early twentieth centuries. John Hart Ely famously articulated this claim to legitimacy in his defense of the Warren Court.[28] The Warren Court's rulings on racial equality, voting rights, and the handling of evidence all fell within this overarching concern with process. They were evaluations of laws generated by a deeply flawed democratic process, one that systematically excluded particular voices. Judicial review was legitimate for Ely insofar as the Warren Court rulings reinforced representation and the participatory process. And, "lawyers are experts on process writ small, the processes by which facts are found and contending parties are allowed to present their claims. And to a degree they are experts on process writ larger, the processes by which issues of public policy are fairly determined."[29] Ely's theory of judicial legitimacy replaced expertise in legal text with expertise in political process to justify the Court's role.[30]

Ely, like many other scholars, offered his justification of judicial decision making as a response to the Court's institutional countermajoritarian potential and to public criticism of the Court's illegitimacy within a democracy. The legitimacy theory he proffered was not meant to suggest that it was one the justices themselves consciously adopted or advocated.[31] Instead, it was a justification of judicial legitimacy put forward in public discourse that was not grounded in formalist textualism. When the political process malfunctioned under plausible circumstances imagined by Stone in the fourth footnote, the Court would not be deferential to the legislature as it was in *Carolene*.

Blurred Lines: Conflating Suspect Class and Suspect Classification and Eroding Tiers of Scrutiny

Carolene's fourth footnote essentially stated that judges must attend to the possibility that democratic deliberation occurred in a context where, despite formal rules to the contrary, inequality of access and voice persisted. In that circumstance, judges must evaluate the process for signs that the resultant law unduly subordinates particular classes contrary to the Constitution's equal protection clause. *Carolene* laid out a path to enforce the Fourteenth Amendment's commandment against subordination.

The qualities of those who might suffer unjust subordination were hardly specific. The footnote provided loose parameters—discrete and insular minorities suffering a history of prejudice—to identify groups that might be eligible for special consideration when a law infringes upon its exercise of rights. Consequently, the principles laid down in the footnote have often been altered and twisted to apply to various group identities that may or may not be insular or discrete, e.g., women (who may be discrete but not insular) or gays (who may be insular in some circumstances but not discrete), but that may maintain a clear claim on suffering discrimination and consequent inequalities and unjust subordination.[32]

That the Fourteenth Amendment's equal protection clause articulates an antisubordination principle is hotly contested. Some suggest that the amendment stands for an anticlassification principle. And, many contend that the antisubordination principle, which would of necessity require classification in order to identify those groups subordinated or dominated by unjust law, is wholly antithetical to the amendment's alleged anticlassification imperative.[33] Of course, if the Fourteenth

Amendment strikes against classification, then the entire jurisprudential development of suspect class and scrutiny levels is deeply shaken. Some justices on the current Roberts Court support the theory that the equal protection clause requires anticlassification or color-blindness.[34] Chief Justice Roberts declared as much in his plurality opinion for the Court when striking down integrative school busing systems in 2007: "'Our Constitution is color-blind.' . . . The way to stop discriminating on the basis of race is to stop discriminating on the basis of race."[35] When offering this decontextualized truism, Roberts referenced Justice John Marshall Harlan's solitary dissent in *Plessy v. Ferguson*: "There is no caste here. Our constitution is color-blind, and neither knows nor tolerates classes among citizens. In respect of civil rights, all citizens are equal before the law."[36] Roberts interpreted Harlan's characterization of equality before the law to demand color-blindness. Additionally, insofar as *Plessy* maintained the constitutionality of racial segregation, and *Brown v. Board of Education* struck down such segregation in public education, the meaning of *Brown* must, by this logic, be congruent with the Harlan dissent.[37] Put differently, the *Brown* ruling must embrace color-blindness. Justice Clarence Thomas made this connection explicit when he challenged the four dissenters in *Parents Involved* who sought to maintain the statutory busing scheme under the principle that the Fourteenth Amendment permitted race consciousness so long as that race consciousness aimed to remedy racial discrimination or subordination. According to Thomas,

> Most of the dissent's criticisms of today's result can be traced to its rejection of the color-blind Constitution. The dissent attempts to marginalize the notion of a color-blind Constitution by consigning it to me and Members of today's plurality. But I am quite comfortable in the company I keep. My view of the Constitution is Justice Harlan's view in *Plessy*: "Our Constitution is color-blind, and neither knows nor tolerates classes among citizens." And my view was the rallying cry for the lawyers who litigated *Brown*. See, e.g., Brief for Appellants in *Brown v. Board of Education*, O.T. 1953, Nos. 1, 2, and 4. P. 65 ("That the Constitution is color blind is our dedicated belief."); Brief for Appellants in *Brown v. Board of Education*, O.T. 1952 No. 1, p. 5 ("The Fourteenth Amendment precludes a state from imposing distinctions or classifications based upon race and color alone.").[38]

Yet, in interpreting *Brown* thus, Thomas ignored the context in which the NAACP lawyers challenging school segregation put forward their color-blind position. He ignored how the rhetoric of color-blindness was used to counter a status quo of unequal educational access suffered by the discrete and insular minority of African American school-children. Color-blindness was a vehicle through which existing law that subordinated on the basis of race might be achieved. It was hardly meant to require total blindness to racial identity and historical and sociological context. Thomas noted that the NAACP Legal Defense Fund (LDF) did advocate color-blindness, but he paid no attention to the context of that advocacy. Racial classification had been utilized to subordinate by maintaining, in part, discriminatory antimiscegenation laws. To challenge these laws that saw color in order to subordinate by color, color-blindness was the obvious alternative; but, a general color-blindness or anticlassification principle that would pay no attention to contextual inequalities of power, access, and voice is not supportable as a matter of constitutional history.[39] And, a wholly color-blind reading of *Brown* is "entirely inconsistent with historical context."[40] As one legal scholar suggests, "At a time when government-imposed subordination of blacks to whites was legitimately recognized in the Supreme Court's black letter law, the idea that some justices on the Court would one day use their plea for a 'color-blind constitution' to support the Court's rejection of any anti-subordination reading of the Fourteenth Amendment would have appeared outright ludicrous."[41] Thomas's interpretation is only accomplished by wrenching the NAACP LDF strategy from the historical context in which it was designed and articulated.

Thomas's and Roberts's reliance on what amounts to a sound bite of Harlan's *Plessy* dissent ignores the full opinion, which articulated that the Fourteenth Amendment was meant to address the past subordination of African Americans. Harlan referenced another case, *Strauder v. West Virginia*,[42] which he maintained rendered the proper interpretation of the Fourteenth Amendment as color conscious and as aimed to counter subordination of discriminated-against minorities:

> We also said: "The words of the amendment it is true, are prohibitory, but they contain a necessary implication of a positive immunity or right, most valuable to the colored race,—the right to exemption from un-

friendly legislation against them distinctively as colored; exemption from legal discriminations, implying inferiority in civil society, lessening the security of their enjoyment of the rights which others enjoy; and discriminations which are steps toward reducing them to the condition of a subject race."[43]

Strauder struck down a state law banning African American participation on juries. In *Strauder*, the Court ruled that the original purpose of the Fourteenth Amendment was to ensure that no law could be made against African Americans on account of their race. No law could strip them of their equal duties and responsibilities of republican citizenship, like jury duty, on the basis of their racial identity. *Strauder* stood for a color-conscious Constitution insofar as such consciousness would promote equality by challenging existing laws that seek to subordinate. Or, as Judge John Minor Wisdom would suggest nearly ninety years later, the Constitution required color-consciousness when attempting to undo legacies of subordination and color-blindness in order to ensure that no further laws are grounded in discriminatory classification schemes: "The Constitution is both color blind and color conscious. . . . [A] classification that denies a benefit, causes harm, or imposes a burden must not be based on race. In that sense the Constitution is color blind. But the Constitution is color conscious to prevent discrimination being perpetuated and to undo the effects of past discrimination."[44]

The *Strauder* ruling was consistent with the first Supreme Court decision to interpret the Fourteenth Amendment, *The Slaughterhouse Cases of 1873*. A divided Court ruled that the amendment was deeply racially conscious and intended to challenge the legal infrastructure that subordinated African Americans. In that case, white butchers challenged a Louisiana statute requiring that all butchers move their trade outside city limits and within facilities built by the Crescent City Live-Stock Landing and Slaughter-House Company. The butchers contended that the law violated their rights under the Thirteenth and Fourteenth Amendments.[45] The Court clarified what it saw as the amendments' intent:

> The most cursory glance at these articles discloses a unity of purpose, when taken in connection with the history of the times, which cannot fail to have an important bearing on any question of doubt concerning their

true meaning. . . . [A]nd on the most casual examination of the language of these amendments, no one can fail to be impressed with the one pervading purpose found in them all, lying at the foundation of each, and without which none of them would have been even suggested; we mean the freedom of the slave race, the security and firm establishment of that freedom, and the protection of the newly-made freeman and citizen from the oppressions of those who had formerly exercised unlimited dominion over him. . . . We do not say that no one else but the negro can share in this protection. Both the language and spirit of the articles are to have their fair and just weight in any question of construction. . . . But what we do say, and what we wish to be understood, is, that in any fair and just construction of any section or phrase of these amendments, it is necessary to look to the purpose which we have said was the pervading spirit of them all, the evil which they were designed to remedy, and the process of continued addition to the Constitution, until that purpose was supposed to be accomplished, as far as constitutional law can accomplish it.[46]

The Court's attention to context behooves an examination of the racially conscious laws that Congress continued to pass in order to continue its antisubordination impulse.[47] These included a federal law to provide money to "destitute colored women and children," as well as a statute to provide material resources to poor "colored" people residing in the District of Columbia.[48] And, the design and purpose of the Freedman's Bureau, which dispensed material resources to former slaves to provide some economic security, was grounded in color awareness and antisubordination.[49] The particular attention toward discrete and insular minorities, which Justice Stone's fourth footnote of *Carolene* articulated, falls in line with judicial precedent and congressional action aimed to undermine any subordinating effects of law. The footnote and the scrutiny doctrine for which it laid the foundation were deeply rooted in an interpretation of the Fourteenth Amendment as racially conscious and meant to prohibit laws that would reinforce the subordination of a historically subject and disadvantaged class, such as African Americans, through law.

By contrast, the color-blind theory of the Fourteenth Amendment's equal protection clause rests, in part, on the reconfiguration of the object toward which the judiciary might be suspect, from suspect class to suspect classification. The *Carolene* footnote indicated that higher scrutiny should be applied to laws that create or maintain "prejudice against discrete and insular minorities." The doctrine has since developed into the identification of "suspect classes," which must exhibit at least four characteristics: immutability, irrelevance, history of discrimination, and political powerlessness.[50] A suspect class is marked by a characteristic that is unchangeable or immutable and that is irrelevant to contributing successfully to society. Race and sex are so considered. Age, blood type, and hair color, while also immutable and irrelevant, are not. This is the case because the Court has contended that there is no evidence of consistent discrimination against or political powerlessness of people of a particular hair color, blood type, or age.[51]

But, while the Court maintains the practice of higher scrutiny, it has applied higher scrutiny not to laws affecting those *classes* but to laws making *classifications*. Contrary to footnote four, color-blind theory ignores histories of discrimination and political powerlessness. Rather, it maintains that any racial classification, regardless of the law's purpose, is inherently suspect. According to one scholar, "the Court now incorrectly defines racial discrimination to mean any racial distinction."[52] Color-blind theory treats racial classification as suspect rather than treating particular classes of individuals as embedded in a configuration of unjust yet powerful inequalities.

That conflation of concern for racial subordination or discrimination with any racial distinction or classification in the law is evident in a variety of affirmative action rulings, such as *Grutter v. Bollinger*. In that ruling, the Court permitted race consciousness in higher education admissions so long as it was narrowly tailored to achieve the compelling interest of diversity in educational settings. However, the Court included a paradoxical statement outlining that such race-conscious policies might be time-limited and ultimately unnecessary in the future, thereby holding out for a full realization of color-blind equality, or at least suggesting that color-blindness and anticlassification would be the end result of the Fourteenth Amendment's aim of equal protection.[53]

The transition to and ultimately conflation of suspect class, i.e., a discrete and insular minority, with suspect classification, i.e., racial classifications more generally, can be at least dated to the 1989 ruling *City of Richmond v. J. A. Croson Co.*[54] The Court struck down Richmond's Minority Business Utilization Plan, which required that the city hire a certain percentage of Minority Business Enterprises. In this decision, Justice Sandra Day O'Connor, with separate concurrences from Justice Scalia and Kennedy, interpreted the Fourteenth Amendment's antisubordination commitment not as a remedial responsibility but instead as requiring race neutrality. As a result, any racial classification becomes inherently suspect. According to O'Connor, "the standard of review under the Equal Protection Clause is not dependent on the race of those burdened or benefited by a particular classification."[55] O'Connor defended her position by citing Justice Powell's ruling in *Regents of the University of California v. Bakke* that "[t]he guarantee of equal protection cannot mean one thing when applied to one individual and something else when applied to a person of another color."[56] While Powell's statement accords with the meaning of equality, his words belie his shift from suspect class to suspect classification. Powell views the existing law, which constructed a racial quota for university admission, as invoking an irrelevant classification: race.

Similarly, by focusing on the classification in the law, i.e., race, rather than the class the law is meant to support by guarding against subordination, i.e., African Americans, Justices Kennedy and Scalia concurred with O'Connor's striking of the Richmond ordinance. For Kennedy, "The moral imperative of racial neutrality is the driving force of the Equal Protection Clause."[57] And, for Scalia, "strict scrutiny must be applied to all governmental classification by race, whether or not its asserted purpose is 'remedial' or 'benign.'"[58]

Justice Thurgood Marshall, who adhered to the antisubordination and racial consciousness that followed from the Court's original interpretation of the Fourteenth Amendment and as further articulated in the *Carolene* footnote, challenged this shift from class to classification. Addressing the former, African Americans as a suspect class or, in Stone's earlier terminology, as a "discrete and insular minority," permitted government action that challenged the dysfunction of extant politico-economic biases. According to Marshall, "A profound difference separates government actions that themselves are racist, and governmental actions that seek to remedy the effects of prior racism or to prevent neutral governmental activity from perpetuating the effects of such racism."[59] The Court's shift to classification did not allow the distinction that Marshall sought to maintain.

O'Connor further claimed that Richmond's set-aside subordinated the white population, making it more difficult to secure government contracts. This position relied on the assumption that African Americans and whites were on equal footing. To substantiate this contention, O'Connor pointed to the demographics of the governing authority: "In this case, blacks comprise approximately 50% of the population of the city of Richmond. Five of the nine seats on the City Council are held by blacks."[60] Such statistics hardly indicated a politically powerless minority. By contrast, Marshall drew attention to the underrepresentation of minority business in the construction field, which the law sought to remedy:

> While I agree that the numerical and political supremacy of a given racial group is a factor bearing upon the level of scrutiny to be applied, this Court has never held that numerical inferiority, standing alone, makes a racial group "suspect" and thus entitled to strict scrutiny review. Rather, we have identified other "traditional indicia of suspectness": whether a group has been "saddled with such disabilities, or subjected to a history of purposeful unequal treatment, or relegated to such a position of political powerlessness as to command extraordinary protection from the majoritarian political process."[61]

Marshall attempted to retain the focus on suspect class, on a group of individuals with a common characteristic used to subjugate them in full contradiction of equal protection. The majority's focus on classification ignored the history of discrimination, the historical context of Richmond itself, citing only present circumstance as evidence of equality that would be the foundation for color-blindness henceforth.

By citing that the white population constituted a little less than half of the city's population and represented a minority of the nine-member city council, O'Connor cast the white population of Richmond as a minority, refusing to acknowledge sustained legacies of unequal access to politico-economic power. Justice Marshall was so incensed because O'Connor utilized the doctrine of strict scrutiny to an antithetical end of undermining laws that would remedy circumstances of power imbalance that perpetuate unequal treatment of insular and discrete minorities. O'Connor's entrepreneurial rhetorical shift represents what political development scholar Stephen Skowronek has called "the audacity to be found in the play of ideas over time, the practice of employing them at opposite ends of the ideological spectrum, their daring defiance of set purposes."[62] By maintaining the logic of antisubordination, but redirecting it toward the white population rather than the historically disadvantaged and politically powerless African American population, O'Connor altered the application of the principle. No longer aimed to support a discrete and insular minority in a circumstance of unequal power distribution and malfunctioning pluralism, it was targeted to challenge any racial classification more broadly.

The inversion of suspect-class doctrine, a doctrine grounded in legal realism and Progressive justification of judicial expertise, into an antithetical suspect classification and color-blind theory would pervert the entire logic and objective of tiered scrutiny, which was meant to regard laws that target minorities as more suspect. Anticlassification does not permit the identification of suspect classes because such identification, by definition, requires classification. But, this jurisprudential tradition has not only been warped to new and opposite purpose by this move from suspect class to suspect classification. It has also been muddled by the purposive blurring of boundaries that mark the forms of scrutiny applied.

This second form of muddling is evident in the blurred distinction between strict scrutiny and intermediate or heightened scrutiny. Strict scrutiny requires that a law be narrowly tailored to achieve a compelling government purpose in order to pass constitutional muster. Intermediate scrutiny is a lower threshold, which requires that a law be substantially related to an important government interest. Intermediate scrutiny has historically applied to sex classification and has been used to nullify laws that rely on stereotypically gendered assumptions about sex roles or that generalize about sex differences in ways that preclude equal opportunity. In 1971, the Court ruled in *Reed v. Reed* that the rational basis test would not be met in cases of gender-based classifications; specifically, a state could not prefer men to women in the management of estates solely on the claim that the gender preference encouraged administrative efficiency.[63] In 1973, the Court elaborated its position in *Frontiero v. Richardson*. While a plurality urged that sex discrimination be treated like racial discrimination and thereby trigger strict scrutiny, the law in question, which required additional proof of dependency by male spouses of female military service members, was struck down on a rational basis standard.[64] In 1976 the Court fashioned a test for gender discrimination to fall between rational basis and strict scrutiny; the Court struck down a law that permitted women to buy alcohol at age eighteen while restricting the sale to men until the age of twenty-one.[65]

In applying this intermediate threshold in 1996 to evaluate whether the Virginia Military Institute could maintain its status as a male-only institution, the Court ruled against Virginia. Justice Ruth Bader Ginsburg cited the intermediate scrutiny standard articulated in *Craig v. Boren* twenty years earlier, but added that "[f]ocusing on the differential treatment or the denial of opportunity for which relief is sought, the reviewing court must determine whether the proffered justification is 'exceedingly persuasive.'"[66] In dissent, Justice Scalia contended that this phrase, in essence, raised sex-based classifications in the law to strict scrutiny, which the United States had so urged in oral and written argument, but which Ginsburg's ruling did not explicitly address. According to Scalia,

> The Court while making no reference to the Government's argument, effectively accepts it. . . . Only the amorphous "exceedingly persuasive justification" phrase, and not the standard elaboration of intermediate scrutiny, can be made to yield the conclusion that VMI's single-sex composition is unconstitutional because there exist several women (or, one would have to conclude under the Court's reasoning, a single woman) willing and able to undertake VMI's program. Intermediate scrutiny has never required a least-restrictive means analysis but only a "substantial relation" between the classification and the state interests that it serves.[67]

Similarly, although he concurred in judgment, Chief Justice William Rehnquist expressed concern over the phrase "exceedingly persuasive justification." The new language seemed to raise the level of scrutiny surreptitiously. For Rehnquist, "the Court thereby introduces an element of uncertainty respecting the appropriate test." The new phraseology abandoned the standards of "important government objective" and "substantially related," which, Rehnquist admitted, "are hardly models of precision" but "have more content and specificity" than the new phrase.[68]

The *Virginia* ruling has been characterized as raising the standard of scrutiny applied to sex-based classifications to somewhere between intermediate and strict scrutiny. The new standard has been called "intermediate review 'with teeth,'" indicating that it has greater bite than the older standard.[69] Furthermore, the Court's ruling emphasized the historical context of gender discrimination against women even without a particular plaintiff establishing a specific claim of discrimination: "By its overview of history and its focus on the place of VMI in the higher education culture of Virginia, the Court constructed a contextualized and historical narrative of women's exclusion from VMI in contrast to the defendants' decontextualized and ahistorical one."[70] This emphasis on context contrasts with the move the Court had previously made to decontextualize racial discrimination in favor of a color-blind theory of race neutrality.

Muddled Scrutiny in Gay Rights Rulings: The Threshold of Human Dignity

During the same term as the *Virginia* ruling, the Court further blurred the tiers of scrutiny by seemingly raising the level of scrutiny applied to laws that discriminated against gays, lesbians, and bisexuals. In *Romer v. Evans*, the Supreme Court invalidated an amendment to the Colorado constitution that prohibited any state or local executive, legislative, or judicial action that might protect gays, lesbians, or bisexuals from discrimination.[71] *Romer* represented the first time the Court considered sexual orientation under the equal protection clause rather than under the due process clause, suggesting a construction of sexuality as beyond a privacy concern. Furthermore, the ruling, written by Justice Kennedy, indicated that the amendment unjustly imposed a "broad and undifferentiated disability on a single named group," essentially cutting that group out of any democratic process.[72] And, the imposition was so broad that it could not be explained by any other motive "but animus toward the class it affects."[73]

Romer identified gays, lesbians, and bisexuals as a class (rather than homosexuality as a behavior) and refused to accept any of Colorado's justifications as rationally related to a legitimate government purpose. Ultimately, the ruling was drafted in language that invoked the rational basis standard. The Court declared the amendment to be a "status-based enactment divorced from any factual context from which we could discern a relationship to legitimate state interests; it is a classification of persons undertaken for its own sake, something the Equal Protection Clause does not permit."[74] Yet, since Kennedy accepted that gays, lesbians, and bisexuals constituted a named class of people that the state targeted for discrimination, *Romer* also appeared to identify some of the basic elements that might trigger heightened scrutiny. Indeed, just as Scalia contended that Ginsburg had raised the scrutiny threshold in *Virginia*, he argued that Kennedy had done so in *Romer*. He contended that the animus expressed in the amendment was "moral disapproval of homosexual conduct," which fell within the constitutional range as permitted by rational basis review.[75]

Scholars have drawn parallels between *Romer* and *Reed* insofar as neither explicitly raised the level of scrutiny applied to the class of individuals at the heart of the case. *Reed* laid the foundation for the adoption of intermediate scrutiny in *Frontiero*, and so it was presumed that *Romer* would likewise lay the foundation for a higher scrutiny level for gays and lesbians.[76] Cass Sunstein focused on the Court's redefinition of homosexual from behavior to identity to highlight the implication that this class of persons had suffered a recognized history of discrimination. For Sunstein, gays, lesbians, and bisexuals are

> subject to a deeper kind of social antagonism, connected not only with their acts but also with their identity. It is this status feature that links discrimination on the basis of sexual orientation with discrimination on the basis of race or sex. . . . [Amendment 2 demonstrates] a desire to isolate and seal off members of a despised group whose characteristics are thought to be in some sense contaminating or corrosive.[77]

Oher scholars suggest that *Romer* makes a similar analogy to racial and sexual discrimination via a pariah principle, or that "gays and lesbians are a group that cannot be relegated to outcast status."[78] Badges of inferiority are not constitutionally permissible, and Kennedy's ruling asserts that Amendment 2 so separates gays and lesbians from the political community as to mark them as sufficiently inferior and second class.[79] Amendment 2, in other words, achieves a similar objective as that of the jury exclusion statute, which the Court struck down in *Strauder*.

Nevertheless, despite recognizing gays and lesbians as a discriminated-against class, *Romer* did not explicitly raise the level of scrutiny. Indeed, that it did not is evidenced in calls from scholars that "the Supreme Court not only ought to make gay men and lesbians a suspect or quasi-suspect class, but . . . has in practice already done so, albeit without the sufficient binding force of precedent."[80] Furthermore, *Romer* has not functioned like *Reed*; *Romer* did not lead to the eventual explicit articulation of higher scrutiny for gays, lesbians, bisexuals, or transgenders.

And, neither did *Lawrence* or *Windsor*. In these two rulings, the Court's reasoning relied less on a formulaic categorization of suspect class or classification (which unnerved Justice Scalia as the passage opening this chapter indicates) and more on a basic claim of human dignity and characterizations of the law under review as motivated by no other purpose than animus. The reference to animus would suggest that the law under review did not even meet the lowest standard of legitimacy, thereby indicating that it did not withstand rational basis review. *Lawrence*, of course, found that state bans on consensual same-sex sexual intercourse unconstitutionally violated a fundamental right to sexual privacy. Nevertheless, the Court's ruling, authored by Justice Kennedy, did not specify whether or not strict scrutiny was applied to evaluate the state bans, which is the standard approach when evaluating an unenumerated fundamental right such as sexual privacy.[81] As Justice Scalia pointed out in his dissent,

> Though there is discussion of "fundamental proposition[s]," . . . and "fundamental decisions" . . . nowhere does the Court's opinion declare that homosexual sodomy is a "fundamental right" under the Due Process Clause; nor does it subject the Texas law to the standard of review that would be appropriate (strict scrutiny) if homosexual sodomy *were* a "fundamental right." Thus, while overruling the *outcome* of *Bowers*, the Court leaves strangely untouched its central legal conclusion: "[R]espondents would have us announce . . . a fundamental right to engage in homosexual sodomy. This we are quite unwilling to do." Instead the Court simply

describes petitioners' conduct as "an exercise of their liberty"—which it undoubtedly is—and proceeds to apply an unheard-of form of rational-basis review that will have far reaching implications beyond this case.[82]

Indeed, rather than adhering to the language and formulaic construction of tiered scrutiny, Kennedy waxed poetic that the criminalization statutes in question denied gays and lesbians basic human dignity:

> It suffices for us to acknowledge that adults may choose to enter upon this relationship in the confines of their homes and their own private lives and still retain their dignity as free persons. When sexuality finds overt expression in intimate conduct with another person, the conduct can be but one element in a personal bond that is more enduring. The liberty protected by the Constitution allows homosexual persons the right to make this choice.[83]

In other words, in *Lawrence*, Kennedy maintained his practice of refusing to specify the level of scrutiny applied. These laws—whether the Colorado Amendment 2 or the remaining fourteen sodomy-criminalization statutes—were struck down without gays and lesbians being named as a suspect class or sexual orientation being identified as a suspect classification. Rather, the Court relied on dignity as an operative concept: laws that violate dignity are grounded in no other motivation than animus and are therefore unconstitutional. Consequently, even if Kennedy, since *Romer*, is inclined to consider gays and lesbians a suspect class insofar as that class suffers a history of discrimination, could be considered politically disadvantaged, and is marked by a trait that is either immutable or, at least, sufficiently irrelevant to justify exclusion, he has treated laws that classify by sexual orientation under rational basis review.

The muddling of scrutiny—made manifest in this confusion of class and classification, this creation of additional standards of review between the three tiers, and the invocation of a generalized claim to human dignity that does not adhere to the parameters and language of the scrutiny thresholds—is also evident in abortion rulings by Kennedy, especially *Gonzalez v. Carhart*.[84] This ruling upheld the Federal Partial-Birth Abortion Ban Act of 2003, which banned a particular late-term abortion procedure, known as dilate and extract (D&X) or intact dilate

and evacuate (D&E).[85] While abortion access had been, to this point, litigated under the substantive due process doctrine of privacy and thereby
considered a fundamental right, Kennedy reviewed this federal statute
under the lowest threshold of rational basis review rather than the highest of strict scrutiny. He justified this move by contending that at stake
was not a right to abortion access, but the state's right to ban a particular
medical procedure. Such a ban fell within the domain of government
power to regulate so long as the regulation had a rational relationship to
a legitimate purpose: "Where it has a rational basis to act, and it does not
impose an undue burden, the State may use its regulatory power to bar
certain procedures and substitute others, all in furtherance of its legitimate interests in regulating the medical profession in order to promote
respect for life, including life of the unborn."[86] And, Kennedy once more
spoke to a need to maintain human dignity. He characterized the federal statute as "express[ing] respect for the dignity of human life."[87] Of
course, Kennedy's dignity concern was limited in scope and application.
According to one legal scholar, "the dignity interests of women confronted with an unwanted pregnancy went largely unacknowledged."[88]
Others noted that the ruling is "remarkable" for "its almost complete
indifference toward the holders of those rights: women" and that consequently, "Abortions seem only, in the eyes of the Supreme Court to
involve the 'abortion doctor,' 'the fetus,' and 'the cervix.'"[89]

In her dissent, Justice Ginsburg focuses on the muddling that followed from Kennedy's invocation of rational basis instead of strict scrutiny. In no other case had abortion statutes been so reviewed:

> Today's decision is alarming. . . . It blurs the line, firmly drawn in *Casey*,
> between previability and postviability abortions. And, for the first time
> since *Roe*, the Court blesses a prohibition with no exception safeguard-
> ing a woman's health. I dissent from the Court's disposition. Retreating
> from prior rulings that abortion restrictions cannot be imposed absent
> an exception safeguarding a woman's health, the Court upholds an Act
> that surely would not survive under the close scrutiny that previously
> attended state-decreed limitations on a woman's reproductive choices.[90]

In this dissent, by identifying how the Court manipulated doctrine
to achieve an antithetical end, Ginsburg occupied the role played by

Marshall in *Crosson*. In the one case, the historical context of an insular and discrete minority was ignored and an abstracted conception of racial classification applied. In the other, the historical context of a fundamental right was ignored and an abstracted medical procedure invalidated.

Kennedy's reliance on an ambiguous, amorphous, and capacious notion of human dignity surfaced once more in his ruling for the Court in *Windsor*. In determining the unconstitutionality of Section 3 of DOMA and ruling that the federal government must recognize same-sex marriage where it is so recognized by state governments, Kennedy once again framed the requirement as necessitated by human dignity. He began by noting, "It seems fair to conclude that, until recent years, many citizens had not even considered the possibility that two persons of the same sex might aspire to occupy the same status and dignity as that of a man and woman in lawful marriage."[91] He stipulated that when a state offers the recognition of marriage to a class of persons, it "confer[s] upon them a dignity and status of immense import."[92] In so doing, the state enhances the "recognition, dignity, and protection of the class in their own community."[93] He then characterized DOMA as creating an "injury and indignity" that "is a deprivation of an essential part of liberty protected by the Fifth Amendment."[94] He considered New York's decision to recognize same-sex marriage as extending "further protection and dignity to that bond," and said that it represented a determination by the state that same-sex couples were "worthy of dignity in the community equal with all other marriages."[95] He contended, "The history of DOMA's enactment and its own text demonstrate that interference with the equal dignity of same-sex marriages, a dignity conferred by the States in the exercise of their sovereign power, was more than an incidental effect of the federal statute."[96] He argued that marriage creates responsibilities and rights that "enhance the dignity and integrity of the person" and that DOMA denies.[97] Finally, he declared the statute invalid because "no legitimate purpose overcomes the purpose and effect to disparage and to injure those whom the State, by its marriage laws, sought to protect in personhood and dignity."[98] While Kennedy utilized the phrase "legitimate purpose," his reliance on human dignity elides the formal structure of the scrutiny tiers. He did not articulate the level of scrutiny applied. And, once again, Justice Scalia harped on the evasion.

Windsor did not compel states to recognize same-sex marriage. It ruled only that federal refusal to recognize same-sex marriage violated human dignity and that congressional support of DOMA could only be explained by resort to animus toward those individuals seeking to enter a same-sex marriage:

> DOMA's unusual deviation from the usual tradition of recognizing and accepting state definitions of marriage here operates to deprive same-sex couples of the benefits and responsibilities that come with the federal recognition of their marriages. This is strong evidence of a law having the purpose and effect of disapproval of that class. The avowed purpose and practical effect of the law here in question are to impose a disadvantage, a separate status, and so a stigma upon all who enter into same-sex marriages made lawful by the unquestioned authority of the States. . . . The history of DOMA's enactment and its own text demonstrate that interference with the equal dignity of same-sex marriages, a dignity conferred by the States in the exercise of their sovereign power, was more than an incidental effect of the federal statute. It was its essence.[99]

And, as in *Lawrence*, Kennedy did not specify the level of review explicitly. Given his discussion of animus, dignity, and legitimate government purpose, the ruling, however, would seem to imply that there is no *rational basis* for the federal government not to recognize same-sex marriage.

Ultimately, despite Judge Stephen Reinhardt's contention in *Abbot* that *Windsor* required heightened scrutiny for laws that classify on the basis of sexual orientation, as discussed in the previous chapter, *Romer*, *Lawrence*, and *Windsor* do not so explicitly indicate. The repeated reliance on a capacious conception of human dignity and the repeated assertion that antigay statutes and amendments have no other motivation than animus would indicate that such statutes cannot meet the lowest threshold of rational basis. In short, gays, lesbians, and bisexuals are not, according to the Supreme Court, a suspect class and neither is sexual orientation a suspect classification. And, importantly, nor do either need to be for antigay laws to be viewed as unconstitutional by the Court's nearly twenty years of consistent rulings since *Romer*.

On June 26, 2015, the second anniversary of the *Windsor* ruling and the twelfth anniversary of the *Lawrence* ruling, Justice Kennedy issued another ruling that would surely endear him to gay and lesbian rights activists and secure his legacy as the stalwart promoter of equal treatment for gay and lesbian Americans. On that day, he delivered the ruling for the five-justice majority in *Obergefell v. Hodges*, which held "that same-sex couples may exercise the fundamental right to marry. No longer may this liberty be denied to them."[100] And, just as in *Lawrence* and *Windsor*, in *Obergefell*, Kennedy premised the decision on claims to dignity; he defined marriage as a union that "always has promised nobility and dignity to all persons, without regard to their station in life."[101] Ironically, the decision that guarantees marriage equality engaged in little to no traditional equal protection analysis. Nowhere in the ruling was there a single mention of suspect-class or higher-scrutiny application. Even as Kennedy acknowledged the equal protection claim at stake—"The right of same-sex couples to marry that is part of the liberty promised by the Fourteenth Amendment is derived, too, from that Amendment's guarantee of the equal protection of the laws"[102]—he subsumed the matter of equal treatment within the due process claim to liberty: "It is now clear that the challenged laws burden the liberty of same-sex couples, and it must be further acknowledged that they abridge central precepts of equality. Here the marriage laws enforced by the respondents are in essence unequal: same-sex couples are denied all the benefits afforded to opposite-sex couples and are barred from exercising a fundamental right."[103] By subsuming the question of equal protection within the due process guarantee of a fundamental right to marry, Kennedy avoided entirely any discussion of suspect class status or tiered scrutiny. The Court's role in recognizing insular and discrete minorities and countering discrimination against them by being their voice in a potentially dysfunctional pluralism that renders them powerless is just so twentieth century.

Once again the Court refused to apply suspect-class status to gays or lesbians or to consider sexual orientation a suspect classification. This was perhaps all the more perplexing as the ruling for the majority seemingly identified many of the characteristics that define suspect class. First, Kennedy recognized a history of enduring unjust discrimination:

> Until the mid-20th century, same-sex intimacy long had been condemned as immoral by the state itself in most Western nations, a belief often embodied in the criminal law. For this reason, among others, many

persons did not deem homosexuals to have dignity in their own distinct identity. A truthful declaration by same-sex couples of what was in their hearts had to remain unspoken. Even when a greater awareness of the humanity and integrity of homosexual persons came in the period after World War II, the argument that gays and lesbians had a just claim to dignity was in conflict with both law and widespread social conventions. Same-sex intimacy remained a crime in many States. Gays and lesbians were prohibited from most government employment, barred from military service, excluded under immigration laws, targeted by police, and burdened in their rights to associate.[104]

Second, unlike in any previous ruling, Kennedy defined sexuality as an immutable trait: "Far from seeking to devalue marriage, the petitioners seek it for themselves because of their respect—and need—for its privileges and responsibilities. And their *immutable nature* dictates that same-sex marriage is their only real path to this profound commitment."[105]

Nevertheless, despite laying out what would seem a systematic identification of suspect-class characteristics, Kennedy grounded the ruling in a distinct justification. The central principle at the foundation of *Obergefell*'s requirement of nation-wide marriage recognition is the dignity that inheres in marriage and the indignity that the state permits when it excludes loving couples from that status. To say that the due process clause protects fundamental liberties is to say, according to Kennedy, that this clause secures liberties that "extend to certain personal choices central to individual dignity and autonomy, including intimate choices that define personal identity and beliefs."[106] And, this right to marry—even if it has not historically been granted to same-sex couples—is so fundamental that the state cannot legitimately use that history as a limiting factor: "If rights were defined by who exercised them in the past, then received practices could serve as their own continued justification and new groups could not invoke rights once denied. This Court has rejected that approach, both with respect to the right to marry and the rights of gays and lesbians."[107]

In sharp contrast to many of the state supreme court rulings on marriage equality reviewed in chapter 6, the ruling in *Obergefell* is direct and its rationale singular. It does not rest on multiple claims, e.g., that there exist both a fundamental rights violation and an equal protection violation given a certain scrutiny applied. It engages in none of the trappings of suspect-class and scrutiny doctrine.[108] Despite its recognizing histories of discrimination, there is no formulaic identification of four distinguishable traits that would render a class suspect and call for higher scrutiny of the state's reasons for limiting access to marriage. And, the Court engages in none of the detailed abstractions that the California Supreme Court did in 2008 to demonstrate how defining marriage as only opposite-sex misses the point of what is at stake in the definition of marriage itself. Instead, it stated quite simply that the petitioners "ask for equal dignity in the eyes of the law. The Constitution grants them that right."[109] In so ruling, the Court has made a profound move in the continued erosion and avoidance of scrutiny doctrine.

Conclusion

The refusal to grant gays, lesbians, and bisexuals a suspect-class designation, even though that class of individuals fits the standard characteristics of a suspect class, as Attorney General Holder expressly contends and as Justice Kennedy would seem to suggest from *Romer* through *Obergefell*, reveals much not only about how the Court views gays, lesbians, and bisexuals but also about how it considers its own expertise and purpose, considerations that animated the development of the tiered-scrutiny framework. This chapter explored that development, and it located the refusal to apply higher scrutiny to sexual-orientation classifications—as well as a general resistance to extending scrutiny beyond its current parameters—to the Court's uneasiness with the original impulse behind scrutiny. That uneasiness is evident in the shift from class to classification in the application of scrutiny and in the blurring of lines among the three established tiers.

The Court's resistance to developing and applying scrutiny ironically worked to the benefit of some gay rights claims. To put this claim in sharper focus, strict scrutiny ironically permits racial discrimination; it only maintains that such discrimination must be narrowly tailored to achieve a compelling government interest or that the discrimination is the only means by which the state can accomplish an exceedingly important objective. As political theorist and legal scholar Sonu Bedi has cogently argued, subjecting racial classifications to strict scrutiny perversely "rationalizes racism" because doing so

> gives credence to the bogus claims of racism. It suggests that racist laws and policies are based on something other than animus or mere prejudice. . . . [V]ia its doctrine of strict scrutiny, constitutional law implies that it is not groundless to claim that race tracks a kind of status or hierarchy. Requiring strict scrutiny . . . perversely errs on the side of suggesting that racist beliefs are not arbitrary, are not based on animus, that these laws are not based on constitutionally inadmissible purpose.[110]

By contrast, the gay rights jurisprudence points in the other direction. By repeatedly holding state laws and state constitutional amendments to something that bears more resemblance to a rational basis standard than not, the Court has declared that there is simply no rational justification for antigay law, that such law in no way is connected to an observed or hypothesized legitimate government purpose, and that the law has no other foundation than animus. Striking down antigay law by rational basis review would seemingly leave little room for antigay discrimination (although, as discussed in the conclusion, room still exists); striking down racist law by strict scrutiny leaves a window for racial prejudice to survive. Ironically, by losing the strategy of raising the scrutiny level of their claims, gay rights advocates have secured more stable footing for their recognition as equal citizens.

The legal developments traced in this chapter indicate that rationales at the foundation of Fourteenth Amendment gay rights victories are distinct from the equal protection doctrine as developed in race- and sex-equality jurisprudence. The former may signal the development of a neoliberal jurisprudence, one that perpetuates the "blind" or anticlassification understanding of the Fourteenth Amendment. The collapse of scrutiny, the collapse of racial liberalism, and the rise of formal principles of equality and anticlassification made manifest in *Romer, Lawrence,* and *Windsor* all indicate the judicial ascendancy of what Jodi Melamed has termed "neoliberal multiculturalism," or a context in which freedom and choice are formally made available while "racism constantly appears as disappearing . . . even as it takes on new forms that signify as nonracist or even anti-racist."[111] David Eng reads this particular neoliberalism as evident in the juxtaposition of *Lawrence* and the anti–affirmative action ruling of *Gratz v. Bollinger*, which were announced within days of each other.[112] The slow demise of affirmative action is politically and legally premised on the very logic that undergirds this abstracted anti-classification reading of the Fourteenth Amendment, which supports gay and lesbian victories at Court. According to Eng, "racial liberation is configured as a politics of the past, while queer liberalism is configured as a politics of the present. Racial liberation is thus deemed a completed project . . . [and] the emergence of queer liberalism underwrites the simultaneous demise of affirmative action. In short, queer liberalism becomes thinkable precisely because racial equality has been settled and achieved."[113] But more than a normative concept marking boundaries of inclusion and exclusion or a stage in the teleological development of constitutional rights—i.e., first African Americans', then women's rights, and now LGBT rights made so popular in contemporary political rhetoric[114]—Eng contends that queer liberalism is premised upon the anticlassification and color-blindness of contemporary renderings of Fourteenth Amendment equal protection such that it "functions not in opposition to but with the logic of colorblindness that deems the racial project historically 'complete.'"[115] Queer liberalism is neoliberalism, and that is the principle guiding Kennedy's rulings in *Lawrence, Windsor,* and *Obergefell.*

Kennedy's emphasis on an amorphous conception of human dignity—even as it has curbed abortion access, supported gay rights as opposed to more radically queer aims, and lent support to anti–affirmative action claims—indicates that the contemporary Court is "much more sympathetic to 'liberty' claims about freedoms we all hold than to 'equality' claims asserted by a subset of the population." As Kenji Yoshino has argued, suspect-class designation compels the Court into an uncomfortable position of "picking favorites among groups," of recognizing citizens as constituted by particular contexts.[116] The traceable process of muddling the suspect-class doctrine further indicates an unwillingness to engage in the contextual antisubordination analytical project. The Court's attempts to articulate a due process guarantee to dignity suggest that justices are unwilling or unable to identify who is harmed or excluded in a democratic process. It no longer seeks to engage in any evaluation of power differentials in extant democratic pluralism. It seeks merely to hold equality as a textual ideal.

Kennedy has yet to develop the implications of dignity as a coherent alternative—either as a doctrinal pathway or as a new means to justify judicial legitimacy—and so its possibilities remain unclear. And, already, some scholars have suggested that it has the dangerous potential of supporting some of those the state deems worthy and denigrating those it does not.[117] Nevertheless, the erosion of scrutiny and suspect-class doctrine not only indicates the erosion of an interpretive tool that defined Fourteenth Amendment jurisprudence for much of the twentieth century, but it also suggests other important developmental conclusions. It illustrates two important dynamics of ideational change over time. First, transformation of suspect class into suspect classification and thus the transformation of an antisubordination principle into an anticlassification principle over time demonstrate how ideas can be put in the service of ends antithetical to their original animating purpose. This is a key mechanism of ideational change in the APD literature. Second, the consistent refusal to recognize gays and lesbians as a suspect class or sexual orientation as a suspect classification—evident over nearly two decades of jurisprudence—suggests the makings of a durable shift in jurisprudential thinking. The limits of equal protection and scrutiny doctrine are exposed. And, the new way to recognize and remedy inequality through a due process rationale linked to dignity is in the making.

The Court, now well into the twenty-first century, is potentially jettisoning a legitimating theory that animated so much of its twentieth-century jurisprudence. Since scrutiny doctrine—one doctrine to have come out of and represent the assumptions, principles, and aspirations of the Progressive Court—is grounded in the Progressive understanding of judicial expertise, the Court is also, in effect, admitting that it can but may no longer desire to identify who is harmed or excluded in a democratic process.[118] It is admitting that it no longer can or wants to consider context and history, adhering only to formal rules of seeming neutrality.[119] It can no longer ground its authority then in this particular form of expertise. This move may have effects not only for our understanding of gay and lesbian status at court but also for how the Court continues to consider the groundings of its own institutional legitimacy.

Conclusion

To Be Whole

It now seems certain that before too many years elapse, the
Supreme Court will be forced to acknowledge the logic of
its own jurisprudence on same-sex marriage and redefine
marriage to include gay couples in all 50 states. . . . We are
not really having an argument about same-sex marriage
anymore. . . . Instead, all that's left is the timing of the final
victory—and for the defeated to find out what settlement the
victors will impose.

—Ross Douthat, "The Terms of Our Surrender," 2014[1]

During the spring of 2014, federal district courts continued to strike
down state bans on same-sex-marriage recognition.[2] While the string
of wins for marriage equality since *United States v. Windsor* continued unabated into this season, one of these victories, *Whitehead v.
Wolf*, issued by a federal district court in Pennsylvania, brought the
fragmented nature of gay and lesbian citizenship into fresh relief. As
mentioned in the introduction of this book, prior to this ruling, if gays
or lesbians lived in a state with marriage recognition, they also lived in
a state that protected individuals from discrimination on the basis of
sexual orientation in the workplace and in public accommodations, and
protected parental and adoption rights of same-sex couples. However,
that pattern shifted after *Whitehead*, and the Supreme Court exacerbated
it by its ruling in *Obergefell*. As of June 26, 2015, the Court recognized a
right to marriage for gays and lesbians, and yet public acknowledgment
of that marriage may endanger one's livelihood—insofar as there exist
no protections against employment discrimination on the basis of sexual
orientation—in twenty-eight states. Marriage may endanger one's fair
access to housing in twenty-eight states. And, marriage may endanger

one's fair access to public accommodations in twenty-nine states. A gay man or lesbian may get married on Sunday and may theoretically lose his or her job and home on Monday.

The spring of 2014 indicated increasing public acceptance of same-sex marriage. First, conservative *New York Times* columnist Ross Douthat declared that forces arrayed against same-sex marriage had lost. In his assessment, a Supreme Court ruling establishing marriage recognition throughout the land was merely a matter of time. Second, the graham cracker manufacturer, Honey Maid, released a new advertising campaign titled "This Is Wholesome," which depicted a variety of families.[3] One commercial centered on a married gay couple with two children.[4] A son described his two dads, the dads narrated how they fell in love, and all spoke to how they made a family. By spring 2014, in political commentary and pop culture, same-sex marriage and same-sex parenting were increasingly recognized as reality.

Nevertheless, these two cultural developments, like the *Whitehead* ruling, brought to the fore the fragmented and unstable nature of gay and lesbian citizenship insofar as they each revealed the tenuous, fragile, and incomplete recognition of citizenship status across space, time, and issue. While *Whitehead*, Douthat, and Honey Maid's recognitions each marked significant shifts in whether and how gay and lesbian families are acknowledged, they also highlighted this book's central theme: given the polity's fracture, fragmentation, and internal institutional and ideational tensions, extensions of acknowledgment, or of how a citizen may be recognized in full dimension, are likely not to occur all at once or fully congruently. Insofar as the normal condition of the polity is marked by fragmentation and disjuncture, so too may citizenship status be. This chapter reviews these three developments—Douthat's commentary, the Honey Maid campaign, and the disjuncture in state recognition of marriage and protections against employment discrimination—to illustrate the relevance and persistence of fragmented citizenship. It then summarizes the book's primary arguments and findings.

The Limits of Recognition and Equality

In concluding that same-sex marriage was inevitable, Douthat lamented the way individuals with religious beliefs against homosexuality are likely to be trampled by a growing regulatory framework that disrespects this belief. As evidence, he discussed the outcome in Arizona where Governor Jan Brewer, after much public pressure, vetoed legislation that would permit business owners to rely on religious belief as justification when refusing to serve LGBT customers. According to Douthat, "What makes this response particularly instructive is that such bills have been seen, in the past, as a way for religious conservatives to negotiate surrender—to accept same-sex marriage's inevitability while carving out protections for dissent. But now, apparently, the official line is that *you bigots don't get to negotiate anymore.*" Douthat was offended that religious believers could be characterized as "bigots" even as he conceded, "Christians had plenty of opportunities—thousands of years' worth—to treat gay people with real charity, and far too often chose intolerance. (And still do, in many instances and places.)" Respect for dissent is the casualty, and thus democratic political culture more broadly, in Douthat's reading of the circumstances. And, yet, the pressure that preceded and perhaps compelled Governor Brewer's veto would seem to illustrate the very dynamics that Douthat would otherwise embrace in the place of formal regulatory policy. He called for a free market of political ideas as much as he advocated a free market of consumer goods and services. In imagining his ideal, he wrote, "And where conflicts arise—in a case where, say, a Mormon caterer or a Catholic photographer objected to working at a same-sex wedding—gay rights supporters would heed the advice of gay marriage's intellectual progenitor, Andrew Sullivan, and let the dissenters opt out 'in the name of their freedom—and ours.'"[5]

Capitalism had political effects, just not ones that Douthat would endorse. Fortune 500 firms like Apple, Delta, Yelp, and Arizona-based PetSmart banded together to demonstrate that, in the words of PetSmart's chief executive officer, David Lenhardt, the legislation was "bad for Arizona business. We think it's bad for the people of Arizona."[6] Consequently, even as Douthat recognized that it remains legal to discriminate against LGBT persons in Arizona with or without this legislation—and this is because sexual orientation and gender identity are not protected categories in Arizona—the market's response to this legislation would seem to foreclose its cultural legitimacy. Similar patterns of corporate hostility to seemingly antigay laws would rapidly develop a year later in Indiana. The public pressure that preceded the

Arizona veto and that followed the Indiana law indicates that the potential for widespread discrimination against LGBT persons is curbed even in the absence of laws formally banning it.

Pressures against discrimination do exist without formal law. But, it remains legal to discriminate on the basis of sexual orientation and gender identity in Arizona and Indiana, and these states are not in the minority. All Governor Brewer's veto accomplished was to ban a particular justification for discrimination; the possibility of being free to discriminate against LGBT persons remains intact. And the potential to prevent bans on such discrimination was potentially buttressed by the Supreme Court in 2014.

The Court's ruling in *Burwell v. Hobby Lobby* permitted privately owned corporations to not cover the costs of contraception, as mandated by the Patient Protection and Affordable Care Act, should provision violate owners' religious beliefs.[7] The ruling could more broadly mean that privately held corporations could not be required by the state to engage in acts that violate the religious beliefs of the corporate owners.[8] Implications for gay and lesbian rights claims are obvious: an employer could legally fire a gay or lesbian employee and claim cover of religious belief. As getting married to a same-sex partner expresses gay or lesbian identity, getting married potentially threatens livelihoods in certain states.[9] In *Hobby Lobby* Justice Alito, writing for the majority, indicated that the decision offered no cover for discrimination since "the Government has a compelling interest in providing equal opportunity to participate in the workforce without regard to race, and prohibitions on racial discrimination are precisely tailored to achieve that critical goal."[10] However, as the federal government and many states do not ban employment discrimination on the basis of sexual orientation or gender identity, the ruling creates a very real potential to which Alito's assurance does not speak.

And, this possibility is left open in the Court's 2015 ruling in *Obergefell v. Hodges*, which required all states to recognize same-sex marriages. In that decision, Justice Kennedy writes, "The First Amendment ensures that religious organizations and persons are given proper protection as they seek to teach the principles that are so fulfilling and so central to their lives and faiths, and to their own deep aspirations to continue the family structure they have long revered."[11] If recognizing same-sex marriage is contrary to one's faith, then can private companies—whether they be businesses, schools, housing complexes, etc.—openly discriminate against gays and lesbians given the absence of explicit federal protections for sexual orientation or gender identity in federal employment, housing, and public accommodations statutes?

The Equal Employment Opportunity Commission (EEOC) ruled in July 2015 that the existing Civil Rights Act (CRA) Title VII protections against discrimination based on sex also protect against sexual-orientation discrimination and thereby potentially meet the concern produced by *Hobby Lobby*.[12] In other words, while there are no explicit federal protections against sexual-orientation or gender-identity discrimination in the workplace—there is no ENDA—the EEOC has ruled that an explicit ENDA is unnecessary. Instead, the EEOC reads gender-identity and sexual-orientation discrimination as being grounded in illegitimate sex stereotyping and thus already covered by the CRA's ban on sex discrimination:

> Allegations of discrimination on the basis of sexual orientation necessarily state a claim of discrimination he or she experienced was sex discrimination because it involved treatment that would not have occurred but for the individual's sex; because it was based on the sex of the person(s) the individual associates with; and/or because it was premised on the fundamental sex stereotype, norm or expectation that individuals should be attracted only to those of the opposite sex. Agencies should treat claims of sexual orientation discrimination as complaints of sex discrimination under Title VII and process such complaints through the ordinary Section 1614 process.[13]

Thus, the ruling suggests that the answer to the above question leans toward no, but the ruling is limited. First, the EEOC decision only covers employment rights, not housing or public accommodations claims. Second, it is subject to possible and probable Supreme Court review. And, Justice Kennedy's ambiguous and expansive conception of human dignity, as discussed in chapter 7, could support the very legislation that Brewer vetoed and that passed in Indiana precisely because it pits one conception of dignity—that of the religious believer—against another—that of the individual seeking to earn a living free from discrimination.

While human dignity may be manifest in the freedom to live free of discrimination that creates psychological and material harm, dignity may also be made manifest in an ability to live in accordance with the dictates of one's conscience. And, when the Court has construed gay rights claims to conflict with First Amendment claims to freedom of expression, the former have not been validated.[14] Who has a greater claim on free expression as constitutive of dignity: the LGBT person who seeks to live free from prejudice or the religious believer who seeks also to live openly and free from prejudice? The due process liberty rationales Kennedy has offered to overturn homosexual criminalization in *Lawrence*, to require federal recognition of same-sex marriage in *Windsor*, and to require nation-wide state recognition of marriage in *Obergefell* may not provide strong foundation for protections from discrimination in employment, housing, or public accommodations. The former rest on a liberty claim whereas the latter have traditionally rested on an equal protection foundation, a doctrinal path rarely taken in the gay rights jurisprudence developed by Kennedy. Just as Kennedy's reliance on dignity as a substitute for the formulaic application of scrutiny curbed abortion access, so it could be used to curb gay rights claims, particularly those that take expression of sexual identity beyond the conceptual bounds of the heteronormative household and family. Market mechanisms may draw attention to this discrimination, but they are not enough to protect LGBT persons from it.

Formal law is necessary even as it may not be fully sufficient, as this book has argued throughout, to eradicate persistent inequalities. And, this claim is exemplified by the Honey Maid campaign, which ends with the tagline, "This Is Wholesome." The ad provocatively relies on the dual meaning of "wholesome," first as beneficial to good health and second as morally good. In showcasing a gay family as being equally morally good as a straight family, the ad counters harmful yet consistently prevalent conceptions of gay identities as immoral.[15]

The ad also marks an anniversary of sorts, which serves to highlight progress made. In 1994, twenty years before the Honey Maid ad, the furniture manufacturer Ikea launched its then-controversial commercial depicting a gay male couple considering the purchase of a dining room table.[16] The Ikea commercial treated the men a bit tentatively, highlighting how they were investing in a dining table. Their relationship was loving and playful, but always contingent, perhaps dissoluble at any moment. Furniture, after all, can always be split up or sold off in the event of a breakup. By contrast, the Honey Maid ad references more indications of longevity and stability. The couple has two children. The camera zooms in on their wedding bands. The men speak of the permanence of their union; they are married, a status hardly possible even a few years previously, as the men admit. In recounting the story of how they met and fell in love, one husband remarks, "what's interesting is that you said you knew you were going to marry me, but that wasn't in our thought then." The other husband comments, "Like having a mortgage together was what marriage used to be for gay people, so that's what I thought." What it means to be a gay citizen has expanded: I can be recognized as married in all fifty states and the District of Columbia.

The ad, nevertheless, demonstrated how equality is deeply contextual and hardly universal. If these men were recognized as married at the time the commercial was aired in March 2014, they had to live in one of just over twenty states that recognized their marriage. Or, if they had sought to wed and live in the other states that did not recognize their marriage, they needed to be affluent enough to travel to a state where they could be married so that they could at least access federal recognition if not state recognition. This family also would have to avoid living in the numerous states that have or are considering legislation permitting religious justification for antigay discrimination.[17] Of course, even without such laws, to be fully and equally recognized this family needs to live in one of the only twenty-two states that ban employment discrimination on the basis of sexual orientation, so that they are financially secure enough to maintain a healthy home for their two sons. And, this family would need to live in one of thirty-eight states that explicitly allow joint adoption, thereby enabling gay adoption. Or, at least, viewers must assume that this family has the financial wherewithal to draft and pay for enough legal documents so that they can privately secure their responsibilities to one another when the state denies them this. In short, the ad, so much a marker of progress, is also very much a display of the contingency and instability that define the lives of gay and lesbian citizens.

This status is not only a consequence of federalism and consequent policy differences across space. Rather, as this book has endeavored to demonstrate, shifts toward equality in one policy domain can reveal unseen or unacknowledged inequalities within that domain or across other domains. As discussed in chapter 1, repealing the ban on openly lesbian, gay, or bisexual soldiers in the U.S. military did not ensure equality. Granting same-sex-marriage recognition has not guaranteed to same-sex families with children protections equal to those experienced by cross-sex families. And, the *Hobby Lobby* ruling only further showcases this clashing of regulatory orders and the consequent instability generated for citizens' lives: the ruling highlights once more how changes toward equality in one set of governing orders (marriage) can create conflict with others (laws regulating religious expression and employment). Change is not comprehensive; policy shifts in one domain do not ensure equality across all. Thus, it is hardly surprising that only hours after a federal district court judge ruled in *Whitehead* that Pennsylvania's statutory ban on same-sex marriage violated the due process and equal protection guarantees of the Constitution's Fourteenth Amendment, the National Gay and Lesbian Task Force (now the National LGBTQ Task Force) tweeted, "As we celebrate marriage in #Pennsylvania, we cannot forget the other LGBT issues we're fighting for. What's your #morethanmarriage?"[18]

Themes and Extensions

A basic tenet of APD scholarship is that the laws and policies that structure citizens' lives are never developed all at once; governance is not invented on a clean slate. More often than not political change is incremental, limited, and, layered. A change in one domain of governance, like marriage laws, might have unanticipated effects on a different already existing domain of governance, like employment law. Consequently, the various policies, laws, and customs that confer the recognition that defines citizenship may not be congruent with one another. In this book, I have applied the APD characterization of the polity—as multiple and potentially clashing entities pursuing different projects, originating at different times, and offering distinct forms of regulatory recognition to the same individual—to an underexamined area within APD scholarship: gay and lesbian politics. I have attempted to show how this conception of the fragmented polity yields a citizenship—defined as a status that follows from regulatory recognition first and then is performed through the claiming of rights and responsibilities—that is itself fractured as its meanings differ across space, time, and policy issue. This book illuminates aspects of gays', lesbians', and bisexuals' experience that would remain invisible if we adopted notions of freedom and citizenship that rest only on the rights of the individual. And, it shows how the concerns of APD scholars render a new history of sexuality politics as well as how attention to sexuality opens up to new analysis the development of governing authorities.

A central question in political science is how the state treats the governed by selectively administering rights to different groups. The rights of citizenship are not uniformly distributed, but instead selectively awarded to those the state deems worthy. By focusing less on the social-movement struggle for equal rights and attending instead to the state's authority to recognize persons or citizens, this book endeavors to bring concerns of gay and lesbian studies further into the political scientific study of institutional and ideational development and thereby respond to the call to center LGBT politics as a lens through which questions of political development can be viewed and new insights into those topics gleaned.

Furthermore, the book has attempted to enrich empirically the normative discussion of citizenship by buttressing the claim that citizenship is grounded in a requirement of recognition. It has detailed how the limits and distinctions in recognition granted to gay and lesbian citizens over time, across space, and by policy issue or concern yield a fragmented citizenship. Some authorities within the state—judicial power, executive authority, and legislative authority—as well as nonstate entities—news media, popular media, and private firms—have shifted in their forms of acknowledgment, bringing into focus how these distinct and incongruous authorities create complex, contradictory political identities for gays and lesbians whose access to the rights and responsibilities that follow from personhood and citizenship status remains circumscribed.

The content and meaning of citizenship is context dependent. As Judith Shklar reminds us, "citizenship is not a notion that can be discussed intelligibly in a static and empty social space."[19] As that context shifts, the meaning of citizenship shifts as well. Examining that context—the development of public and private governing authorities that grant the recognition and provide the standing that give citizenship meaning—has been this book's overarching goal. And, what has been illustrated is that the status of the lesbian and gay citizen is just as fragmented as the polity. It is far from wholly or consistently recognized. This differential status of recognition is a consequence of the very dynamics of political change, which are not comprehensive, yield unexpected results, and do not clearly move in a singularly progressive direction. Instead, the normal condition of the polity, as Orren and Skowronek describe it, as composed of multiple incongruous authorities operating simultaneously fragments the citizenship status of gay and lesbian Americans. The meaning and content of their citizenship status is fractured by the normal condition of the polity.

There is a gap in our understanding of relationships between the deliberate, purposeful construction of homosexuality as a personage and the building of state regulatory apparatus. This book has contended that drawing out these connections may not only indicate how the one is implicated in the other but also raise questions about how sexuality has been framed and utilized for a variety of political ends. This link is apparent in the parallel construction of homosexual identity as a threat to nation building, i.e., the first modality of recognition detailed in this book, and the development of immigration infrastructure that could recognize the markers of the homosexual threat and keep it beyond the boundaries of the nation, as discussed in chapter 2. Homosexuality was constructed, in part, to define what could not be included in the Progressive Era notion of healthy citizenship and community, and this idea that homosexuality threatened national community persisted well beyond the point when Progressive notions of eugenics fell into disrepute.[20] But homosexuality has been framed in distinct ways to serve different ends in contemporary politics as well. As detailed in chapters 3 and 4, activists have defined gay identities differently in order to achieve government recognition, and such framing has been exclusionary, often foreclosing acceptance of the gender nonnormative or the more queerly transgressive.[21] Most recently the Court's recognition of gay identities as moving from sexual act to personal identity to relationship serves the political aim of recognition, but it does so on terrain that is fundamentally grounded in norms that are classist, gendered, and heterosexist. In other words, as access to marriage expands, it only folds within it those who hold closely to the gendered and often racialized roles of an idealized heterosexual fantasy-as-tradition.[22]

Attention to distinct political constructions of sexuality, made more transparent in this book through the schematic use of distinct modalities of regulatory recognition, suggests the need to elongate the historical perspective. Sociological and historical literature has highlighted pre-Stonewall mobilization to showcase how gay rights activism did not simply burst onto the scene in 1969, taking its cue from the African American civil rights and second wave feminist movements that preceded it. Yet, only recently has gay or lesbian identity construction been linked to the rise of the national administrative state in the early twentieth century, before any recognizably modern gay rights movement formed.

Disaggregating recognition of gay and lesbian lives to a set of distinct modalities also makes evident the way different authorities can engage different modalities often simultaneously. This lays bare the stickiness of certain constructions of identity and the kinds of entrepreneurial moves made to shift these conceptions. These dynamics are perhaps most recently evident in the distinct ways in which different branches of the federal government have argued in favor of both same-sex marriage and protections against discrimination based on sexual orientation. The executive branch, through the Department of Justice, has employed the entrenched equal protection jurisprudence of suspect-class status and folded gays and lesbians within that framework. And, the EEOC, in an argument reminiscent of that put forward by the Hawaii Supreme Court in *Baehr*, reads sexual-orientation discrimination as a variation of sex discrimination, obviating the need for explicitly naming sexual-orientation discrimination as a distinct act (a move, I have argued, that while strategically understandable, also relies on a blindness to the distinct histories of discrimination faced by gays and lesbians). Meanwhile, the Supreme Court jurisprudential path to gay rights cut by Justice Kennedy has engaged none of the traditional equal protection jurisprudence, instead carving out a new rationale grounded in universalistic claims to dignity. That the executive branch and the states rely on older notions as the Court blazes a seemingly new trail reveals both the ideational durability as well as the role of entrepreneurial arguments central to tracing out the changes over time that mark American political development.

In addition, by focusing on modalities of recognition conferred by regulatory authorities, this book has brought into clearer relief the distinct roles played by different branches in recognizing gay and lesbian personhood and citizenship, and it has indicated that these roles are often counter to conventional wisdom. Attending to the modality of privatization of same-sex relationships that took hold especially in the 1990s locates the Supreme Court as the *last* mover in its *Romer* and *Lawrence* rulings.[23] This positioning would seem to at least complicate if not undermine accusations of judicial activism. The military first adopted this position of privatization through the executive order of Don't Ask Don't Tell, which was later reconfigured as congressional statute. The executive and legislative branches reinforced this modality of privatization by passing the Defense of Marriage Act. The Court adopted privatization of homosexual identity and same-sex relations only *after* that modality gained traction through executive and legislative action. Similarly, the Supreme Court, should it eventually consider gays and lesbians a suspect class or sexual orientation a suspect classification—in the context of recognizing same-sex marriage—would only be following the paths blazed not only by state judges and lower federal judges but by the Obama administration.

This book has also aimed to foreground the way intersectional notions of identity play out in the conceptualization and acknowledgment of gay and lesbian identities. By "intersectional," I mean not only that identities are multiple (racial, age, ethnic, sexual, gender, class, political, etc.), contextual (particular identities may be more salient in particular spaces, places, and times), and fluid (individuals may or may not be able to move from one identity to another in different contexts) such that individuals may be discriminated against or marginalized on a variety of distinct identity dimensions. I also contend that the histories of discrimination and refusal to recognize personhood or citizenship status of gays and lesbians draws upon the logics of prejudice and systemic bias that have been made manifest in refusals to recognize many others. The fourth modality of privatization in particular reveals connections across disparate areas of Supreme Court jurisprudence: race equality, sexuality, and employment law, to name a few. The possibilities of intersectional analysis are laid bare in the emerging jurisprudence of blindness. The Court majority, in cases involving racial discrimination and antigay discrimination, endorses formal equality without recognizing the context on which the claims of inequality, in fact, rest and only through which are intelligible. For the Court majority, the vestiges of inequality are only perpetuated by seeing race; blindness to such characteristics ensures equal treatment. The state refuses to acknowledge the citizen as anything but abstracted, ripping her from historical, racial, or sexual context, ripping her from the contours and context of experience that define her as an individual demanding the dignity of recognition. The jurisprudence of blindness—whether it is locking gay sexualities behind the bedroom door, grappling with histories of discrimination that underlay the refusal to recognize relationships, or refusing to recognize the context and meanings of racial identity—has been on full display since the *Lawrence* ruling.

This book has explored how homosexuality has been regulated differently over time and calls for expanding the scope of the "political" in American "political" development since many of those earliest recognitions came from the private sector. Each distinct modality of recognizing the lesbian and gay subject differently highlighted the need to assess the private sector's role in policy development and change. Consequently, nonstate, particularly private corporate, actors were brought more fully into the study of development. The rise of corporate human resource policies reflective of cultural acceptance of gays and lesbians, in particular, needs to be examined more systematically, especially with respect to the question of whether they influence the possibility and direction of policy, institutional, and ideational development. As the order of authority with which one primarily interacts over the course of the life cycle can change as the individual's primary set of identities changes, it is necessary to evaluate multiple sites of regulatory power. As an individual's needs and consequent interactions with state and private power shift as age, marital and parental status, and employment change over time, her interactions with distinct fields and sources of power, recognition, right, and domination will be temporally and spatially contextual.

Despite this book's exclusive focus on U.S. histories, the critical developmental insight—the polity as made up of multiple clashing orders—is in no way a phenomenon limited to the United States. While it may be more evident in more decentralized federalist systems, it is a function of political change, change that is always incomplete and hardly comprehensive. Given possibilities of developmental congruence, there is ample reason to explore how the fracturing of citizenship may be evident cross-nationally. Countries that have similarly attempted to provide equal access to the military and various forms of relationship recognition to gay and lesbian citizens, among others, may be a place to start.

Finally, just as the idea of sexuality orders discussed in this book draws on Desmond King and Rogers Smith's notion of racial orders, mentioned in chapter 1, there is no reason to contend that fragmented citizenship, or the idea that regulatory recognition of an individual's status can vary across time, across space at a given moment in time, and by policy domain, e.g., parental rights, employment protection, criminal status, marital recognition, etc., is a phenomenon limited to gays, lesbians, bisexuals, or transgendered persons. Rather, the case of lesbian, gay, and bisexual recognitions was utilized to demonstrate how APD concepts can be fruitfully applied to yield new insights and thus, how much can be gained by increased developmental attention to gay and lesbian politics.

But one claim remained consistent throughout: citizenship, in this book, is not, or is not only, a liberal idea that draws on preexisting or natural rights or the republican notion that emphasizes democratic and civic responsibilities. Instead, if citizenship is a constructed, relational, and institutionally recognized status on which the substantive claim to rights and the substantive enactment of responsibilities is predicated, then public and private regulatory authorities that perform that recognition influence what a citizen's status may entail. If the sets of institutions, ideas, rules, and norms on which citizenship derives its meaning are often in tension with one another, as developmental theories of political change suggest, then citizenship itself is perhaps better conceptualized as often and even primarily unstable as well. A developmental definition of the polity as fragmented, disjointed, and internally incongruous provides a possible conception of citizenship in the same terms, and detailing the history of regulatory recognitions of gay and lesbian personhood and citizenship highlights the congruent fragmentation.

This developmental conception of the polity as fragmented—the components of which may grate against each other, creating unanticipated frictions—and the parallel conception of fragmented citizenship that follows are potentially in tension with the national and holistic conception of citizenship that may follow from the Fourteenth Amendment's guarantees of rights, liberties, and equality. Do we operate under two constitutional framings of citizenship, an antebellum conception and a post–Fourteenth Amendment notion whereby the latter was layered upon the other, not successfully wiping the slate clean of the older notion precisely because it grated against governing orders of racism and other hierarchic relations to which powerful interests held fast?

If the Fourteenth Amendment's guarantees of due process, equal protection, and the privileges and immunities of citizenship do compel a *whole* citizen, one who is federally cognizable and supported in *all* her rights, the amendment's meaning in light of a developmental conception of the polity also raises a set of questions: Can the fragmented citizen become whole, or at least wholly recognized by public and private regulatory authorities given the condition of the polity as always necessarily comprised of laws, policies, ideas, and institutions in tension? Is this an unresolved and, indeed, unresolvable fundamental tension—between the experience of governance and the idealistic aspiration of governance—that drives political development? In short, the Constitution would seem to be the fullest expression of the key insight of American political development, namely, politics as the manifestation of incomplete ideas and institutions, as new premises layered upon old without erasure of that which came before, thereby producing instabilities and frictions. These frictions have a direct impact on the enactment of citizenship and on the recognition of personhood. Insofar as the meanings of personhood and citizenship flow from constitutional recognition, our fractured Constitution, produced over time with new ideas in tension with older ones that still hold in the cultural imagination, yields a fragmented citizen. This is not a normative critique but an empirical reality, one aptly illustrated by the historical and contemporary status of gay and lesbian Americans.

NOTES

INTRODUCTION

1 Wilpert quoted in Stephen Ohlemacher, "Tax Day Gets Complicated for Same-Sex Couples in States That Don't Recognize Their Marriages," *Fox Business*, 15 April 2015, http://www.foxbusiness.com/markets/2015/04/11/tax-day-gets-complicated-for-same-sex-couples-in-states-that-dont-recognize/ (accessed 24 May 2015).

2 Oesterle quoted in Hannah Bae, Ben Rooney, and Aaron Smith, "Indiana Backlash: Opposition to Anti-Gay Law Grows," *CNNMoney*, 29 March 2015, http://money.cnn.com/2015/03/28/news/companies/angies-list-indiana-gay-discrimination/index.html?sr=fbmoney032915indiana1030story (accessed 24 May 2015).

3 Donald Verrilli, *Obergefell v. Hodges* Docket Number: 14-556-Question-1. Date Argued: 28 April 2015, http://www.supremecourt.gov/oral_arguments/audio/2014/14-556-q1 (accessed 24 May 2015).

4 Scott Clement and Robert Barnes, "Poll: Gay Marriage Support at Record High," *Washington Post*, 23 April 2015.

5 Ohlemacher (2015).

6 Wells Fargo Advisors, *Out*, June/July 2013, 35.

7 *United States v. Windsor*, 570 U.S. ____ (2013), 25–26.

8 "Treasury and IRS Announce That All Legal Same-Sex Marriages Will Be Recognized for Federal Tax Purposes: Ruling Provides Certainty, Benefits, and Protections under Federal Tax Law for Same-Sex Married Couples," *Internal Revenue Service*, 29 August 2013, http://www.irs.gov/uac/Newsroom/Treasury-and-IRS-Announce-That-All-Legal-Same-Sex-Marriages-Will-Be-Recognized-For-Federal-Tax-Purposes%3B-Ruling-Provides-Certainty,-Benefits-and-Protections-Under-Federal-Tax-Law-for-Same-Sex-Married-Couples (accessed 24 May 2015).

9 Those states are Alabama, Arkansas, Georgia, Kentucky, Louisiana, Michigan, Mississippi, Nebraska, North Dakota, Ohio, South Dakota, Tennessee, and Texas. Missouri currently recognizes marriages celebrated initially out of state. In Kansas, local jurisdictions are issuing marriage licenses to same-sex couples, but these marriages are not currently recognized by the state governments. Information is accurate as of 24 May 2015.

10 Ben Steverman, "Gay Couples' Tax-Season Nightmares Continue," *Bloomberg.com*, 17 February 2015, http://www.bloomberg.com/news/articles/2015-02-17/gay-couples-tax-season-nightmares-continue (accessed 24 May 2015).

11 Throughout this book I utilize the acronym LGBT to define the contemporary movement for equal rights for lesbian, gay, bisexual, and transgender people. Nevertheless, since the aim of the book is to examine change in regulatory recognition of these identities over time, I attempt to reflect the gradual and often contentious inclusion of the "B" and the "T" over time. As a result, in many cases the book reflects the absence of attention by public and private governing authorities to transgender inclusion and equality. The deliberate exclusion of transgender individuals from the full removal of the ban on openly gay, lesbian, and bisexual soldiers, as discussed in chapter 1, is a case in point.

12 Deborah Gould, *Moving Politics: Emotion and ACT UP's Fight against AIDS* (Chicago: University of Chicago Press, 2009), 58. On gay shame as grounded in nonrecognition, see Eve Kosofsky Sedgwick, *Touching Feelings: Affect, Pedagogy, Performativity* (Durham, NC: Duke University Press, 2003).

13 See David Harvey, *A Brief History of Neoliberalism* (New York: Oxford University Press, 2005).

14 Steverman (2015).

15 Ibid.

16 Wilbert quoted in Ohlemacher (2015).

17 Anthony Kennedy, *Obergefell v. Hodges* Docket Number: 14-556-Question-1. Date Argued: 28 April 2015, http://www.supremecourt.gov/oral_arguments/audio/2014/14-556-q1 (accessed 24 May 2015).

18 John Roberts, *Obergefell v. Hodges* Docket Number: 14-556-Question-1. Date Argued: 28 April 2015, http://www.supremecourt.gov/oral_arguments/audio/2014/14-556-q1 (accessed 24 May 2015).

19 On public support for same-sex marriage, see Justin McCarthy, "Record-High 60% of Americans Support Same-Sex Marriage," *Gallup.com*, 19 May 2015, http://www.gallup.com/poll/183272/record-high-americans-support-sex-marriage.aspx (accessed 24 May 2015). On the pace of court rulings after *Windsor* see Garrett Epps, "Is Tennessee's Ruling against Gay Marriage a Setback for the Cause?" *Atlantic*, 13 August 2014.

20 *United States v. Windsor*, 570 U.S. _____ (2013), 23.

21 Ibid., 24. Citations omitted.

22 Ibid., 25.

23 John Bursch quoted in Amy Davidson, "The Here and Now of Same-Sex Marriage," *New Yorker*, 28 April 2015.

24 Kennedy quoted in ibid.

25 See generally Tina Fetner, "Working Anita Bryant: The Impact of Christian Anti-Gay Activism on Lesbian and Gay Movement Claims," *Social Problems* 48 (3) (2001): 411–28.

26 Richard Perez-Peña and Ashley Southall, "Indiana Legislators Say They'll Clarify Beliefs Law," *New York Times*, 30 March 2015.

27 Kristen Guerra and Tim Evans, "RFRA Revision Does Not Widely Extend Discrimination Protections for LGBT, Experts Say," *IndyStar*, 6 April 2015.

28 Bae, Rooney, and Smith (2015). Tim Cook, "Pro-Discrimination 'Religious Freedom' Laws Are Dangerous," *Washington Post*, 29 March 2015.

29 Rogers M. Smith, *Civic Ideals: Conflicting Visions of Citizenship in U.S. History* (New Haven, CT: Yale University Press, 1997), 14.

30 Linda Bosniak, "Universal Citizenship and the Problem of Alienage," *Northwestern University Law Review* 94 (2000).

31 Mary Ann Glendon, *Rights Talk: The Impoverishment of Political Discourse* (New York: Free Press, 1993); Stephen Macedo, *Liberal Virtues: Citizenship, Virtue, and Community* (New York: Oxford University Press, 1990); Jason Pierceson, *Courts, Liberalism, and Rights: Gay Law and Politics in the United States and Canada* (Philadelphia: Temple University Press, 2005).

32 Roger Brubaker and Frederick Cooper, "Beyond Identity," *Theory and Society* 29 (2000): 1–47; and Judith Shklar, *American Citizenship: The Quest for Inclusion* (Cambridge, MA: Harvard University Press, 1991).

33 Shane Phelan, *Sexual Strangers: Gays, Lesbians, and Dilemmas of Citizenship* (Philadelphia: Temple University Press, 2001), 17.

34 Ibid., 139–40. Emphasis added.

35 Ibid., 14.

36 Ibid.

37 See Seyla Benhabib, *The Reluctant Modernism of Hannah Arendt* (Newbury Park, CA: Sage, 1992); and Bonnie Honig, *Feminist Interpretations of Hannah Arendt* (University Park: Pennsylvania State University Press, 1995).

38 Suzanne Mettler, *Soldiers to Citizens: The G.I. Bill and the Making of the Greatest Generation* (New York: Oxford University Press, 2005); Rogers Smith, *Civic Ideals: Conflicting Visions of Citizenship in U.S. History* (New Haven, CT: Yale University Press, 1997).

39 Suzanne Mettler and Andrew Milstein, "American Political Development from Citizens' Perspective: Tracking Federal Government's Presence in Individual Lives over Time," *Studies in American Political Development* 21 (2001): 110–11.

40 Gary Mucciaroni, "The Study of LGBT Politics and Its Contributions to Political Science," *PS: Political Science & Politics* 44 (January 2011).

41 Rogers Smith, "Beyond Tocqueville, Myrdal, and Hartz: The Multiple Traditions in America," *American Political Science Review* 87 (September 1993): 549–50.

42 Joseph Lowndes, Julie Novkov, and Dorian Warren, "Race and American Political Development," in *Race and American Political Development*, Lowndes, Novkov, and Warren, eds. (New York: Routledge, 2008), 13.

43 Marriage data from "Same-Sex Marriage State-by-State," Pew Forum, 20 October 2014, http://www.pewforum.org/2014/10/20/same-sex-marriage-state-by-state/ (accessed 23 October 2014). Employment statute data from "Statewide Employment Laws and Policies," Human Rights Campaign, updated 9 October 2014, http://hrc-assets.s3-website-us-east-1.amazonaws.com//files/assets/resources/statewide_employment_10-2014.pdf (accessed 16 October 2014). Adoption laws (either second-parent/step-parent or joint) vary widely. On joint, see "Parenting

Laws: Joint Adoption," Human Rights Campaign, updated 10 June 2014, http://
hrc-assets.s3-website-us-east-1.amazonaws.com//files/assets/resources/parent-
ing_joint-adoption_082013.pdf. On second-parent adoption, see "Parenting Laws:
Second Parent or Step-parent Adoption," Human Rights Campaign, updated 10
June 2014, http://hrc-assets.s3-website-us-east-1.amazonaws.com//files/assets/re-
sources/parenting_second-parent-adoption_2-2014.pdf. The Utah State Supreme
Court lifted a stay on a ruling permitting same-sex parental adoption on October
23, 2014. Molly Reilly, "Utah Supreme Court Lifts Hold on Same-Sex Adoptions,"
Huffington Post, 23 October 2014, http://www.huffingtonpost.com/2014/10/23/
utah-same-sex-adoptions_n_6037978.html (accessed 23 October 2014). "Status
Undefined" means that second-parent adoption, meaning adopting the child of
one's partner, and joint adoption, which means adopting a child from its biological parents or from the state, are not clearly defined in the context of same-sex
couples. In other words, there is no explicit allowance for same-sex adoption but
also no explicit ban.

44 Paul Pierson, "Fragmented Welfare States: Federal Institutions and the Development of Social Policy," *Governance* 8 (October 1995).

45 Karen Orren and Stephen Skowronek, *The Search for American Political Development* (New York: Cambridge University Press, 2004), 112.

46 Paul Pierson, *Politics in Time: History, Institutions, and Social Analysis* (Princeton,
NJ: Princeton University Press, 2004), 136.

47 See Stephen Skowronek and Matthew Glassman, eds., *Formative Acts: American
Politics in the Making* (Philadelphia: University of Pennsylvania Press, 2008).

48 Orren and Skowronek (2004), 7.

49 Ibid.

50 The U.S. Constitution speaks of persons and citizens. The Fourteenth Amendment indicates:

> All persons born or naturalized in the United States, and subject to the
> jurisdiction thereof, are citizens of the United States and of the State wherein
> they reside. No State shall make or enforce any law which shall abridge the
> privileges or immunities of citizens of the United States; nor shall any State
> deprive any person of life, liberty, or property, without due process of law; nor
> deny to any person within its jurisdiction the equal protection of the laws.

Since the *Slaughterhouse Cases of 1873*, "the privileges or immunities of citizenship" has been read as a meaningless clause, an idea contested in this book's
conclusion. By distinguishing personhood from citizenship, I am attempting to
draw attention to how homosexuality shifted in the eyes of various governing authorities from act to identity or status. The homosexual person could be granted
aspects of citizenship if not full citizenship, but the homosexual act could not.

51 Phelan (2001), 37.

52 David S. Meyer and Suzanne Staggnborg, "Movements, Countermovements, and
the Structure of Political Opportunity," *American Journal of Sociology* 101 (May

1996): 1628–60; Fetner (2001); Stephen M. Engel, *Social Movement Theory and the Gay and Lesbian Movement* (New York: Cambridge University Press, 2001).

53 Timothy E. Cook, "The Empirical Study of Lesbian, Gay, and Bisexual Politics: Assessing the First Wave of Research," *American Political Science Review* 93 (1999): 679.

54 Richard Valelly, "LGBT Politics and American Political Development," *Annual Review of Political Science* 15 (2012): 316. On social movement studies, see Amin Ghaziani, *The Dividends of Dissent: How Conflict and Culture Work in Lesbian and Gay Marches on Washington* (Chicago: University of Chicago Press, 2008); Craig Rimmerman, *From Identity to Politics: The Lesbian and Gay Movements in the United States* (Philadelphia: Temple University Press, 2002). On public opinion studies see Paul R. Brewer, *Value War: Public Opinion and the Politics of Gay Rights* (Lanham, MD: Rowman & Littlefield, 2008); Gary Mucciaroni, *Same Sex, Different Politics: Success and Failure in the Struggles over Gay Rights* (Chicago: University of Chicago Press, 2008); Nathaniel Persily, Jack Citrin, and Patrick J. Egan, eds., *Public Opinion and Constitutional Controversy* (New York: Oxford University Press, 2008). On judicial politics see Ellen Ann Andersen, *Out of the Closets and into the Courts* (Ann Arbor: University of Michigan Press, 2006); and William Eskridge Jr., *Gaylaw: Challenging the Apartheid of the Closet* (Cambridge, MA: Harvard University Press, 1999).

55 See Julie Novkov and Scott Barclay, "Lesbians, Gays, Bisexuals, and the Transgendered in Political Science: Report on a Discipline-Wide Survey," *PS: Political Science and Politics* 42 (1) (2010): 95–106; and Mucciaroni (2011).

56 Valelly (2012), 316. Valelly's citations refer to Stephen M. Engel, "Organizational Identity as a Constraint on Strategic Action: A Comparative Analysis of Gay and Lesbian Interest Groups," *Studies in American Political Development* 21 (2007): 66–91; and J. Bell, "'To Strive for Economic and Social Justice': Welfare, Sexuality, and Liberal Politics in San Francisco in the 1960s," *Journal of Policy History* 22 (2010): 193–225. There are at least two notable exceptions to Valelly's broadly accurate assessment of APD. First, responding to the research gap described above, Margot Canaday conducted extensive research on how the administrative state built a sexuality regime over the course of the early twentieth century. See Margot Canaday, *The Straight State: Sexuality and Citizenship in Twentieth-Century America* (Princeton, NJ: Princeton University Press, 2009). Also, Kevin Murphy has shown how Progressive Era (1890–1920) political rhetoric, in order to stigmatize political opponents, employed the image of the overly sensitive and inward-focused "mollycoddle," who bore similarities to the emerging homosexual of the period. In other words, the political construction of sexuality, and in particular of manhood, overlaps and intersects with the Progressive nationalist aims of what Stephen Skowronek (1982) has documented as building a new American state. See Kevin P. Murphy, *Political Manhood: Redbloods, Mollycoddles, and the Politics of Progressive Era Reform* (New York: Columbia University Press, 2008). Stephen

Skowronek, *Building a New American State* (New York: Cambridge University Press, 1982).

57 Dara Strolovitch, *Affirmative Advocacy* (Chicago: University of Chicago Press, 2008), 24.

58 Dara Strolovitch, "Intersectionality in Time: Sexuality and the Shifting Boundaries of Intersectional Marginalization," *Politics & Gender* 8 (3) (2012): 386–96.

59 Julie Novkov, "The Miscegenation/Same-Sex Marriage Analogy: What Can We Learn from Legal History?" *Law & Social Inquiry* 33 (2008): 360.

60 David M. Halperin, "How to Do the History of Male Homosexuality," *GLQ: A Journal of Lesbian and Gay Studies* 6 (1) (2000): 87.

CHAPTER 1. FROM INDIVIDUAL RIGHTS TO INSTITUTIONAL RECOGNITIONS

1 Judith N. Shklar, *American Citizenship: The Quest for Inclusion* (Cambridge, MA: Harvard University Press, 1991), 1.

2 Karen Orren and Stephen Skowronek, *The Search for American Political Development* (New York: Cambridge University Press, 2004), 112.

3 On gay- and lesbian-rights strategies as utilizing a quasi-ethnic master frame drawing upon the civil rights movement of the 1950s and 1960s, see Steven Epstein, "Gay and Lesbian Movements in the United States: Dilemmas of Identity, Diversity, and Political Strategy," in *The Global Emergence of Gay and Lesbian Politics: National Imprints of a Worldwide Movement*, Barry D. Adam, Jan Willem Duyvendak, and Andre Krouwel, eds. (Philadelphia: Temple University Press, 1999).

4 Barack Obama, "Inaugural Address." Online by Gerhard Peters and John T. Woolley, *The American Presidency Project*, 21 January 2013. http://www.presidency.ucsb.edu/ws/?pid=102827.

5 See Martin Duberman, *Stonewall* (New York: Penguin, 1994).

6 Shushanna Walshe, "Obama Makes History by Citing Gay Rights in Inaugural Address," *ABC News*, 21 January 2013, http://abcnews.go.com/Politics/obama-makes-history-citing-gay-rights-inaugural-address/story?id=18275341; Liz Halloran, "Stonewall? Explaining Obama's Historic Gay-Rights Reference," *NPR*, 22 January 2013, http://www.npr.org/blogs/itsallpolitics/2013/01/22/169984209/stonewall-explaining-obamas-historic-gay-rights-reference; Moni Basu, "Obama Embraces Key Social Justice Movements in Inaugural Address," *CNN*, 21 January 2013, http://inamerica.blogs.cnn.com/2013/01/21/obama-embraces-key-social-justice-movements-in-inaugural-address/ (all accessed 22 October 2013).

7 For discussion of pre-Stonewall mobilization after the Second World War, see Barry Adam, *The Rise of a Gay and Lesbian Movement* (New York: Twayne, 1995); John D'Emilio, *Sexual Politics, Sexual Communities: The Making of a Homosexual Minority in the United States, 1940–1970* (Chicago: University of Chicago Press, 1983). For discussion of post-Stonewall gay liberation, see Steve Valocchi, "Individual Identities, Collective Identities, and Organizational Structure: The

Relationship of the Political Left and Gay Liberation in the United States," *Socio-logical Perspectives* 44 (Winter 2001): 445–67. For discussion of media and popular cultural attention to gay and lesbian rights claims in the 1990s, see chapters 6 and 8 of Amin Ghaziani, *The Dividends of Dissent: How Conflict and Culture Work in Lesbian and Gay Marches on Washington* (Chicago: University of Chicago Press, 2008).

8 More radical elements, such as liberationist and queer communities, have advo-cated abandoning the conception of citizenship as equal rights and have offered a more thoroughgoing critique of the liberal claim for inclusion. Thus they have refused to engage in the normalization of homosexuality such that the gay couple is "just like" the straight couple. Nevertheless, as Steven Seidman points out, queer critique that undermines the moral distaste for queer sex still "adopt[s] a normative position that draws heavily on liberal notions of bodily integrity and privacy. . . . [S]exual citizenship entails a robust defense of a private sphere that is juridically and socially protected from interference by the state and other citi-zens." Seidman, "From Identity to Queer Politics: Shifts in Normative Heterosexu-ality and the Meaning of Citizenship," *Citizenship Studies* 5 (3) (2001): 327.

9 See D'Emilio (1983).

10 James A. Morone, *Hellfire Nation: The Politics of Sin in American History* (New Haven, CT: Yale University Press, 2003), 8.

11 Rogers Smith, "Beyond Tocqueville, Myrdal, and Hartz: The Multiple Traditions in America," *American Political Science Review* 87 (September 1993): 550.

12 See Stuart A. Sheingold, *The Politics of Rights: Lawyers, Public Policy, and Political Change*, 2nd ed. (Ann Arbor: University of Michigan Press, 2004). On limits of litigation, see Gerald Rosenberg, *The Hollow Hope: Can Courts Bring about Social Change?* 2nd ed. (Chicago: University of Chicago Press, 2008). For a critical response see Tom Keck, "Beyond Backlash: Assessing the Impact of Judicial Decisions on LGBT Rights," *Law & Society Review* 43 (1) (2009): 151–85; and Matthew E. K. Hall, *The Nature of Supreme Court Power* (New York: Cambridge University Press, 2011).

13 Louis Hartz, *The Liberal Tradition in America* (New York: Harcourt, Brace, & World, 1955). Rogers Smith (1993) has suggested that the political culture is best conceptualized as comprised of multiple traditions—a liberal tradition, a republi-can tradition, and a tradition of identity-based prejudice—any of which might be drawn upon at a given moment to support policy change.

14 T. H. Marshall, *Class, Citizenship, and Social Development* (New York: Doubleday, 1965).

15 Elizabeth F. Cohen, *Semi-Citizenship in Democratic Politics* (New York: Cam-bridge University Press, 2009), 6.

16 Ibid.

17 Ibid., 193–203.

18 On French republicanism see Roger Brubaker, *Citizenship and Nationhood in France and Germany* (Cambridge, MA: Harvard University Press, 1992). On the rhetoric of republicanism during the debates on the PaCS, see Eric Fassin, "Same

Sex, Different Politics: 'Gay Marriage' Debates in France and the United States," *Public Culture* 13 (Spring 2001): 215–32.

19 Carl F. Stychin, "Civil Solidarity or Fragmented Identities? The Politics of Sexuality and Citizenship in France," *Social and Legal Studies* 10 (3) (2001): 347–75.

20 Will Kymlicka, *Contemporary Political Philosophy: An Introduction*, 2nd ed. (New York: Oxford University Press, 2002), 284.

21 See John Dryzek, *Deliberative Democracy and Beyond: Liberals, Critics, Contestations* (New York: Oxford University Press, 2000).

22 Shklar (1991), 9.

23 Iris Marion Young, *Justice and the Politics of Difference* (Princeton, NJ: Princeton University Press, 1990), 60.

24 Shane Phelan, *Sexual Strangers: Gays, Lesbians, and Dilemmas of Citizenship* (Philadelphia: Temple University Press, 2001), 5.

25 Ibid.

26 Mary Ann Glendon, "Rights in Twentieth-Century Constitutions: The Case of Welfare Rights," *Journal of Policy History* 6 (1) (1994): 140–56.

27 Shklar (1991), 63.

28 Some scholars have reached beyond Shklar's emphasis on labor as productive and focused on the marketplace as a venue for enacting citizenship. Consequently, citizenship is enacted through material consumption. See Kate Soper and Frank Trentmann, eds., *Citizenship and Consumption* (New York: Palgrave Macmillan, 2008). Indeed, institutions of collective gay and lesbian identity formation, such as bars, bookstores, cafes, clubs, magazines, and websites, have been criticized for their connections to profit motive and market imperatives because they appeal to and reproduce as universalistic the identities of those who can afford to consume: "the institutions of queer culture have been dominated by those with capital: typically, middle-class white men." Michael Warner, *Fear of a Queer Planet: Queer Politics and Social Theory* (Minneapolis: University of Minnesota Press, 1993), xvii. See also Rosemary Hennessey, "Queer Visibility in Commodity Culture," *Cultural Critique* 29 (Winter 1994).

29 Shklar (1991), 67.

30 Ibid., 84.

31 Phelan (2001), 37.

32 James C. Scott, *Seeing Like a State: How Certain Schemes to Improve the Human Condition Have Failed* (New Haven, CT: Yale University Press, 1998).

33 David Halperin, *How to Do the History of Homosexuality* (Chicago: University of Chicago Press, 2002), 106.

34 Eve Kosofsky Sedgwick, *Epistemology of the Closet* (Berkeley: University of California Press, 1990), 85.

35 Gerald Berk, Dennis C. Galvan, and Victoria Hattam, eds., *Political Creativity: Reconfiguring Institutional Order and Change* (Philadelphia: University of Pennsylvania Press, 2013).

36 Orren and Skowronek (2004), 1.

37 Karen Orren and Stephen Skowronek, "Beyond the Iconography of Order: Notes for a 'New Institutionalism,'" in *The Dynamics of American Politics: Approaches and Interpretations*, Lawrence C. Dodd and Calvin Jilson, eds. (Boulder, CO: Westview, 1994); Robert C. Lieberman, "Ideas, Institutions, and Political Order: Explaining Political Change," *American Political Science Review* 96 (December 2002): 697.

38 See Lieberman (2002), 700–705.

39 David Plotke, *Building a Democratic Political Order: Reshaping American Liberalism in the 1930s and 1940s* (New York: Cambridge University Press, 1996), 1.

40 Orren and Skowronek (2004), 143–55. See also Karen Orren, *Belated Feudalism: Labor, Law, and Liberal Development in the United States* (New York: Cambridge University Press, 1992).

41 Ibid., 702.

42 Lieberman (2002), 702.

43 Desmond King and Rogers Smith, "Racial Orders in American Political Development," *American Political Science Review* 99 (February 2005): 75.

44 Ibid.

45 Orren and Skowronek (2004), 20–21; Lieberman (2002), 703.

46 Eric Schickler, *Disjointed Pluralism: Institutional Innovation and the Development of the U.S. Congress* (Princeton, NJ: Princeton University Press, 2001).

47 Daniel Beland, "Ideas and Institutional Change in Social Security: Conversion, Layering, and Policy Drift," *Social Science Quarterly* 88 (2007): 20–38; Lieberman (2002).

48 Paul Frymer, "Law and American Political Development," *Law & Social Inquiry* 33 (Summer 2008): 786.

49 Jacob Hacker, "The Historical Logic of National Health Insurance: Structure and Sequence in the Development of British, Canadian, and U.S. Medical Policy," *Studies in American Political Development* 12 (1998): 57–130; Paul Pierson, *Politics in Time: History, Institutions, and Social Analysis* (Princeton, NJ: Princeton University Press, 2004).

50 Andrea Louise Campbell, *How Policies Make Citizens: Senior Political Activism and the American Welfare State* (Princeton, NJ: Princeton University Press, 2003); Suzanne Mettler, "Bringing the State Back into Civic Engagement: Policy Feedback Effects of the G.I. Bill for World War II Veterans," *American Political Science Review* 96 (2002): 351–65; Joe Soss and Sanford F. Schram, "A Public Transformed? Welfare Reform as Policy Feedback," *American Political Science Review* 101 (2007): 111–27.

51 Schickler (2001).

52 Beland (2007); Jacob Hacker and Paul Pierson, "Winner-Take-All Politics: Public Policy, Political Organization, and the Precipitous Rise of Top Incomes in the United States," *Politics & Society* 38 (2010): 152–204.

53 Daniel P. Carpenter, *The Forging of Bureaucratic Autonomy: Reputations, Networks, and Policy Innovation in Executive Agencies, 1862–1928* (Princeton, NJ: Princeton University Press, 2001); Adam Sheingate, "Political Entrepreneurship,

Institutional Change, and American Political Development," *Studies in American Political Development* 17 (2003): 185–203; and Stephen Skowronek and Matthew Glassman, eds., *Formative Acts: American Politics in the Making* (Philadelphia: University of Pennsylvania Press, 2007).

54 Orren and Skowronek (2004), 1.

55 Ibid.

56 Naomi Murakawa, "The Origins of the Carceral Crisis: Racial Order as 'Law and Order' in Postwar American Politics," in *Race and American Political Development*, Joseph Lowndes, Julie Novkov, and Dorian T. Warren, eds. (New York: Routledge, 2008), 236.

57 See Derrick A. Bell, "Who's Afraid of Critical Race Theory?" *University of Illinois Law Review* 4 (1995) (4): 893–910.

58 Paul Frymer, *Black and Blue: African Americans, the Labor Movement, and the Decline of the Democratic Party* (Princeton, NJ: Princeton University Press, 2008), 102.

59 Michael C. Dawson and Cathy Cohen, "Problems in the Study of the Politics of Race," in *Political Science: The State of the Discipline*, Ira Katznelson and Helen V. Milner, eds. (New York: Norton, 2002), 490.

60 Warner (1993), xvii.

61 Kenji Yoshino, *Covering: The Hidden Assault on Our Civil Rights* (New York: Random House, 2006).

62 Victoria Hattam, *In the Shadow of Race: Jews, Latinos, and Immigrant Politics in the United States* (Chicago: University of Chicago Press, 2007).

63 Michael Warner, "Introduction," in *Fear of a Queer Planet: Queer Politics and Social Theory*, Michael Warner, ed. (Minneapolis: University of Minnesota Press, 1993), xv–xvi.

64 Dara Strolovich, "Intersectionality in Time: Sexuality and the Shifting Boundaries of Intersectional Marginalization," *Politics & Gender* 8 (3) (2012): 386–96.

65 Elizabeth Freeman, "Introduction," *GLQ: A Journal of Lesbian and Gay Studies* 13 ("Queer Temporalities" issue) (2007): 159; see also Judith Halberstam, *In a Queer Time and Place* (New York: NYU Press, 2005).

66 I use the verb "to queer" to mean challenging not only sexual norms but any institutionalization of norm and identity that disempowers. As Warner (1993) writes, "For both academics and activists, 'queer' gets a critical edge by defining itself against the normal rather than the heterosexual, and normal includes normal business in the academy" (xxvi).

67 Orren and Skowronek (2004), 130.

68 Ibid., 123.

69 Richard Valelly, "LGBT Politics and American Political Development," *Annual Review of Political Science* 15 (2012): 316.

70 Examples of periodization in the literature include John Gerring, *Party Ideologies in America, 1828–1996* (New York: Cambridge University Press, 1998); Stephen Skowronek, *The Politics Presidents Make: Leadership from John Adams to Bill Clinton* (Cambridge, MA: Belknap Press of Harvard University, 1998); and James L.

Sundquist, *Dynamics of the Party System: Alignment and Realignment of Political Parties in the United States* (Washington, DC: Brookings Institution Press, 1983).

71 Orren and Skowronek (2004), 124.

72 Ibid., 123.

73 Ibid., 92.

74 On evaluating power as contextual within a human life cycle framework, see Ian Shapiro, *Democratic Justice* (New Haven, CT: Yale University Press, 1999), 24–28.

75 Antonio Gramsci, *Selections from the Prison Notebooks*, Quintin Hoare and Geoffrey Nowell Smith, eds. (New York: International Publishers, 1971).

76 Margot Canaday, *The Straight State: Sexuality and Citizenship in Twentieth-Century America* (Princeton, NJ: Princeton University Press, 2009).

77 Valelly (2012).

78 Ibid., 317.

79 David Bell and Jon Binnie, *The Sexual Citizen: Queer Politics and Beyond* (Cambridge: Polity, 2000); and Linda K. Kerber, "The Meanings of Citizenship," *Journal of American History* 84 (1997): 833–54.

80 Nancy F. Cott, "Marriage and Women's Citizenship in the United States," *American Historical Review* 103 (1998): 1441.

81 Cohen (2009), 8.

82 Hacker (1998), 59.

83 Orren and Skowronek (2004), 23.

84 David Rayside, *On the Fringe: Gays and Lesbians in Politics* (Ithaca, NY: Cornell University Press, 1998), 219; Chai Feldblum, "The Federal Gay Rights Bill: From Bella to ENDA," in *Creating Change: Sexuality, Public Policy, and Civil Rights*, J. D'Emilio, W. Turner, and U. Vaid, eds. (New York: St. Martin's, 2000), 174.

85 Suzanne Mettler, *Soldiers to Citizens: The G.I. Bill and the Making of the Greatest Generation* (New York: Oxford University Press, 2005).

86 Nancy F. Cott, *Public Vows: A History of Marriage and Nation* (Cambridge, MA: Harvard University Press, 2000); Peggy Pascoe, *What Comes Naturally: Miscegenation Law and the Making of Race in America* (New York: Oxford University Press, 2009); Priscilla Yamin, *American Marriage: A Political Institution* (Philadelphia: University of Pennsylvania Press, 2012).

87 Stephen Skowronek, *Building a New American State: The Expansion of National Administrative Capacities, 1877–1920* (New York: Cambridge University Press, 1982); Canaday (2009); Yamin (2012); Dorit Geva, *Conscription, Family, and the Modern State: A Comparative Study of France and the United States* (New York: Cambridge University Press, 2013).

88 Ash Carter, Secretary of Defense, "Remarks at LGBT Pride Month Ceremony," delivered 9 June 2015, http://www.defense.gov/Speeches/Speech.aspx?SpeechID=1947 (accessed 12 June 2015).

89 Chai R. Feldblum, "The Federal Gay Rights Bill: From Bella to ENDA," *Creating Change: Sexuality, Public Policy, and Civil Rights*, John D'Emilio, William B. Turner, and Urvashi Vaid, eds. (New York: St. Martin's, 2000), 152–87; Nathaniel

Frank, *Unfriendly Fire: How the Gay Ban Undermines the Military and Weakens America* (New York: St. Martin's, 2009); L. Morales, "In U.S., Broad, Steady Support for Openly Gay Service Members," *Gallup.com*, 10 May 2010.

90 The Don't Ask, Don't Tell Repeal Act of 2010 (H.R. 2965, S. 4023). See D. Burrelli, "'Don't Ask, Don't Tell': The Law and Military Policy on Same-Sex Behavior," Congressional Research Service 7-5700, 14 October 2010; A. Nicholson, *Fighting to Serve: Behind the Scenes in the War to Repeal "Don't Ask, Don't Tell"* (Chicago: Chicago Review Press, 2012).

91 *United States v. Windsor*, 570 U.S. ___ (2013).

92 *Servicemembers Legal Defense Fund*, http://www.sldn.org/pages/benefits-and-pay (accessed 12 February 2013).

93 *Federal Register*, 20 July 2012, http://www.gpo.gov/fdsys/pkg/FR-2012-07-20/pdf/2012-17536.pdf.

94 I thank James Durant III, Chief Counsel, U.S. Department of Energy–Office of Science, for bringing this distinction to my attention at the Law and Bias conference hosted by the American Bar Foundation on 9 May 2015.

95 Leon Panetta, Secretary of Defense, "Memorandum for Secretaries of the Military Departments Acting Under Secretary of Defense for Personnel and Readiness, Subject: Extending Benefits to Same-Sex Domestic Partners of Military Members," *U.S. Department of Defense*, 11 February 2013. http://www.defense.gov/news/same-sexbenefitsmemo.pdf (accessed 31 May 2013).

96 Ibid.

97 Ibid.

98 Orren and Skowronek (2004), 108.

99 Chuck Hagel, Secretary of Defense, "Memorandum for Secretaries of the Military Departments, Under Secretary of Defense for Personnel and Readiness, Subject: Extending Benefits to Same-Sex Spouses of Military Members," 13 August 2013, http://militarypartners.org/wp-content/uploads/2013/08/Extending-Benefits-to-Same-Sex-Spouses-of-Military-Members.pdf.

100 Adam Smith, Ranking Member of the House Armed Services Committee, and Carl Levin, Chairman of the Senate Armed Service Committee, to The Honorable Chuck Hagel, Secretary of Defense, "Delay in Processing of Military Benefits to Same-Sex Spouses of Members of the National Guard":

Recently, the states of Texas, Mississippi, Louisiana, and Oklahoma have refused to issue or have stopped issuing ID cards in state facilities to same-sex spouses of service members. Citing statewide bans on marriage for same-sex couples, local policy makers have forced these spouses to travel to federal military installations to apply for their military benefits. . . . We urge you to issue further guidance in this matter, reaffirming that all married military couples must be treated equally, and clarifying that state National Guards, because they are funded in large part by federal tax dollars, cannot choose to ignore this order by denying some lawfully married couples equal access to the federal benefits to which they are entitled.

American Military Partner Association, 30 September 2013, http://militarypart-ners.org/wp-content/uploads/2012/12/Smith-Levin-Letter-to-Hagel-9-30-13.pdf (accessed 14 February 2014). In a speech before the Anti-Defamation League of New York in late October 2013, Hagel stated that nine states were currently violating federal law: "All spouses of service members are entitled to Department of Defense ID cards, and the benefits that come with them. But several states are refusing to issue these IDs to same-sex spouses at National Guard facilities." He added, "not only does this violate the states' obligations under federal law, their actions have created hardship and inequality by forcing couples to travel long distances to federal military bases to obtain the ID cards they're entitled to. This is wrong. It causes division among the ranks, and it furthers prejudice, which the Department of Defense has fought to extinguish." Hagel, quoted in Agence France-Presse, "Chuck Hagel Scolds States for Not Recognizing Military Benefits for Same-Sex Marriages," *Raw Story*, 31 October 2013, http://www.rawstory.com/rs/2013/10/31/chuck-hagel-scolds-states-for-not-recognizing-military-benefits-for-same-sex-marriages/ (accessed 14 February 2014).

101 Robert Burns, "Chuck Hagel Blasts States on Gay Marriage Benefits Policy," *Huffington Post*, 31 October 2013, http://www.huffingtonpost.com/2013/10/31/chuck-hagel-gay-marriage-benefits_n_4185294.html (accessed 5 February 2014).

102 Richard A. Oppel Jr., "Texas and 5 Other States Resist Processing Benefits for Gay Couples," *New York Times*, 10 November 2013.

103 Pascoe (2009), 191.

104 Ibid., 195–98.

105 Franklin H. Williams to John W. Morris, 23 March 1948, fr. 117, Part 9, Series B, Reel 15, Papers of the NAACP, Microfilm Edition, quoted in Pascoe (2009), 199.

106 Josh Hicks, "Texas Processing Military Benefits for Gay Spouses under Pentagon Deal," *Washington Post*, 27 November 2013.

107 Fallin quoted in Zach Ford, "Oklahoma Drops National Guard Benefits for All Couples to Avoid Serving Same-Sex Couples," *thinkprogress.org*, 19 November 2013, http://thinkprogress.org/lgbt/2013/11/19/2970531/oklahoma-national-guard/ (accessed 5 February 2014).

108 While the DoD exemplifies political creativity to work around the law to implement a federal modality of recognizing same-sex marriages, Oklahoma and other states also engage in political creativity to avoid that form of regulatory recognition. Each action can be defended as legal and constitutional under the *Windsor* framework, but they also indicate that political creativity is not normatively good or bad. Oklahoma's actions resemble Prince Edward County, Virginia's massive resistance to school desegregation when it shut down its public schools (offering tuition grants to white students to attend private school). Oklahoma is pursuing this strategy with regard to marriage recognition as well. Rather than be judicially compelled to recognize same-sex marriage, as a federal judge ruled the state ban unconstitutional in January 2014, the state government is considering legislation that would enable

it not to recognize any marriages. Heide Brandes, "U.S. Judge Rules Oklahoma Gay Marriage Ban Unconstitutional," *Chicago Tribune*, 14 January 2014; Michael Konopasek, "Lawmakers Consider Preventing ALL Marriage in Oklahoma," *News9. com*, 24 January 2014, http://www.news9.com/story/24543033/lawmakers-consider-preventing-all-marriage-in-oklahoma (accessed 5 February 2014).

109 Hagel, 13 August 2013.

110 Jessica L. Write, Acting Under Secretary of Defense, "Memorandum for Secretaries of the Military Departments Chiefs of the Military Services," Subject: Clarifying Policy—Administrative Absence to Obtain a Legal Marriage, 4 September 2013, available online.

111 Ibid.

112 "U.S. Army Chaplain Corps (DACH)," *U.S. Army Chaplain Corps*, http://www.army.mil/chaplaincorps/ (accessed 21 November 2013).

113 "Stronger Relationships Mean a Stronger Army," *Army Strong Bonds Program*, http://www.strongbonds.org/skins/strongbonds/home.aspx (accessed 21 November 2013).

114 Joe Gould, "Gay Army Couple Says Chaplain Barred Them from Marriage Retreat," *Military Times*, 21 November 2013.

115 SDGLN Staff, "Same-Gender Couple Not Allowed in Army's Marriage Enrichment Program," *San Diego Gay & Lesbian News, SDGLN.com*, 21 November 2013.

116 See John D. Laing and Page Matthew Brooks, ed., *Don't Ask, Don't Tell: Homosexuality, Chaplaincy, and the Modern Military* (Eugene, OR: Resource Publications, 2013).

117 Douglas L. Carver, "Foreword," in *Don't Ask, Don't Tell: Homosexuality, Chaplaincy, and the Modern Military*, John D. Laing and Page Matthew Brooks, eds. (Eugene, OR: Resource Publications, 2013), xiv.

118 Douglas Lee, John D. Laing, and Page Matthew Brooks, "Introduction: 'Don't Ask, Don't Tell!' (Don't Care?)," in *Don't Ask, Don't Tell: Homosexuality, Chaplaincy, and the Modern Military*, John D. Laing and Page Matthew Brooks, eds. (Eugene, OR: Resource Publications, 2013), 1, 3.

119 John D. Laing, "Virtue or Obedience? Homosexuality, Repeal of DADT, and Chaplains," in *Don't Ask, Don't Tell: Homosexuality, Chaplaincy, and the Modern Military*, John D. Laing and Page Matthew Brooks, eds. (Eugene, OR: Resource Publications, 2013), 126.

120 Letter to President Barack Obama and Dr. Robert M. Gates, 16 September 2010, http://adfwebadmin.com/userfiles/file/DADTletter%209_16_10.pdf (accessed 16 February 2014); see also Tom Breen, "Retired Chaplains: Preserve 'Don't Ask,'" *Washington Post*, 29 October 2010.

121 Gordon Lingenschmitt, former naval chaplain, quoted in Laing (2013), 128.

122 Laing (2013), 131; and Dennis Camp, retired army chaplain, quoted in Barbara Bradley Hagerty, "Chaplains Worry about Careers If 'Don't Ask' Is Lifted," *NPR*, 9 November 2010, http://www.npr.org/2010/12/09/131918799/chaplains-worry-about-careers-if-don-t-ask-is-lifted (accessed 16 February 2014).

123 Laing denies the foundational thesis of this project, namely, that homosexuality is an identity constructed by public and private regulatory authorities, one that changes over time and is adopted by citizens. By contrast, Laing contends that homosexuality is an identity that is defined only in terms of object, or that the homosexual is homosexual insofar as he or she desires a same-sex partner. He argues that while "some may wish to respond that this kind of self-identity was somehow thrust upon homosexuals by an often hostile and even violent society," he maintains that "this claim cannot be sustained for self-perception comes not from without, but from within. External factors can have an influencing effect, but can never be determinative." If then homosexuality is a personal identity defined primarily by its object, then it "works against the virtue of selflessness and instead cultivates selfishness." See Laing (2013), 151–52. Of course, this contention refuses to take seriously the conservative argument that same-sex marriage guards against such selfishness, but more importantly that heterosexuality is also defined by object desire and that homosexuality is only so denoted because its object of desire is the primary quality distinguishing it from the majority. That distinction remains imposed by that majority through various institutional mechanisms, as this book demonstrates.

124 See Douglas Laycock, Antony R. Picarello Jr., and Robin Fretwell Wilson, eds., *Same-Sex Marriage and Religious Liberty: Emerging Conflicts* (Lanham, MD: Rowman & Littlefield, 2008).

125 As of May 2015, military policy permitted access to service but does not explicitly indicate that promotion within service will be considered without regard to sexual orientation. See Gordon England, Deputy Secretary of Defense, Department of Defense Directive, "Diversity Management and Equal Opportunity (EO) in the Department of Defense" (Number 1020.02), *Defense Technical Information Center*, 5 February 2009, http://www.dtic.mil/whs/directives/corres/pdf/102002p.pdf (accessed 21 November 2013).

126 Carter quoted in Terri Moon Cronk, "Carter: Diversity, Inclusion Critical to Force of Future," *DoD News*, 9 June 2015, http://www.defense.gov/News-Article-View/Article/604799 (accessed 10 June 2015).

127 Warner (1993), xix.

128 Cott (2000); Pascoe (2009); Yamin (2012).

129 William Eskridge Jr. and Darren R. Spedale, *Gay Marriage: For Better or for Worse? What We've Learned from the Evidence* (New York: Oxford University Press, 2009), 247.

130 The answer appears to depend on the particular benefit at issue. On Friday, August 9, 2013, the Social Security Administration announced that it would only permit payment of claims for same-sex couples married and residing in states that recognize the marriage; a couple married in Massachusetts who moves to Texas or a couple married in New York but residing in New Jersey would not be eligible for federal Social Security payments. See *Program Operations Manual System*, chapter 002, subchapter 10, "*Windsor* Same-Sex Marriage Claims,"

https://secure.ssa.gov/apps10/public/reference.nsf/links/08092013111040AM. However, the same-sex spouse of a military service member will be eligible for healthcare, housing, and other benefits that opposite-sex spouses receive as of September 3, 2013. See Robert Burns, "Pentagon to Extend Benefits to Gay Spouses," *Huffington Post*, 14 August 2013, http://www.huffingtonpost.com/2013/08/14/pentagon-gay-benefits_n_3756266.html (assessed 26 June 2014).

131 Attorney General Eric Holder to President of the United States, Barack Obama, "Implementation of *United States v. Windsor*," *Department of Justice*, 20 June 2014, http://www.justice.gov/iso/opa/resources/9722014620103930904785.pdf (accessed 26 June 2014), 2–3.

132 Ibid., 3.

133 Ibid., 2.

134 Ibid., 3.

135 See Joanna L. Grossman, "Resurrecting Comity: Re-Visiting the Problem of Non-Uniform Marriage Laws," *Oregon Law Review* 84 (2004).

136 Josh Hicks, "Federal Benefits Won't Extend to Domestic Partners under DOMA Ruling," *Washington Post*, 8 July 2013.

137 Holder to Obama, "Implementation of *United States v. Windsor*," 13.

138 Matt Friedman, "N.J. Assemblymen Want to Convert Civil Unions into Marriages," *NJ.com*, 17 December 2013, http://www.nj.com/politics/index.ssf/2013/12/nj_assemblyman_wants_to_convert_civil_unions_into_marriages.html (accessed 5 February 2013).

139 Annie Lowrey, "Gay Marriages Get Recognition of the IRS," *New York Times*, 29 August 2013.

140 See Stephen Skowronek's characterization of late-nineteenth-century administrative state development as a "pattern of patchwork reforms" followed by attempts at more wholesale "reconstitution" during the early twentieth century. Skowronek (1982), 46, 165–76.

141 Orren and Skowronek (2004), 20.

142 For oral argument, http://www.oyez.org/cases/2010-2019/2012/2012_12_307 (accessed 11 February 2014). See amicus brief filed by the American Sociological Association on whether same-sex parents harm children.

143 *United States v. Windsor*, 570 U.S. ____ (2013), 23.

144 Data for 2014 are from the "Parenting Laws: Second Parent or Stepparent Adoption," *Human Rights Campaign*, http://hrc-assets.s3-website-us-east-1.amazonaws.com//files/assets/resources/second_parent_adoption_6-10-2014.pdf (accessed 18 June 2014).

145 In 2006, nineteen legislative proposals to prevent same-sex parenting were introduced in ten states; however, only Utah's proposal was passed into law.

146 Human Rights Campaign, "Equality from State to State," 2007, 37.

147 *Arkansas Department of Human Services v. Cole*, 2011 Ark. 145.

148 Michelangelo Signorile, Jason Hanna, and Joe Riggs, "Texas Gay Fathers, Denied Legal Parenthood of Twin Sons," *Huffington Post*, 18 June 2014, http://www.huffingtonpost.com/2014/06/18/jason-hanna-and-joe-riggs_n_5506720.html (accessed 18 June 2014).

149 Hanna quoted in ibid.

150 Ibid., 115.

151 Jens Manuel Krogstad, "Moms: Put Us Both on Birth Certificate," *Des Moines Register*, 7 March 2011.

152 American Civil Liberties Union, "ACLU Files Amicus Brief in Same-Sex Parents Birth Certificate Case," 22 May 2012, https://www.aclu.org/news/aclu-files-amicus-brief-same-sex-parents-birth-certificate-case

153 *Gartner and Gartner v. Iowa Department of Public Health*, No. 12-0234, 3 May 2013.

154 James C. McKinley Jr., "N.Y. Judge Alarms Gay Parents by Finding Marriage Law Negates Need for Adoption," *New York Times*, 28 January 2014.

155 Judge Margarita Lopez Torrez quoted in ibid.

156 Ibid.

157 Sommer quoted in ibid.

158 Alison Gash, *Below the Radar: How Silence Can Save Civil Rights* (New York: Oxford University Press, 2015).

159 Ibid.

160 Marc Stein, *Rethinking the Gay and Lesbian Movement* (New York: Routledge, 2012).

161 Linda Hirschman, *Victory: The Triumphant Gay Revolution* (New York: Harper, 2012).

162 On other issues defining the LGBTQ-rights movements, see "7 LGBT Issues That Matter More Than Marriage," *Buzzfeed.com*, 11 October 2013, http://www.buzzfeed.com/hfetter/7-lgbt-issues-that-matter-more-than-marriage-fk74 (accessed 15 October 2013).

163 Lieberman (2002), 704.

164 Ibid.

165 For various examples of rhetorical shifting of original meanings to use in the service of unanticipated ends, see Stephen Skowronek, "The Reassociation of Ideas and Purposes: Racism, Liberalism, and the American Political Tradition," *American Political Science Review* 100 (2006): 385–401.

166 On exogenous shocks as transformational see Pierson (2004) and Frank R. Baumgartner and Bryan D. Jones, *Agendas and Instability in American Politics*, 2nd ed. (Chicago: University of Chicago Press, 2009); on the leveraging of crisis to afford new meanings for old concepts see J. David Greenstone, *The Lincoln Persuasion* (Princeton, NJ: Princeton University Press, 1994).

167 On institutions and rules as constraints see Peter A. Hall, "Historical Institutionalism in Rationalist and Sociological Perspective," in *Explaining Institutional*

Change: Ambiguity, Agency, and Power, James Mahoney and Kathleen Thelen, eds. (Cambridge: Cambridge University Press, 2010). On resource investments in institutions being able to enhance capacity rather than constrain or even close pathways to reform, see Daniel J. Galvin, "The Transformation of Political Institutions: Investments in Institutional Resources and Gradual Change in the National Party Committees," *Studies in American Political Development* 26 (1) (2012).

168 Scott (1998), 80.

169 Cohen (2009), 14.

CHAPTER 2. EXCLUDING THE HOMOSEXUAL

1 G. Frank Lydston, *The Diseases of Society (The Vice and Crime Problem)* (Philadelphia: Lippincott, 1904), 421.

2 *Employment of Homosexuals and Other Sex Perverts in Government*, Subcommittee on Investigations, Committee on Expenditures in the Executive Department, United States Senate, 81st Congress, 2nd Session, 15 December 1950, 2.

3 Michel Foucault, *The History of Sexuality*. Volume 1, *An Introduction* (New York: Vintage, 1978), 43.

4 See William N. Eskridge Jr., *Dishonorable Passions: Sodomy Laws in America, 1861–2003* (New York: Viking, 2008), 16–23, 49–59.

5 The notion of the homosexual person as a late-nineteenth-century construct has been challenged. See John Boswell, "Revolutions, Universals, and Sexual Categories," in *Hidden from History: Reclaiming the Gay and Lesbian Past*, George Chauncey, Martin Duberman, and Martha Vicinus, eds (New York: Penguin, 1990); Jonathan Ned Katz, *Love Stories: Sex between Men before Homosexuality* (Chicago: University of Chicago Press, 2001).

6 Jonathan Ned Katz, *The Invention of Heterosexuality* (Chicago: University of Chicago Press, 1995), 14.

7 This scholarship tends to emphasize the urbanization, industrialization, and modernization that provided the foundation for a same-sex intimate subculture. See John D'Emilio, *Sexual Politics, Sexual Communities: The Making of a Homosexual Minority in the United States, 1940–1970* (Chicago: University of Chicago Press, 1983). George Chauncey describes a more dialectic process between urban subculture and the new medical discourse of homosexuality in which the one informed the development and perpetuation of the other. See George Chauncey, *Gay New York: Gender, Urban Culture, and the Making of the Gay Male World, 1890–1940* (New York: BasicBooks, 1994).

8 See Eve Kosofsky Sedgwick, *Epistemology of the Closet* (Berkeley: University of California Press, 1990); David Halperin, *How to Do the History of Homosexuality* (Chicago: University of Chicago Press, 2002); and Chauncey (1994).

9 Scott Bravmann, *Queer Fictions of the Past: History, Culture, and Difference* (New York: Cambridge University Press, 1997), x.

10 Dana Seitler, "Queer Physiognomies; or, How Many Ways Can We Do the History of Sexuality?" *Criticism* 46 (Winter 2004): 77.

11 Jay Hatheway finds evidence that homosexuals self-identified as "pansies" and "mollies"; George Chauncey refers to what I call the modern homosexual as the "fairy"; and, Kevin Murphy identifies the identifier "mollycoddle," from which was derived "mollies." See Jay Hatheway, *The Gilded Age Construction of Modern American Homophobia* (New York: Palgrave Macmillan, 2003); Chauncey (1994); and Kevin P. Murphy, *Political Manhood: Red Bloods, Mollycoddles, and the Politics of Progressive Era Reform* (New York: Columbia University Press, 2008).

12 German, English, and American sexologists differently named same-sex erotic desire. Karl Heinrich Ulrichs referred to individuals with this feeling as "Urnings"; Krafft-Ebing called exclusive homosexuals "Urnings" and referred to all others as "psycho-sexual hermaphrodites"; Edward Spitzka referred to homosexuals as displaying contrary sexual feeling or simply as perverted. Havelock Ellis referred to same-sex attraction as "sexual inversion." See Karl Heinrich Ulrichs, *The Riddle of "Man-Manly" Love*, trans. Michael A. Lomardi-Nash with a foreword by Vern L. Bullough (Buffalo, NY: Prometheus Books, 1994), 1: 34; Richard von Krafft-Ebing, *Psychopathia Sexualis with Especial Reference to the Antipathetic Sexual Instinct: A Medico-Forensic Study* (Philadelphia: F. A. Davis, 1892; E. C. Sptizka, "A Historical Case of Sexual Perversion," *Chicago Medical Review* 4 (4) (20 August 1881); Havelock Ellis, "Sexual Inversion in Men," *Alienist and Neurologist* 17 (2) (April 1896).

13 H. G. Cocks, "Modernity and the Self in the History of Sexuality," *Historical Journal* 49 (2006): 1220, summarizing Judith M. Bennett's insight in her "'Lesbian-like' and the Social History of Lesbianism," *Journal of the History of Sexuality* 9 (2000): 1-24.

14 I am utilizing Hugh Heclo's notion of how the institutions of the state "puzzle before they power." Heclo, *Modern Social Politics in Britain and Sweden: From Relief to Income Maintenance* (New Haven, CT: Yale University Press, 1974), 305.

15 Robert H. Wiebe, *The Search for Order, 1877-1920* (New York: Hill and Wang, 1967).

16 Margot Canaday offers a similar argument in her book *The Straight State: Sexuality and Citizenship in Twentieth-Century America* (Princeton, NJ: Princeton University Press, 2009).

17 David K. Johnson, *The Lavender Scare: The Cold War Persecution of Gays and Lesbians in the Federal Government* (Chicago: University of Chicago Press, 2004).

18 Act of 1533, 25 Henry VIII, chapter 6 (England), discussed in Francois Lafitte, "Homosexuality and the Law," *Journal of British Delinquency* 9 (1958): 8-14.

19 William Blackstone, *Commentaries on the Laws of England* (in two volumes), volume 2 (New York: E. Duyckinck, G. Long, Collins & Hannay, Collins & Co., 1827), 159.

20 Ibid., 17-18. Primary documents banning sodomy from colonial Rhode Island, New Haven, and Massachusetts can be found in Jonathan Ned Katz, *Gay/Lesbian Almanac* (New York: Carroll & Graf, 1994), 91, 101-2, and 85-86, respectively.

21 For the Virginia law, see Katz, *Gay/Lesbian Almanac* (1994), 68.

22 William B. Reubenstein, ed., *Cases and Materials on Sexual Orientation and the Law*, 2nd ed. (St. Paul, MN: West, 1997), 81.

23 Caroline Bingham, "Seventeenth-Century Attitudes toward Deviant Sex," *Journal of Interdisciplinary History* 1 (1971): 447–68; Louis Crompton, "Homosexuals and the Death Penalty in Colonial America," *Journal of Homosexuality* 1 (1976): 277–93.

24 See Eskridge (2008).

25 Ibid., 16.

26 Brief *Amicus Curae* of Professors of History George Chauncey et al., *Lawrence v. Texas*, No. 02-102 (16 January 2003), 8.

27 For a discussion of the homoerotic correspondence between Whitman and the journalist Charles Warren Stoddard, see Jonathan Ned Katz, *Love Stories: Sex between Men before Homosexuality* (Chicago: University of Chicago Press, 2001), 178–87.

28 John Champagne, "Walt Whitman, Our Great Gay Poet?" *Journal of Homosexuality* 55 (4) (2008): 648–64. See also D. Hennessy, "Pedagogy and the Good G(r)ay Poet: Teaching Sexuality in Whitman's Texts," *Egotistics* 2 (1) (2002): 1–14.

29 Eskridge (2008), 20.

30 Ibid., 21.

31 Katz (2001), 402–6.

32 Eskridge (2008), 21.

33 Ibid., 51–52.

34 Ibid., 51.

35 Jennifer Terry, *An American Obsession: Science, Medicine, and Homosexuality in Modern Society* (Chicago: University of Chicago Press, 1999), 268.

36 William Eskridge Jr., *Gaylaw: Challenging the Apartheid of the Closet* (Cambridge, MA: Harvard University Press, 1999), 78–80.

37 Ibid., 76–78, 95–96. See Patricia Cain, "Litigating for Gay and Lesbian Rights: A Legal History," *Virginia Law Review* 79 (October 1993); and David K. Johnson, "Physique Pioneers: The Politics of 1960s Gay Consumer Culture," *Journal of Social History* 43 (Summer 2010).

38 *One, Inc. v. Olesen*, 355 U.S. 371 (1958); see further discussion in chapter 4.

39 On how the description of the new homosexual invoked assumptions of evolutionary race theory, see Siobhan Somerville, "Scientific Racism and the Emergence of the Homosexual Body," *Journal of the History of Sexuality* 5 (October 1994).

40 Hatheway (2003), 65.

41 See Stephen Skowronek, Stephen Engel, and Bruce Ackerman, eds., *The Progressives' Century: Democratic Reform and Constitutional Governance in the United States* (New Haven, CT: Yale University Press, forthcoming 2016).

42 See Franklin Giddings, *Elements of Sociology* (New York: Macmillan, 1898), 155–57; and Arthur Hadley, *The Education of the American Citizen* (New York: Scribner's, 1901), 25.

43 Eldon Eisenach, *The Lost Promise of Progressivism* (Lawrence: University Press of Kansas, 1994), 77.

44 See generally, Stephen Jay Gould, *The Mismeasure of Man*, rev. ed. (New York: Norton, 1996).

45 John W. Burgess, "The Ideal of the American Commonwealth," *Political Science Quarterly* 10 (3) (September 1895): 404, 405–7.

46 See Michael McGerr, *A Fierce Discontent: The Rise and Fall of the Progressive Movement in America* (New York: Oxford University Press, 2003), especially chapter 6.

47 For a discussion of the social Darwinist premises that underlay congressional debate on the Chinese Exclusion Acts, see Rogers Smith, "Beyond Tocqueville, Myrdal, and Hartz: The Multiple Traditions in America," *American Political Science Review* 87 (3) (September 1993): 559–62. On antimiscegenation laws as added to state codes to promote Progressive aims toward a particular community, see Peggy Pascoe, "Miscegenation Law, Court Cases, and Ideologies of 'Race' in Twentieth-Century America," *Journal of American History* 83 (June 1996): 44–69.

48 John W. Burgess, *The Civil War and the Constitution, 1859–1865* (New York: Scribner's, 1901), 135.

49 David M. Halperin, "How to Do the History of Male Homosexuality," *GLQ: A Journal of Lesbian and Gay Studies* 6 (1) (2000): 104.

50 Somerville (1994), 247.

51 Krafft-Ebing (1893), 1.

52 James G. Kiernan, "Sexual Perversion and the Whitehead Murders," *Medical Standard* 4 (5) (November 1888): 129.

53 James G. Kiernan, "Responsibility in Sexual Perversion," *Chicago Medical Recorder* (May 1892): 194.

54 George M. Beard, *Sexual Neurasthenia: Its Hygiene, Causes, Symptoms, and Treatment* (New York: E. B. Treat, 1898; reprint New York: Arno Press, 1972), 15.

55 Ibid.

56 Charles Gilbert Chaddock, "Sexual Crimes," in *A System of Legal Medicine*, Allen McLane Hamilton, ed. (New York: E. B. Treat, 1894).

57 Lydston (1904), 36.

58 Ibid.

59 Matthew F. Jacobson, *Barbarian Virtues: The United States Encounters Foreign Peoples at Home and Abroad, 1876–1917* (New York: Hill and Wang, 2000), 3–5.

60 Hatheway (2003), 99.

61 Krafft-Ebing (1893), iv.

62 Havelock Ellis, "A Note on the Treatment of Sexual Inversion," *Alienist and Neurologist* 17 (3) (July 1896): 261.

63 See Evelyn Hooker, "A Preliminary Analysis of Group Behavior of Homosexuals," *Journal of Psychology: Interdisciplinary and Applied* 42 (2) (1956): 217–25; and Evelyn Hooker, "The Adjustment of the Male Overt Homosexual," *Journal of Projective Techniques* 21 (1) (1957): 18–31. See Henry L. Minton, *Departing from Deviance: A History of Homosexual Rights and Emancipatory Science in America* (Chicago: University of Chicago Press, 2002), chapter 8.

64 Kiernan (1892), 207.

65 Ibid., 210.

66 Chaddock (1894), 272.

67 Hatheway (2003), 121.

68 Lydston (1904), 13.

69 Ibid., 560–66.

70 Ibid., 557.

71 Ibid., 54.

72 Ibid., 404.

73 Ibid., 375.

74 Canaday (2009), 4.

75 Stephen Skowronek, *Building a New American State: The Expansion of National Administrative Capacities, 1877–1920* (New York: Cambridge University Press, 1982); Theda Skocpol, *Protecting Soldiers and Mothers: The Political Origins of Social Policy in the United States* (Cambridge, MA: Belknap Press of Harvard University Press, 1995).

76 Canaday (2009), 21.

77 Ibid.

78 Ibid., 23.

79 Ibid., 34.

80 Terry (1999).

81 Nancy Cott, "Marriage and Women's Citizenship in the United States, 1830–1934," *American Historical Review* 103 (5) (December 1998): 1453.

82 Canaday (2009), 34–51.

83 File no. 53248/18, box 351, Records of the INS, RG 85. Quoted in Canaday (2009), 35.

84 Canaday (2009), 36.

85 Ibid., 36–38.

86 File no. 53710/373, box 622, Records of the INS, RG 85. Quoted in Canaday (2009), 37.

87 Ibid.

88 Canaday (2009), 48–51.

89 File no. 54134/62A, box 869, Records of the INS, RG 85. Quoted in Canaday (2009), 50.

90 Ibid.

91 Canaday (2009), 53.

92 Ibid., 23.

93 Randy Shilts, *Conduct Unbecoming: Gays and Lesbians in the U.S. Military, Vietnam to the Persian Gulf* (New York: St. Martin's, 1993).

94 David F. Burrelli, "The Debate on Homosexuals in the Military," in *Gays and Lesbians in the Military*, Wilbur J. Scott and Carson Stanley, eds. (New York: de Gruyter, 1994).

95 Canaday (2009), 59–90

96 Shilts (1993); Alan Berube, *Coming Out under Fire: The History of Gay Men and Women in World War Two* (New York: Plume, 1991); Francine D'Amico, "Sex/uality and Military Service," in *The Politics of Gay Rights*, Craig Rimmerman,

Kenneth D. Wald, and Clyde Wilcox, eds. (Chicago: University of Chicago Press, 2000).

97 D'Emilio (1983), 31.

98 Ibid., 24.

99 Berube (1991), 33.

100 Ibid., 147.

101 Chief of Naval Personnel to Commandant, U.S. Marine Corps, "Proposed Procedure for the Disposition of the Cases of Homosexuality," July 22, 1942, file no. P12-7, box 845, General Correspondence 1925–1940, Records of the Bureau of Naval Personnel, RG 24, National Archives, College Park, MD. Quoted in Canaday (2009), 147.

102 Canaday (2009), 147.

103 Memorandum from Colonel John M. Weir to Director of Military Personnel, "Sodomists," December 17, 1942, decimal 250.1, box 438, G-1 Personnel decimal file 1942–1946, Records of the War Department General Staff, RG 165. Quoted in Canaday (2009), 147.

104 Berube (1991), 139–43.

105 Margot Canaday, "Building a Straight State: Sexuality and Social Citizenship under the 1944 G.I. Bill," *Journal of American History* 90 (December 2003): 942.

106 U.S. Congress, House, Committee on Military Affairs, *Blue Discharges*, 79th Congress, 2nd Session, 30 January 1946.

107 U.S. Congress, Senate, Committee on Finance, *Providing Federal Government Aid for the Readjustment in Civilian Life of Returning World War II Veterans*, 78th Congress, 2nd Session, March 18, 1944, 15.

108 Frank T. Hines to Secretary of the Navy James Forrestal, August 9, 1944, Policy Series 807, Records of the Department of Veterans Affairs, RG 15. Quoted in Canaday (2009), 149.

109 Frank T. Hines, "Legal Bars under Section 300, Public No. 346, 78th Congress, and Character of Discharge under Public No. 2, 73rd Congress, as Amended, and Public No. 346, 78th Congress," October 30, 1944, Policy Series 800.04. volume 2, Records of the Department of Veterans Affairs, RG 15. Quoted in Canaday (2009), 149.

110 Ibid., 249.

111 U.S. Congress, House, *Blue Discharges*, 8–9.

112 Canaday (2009), 150.

113 Robert C. Lieberman, *Shifting the Color Line: Race and the American Welfare State* (Cambridge, MA: Harvard University Press, 2001), 7–8.

114 Ira Katznelson, *When Affirmative Action Was White: The Untold History of Racial Inequality in Twentieth-Century America* (New York: Norton, 2006), 124.

115 Canaday (2009), 150.

116 D'Amico (2000).

117 Barry Adam, *The Rise of the Gay and Lesbian Movement* (New York: Twayne, 1995); David K. Johnson, *The Lavender Scare: The Cold War Persecution of Gays and Lesbians in the Federal Government* (Chicago: University of Chicago Press, 2004).

118 John D'Emilio, "The Homosexual Menace: The Politics of Sexuality in Cold War America," in *Passion and Power: Sexuality in History*, Kathy Peiss and Christina Simmons, eds. (Philadelphia: Temple University Press, 1989), 226–40.

119 Andrea Friedman, "The Smearing of Joe McCarthy: The Lavender Scare, Gossip, and Cold War Politics," *American Quarterly* 57 (December 2005): 1105.

120 Ibid.

121 Johnson (2004), 21; and William N. Eskridge Jr., *Gaylaw: Challenging the Apartheid of the Closet* (Cambridge, MA: Harvard University Press, 1999), 68.

122 Johnson (2004), 21.

123 Ibid.

124 Eskridge (1999), 68.

125 Johnson (2004), 21.

126 Joseph McCarthy, "Speech at Wheeling, West Virginia, February 9, 1950," in *In Our Own Words: Extraordinary Speeches of the American Century*, Andrew Carroll, Robert Torricelli, and Doris Kearns Goodwin, eds. (New York: Washington Square Press, 2000).

127 Full text of the hearing is in *Congressional Record*, Senate, Subcommittee of the Committee on Appropriations, Departments of State, Justice, Commerce, and the Judiciary Appropriations for 1951, 81st Congress, 2nd Session, 28 February 1950, 581–603.

128 Quoted in Johnson (2004), 23.

129 Full text of the hearing is in *Congressional Record*, Senate, Subcommittee of the Committee on Appropriations, Departments of State, Justice, Commerce, and the Judiciary Appropriations for 1951, 81st Congress, 2nd Session, 28 February 1950, 581–603.

130 Johnson (2004), 18.

131 *Congressional Record*, Senate, 81st Congress, Second Session, 5704.

132 Ibid.

133 Ibid.

134 Ibid., 5711.

135 Ibid.

136 Ibid., 5712.

137 Gabrielson quoted in Adam (1995), 62.

138 Gabrielson quoted in "Perverts Called Government Peril," *New York Times*, 19 April 1950, 25, reproduced in Larry Gross and James D. Woods, *The Columbia Reader on Lesbians and Gay Men in Media, Society, and Politics* (New York: Columbia University Press, 1999), 355.

139 Ibid.

140 U.S. Congress, Senate, *State Department Employee Loyalty Investigation*, Report no. 2108, Committee on Foreign Relations, 81st Congress, 2nd Session, 20 July 1950.

141 *Congressional Record*, Senate, 81st Congress, Second Session, 10792.

142 Ibid., 10816.

143 U.S. Congress, Senate, *Report of Subcommittee of Subcommittee on Appropriations for the District of Columbia Made by the Chairman, the Senior Senator from the*

State of Alabama, Mr. Hill, with Reference to Testimony on Subversive Activity and Homosexuals in the Government Service, 81st Congress, 2nd Session, May 1950.

144 U.S. Congress, Senate, *Report of the Investigation of the Junior Senator of Nebraska, a Member of the Subcommittee Appointed by the Subcommittee on Appropriations for the District of Columbia, on the Infiltration of Subversives and Moral Perverts into the Executive Branch of the United States Government*, 81st Congress, 2nd Session, May 1950.

145 *Congressional Record*, Senate, 81st Congress, Second Session, 17329–30.

146 Johnson (2004), 104–5.

147 Ibid., 106.

148 Flanagan quoted in ibid., 107.

149 Ibid., 108–12. The link between homosexuality and security risk stems, at least in part, from a rather dubious claim that homosexuals would be more susceptible to blackmail or were more emotionally unstable and thereby more likely to spill state secrets. See James D. Steakley, "Iconography of a Scandal: Political Cartoons and the Eulenburg Affair in Wilhelmin Germany," in *Hidden from History: Reclaiming the Gay and Lesbian Past*, Martin Duberman, Martha Vicinus, and George Chauncey, eds. (New York: American Library, 1989), 233–57.

150 Johnson (2004), 113.

151 United States Subcommittee of the Committee on Expenditures in the Executive Department, "Employment of Homosexuals and Other Sex Perverts in the U.S. Government" (1951), in *We Are Everywhere*, Mark Blasius and Shane Phelan, eds. (New York: Routledge, 1997), 244.

152 Johnson (2004), 123.

153 Ibid., 120–21.

154 D'Emilio (1983), 44.

155 Johnson (2004), 136.

156 Adam Yarmolinsky, *Case Studies in Personnel Security* (Washington, DC: Bureau of National Affairs, 1955); Eleanor Bontecou, *The Federal Loyalty-Security Program* (Ithaca, NY: Cornell University Press, 1953).

157 Quoted in Johnson (2004), 143–44.

158 David M. Barnett, "Secrecy, Security, and Sex: The NSA, Congress, and the Martin-Mitchell Defections," *International Journal of Intelligence and Counterintelligence* 22 (2009): 699–729.

159 Johnson (2004), 146.

160 *Norton v. Macy*, 417 F.2d 1161 (1969).

161 *Schlegel v. United States*, 416 F.2d 1372 (1969).

162 Gregory B. Lewis, "Lifting the Ban on Gays in the Civil Service: Federal Policy toward Gay and Lesbian Employees since the Cold War," *Public Administration Review* 51 (1997): 392.

163 Martin Duberman, *Stonewall* (New York: Plume, 1993), xvii.

164 Michael J. Bosia and Meredith Weiss, "Political Homophobia in Comparative Perspective," in Michael Bosia and Meredith Weiss, eds., *Homophobia Goes Global:*

States, Movements, and the Diffusion of Oppression (Champaign: University of Illinois Press, 2013).

165 Richard Valelly, "Uncle Sam's Closet: The American State and Sexual Orientation" (2013), manuscript on file with author, 8. See also George Chauncey, "'What Gay Studies Taught the Court': The Historians' Amicus Brief in *Lawrence v. Texas*," *GLQ: A Journal of Lesbian and Gay Studies* 10 (3) (2004): 509–38.

166 John D'Emilio, "The Homosexual Menace: The Politics of Sexuality in Cold War America," in *Making Trouble: Essays on Gay History, Politics, and the University* (New York: Routledge, 1992), 68.

167 Valelly (2013), 31–49.

168 Ibid., 39–47.

169 Richard Hofstadter, *Anti-Intellectualism in American Life* (New York: Knopf, 1962), 189.

170 Ibid., 188.

171 Ibid. The definition was offered by Senator Ingalls of Kansas. *Congressional Record*, 49th Congress, 1st Session, 2786, 26 March 1888.

172 Terry (1999), 35.

173 Murphy (2008), 14.

174 Ibid., 21–23.

175 Elliott J. Gorn, *The Manly Art: Bare Knuckle Prize Fighting in America* (Ithaca, NY: Cornell University Press, 1990), 252.

176 See, for example, George Washington Plunkitt's critique of mugwumps and corresponding defense of the machine politics of Tammany Hall, suggesting that if the mugwumps had their way, "Tammany might win an election once in four thousand years" and contending that college-educated mugwumps hardly understood what politics was about: "Some young men think they can learn how to be successful in politics from books, and they cram their heads with all sorts of college rot. . . . In fact, a young man who has gone through the college course is handicapped at the outset. He may succeed in politics, but the chances are 100 to 1 against him." Quoted in William L. Riordon, *Plunkitt of Tammany Hall* (New York, 1905), 60, 10.

177 Murphy (2008), 54–59.

178 Murphy (2008), 40.

179 Ibid., 55.

180 Ibid., 54–59, 189–90. On Roosevelt and ideas of masculinity, see Sarah Watts, *Rough Rider in the White House: Theodore Roosevelt and the Politics of Desire* (Chicago: University of Chicago Press, 2003), 79–122.

181 Theodore Roosevelt, "An Address Delivered at the Harvard Union," 7 February 1907, in Donald George Wilhelm, *Theodore Roosevelt as an Undergraduate* (Boston: John W. Luce, 1910), 84.

182 Editorial in the *Minneapolis Journal*, 14 April 1907, quoted in Murphy (2008), 11.

183 Gail Bederman, *Manliness and Civilization: A Cultural History of Gender and Race in the United States, 1880–1917* (Chicago: University of Chicago Press, 1995), 1–44.

184 Theodore Roosevelt, "Latitude and Longitude among Reformers," *Century* (June 1900), reprinted in Theodore Roosevelt, *The Strenuous Life* (New York: Century, 1905), 41–60.

185 Roosevelt (1907), 85.

186 Theodore Roosevelt, "First Annual Message," December 3, 1901. Online by Gerhard Peters and John T. Woolley, *American Presidency Project*, http://www.presidency.ucsb.edu/ws/?pid=29542.

187 Ibid.

188 Terence Kissack, *Free Comrades: Anarchism and Homosexuality in the United States, 1895–1917* (Oakland, CA: AK Press, 2008), 3.

189 Ibid., 45.

190 Benjamin R. Tucker, "The Criminal Jailers of Oscar Wilde," *Liberty*, 15 June 1895, 4–5.

191 Goldman to Hirschfeld, January 1923, quoted in Kissak (2008), 6.

192 Margaret Marsh, *Anarchist Women, 1870–1920* (Philadelphia: Temple University Press, 1981), 69–70.

193 Kissak (2008), 153–56.

194 Ibid., 157.

195 Quoted in Marian J. Morton, *Emma Goldman and the American Left: Nowhere at Home* (New York: Twayne, 1992), 138.

196 Kissack (2008), 153.

197 Ibid., 156.

198 George Chauncey, "'What Gay Studies Taught the Court': The Historians' Amicus Brief in *Lawrence v. Texas*," *GLQ: A Journal of Lesbian and Gay Studies* 10 (3) (2004): 520.

199 Paul Pierson, *Politics in Time: History, Institutions, and Social Analysis* (Princeton, NJ: Princeton University Press, 2004), 126.

200 Ibid.

201 Michael T. Hannan and John Freeman, *Organizational Ecology* (Cambridge, MA: Harvard University Press, 1989), 23.

CHAPTER 3. GAY IS GOOD

1 Donald Webster Cory (Edward Sagarin), *The Homosexual in America: A Subjective Approach* (1951), excerpted in *We Are Everywhere: A Historical Sourcebook of Gay and Lesbian Politics*, Mark Blasius and Shane Phelan, eds. (New York: Routledge, 1997), 277.

2 *Romer v. Evans*, 517 U.S. 620 (1996).

3 Gail Collins, "The State of Arizona," *New York Times*, 26 February 2014.

4 Cory (1951), 277.

5 "Statement of Purpose of the Mattachine Society" (1951) in *We Are Everywhere*, Mark Blasius and Shane Phelan, eds. (New York: Routledge, 1997), 283–84.

6 John D'Emilio, *Sexual Politics, Sexual Communities: The Making of a Homosexual Minority in the United States, 1940–1970* (Chicago: University of Chicago Press,

1983), 50–89. See also Marc Stein, *Rethinking the Gay and Lesbian Movement* (New York: Routledge, 2012), 41–63.

7   Marilyn Reiger, "Delegates of the Convention," 23 May 1953, quoted in Urvashi Vaid, *Virtual Equality: The Mainstreaming of Gay and Lesbian Liberation* (New York: Anchor Books, 1995), 53–54.

8   Karen Orren and Stephen Skowronek, *The Search for American Political Development* (New York: Cambridge University Press, 2004), 123.

9   On path dependent development of constitutional interpretation see Mark Graber, "Legal, Strategic, or Legal Strategy: Deciding to Decide during the Civil War and Reconstruction," in *The Supreme Court and American Political Development*, Ronald Kahn and Ken I. Kersch, eds. (Lawrence: University Press of Kansas, 2006).

10 *Boutilier v. INS*, 387 U.S. 118 (1967); *Bowers v. Hardwick*, 478 U.S. 186 (1986); *Romer v. Evans*, 517 U.S. 620 (1996).

11 Americans with Disabilities Act (Pub. L. No. 101-336, 104 Stat. 328 [1990]).

12 On Hay's communism and the early Mattachine see Stuart Timmons, *The Trouble with Harry* (Boston: White Crane Books, 2012); and Harry Hay, *Radically Gay: Gay Liberation in the Words of Its Founder* (Boston: Beacon, 1997).

13 Craig M. Loftin, *Masked Voices: Gay Men and Lesbians in Cold War America* (Albany: SUNY Press, 2012), 20.

14 D'Emilio (1983), 80.

15 Daughters of Bilitis, "Statement of Purpose" (1955) in *We Are Everywhere* (1997), 328.

16 Toby Marotta, *The Politics of Homosexuality* (New York: Houghton Mifflin, 1981), 68.

17 "Statement of Beliefs from 1954 Issue of *ONE* Magazine," in *We Are Everywhere* (1997), 309.

18 *We Are Everywhere* (1997), 309.

19 Loftin (2012), 20.

20 Spaces such as gay bars in urban areas functioned as places to meet others, and they proliferated in large and small cities; bar culture built a "nascent post-war community of gay men and women [which] was . . . ripe for political organizing." Vaid (1995), 48.

21 Loftin (2012), 20, 21.

22 Ibid., 21.

23 Kameny quoted in Marotta (1981), 24.

24 Marotta (1981), 48–49.

25 Shirley Willer, "What Concrete Steps Can Be Taken to Further the Homophile Movement," *Ladder* (November 1966): 17–20, quoted in Marotta (1981), 51.

26 Letter from Lietsch to Kameny, 19 June 1968, quoted in Marotta (1981), 61.

27 Kameny quoted in Elizabeth Armstrong, *Forging Gay Identities: Organizing Sexuality in San Francisco, 1954–1994* (Chicago: University of Chicago Press, 2002), 54.

28 Armstrong (2002), 54

29 Quoted in Armstrong (2002), 54.

30 Franklin Kameny, "Gay Is Good" (1969) in *We Are Everywhere* (1997), 376.

31 William N. Eskridge Jr., *Gaylaw: Challenging the Apartheid of the Closet* (Cambridge, MA: Harvard University Press, 1999), 35–36, 69–70, 132–34, 383–84.

32 Margot Canaday, "'Who Is a Homosexual?': The Consolidation of Sexual Identities in Mid-Twentieth-Century American Immigration Law," *Law and Social Inquiry* 28 (2003): 351–86.

33 Andrew M. Boxer and Joseph M. Carrier, "Evelyn Hooker: A Life Remembered," *Journal of Homosexuality* 36 (1) (1998).

34 John Zaller, *The Nature and Origins of Mass Opinion* (New York: Cambridge University Press, 1992), 318.

35 Ellen Andersen, *Out of the Closets and into the Courts* (Ann Arbor: University of Michigan Press, 2006).

36 William Eskridge Jr., *Dishonorable Passions: Sodomy Laws in America, 1861–2003* (New York: Viking, 2008), 118.

37 Blasius and Phelan, eds. (1997), 309.

38 Jonathan Rauch, "The Unknown Supreme Court Decision That Changed Everything for Gays," *Washington Post*, 5 February 2014.

39 *MANual Enterprises v. Day*, 370 U.S. 478 (1962).

40 David K. Johnson, "Physique Pioneers: The Politics of 1960s Gay Consumer Culture," *Journal of Social History* 43 (Summer 2010): 867–68.

41 *Roth v. United States*, 354 U.S. 476 (1957).

42 *Mishkin v. New York*, 383 U.S. 502 (1966). For more detailed discussion of the *ONE*, *MANuel*, and *Mishkin* rulings, see Joyce Murdoch and Deb Price, *Courting Justice: Gay Men and Lesbians v. the Supreme Court* (New York: Basic Books, 2001), 17–141.

43 *Rosenberg v. Fleuti*, 374 U.S. 449 (1963).

44 *Boutilier v. INS*, 387 U.S. 118 (1967).

45 *Lavoie v. INS*, 360 F.2d 27(1966).

46 *Boutilier v. Immigration and Naturalization Service*, 363 F.2d 488 (1966).

47 Marc Stein, *Sexual Injustice: Supreme Court Decisions from* Griswold *to* Roe (Chapel Hill: University of North Carolina Press, 2010), 61.

48 *Boutilier v. Immigration and Naturalization Service*, 363 F.2d 488 (1966), 489–90.

49 Ibid., 495.

50 Stein (2010), 65.

51 Tom Clark Papers, Jamal Center for Legal Research, Tarlton Law Library, University of Texas School of Law, Austin Texas, Box A207, Ullman Critical Abstract, quoted in Stein (2010), 66.

52 Stein (2010), 72–73.

53 *Boutilier v. INS*, 387 U.S. 118 (1967), 122–23.

54 Ibid., 123.

55 Ibid.

56 Ibid.

57 Stein (2010), 171.

58 *Boutilier v. INS*, 387 U.S. 118 (1967), 122.

59 Ibid., 123.

60 Stein (2010), 76; Kameny, "Gay Is Good" (1969) in Blasius and Phelan, eds. (1997), 367.

61 Lady Gaga, "Born This Way," *Streamline*, Interscope, Kon Live (2011).

62 *People v. Ronald Onofre*, 51 N.Y.2d 476 (1980); *Baker v. Wade*, 553 F.Supp. 1121 (N.D.Tex.1982).

63 *Griswold v. Connecticut*, 381 U.S. 479 (1965); *Eisenstadt v. Baird*, 405 U.S. 438 (1972); *Roe v. Wade*, 410 U.S. 113 (1973).

64 Andersen (2006), 70; *Doe v. Commonwealth's Attorney of Richmond*, 425 U.S. 901 (1976).

65 *Baker v. Wade*, 553 F.Supp. 1121 (N.D.Tex.1982), 1140.

66 Andersen (2006), 63.

67 Ibid., 58–97. See also Stein (2012): "gay and lesbian activists could not claim direct credit for all of those successes; in most cases, reform occurred in the context of a general criminal code revision" (103).

68 *Bowers v. Hardwick*, 478 U.S. 186 (1986), 191.

69 Ibid., 190–91.

70 Ibid., 192.

71 *Stanley v. Georgia*, 394 U.S. 557 (1969).

72 *Bowers v. Hardwick*, 478 U.S. 186 (1986), 195.

73 Ibid., Blackmun dissenting, 200.

74 Ibid., 204.

75 Ibid., 206.

76 This passage in *Bowers* is a quotation of an earlier statement by Justice Stevens offered in *Fitzgerald v. Porter Memorial Hospital*, 523 F.2d 716, 719–20 (CA7 1975) (footnotes omitted), cert. denied, 425 U.S. 916 (1976), *Bowers v. Hardwick*, 478 U.S. 186 (1986), 215.

77 For a summary of suspect class and scrutiny doctrine see chapter 6.

78 Deborah Gould, *Moving Politics: Emotion and ACT UP's Fight against AIDS* (Chicago: University of Chicago Press, 2009), 138–39.

79 Stein (2010), 76.

80 *Romer v. Evans*, 517 U.S. 620 (1996); see generally Joseph S. Jackson, "Persons of Equal Worth: *Romer v. Evans* and the Politics of Equal Protection," *UCLA Law Review* 45 (1997); Andrew Koppelman, "*Romer v. Evans* and Invidious Intent," *William & Mary Bill of Rights Journal* 6 (1997).

81 *Romer v. Evans*, 517 U.S. 620 (1996), 624.

82 See generally, Chris Bull and John Gallagher, *Perfect Enemies: The Religious Right, the Gay Movement, and the Politics of the 1990s* (New York: Crown, 1996), 97–124.

83 Jeffrey R. Dudas, "In the Name of Equal Rights: 'Special' Rights and the Politics of Resentment in Post–Civil Rights America," *Law & Society Review* 39 (2005): 723–57.

84 *Romer v. Evans*, 517 U.S. 620 (1996), 624.

85 Ibid., 627.

86 Ibid., 642.

87 Ibid., 641.

88 See Akhil Reed Amar, "Attainder and Amendment 2: *Romer's* Rightness," *Michigan Law Review* 95 (October 1996): 203–35.

89 Jay Michaelson, "On Listening to the Kulturkampf; or, How America Overruled *Bowers v. Hardwick*, Even though *Romer v. Evans* Didn't," *Duke Law Journal* (2000): 1559–1618.

90 Robert H. Bork, *Slouching towards Gomorrah* (New York: Reagan Books, 1996); Ronald Dworkin, "Sex, Death, and the Courts," *New York Review of Books*, 8 August 1996, 48–50; Thomas C. Grey, "*Bowers v. Hardwick* Diminished," *University of Colorado Law Review* 68 (1997): 373–86.

91 On the distinction between homosexuality as conduct and homosexuality as character see generally Janet E. Halley, "The Politics of the Closet: Toward Equal Protection for Gay, Lesbian, and Bisexual Identity," *UCLA Law Review* 36 (1989): 915–76.

92 Canaday (2003), 383.

93 Ibid., 353.

94 GLF Statement of Purpose, 31 July 1969, quoted in John D'Emilio and Estelle B. Freedman, *Intimate Matters: A History of Sexuality in America* (Chicago: University of Chicago Press, 1988), 322.

95 On comparisons between the GLF and GAA see Dudley Clendinen and Adam Nagourney, *Out for Good: The Struggle to Build a Gay Rights Movement in America* (New York: Simon & Schuster, 1999), 50–56; Marotta (1981), 88–91; Adam (1995), 86–87; Steven Seidman, "Identity and Politics in a 'Postmodern' Gay Culture: Some Historical and Conceptual Notes," in *Fear of a Queer Planet*, Michael Warner, ed. (Minneapolis: University of Minnesota Press, 1994), 109–13. On GLF's structure and relationship to the New Left, see Steve Valocchi, "Individual Identities, Collective Identities, and Organizational Structure: The Relationship of the Political Left and Gay Liberation in the United States," *Sociological Perspectives* 44 (4) (2001): 445–67.

96 Stein (2012), 102–4.

97 Eskridge (1999).

98 Andersen (2006), 78–87.

99 Stein (2012), 126.

100 Robert Benford and David A. Snow, "Framing Processes and Social Movements: An Overview and Assessment," *Annual Review of Sociology* 26 (August 2000); on the legal analogies between gay-rights claims as identity-based claims and women's-rights, religious-rights, and race-equality claims, see David A. J. Richards, *Identity and the Case for Gay Rights: Race, Gender, and Religion as Analogies* (New York: NYU Press, 1999).

101 James W. Button, Barbara A. Rienzo, and Kenneth Wald, "The Politics of Gay Rights at the Local and State Level," in *The Politics of Gay Rights*, Craig Rimmer-

man, Kenneth D. Wald, and Clyde Wilcox, eds. (Chicago: University of Chicago Press, 2000); Linda A. Mooney, David Knox, and Caroline Schact, *Understanding Social Problems*, 6th ed. (Belmont, CA: Wadsworth, Cengage Learning, 2009); Craig Rimmerman, *From Identity to Politics: The Lesbian and Gay Movements in the United States* (Philadelphia: Temple University Press, 2002).

102 See Charles W. Gossett, "Dillon's Rule and Gay Rights: State Control over Local Efforts to Protect the Rights of Lesbians and Gay Men," in *Gays and Lesbians in the Democratic Process: Public Policy, Public Opinion, and Political Representation*, Ellen D. B. Riggle and Barry L. Tadlock, eds. (New York: Columbia University Press, 1999).

103 For states that prohibit discrimination in employment on the basis of sexual orientation and/or gender identity, see https://www.aclu.org/map/non-discrimination-laws-state-state-information-map (accessed 22 October 2015).

104 Stein (2012), 139–40. On gay rights mobilization against antigay referenda, see Amy L. Stone, *Gay Rights at the Ballot Box* (Minneapolis: University of Minnesota Press, 2012).

105 Donald P. Haider-Markel and Kenneth J. Meier, "The Politics of Gay and Lesbian Rights: Expanding the Scope of the Conflict," *Journal of Politics* 58 (1996): 332–50.

106 Brad Sears, Nan D. Hunter, and Christy Mallory, *Documenting Discrimination on the Basis of Sexual Orientation and Gender Identity in State Employment* (Williams Institute of the University of California—Los Angeles School of Law, 2009).

107 Alan Johnson, "Kasich Alters Order on Work Rights," *Columbus Dispatch*, 22 January 2011; Eric Resnik, "Kasich Lets LGBT Job Bias Rule Expire," *Gay People's Chronicle*, 14 January 2011.

108 See Jack L. Walker, "The Diffusion of Innovations among the American States," *American Political Science Review* 63 (1969): 880–99.

109 Marieka Klawitter and Brian Hammer, "Spatial and Temporal Diffusion of Local Anti-Discrimination Policies for Sexual Orientation," in *Gays and Lesbians in the Democratic Process: Public Policy, Public Opinion, and Political Representation*, Ellen D. B. Riggle and Barry L. Tadlock, eds. (New York: Columbia University Press, 1999), 32.

110 Ibid., 34.

111 Chai R. Feldblum, "The Federal Gay Rights Bill: From Bella to ENDA," in *Creating Change: Sexuality, Public Policy, and Civil Rights*, John D'Emilio, William B. Turner, and Urvashi Vaid, eds. (New York: St. Martin's, 2000), 152–87.

112 While the number of congressional hearings on gay and lesbian civil rights matters showed a smaller increase from the 1980s through the mid-1990s than in the previous two decades, the number of hearings on AIDS issues outpaced them by as much as 700 percent in particular years. Donald P. Haider-Markel, "Creating Change—Holding the Line: Agenda Setting on Lesbian and Gay Issues at the National Level," in *Gays and Lesbians in the Democratic Process* (1999), 249–54.

113 See Vaid (1995), 69–105; and Mark Carl Rom, "Gays and AIDS: Democratizing Disease?" in *The Politics of Gay Rights*, Craig Rimmerman, Kenneth D. Wald, and Clyde Wilcox, eds. (Chicago: University of Chicago Press, 2000), 217–48.

114 Quoted in Vaid (1995), 90.

115 Leo Bersani, *Homos* (Cambridge, MA: Harvard University Press, 1995), 21.

116 Carl Stychin, *Law's Desire: Sexuality and the Limits of Justice* (New York: Routledge, 1995), 53.

117 See Gould (2009).

118 Eric E. Rofes, "Gay Lib vs. AIDS: Averting Civil War in the 1990s," *Out/Look* (1990) in Blasius and Phelan (1997), 652–59.

119 Vaid (1995), 91.

120 David Rayside, *On the Fringe: Gays and Lesbians in Politics* (Ithaca, NY: Cornell University Press, 1998), 285.

121 Chai R. Feldblum, "The Americans with Disabilities Act Definition of Disability," *Labor Lawyer* 7 (Winter 1991): 20. The three-prong definition of disability is offered at Americans with Disabilities Act of 1990, Pub. L. No. 101-336, Section 3(2), 104 Stat 327, 330 (1990).

122 Arthur Leonard, "Discrimination," in *AIDS Law Today: A New Guide for the Public*, Scott Burris, Harlon L. Dalton, Judith Leonie Miller, and the Yale AIDS Law Project, eds. (New Haven, CT: Yale University Press, 1993), 302.

123 See Steven Epstein, *Impure Science: AIDS, Activism, and the Politics of Knowledge* (Berkeley: University of California Press, 1996).

124 On the social construction of HIV as plague see Cindy Patton, *Sex and Germs: The Politics of AIDS* (Boston: South End, 1985), 5; Janet L. Dolgin, "AIDS: Social Meanings and Legal Ramifications," *Hofstra Law Review* 14 (1985); and Wendy E. Parmet and Daniel J. Jackson, "No Longer Disabled: The Legal Impact of the New Social Construction of HIV," *American Journal of Law & Medicine* 23 (1) (1997): 7–12, 27–29.

125 *Report of the Presidential Commission on the Human Immunodeficiency Virus Epidemic* (June 1988), 119. https://archive.org/details/reportofpresideno0opres.

126 Ibid.

127 Ibid., 119–20.

128 Ibid., 120.

129 See Parmet and Jackson (1997), 11; see also Wendy E. Parmet, "AIDS and Quarantine: The Revival of an Archaic Doctrine," *Hofstra Law Review* 14 (1985): 87, n. 222.

130 Arthur Leonard, "Employment Discrimination against Persons with AIDS," *University of Dayton Law Review* 10 (1985). The idea of disability law including people with AIDS is also addressed by Robert S. Burns, "See AIDS: A Legal Epidemic?" *Akron Law Review* 17 (1984).

131 Pub. L. No. 93-112, 87 Stat. 355 (codified at 29 U.S.C. section 706[8][B]).

132 Leonard (1985), 691.

133 Ibid., 696.

134 *School Board of Nassau County v. Arline*, 480 U.S. 273 (1987), 281.

135 *Memorandum to Arthur B. Culvahouse Jr., Justice Department Memorandum on Application of Rehabilitation Act's Section 504 to HIV Infected Persons*, Daily Lab. Rep. (BNA) No. 195, at D-1 (7 October 1988) quoted in Parmet and Jackson (1997), 16.

136 Parmet and Jackson (1997), 17.

137 42 U.S.C. section 12101(a)(7) (West Supp. 1995).

138 Arlene Mayerson, "The Americans with Disabilities Act: An Historic Overview," *Labor Lawyer 7* (Winter 1991): 7.

139 See generally Rhonda K. Jenkins, "Square Pegs, Round Holes: HIV and the Americans with Disabilities Act," *Southern Illinois University Law Journal* 20: 1996, 637–50.

140 See 136 *Congressional Record* H4623 (12 July 1990) and 136 *Congressional Record* S9696 (13 July 1990).

141 *Doe v. Kohn Nast & Graf, P.C,* 862 F. Supp. 1310 (E.D. Pa. 1994).

142 Ibid., 1319.

143 Ibid., 1320.

144 Ibid., 1321.

145 No. 96-1643, 1997 U.S. App. LEXIS 3870 (1st Circuit, 5 March 1997).

146 Ibid., 21.

147 Parmet and Jackson (1997), 35–36.

148 In dicta in *School Board of Nassau County v. Arline*, Justice Brennan wrote, "society's accumulated myths and fears about disability are as handicapping as are the physical limitations that flow from actual impairment." The effects of discrimination need not rely on a showing of physical impairment but can flow from the assumption that an individual is assumed to be disabled or diseased. Brennan thereby offered one way to understand the third prong—"regarded as"—of the definition of disability in the 1973 Rehabilitation Act (and subsequently in the ADA) that would be more fully inclusive of asymptomatic HIV-positive persons or even gay and bisexual men who might be assumed to be HIV carriers. 480 U.S. 273 (1987), 284. Parmet and Jackson contend that, when writing this part of the ruling, "No doubt he [Brennan] was thinking of HIV" (1997, 15).

149 Vaid (1995), 3.

150 Ed Mickens, *The 100 Best Companies for Gay Men and Lesbians: Plus Options and Opportunities No Matter Where You Work* (New York: Pocket, 1994); Liz Winfield and Susan Spielman, *Straight Talk about Gays in the Workplace: Creating an Inclusive, Productive Environment for Everyone in Your Organization* (New York: Amacom, 1995).

151 For discussion of the HRC's WorkNet database, which preceded its Corporate Equality Index, see Nicole C. Raeburn, *Changing Corporate America from Inside Out: Lesbian and Gay Workplace Rights* (Minneapolis: University of Minnesota Press, 2004).

152 Human Rights Campaign Foundation, "Corporate Equality Index 2015: Rating American Workplaces on Lesbian, Gay, Bisexual, and Transgender Equality," http://www.hrc.org/campaigns/corporate-equality-index.

153 On this debate see Orren and Skowronek (2004), 33–59.

154 On the U.S. welfare state as distinct but not a laggard and rooted in maternalist provisions targeting widows and orphans, see Theda Skocpol, *Protecting Soldiers and Mothers: The Political Origins of Social Policy in the United States* (Cambridge, MA: Belknap Press of Harvard University Press, 1995); on Progressive Era policies see Kenneth Scheve and David Stasavage, "The Political Economy of Religion and Social Insurance in the United States, 1910–1939," *Studies in American Political Development* 20 (Fall 2006); on New Deal policies see Bruce Ackerman, *We the People: Transformations* (Cambridge, MA: Belknap Press of Harvard University Press, 1998).

155 Mary Ann Glendon, "Rights in Twentieth-Century Constitutions," *University of Chicago Law Review* 59 (Winter 1992): 521; see also Mary Ann Glendon, "Rights in Twentieth-Century Constitutions: The Case of Welfare Rights," *Journal of Policy History* 6 (1) (1994): 140–56.

156 Jacob Hacker, "The Historical Logic of National Health Insurance: Structure and Sequence in the Development of British, Canadian, and U.S. Medical Policy," *Studies in American Political Development* 12 (April 1998): 59.

157 Joshua Gamson, "Silence, Death, and the Invisible Enemy: AIDS Activism and Social Movement 'Newness,'" *Social Problems* 36 (1989): 357.

158 Epstein (1996).

159 Jeff Goodwin and James M. Jasper, "Caught in a Winding, Snarling Vine: The Structural Bias of Political Process Theory," *Sociological Forum* 14 (1999); Elisabeth Armstrong and Mary Bernstein, "Culture, Power, and Institutions: A Multi-Institutional Approach to Social Movements," *Sociological Theory* 26 (1) (2008).

160 Raeburn (2004), 23.

161 Eighty-nine percent of Fortune 500 firms included sexual orientation in their nondiscrimination statements in 2014. Sixty-six percent provided health insurance coverage for same-sex partners of employees. HRCF, "Corporate Equality Index 2015," 8.

162 Stein (2012), 74.

163 Raeburn (2004), 8–9; Stein (2012), 129.

164 Raeburn (2004), 23–26.

165 Ibid., 29.

166 Quoted in Arthur C. Bain, "Cracker Barrel Seeks SEC Dismissal of First Gay Rights Shareholder Action," *Gay/Lesbian/Bisexual Corporate Letter*, September–October 1992, 1.

167 Raeburn (2004), 43. See also Vaid (1995), 10.

168 Raeburn (2004), 43.

169 Ibid., 30.

170 Steven Epstein, "Gay and Lesbian Movements in the United States: Dilemmas of Identity, Diversity, and Political Strategy," in *The Global Emergence of Gay and Lesbian Politics: National Imprints on a Worldwide Movement*, Barry D. Adam, Jan

Willem Duyvendak, and Andre Krouwel, eds. (Philadelphia: Temple University Press, 1999), 68. On losses as opportunities for mobilization see Traci M. Sawyers and David S. Meyer, "Missed Opportunities: Social Movement Abeyance and Public Policy," *Social Problems* 46 (1999): 187–206.

171 On the idea of a more radical fringe as leverage to achieve moderate policy reform see Herbert H. Haines, *Black Radicals and the Civil Rights Movement, 1954–1970* (Knoxville: University of Tennessee Press, 1988).

172 Raeburn (2004), 38.

173 Thomas A. Stewart, "Gay in Corporate America," *Fortune*, 16 December 1991.

174 Ibid.

175 Ibid.

176 James O'Toole, "Best Companies List Hits Gay Rights Milestone." *CNNMoney. com*, 20 January 2012, http://money.cnn.com/2012/01/20/pf/jobs/best_companies_gay_rights/index.htm (accessed 5 June 2012).

177 Human Rights Campaign Foundation, "Corporate Equality Index 2015," 9.

178 Raeburn (2004), 1.

179 Paul J. DiMaggio and Walter W. Powell, "The Iron Cage Revisited: Institutional Isomorphism and Collective Rationality in Organizational Fields," in *The New Institutionalism in Organizational Analysis*, Paul J. DiMaggio and Walter W. Powell, eds. (Chicago: University of Chicago Press, 1991).

180 Raeburn (2004), 111.

181 Daryl Herrschaft and Kim I. Mills, *The State of the Workplace for Lesbian, Gay, Bisexual, and Transgender Americans, 2001* (Washington, DC: Human Rights Campaign Foundation, 2001), 31.

182 Raeburn (2004), 7–8.

183 See Alexandra Chasin, *Selling Out: The Gay and Lesbian Movement Goes to Market* (New York: Palgrave, 2000).

184 Katherine Sender, *Business, Not Politics: The Making of the Gay Market* (New York: Columbia University Press, 2004), 3.

185 Raeburn (2004), 70.

186 Tara Siegel Bernard, "Exxon to Extend Health Care to Married Same-Sex Couples," *New York Times*, 27 September 2013.

187 Antonia Juhasz, "What's Wrong with Exxon?" *Advocate*, October/November 2013, 54.

188 Ibid., 56.

189 *United States v. Windsor*, 570 U.S. ___ (2013).

190 Quoted in Siegel Bernard (2013).

191 Siegel Bernard (2013).

192 Quoted in Seigel Bernard (2013).

193 Welbord quoted in Amanda Chatel, "Gay-Friendly Companies: The 7 Most Surprising," *Huffington Post*, 10 September 2013, http://www.huffingtonpost.com/2013/09/10/gay-friendly-companies-surprising-_n_3882854.html (accessed 29 December 2014).

194 Sabin Willett, Counsel of Record, "Brief of 278 Employers and Organizations Representing Employers as Amici Curiae in Support of Respondent Edith Schlain Windsor (Merits Brief)," No 12-307, (2012), 1.

195 Ibid., 13.

196 Ibid., 25–26.

197 Ibid., 14–15.

198 Tara Siegel Bernard, "For Gay Employees, an Equalizer," *New York Times*, 20 May 2011.

199 Ibid.

200 Tara Siegel Bernard, "Yale and Columbia Reimburse Gay Employees for Extra Taxes," *New York Times*, 20 December 2012.

201 Willett (2012), 13.

202 Ibid.

203 Raeburn (2004), 68–72.

204 Ibid., 62–67; on social movement success generating complacency in the context of second-wave feminism, see Verta Taylor and Leila J. Rupp, "Women's Culture and Lesbian Feminist Activism: A Reconsideration of Cultural Feminism," *Signs: Journal of Women in Culture and Society* 19: 1993, 32–61.

205 Between 1977 and 2008, Gallup has asked, "As you may know, there has been considerable discussion in the news regarding the rights of homosexual men and women. In general, do you think homosexuals should or should not have equal rights in terms of job opportunities?" The percentage of respondents answering yes never fell below 56 percent (1977) and reached a consistent high of 88 or 89 percent by 2003. "Gallup Gay and Lesbian Rights," *Gallup. com*, http://www.gallup.com/poll/1651/gay-lesbian-rights.aspx (accessed 31 May 2013).

206 Raeburn (2004), 61.

207 Vaid (1995).

208 On human resource discursive construction of "diversity" see Ellen Berry, *The Enigma of Diversity: The Language of Race and the Limits of Racial Justice* (Chicago: University of Chicago Press, 2015).

209 On "fit" see Skocpol (1995) and discussion in chapter 4 of this book.

210 Canaday (2003), 383.

211 Brian J. Glenn, "The Two Schools of American Political Development," *Political Studies Review* 2 (2004): 153–65.

212 Ibid., 159.

213 On the role of networks and ideational entrepreneurs and strategies taken to destabilize hegemonic ideas, see Steven M. Teles, *The Rise of the Conservative Legal Movement: The Battle for Control of the Law* (Princeton, NJ: Princeton University Press, 2008), 16–21.

214 On empirical examination of backlash and normative warnings against litigation as a mechanism for social change see Gerald Rosenberg, *The Hollow Hope?* 2nd ed. (Chicago: University of Chicago Press, 2008). For a counterpoint, see Laura

Beth Nielsen, "Social Movements, Social Process: A Response to Gerald Rosen-berg," *John Marshall Law Review* 42 (Spring 2009).

215 See Karen Orren and Stephen Skowronek, "Institutions and Intercurrence: Theory Building in the Fullness of Time," *Political Order* (1996): 111–46.

216 Tim Cook, "Tim Cook Speaks Up," *Bloomberg Businessweek*, 30 October 2014.

217 Ibid.

218 Cooper quoted in Daniel D'Addario, "Why Tim Cook's Coming Out Is the Most Meaningful to Date," *Time*, 30 October 2014.

219 Arizona SB 1062 would have amended existing law to permit any individual or legal entity to claim exemption from any state law that constituted an infringe-ment on religious belief or exercise. See Dan Nowicki, Yvonne Wingett Sanchez, and Alia Beard Rau, "Arizona Governor Vetoes Anti-Gay Bill," *Arizona Republic*, 26 February 2014.

CHAPTER 4. RECOGNIZING OURSELVES

1 Richard Goldstein, "Cease Fire!" *Advocate*, 15 February 2000, 36–40.

2 This chapter is a revision of an article published as "Organizational Identity as a Constraint on Strategic Action: A Comparative Analysis of Gay and Lesbian Interest Groups," *Studies in American Political Development* 21 (Spring 2007): 66–91. This version is particularly indebted to the evaluation of the original version offered by Darren Halpin and Carsten Daugbjerg in their article "Identity as Con-straint and Resource in Interest Group Evolution: A Case of Radical Organiza-tional Change," *British Journal of Politics and International Relations* (April 2013).

3 Amin Ghaziani, *The Dividends of Dissent: How Conflict and Culture Work in Lesbian and Gay Marches on Washington* (Chicago: University of Chicago Press, 2008), 235–41.

4 Michael Heaney, "Outside the Issue Niche: The Multidimensionality of Interest Group Identity," *American Politics Research* 32 (2004): 615–16.

5 Francesca Polletta and James M. Jasper, "Collective Identity and Social Move-ments," *Annual Review of Sociology* 27 (August 2001): 293.

6 See Paul Pierson, *Politics in Time: History, Institutions, and Social Analysis* (Princ-eton, NJ: Princeton University Press, 2004), 17–53.

7 See Jess Cagle, "America Sees Shades of Gay: A Once-Invisible Group Finds the Spotlight," *Entertainment Weekly*, 8 September 1995. For summary analysis of increased media exposure of gays and lesbians in the 1990s see Larry Gross, *Up from Invisibility: Gay Men, Lesbians, and the Media in America* (New York: Co-lumbia University Press, 2002) and Ghaziani (2008), 196–203. Note the limits of this visibility, which often represented gays and lesbians as white, socioeconomi-cally well off, and cis-gendered.

8 Craig Rimmerman, *From Identity to Politics: The Lesbian and Gay Movement in the United States* (Philadelphia: Temple University Press, 2002), 310.

9 By 1998 more than two thousand government officials across the United States publicly identified as lesbian or gay. Ellen D. B. Riggle and Barry L. Tadlock,

"Gays and Lesbians in the Democratic Process: Past, Present, and Future," in *Gays and Lesbians in the Democratic Process*, Ellen D. B. Riggle and Barry L. Tadlock, eds. (New York: Columbia University Press, 1999), 1.

10 Marieka Klawitter and Brian Hammer, "Spatial and Temporal Diffusion of Local Government Antidiscrimination Policies for Sexual Orientation," in Riggle and Tadlock, eds. (1999), 23–35.

11 Donald P. Haider-Markel, "Creating Change—Holding the Line: Agenda Setting on Lesbian and Gay Issues at the National Level," in Riggle and Tadlock, eds. (1999), 250, 255.

12 Tyler quoted in Lisa Neff, "Marching On," *Advocate*, 22 June 1999, 40.

13 On political opportunity see Sidney Tarrow, *Power in Movement* (New York: Cambridge University Press, 1994), 17.

14 Success can be a gradient category and need not require the passage or defeat of legislation only. Even in the case of legislative or litigation failure, interest groups may utilize that defeat to mobilize constituencies, fund raise, expand networks, etc.

15 Theda Skocpol, *Protecting Soldiers and Mothers: The Political Origins of Social Policy in the United States* (Cambridge, MA: Belknap Press of Harvard University Press, 1992), 41, 55–56.

16 See, in particular, John D'Emilio, "Organizational Tales: Interpreting the NGLTF Story," in *Creating Change: Sexuality, Public Policy, and Civil Rights*, John D'Emilio, William B. Turner, and Urvashi Vaid, eds. (New York: Doubleday, 2000).

17 See Richard Cortner, "Strategies and Tactics of Litigants in Constitutional Cases," *Journal of Public Law* 17 (1968): 287–307; Jack Greenberg, *Judicial Process and Social Change: Constitutional Litigation* (St. Paul, MN: West, 1974); Herbert Jacob, *Justice in America* (Boston: Little, Brown, 1977); Karen O'Connor, *Women's Organizations' Use of the Courts* (Boston: Lexington Books, 1980).

18 One of the earliest articulations of ideas that coalesced into niche theory was put forward by Peter H. Odegard in his *Pressure Politics: The Story of the Anti-Saloon League* (New York: Columbia University Press, 1928). More recent forms of niche theory examine how niches within a particular policy arena, such as environmental politics, gay and lesbian politics, racial equality politics, immigration politics, women's rights, etc., are filled by different organizations working in the same substantive area. See John Marc Hansen, *Gaining Access: Congress and the Farm Lobby, 1919–1981* (Chicago: University of Chicago Press, 1991).

19 For a critique of this actor-centered functionalism see Paul Pierson, *Politics in Time: History, Institutions, and Social Analysis* (Princeton, NJ: Princeton University Press, 2004), 103–31.

20 Christopher J. Bosso, *Environment, Inc.: From Grassroots to Beltway* (Lawrence: University Press of Kansas, 2005), 148.

21 On the importance of leadership, and how strong leaders are attentive to environmental pressures that may provide opportunities if seized, see Anthony J. Nownes and Daniel Lipinski, "The Population Ecology of Interest Group Death: Gay and

Lesbian Rights Interest Groups in the United States, 1945–98," *British Journal of Political Science* 35 (2005): 303–19.

22 See Verta Taylor and Nancy Whittier, "Analytical Approaches to Social Movement Culture: The Culture of the Women's Movement," in *Social Movements and Culture*, Hank Johnston and Bert Klandermans, eds. (Minneapolis: University of Minnesota Press, 1995); and Steven Epstein, "Gay and Lesbian Movements in the United States: Dilemmas of Identity, Diversity, and Political Strategy," in *The Global Emergence of Gay and Lesbian Politics: National Imprints of a Worldwide Movement*, Barry Adam, Jan Wilem Duyvendak, and Andre Krouwel, eds. (Philadelphia: Temple University Press, 1999).

23 See Verta Taylor and Nancy E. Whittier, "Collective Identity in Social Movement Communities: Lesbian Feminist Mobilization," in *Frontiers in Social Movement Theory*, Aldon D. Morris and Carol M. Mueller, eds. (New Haven, CT: Yale University Press, 1992); Verta Taylor and Leila J. Rupp, "Women's Culture and Lesbian Feminist Activism: A Reconsideration of Cultural Feminism," *Signs* 19 (1) (Autumn 1993): 32–61.

24 Polletta and Jasper (2001), 96–97; Urvashi Vaid, *Virtual Equality: The Mainstreaming of Gay and Lesbian Liberation* (New York: Anchor Books, 1995), 195–209.

25 Polletta and Jasper (2001), 294.

26 See Mary Bernstein, "Celebration and Suppression: The Strategic Uses of Identity by the Lesbian and Gay Movement," *American Journal of Sociology* 103 (1997): 531–65; Mary Bernstein, "Identities and Politics: Toward a Historical Understanding of the Lesbian and Gay Movement," *Social Science History* 26 (2002): 531–81; and, Mary Bernstein, "The Analytic Dimensions of Identity: A Political Identity Framework," in *Identity Work in Social Movements*, Jo Reger, Daniel J. Myers, and Rachel Einwohner, eds. (Minneapolis: University of Minnesota Press, 2008).

27 Bernstein offers tactics of identity deployment beyond critique and education in Bernstein (2008) and, in particular, examines the mechanisms by which these deployments occur, including cultural performance, music, fashion, and interactively or dramaturgically.

28 Bernstein (1997); see also Mary Bernstein and Kristine A. Olsen, "Identity Development and Social Change: Understanding Identity as a Social Movement and Organizational Strategy," *Sociology Compass* 3 (6) (December 2009): 871–83. These strategies clearly resonate with the reform-versus-radicalism strategies that defined much of LGBT movement development since at least the 1950s. See Craig Rimmerman, *The Lesbian and Gay Movements: Assimilation or Liberation?* 2nd ed. (Boulder, CO: Westview, 2015).

29 Bernstein (1997) examines case histories of advocacy for local ordinances in New York, Oregon, and Vermont; see also Mary Bernstein, "The Contradictions of Gay Ethnicity: Forging Identity in Vermont," in *Social Movements: Identity, Culture, and the State*, David S. Meyer, Nancy Whittier, and Belinda Robnett, eds. (New York: Oxford University Press, 2002).

30 On the potential for ballot campaigns as movement building, see Donald P. Haider-Markel, "Lesbian and Gay Politics in the States," in *The Politics of Gay Rights*, Craig Rimmerman, Kenneth D. Wald, and Clyde Wilcox, eds. (Chicago: University of Chicago Press, 2000), 290–346.

31 Amy Stone, *Gay Rights at the Ballot Box* (Minneapolis: University of Minnesota Press, 2012), xvi–xxix; on the instrumental strategies that may harm longer-term coalition building, see Jane Ward, *Respectably Queer: Diversity Culture in LGBT Activist Organizations* (Nashville, TN: Vanderbilt University Press, 2008).

32 Hansen (1991), 13–22.

33 Sidney Verba and Norman H. Nie, *Participation in America: Political Democracy and Social Equality* (New York: Harper & Row, 1972), 160–70.

34 Steven J. Rosenstone and John Mark Hansen, *Mobilization, Participation, and Democracy in America* (New York: Longman, 2003), 78.

35 See *National LGBTQ Task Force*, www.thetaskforc.org, and *Human Rights Campaign*, www.hrc.org.

36 Vaid (1995), 93.

37 See, for example, "NGLTF Statement on Upcoming Supreme Court Hearing of Amendment 2," 21 September 1995, http://www.thetaskforce.org/press/releases/pr248_092195 (accessed 31 January 2014).

38 See "Task Force Action Fund Statement on Administration's Decision to Recognize Utah Same-Sex Marriages," 10 January 2010, http://www.thetaskforce.org/press/release/pr_011014 (accessed 31 January 2014).

39 See "Pat Ballie to Receive Task Force Leather Leadership Award," 8 January 2014, http://www.thetaskforce.org/press/release/pr_010814 (accessed 31 January 2014).

40 *Human Rights Campaign*, www.hrc.org.

41 "Equations," 1998–1999 Annual Report of the Human Rights Campaign, http://www.hrc.org/files/assets/resources/AnnualReport_1999.pdf (accessed 31 January 2014).

42 "Still Building Equality," 2002–2003 Annual Report of the Human Rights Campaign, http://www.hrc.org/files/assets/resources/AnnualReport_2003.pdf (accessed 31 January 2014).

43 Much of the political history of the post-Stonewall LGBT movements categorizes its advocacy organizations as revolutionary or reform oriented. The former include groups like the Gay Liberation Front, the AIDS Coalition to Unleash Power, and Queer Nation. These groups question underlying politico-economic forces that maintain the status quo and call for transformative cultural and institutional change. Reform-oriented organizations tend, by contrast, to work within existing institutions and power relations to seek inclusion; rather than delegitimize those in power, they often attempt to work with them to achieve piecemeal change. For more on the revolution-reform dichotomy see Rimmerman (2002); David Rayside, *On the Fringe: Gays and Lesbians in Politics* (Ithaca, NY: Cornell University Press, 1998), 3–8; Vaid (1995).

44 Phuong Ly, "March Shows Gays Taking Different Roads," *Washington Post*, 29 March 2000, B1; Ann Scales, "Weekend Gay-Rights March Doesn't Sit Well with Some Grass Roots Activists," *Boston Globe*, 29 April 2000, A3; Joshua Gamson, "Who's Millenium March?" *Nation*, 17 April 2000, 16–20.

45 Federation Announces "Equality Begins at Home," NGLTF Press Release, 30 April 1998.

46 Interviews with senior-level staffers in the HRC communication, field, policy, legal, and legislative divisions, 3–4 March 2005.

47 Interview with senior HRC staffer, 4 March 2005.

48 Interviews with senior HRC staffers in the communication, field, policy, legal, and legislative divisions, 3–4 March 2005.

49 Interview with former Task Force senior staffer, 4 March 2005. This individual worked in various positions at the Task Force between 1993 and 2003.

50 Interview with Task Force senior staffer, 22 April 2005.

51 Interview with Task Force senior staffer, 9 March 2005.

52 Interviews with Task Force staffers, 4 March and 9 March 2005.

53 Interview with former Task Force senior staffer, 4 March 2005.

54 Equality Store, *Human Rights Campaign*, shop.hrc.org (accessed 22 September 2015).

55 Dudley Clendinen and Adam Nagourney, *Out for Good: The Struggle to Build a Gay Rights Movement in America* (New York: Simon & Schuster, 1999), 188–99; Rimmerman (2002), 31–32.

56 Clendinen and Nagourney (1999), 195; Rimmerman (2002), 2–7.

57 Clendinen and Nagourney (1999), 243.

58 Ibid.

59 Ibid., 245–60.

60 Vaid (1995), 61.

61 Chai Feldblum, "The Federal Gay Rights Bill: From Bella to ENDA," in *Creating Change: Sexuality, Public Policy, and Civil Rights*, John D'Emilio, William B. Turner, and Urvashi Vaid, eds. (New York: St. Martin's, 2000), 153–59.

62 Valeska quoted in Clendinen and Nagourney (1999), 457.

63 Clendinen and Nagourney (1999), 457.

64 Ibid.

65 Ibid., 433–36.

66 Ibid, 433–45.

67 Ibid., 472–74.

68 Rayside (1998), 301.

69 Interview with HRC senior staffer, 4 March 2005.

70 Rayside (1998), 301–2; Vaid (1995), 1993; Rimmerman (2002), 33.

71 Clendinen and Nagourney (1999), 475–77.

72 Feldblum (2000), 169–74; Clendinen and Nagourney (1999), 488–93.

73 Feldblum (2000), 171.

74 Rayside (1998), 285–86.

75 D'Emilio (2000), 471.

76 Interview with former Task Force staffer, 4 March 2005.

77 Interview with Task Force senior staffer, 9 March 2005.

78 Rayside (1998), 285.

79 Interview with former Task Force staffer, 4 March 2005.

80 Feldblum (2000), 174.

81 See Randy Shilts, *Conduct Unbecoming: Lesbians and Gays in the U.S. Military* (New York: St. Martin's, 1993).

82 William N. Eskridge Jr. and Nan D. Hunter, *Sexuality, Gender, and the Law* (Westbury, NY: Foundation Press, 1997), 372. *Matlovich v. Secretary of the Air Force*, 591 F.2d 852 (1978); *Berg v. Claytor*, 591 F.2d 849 (1978).

83 Vaid (1995), 152.

84 Rimmerman (2002), 57–58; Feldblum (2000), 174–78.

85 Rayside (1998), 219.

86 Gary I. Lehring, *Officially Gay: The Political Construction of Sexuality by the U.S. Military* (Philadelphia: Temple University Press, 2003), 143.

87 Vaid (1995), 153.

88 Ibid., 157.

89 *National LBGTQ Task Force*, http://www.thetaskforce.org/about_us/history (last accessed 31 January 2014).

90 Rayside (1998), 219.

91 Vaid (1995), 159–61.

92 Rayside (1998), 219. On Tsongas, see Steve Endean, *Bringing Lesbians and Gay Rights into the Mainstream: Twenty Years of Progress* (New York: Harrington Park Press, 2006), 219–20, 285–86, and 303–4.

93 Rayside (1998), 219–20.

94 *Human Rights Campaign*, http://www.hrc.org/Content/NavigationMenu.About_HRC/HRC_History_Timeline_1990-2000.htm (accessed 10 April 2005).

95 David Rayside, "The Perils of Congressional Politics," in *Gay Rights, Military Wrongs*, Craig Rimmerman, ed. (New York: Gerald Publishing, 1996): 147–93; see also Vaid (1995), 163–67.

96 Rayside (1998), 242–47; Vaid (1995), 170–71; John Gallagher and Chris Bull, *Perfect Enemies: The Religious Right, the Gay Movement, and the Politics of the 1990s* (New York: Crown, 1996), 151–60.

97 Feldblum (2000), 175.

98 D'Emilio (2000), 478–82.

99 D'Emilio (2000), 479.

100 *National LGBTQ Task Force*, http://www.thetaskforce.org/about_us/history (accessed 22 September 2015.

101 *Human Rights Campaign*, http://www.hrc.org/Content/NavigationMenu.About_HRC/HRC_History_Timeline_1990-2000.htm (accessed 10 April 2005).

102 Rayside (1998), 285, 287; Rimmerman (2002), 33.

103 Feldblum (2000), 180. See also Gregory B. Lewis and Jonathan L. Edelson, "DOMA and ENDA: Congress Votes on Gay Rights," in *Politics of Gay Rights,* Craig A. Rimmerman, Kenneth D. Wald, and Clyde Wilcox, eds. (Chicago: University of Chicago Press, 2000), 201–12. See Employment Non-Discrimination Act of 1994, S. 2239, 103d Cong. (as introduced in Senate, 23 June 1004). This bill was the first iteration of ENDA, which replaced the previous Civil Rights Amendments, which included sexual orientation, to the 1964 Civil Rights Act. See, for example, H.R. Rep. No. 110-406, pt. 1, at 2, 5.

104 Votes on and text of the 1996 version of ENDA are available at https://www.govtrack.us/congress/bills/104/s2056 (accessed 31 January 2014).

105 Feldblum (2000), 183; Lewis and Edelson (2000), 201–12.

106 Feldblum (2000), 184–86.

107 *United States Senate,* http://www.senate.gov/legislative/LIS/roll_call_lists/roll_call_vote_cfm.cfm?congress=104&session=2&vote=00271; and http://proaxis.com/cop/sv960280.htm (accessed 10 April 2005).

108 "Major Gay and Lesbian Conference Set for Minneapolis," 12 April 1990, NGLTF, box 2, folder 32, cited in Michael J. Klarman, *From the Closet to the Altar: Courts, Backlash, and the Struggle for Same-Sex Marriage* (New York: Oxford University Press, 2013), 48.

109 On the case for same-sex marriage, see Evan Wolfson, *Why Marriage Matters: America, Equality, and Gay People's Right to Marry* (New York: Simon & Schuster, 2005). On arguments against same-sex marriage within the sexual-minorities communities, see Mary Bernstein and Verta Taylor, eds., *The Marrying Kind? Debating Same-Sex Marriage within the Lesbian and Gay Movement* (Minneapolis: University of Minnesota Press, 2013).

110 *Richard John Baker v. Gerald R. Nelson,* 291 Minn. 310, 191 N.W.2d 185 (1971). See Martin Dupuis, *Same-Sex Marriage, Legal Mobilization, and the Politics of Rights* (New York: Peter Lang, 2002).

111 *Baehr v. Lewin,* 74 Haw. 530, 852 P.2d 44 (1993); *Baker v. Vermont,* 744 A.2d 864 (Vt. 1999). For a detailed history of the Vermont litigation, see David Moats, *Civil Wars: A Battle for Gay Marriage* (New York: Harcourt, 2004). See also Michael Mello, *Legalizing Gay Marriage* (Philadelphia: Temple University Press, 2004).

112 George Chauncey, *Why Marriage? The History of Shaping Today's Debate over Gay Equality* (New York: Basic Books, 2005), 94.

113 Ibid., 96–111.

114 Casey Charles, *The Sharon Kowalski Case: Lesbian and Gay Rights on Trial* (Lawrence: University Press of Kansas, 2003), 6, 16–20, 29–30, 142–43, 179. *In re Guardianship of Kowalski,* 478 N.W.2d 790 (Minn. App. 1991), 797; see also Klarman (2013), 50; and Chauncey (2004), 111–16.

115 Chauncey (2004), 105–11.

116 Gerald Rosenberg, *The Hollow Hope: Can Courts Bring About Social Change?* 2nd ed. (Chicago: University of Chicago Press, 2008), 357. The significant victory for

anti-same-sex constitutional bans came in 2004, when eleven states passed constitutional amendments in the wake of Massachusetts's *Goodridge v. Department of Public Health* ruling.

117 Interview with HRC senior staffer, 4 March 2005. *Goodridge v. Dept. of Public Health*, 798 N.E.2d 941 (Mass. 2003).

118 Paula Ettelbrick, "Since When Is Marriage a Path to Liberation?" quoted in Eskridge and Hunter (1997), 817. The original exchange was first published as "Gay Marriage: A Must or a Bust?" *Out/Look* (1989): 8–19.

119 Thomas B. Stoddard, "Why Gay People Should Seek the Right to Marry," quoted in Eskridge and Hunter (1997), 819.

120 Ibid., 76.

121 Karen Orren and Stephen Skowronek, *The Search for American Political Development* (New York: Cambridge University Press, 2004), 105.

122 Ibid., 106.

123 The Task Force looks more like Orren and Skowronek's (2004) misfits, which "may succeed in transforming institutional relationship, making the government fit them rather than vice versa" (106). Indeed, from the standpoint of a decade later, as marriage recognition is now law throughout the United States, the exact role and effects of misfits should be the subject of more inquiry.

124 *National LGBTQ Task Force*, http://www.thetaskforce.org/about_us/history (last accessed 29 January 2014).

125 Ibid.

126 "Bush's Support of the Federal Marriage Amendment Deemed a Declaration of War on Gay America," NGLTF Press Release, 16 December 2003, *National LGBTQ*, http://www.thetaskforce.org/press/releases/pr611_121603 (accessed 29 January 2014).

127 For journalistic coverage supporting this thesis see Dante Chinni, "Is the Post-Election Red Tinge a Mandate? Don't Bet on It," *Christian Science Monitor*, 4 November 2004, 9; James Dao, "Same-Sex Marriage Issue Key to Some GOP Races," *New York Times*, 4 November 2004, 4; Howard Manly, "In the End, It Was the Bible, Stupid," *Boston Herald*, 4 November 2004, 55. For journalistic coverage countering this claim, suggesting that these ballot initiatives did not boost the vote for George W. Bush, see Michelangelo Signorile, "Don't Blame the Gays: Why the 'Moral Values' Story Plays Right into the GOP's Hands," *New York Press*, 10 November 2004, 17. For testing of this thesis that finds the ballot initiatives had a statistically significant effect on boosting voter turnout but that other issues mattered more, see Gregory B. Lewis, "Same-Sex Marriage and the 2004 Election," *PS* (April 2004): 195–99.

128 In Georgia (76 percent yes), Kentucky (75 percent yes), Mississippi (86 percent yes), Oklahoma (76 percent yes), and Utah (66 percent yes), the state legislatures placed referendums on the ballot. In Arkansas (75 percent yes), Michigan (56 percent yes), Montana (67 percent yes), North Dakota (73 percent yes), Ohio (62 percent yes), and Oregon (57 percent yes), the measures were brought by citizen initiative.

129 John M. Broder and Katherine Q. Seelye, "Groups Debate Slower Strategy on Gay Rights," *New York Times*, 9 December 2004.

130 Ibid.

131 Evelyn Nieves, "Activists Refuse to Bargain Away Rights," *Washington Post*, 10 December 2004, A2.

132 Where We Stand: A Letter to all Members of Congress, NGLTF Press Release, 10 December 2004, *National Gay and Lesbian Task Force*, http://www.thetaskforce.org/press/releases/pr772_121004 (accessed 31 January 2014).

133 Foreman quoted in ibid.

134 Michael Berman, co-chairperson of the Human Rights Campaign quoted in Broder and Seeyle (2004).

135 Broder and Seeyle (2004).

136 Foreman quoted in Broder and Seeyle (2004).

137 Stephen Skowronek, *The Politics Presidents Make: Leadership from George Washington to Bill Clinton* (Cambridge, MA: Belknap Press of Harvard University Press, 1997), 37.

138 Interview with Task Force senior staffer, 9 March 2005.

139 Interview with Task Force senior staffer, 22 April 2005.

140 Task Force Hails Introduction of Transgender-Inclusive Employment Non-Discrimination Act in U.S. House of Representatives, NGLTF Press Release, 24 April 2007, http://www.thetaskforceactionfund.org/press/2007/042407_trans_inclusion.html (accessed 1 February 2014). In 2007 ENDA finally included transgender as a category of protected identity in addition to sexual orientation. See Employment Non-Discrimination Act of 2007, H.R. 2015, 110th Cong. (as introduced in House, 24 April 2007).

141 Employment Non-Discrimination Act of 2007, H.R. 3685, 110th Cong. (as placed on Senate calendar 13 November 2007) included protections only for sexual orientation; H.R. 3686, 110th Cong (as introduced in the House, 27 September 2007) included protections on the basis of gender identity.

142 A Non-Transgender-Inclusive ENDA? No Way! NGLTF Press Release, 27 September 2007, http://www.thetaskforceactionfund.org/press/2007/092707_trans_enda_inclusion.html (accessed 31 January 2014).

143 Ibid.

144 National Lesbian, Gay, Bisexual, and Transgender Leaders Demand More Time to Secure a Transgender-Inclusive ENDA, NGLTF Press Release, 27 September 2007, http://www.thetaskforceactionfund.org/press/2007/092707_enda_leaders_time.html (accessed 31 January 2014).

145 Task Force, Inc., Responds to Decision to Postpone Hearing on Substitute ENDA Aimed at Stripping Transgender Protections, NGLTF Press Release, 2 October 2007, http://www.thetaskforceactionfund.org/press/2007/100207_enda_postpone.html (accessed 31 January 2014).

146 Task Force, Inc., and More Than 150 Groups Announce Launch of United ENDA, a Nationwide Campaign to Ensure Transgender Protections Remain in Employ-

ment Non-Discrimination Act, NGLTF Press Release, 3 October 2007, http://
www.thetaskforceactionfund.org/press/2007/100307_united_enda.html. For the
text of the October 1, 2007, letter to Congress with all 150 signatories, see http://
www.thetaskforce.org/activist_center/ENDA_oct1_letter (last accessed 31 January
2014).

147 The House approved H.R. 3685, which died in the Senate. House Bill 3686, which
applied to transgenders, died in House committee at the close of the legislative
session.

148 Interview with HRC senior staffer, 3 March 2005.

149 Halpin and Daugbjerg (2013), 6.

150 Ibid., 7.

151 See, for example, P. DiMaggio and W. Powell, "The Iron Cage Revisited: Institutional Isomorphism and Collective Rationality in Organizational Fields," in
The New Institutionalism in Organizational Analysis, W. Powell and P. DiMaggio,
eds. (Chicago: University of Chicago Press, 1991); Douglass North, *Institutions,
Institutional Change, and Economic Performance* (New York: Cambridge University Press, 1990); Daniel Galvin, *Presidential Party Building: Dwight D. Eisenhower
to George W. Bush* (Princeton, NJ: Princeton University Press, 2009); James
Mahoney and Kathleen Thelan, eds., *Explaining Institutional Change: Ambiguity,
Agency, and Power* (New York: Cambridge University Press, 2010).

152 Notable exceptions include Halpin and Daughbjerg (2013) as well as McGee
Young, *Developing Interests: Organizational Change and the Politics of Advocacy*
(Lawrence: University Press of Kansas, 2010).

153 Kathleen Thelen, *How Institutions Evolve: The Political Economy of Skills in Germany, Britain, the United States, and Japan* (Cambridge: Cambridge University
Press, 2004), 212–13.

154 While the case speaks to ideological investment in maintaining connection to an
institutional venue, others have assessed material investment decisions as fostering endogenous transformations of organizational power. See Daniel Galvin, "The
Transformation of Political Institutions: Investments in Institutional Resources
and Gradual Change in the National Party Committees," *Studies in American
Political Development* 26 (Spring 2012): 1–21.

CHAPTER 5. RESPECT FOR PRIVATE LIVES

1 *Lawrence v. Texas*, 539 U.S. 558 (2003), 578–89. Justice Kennedy quoted the first
sentence of this passage from *Planned Parenthood of Southeastern Pennsylvania v.
Casey*, 505 U.S. 833 (1992), 847.

2 Parts of this chapter were published as "Frame Spillover: Media Framing and Public Opinion of a Multifaceted LGBT Rights Agenda," *Law & Social Inquiry* 38 (2)
(Spring 2013): 403–4. That article also contains a discussion of print news media
not included in this chapter, but it does not address this chapter's primary theme:
the development of a unified regulatory recognition of gay sexuality among the
three federal branches between 1993 and 2003.

3   *Bowers v. Hardwick*, 478 U.S. 186 (1986).

4   This equal protection approach was taken by Justice Sandra Day O'Connor, in her concurrence. O'Connor, who was in the majority in *Bowers*, would have struck down the Texas statute but permitted Texas to respond by recriminalizing both same-sex and different-sex sodomy, as the George statute had done.

5   *Lawrence v. Texas*, 539 U.S. 558 (2003), 578.

6   David J. Richards, *The Sodomy Cases:* Bowers v. Hardwick *and* Lawrence v. Texas (Lawrence: University Press of Kansas, 2009), 178.

7   Constitutional protection for sexual and intimate privacy was articulated in the domain of contraception within marriage (*Griswold v. Connecticut*, 381 U.S. 479 [1965]), contraception outside of marriage (*Eisenstadt v. Baird*, 405 U.S. 438 [1972]), and abortion (*Roe v. Wade*, 410 U.S. 113 [1973] and *Planned Parenthood v. Casey*, 505 U.S. 833 [1992]). *Bowers v. Hardwick* has been criticized as a clear outlier of that developing tradition. See William N. Eskridge Jr., "*Hardwick* and Historiography," *University of Illinois Law Review* (2) (1999): 633 ("Although gay people are predictably critical of the decision, respected academic commentators, most of them nongay, have strongly criticized Hardwick as manipulative, ignorant and inefficient, violent, historically inaccurate, misogynistic, authoritarian, and contrary to precedent" [citations omitted]).

8   Dale Carpenter, *Flagrant Conduct: The Story of* Lawrence v. Texas (New York: Norton, 2012), 259.

9   These states included Alabama, Florida, Idaho, Kansas, Louisiana, Michigan, Missouri, Mississippi, North Carolina, Oklahoma, South Carolina, Texas, Utah, and Virginia.

10 *Padula v. Webster*, 822 F. 2d 97 (1987) relied on *Bowers* to uphold the FBI's refusal to hire an otherwise qualified candidate because she was a lesbian. *Woodward v. United States*, 871 F. 2d 1068 (1989) relied on *Bowers* to maintain the navy's discharge of a man due to his homosexuality. *High Tech Gays, et al. v. Defense Industrial Security Clearance Office, et al.*, 895 F.2d 563 (9th Cir. 1990) utilized *Bowers* to maintain the policy of denying security clearance to any gay, lesbian, or bisexual individuals. And, various states relied on *Bowers* to prevent adoption by gay, lesbian, or bisexual individuals. See Ellen Ann Andersen, *Out of the Closets and into the Courts: Legal Opportunity Structure and Gay Rights Litigation* (Ann Arbor: University of Michigan Press, 2005), 93–94.

11 Harlow quoted in Joel Brinkley, "Supreme Court Strikes Down Texas Law Banning Sodomy," *New York Times*, 26 June 2003.

12 Goldberg quoted in Linda Greenhouse, "Justices, 6–3, Legalize Gay Sexual Conduct in Sweeping Reversal of Court's '86 Ruling," *New York Times*, 27 June 2003.

13 *Lawrence v. Texas*, 539 U.S. 558 (2003), 578.

14 See Cathy Harris, "Outing Privacy Litigation: Toward a Contextual Strategy for Lesbian and Gay Rights," *George Washington Law Review* 65 (1996): 248–77; and Catherine MacKinnon, "The Road Not Taken: Sex Equality in *Lawrence v. Texas*," *Ohio State Law Journal* 65 (2004): 1081–94.

15 *Hurley v. Irish-American Gay, Lesbian & Bisexual Group of Boston*, 515 U.S. 557 (1995); *Romer v. Evans*, 517 U.S. 620 (1996); *Boy Scouts of America et al. v. Dale*, 530 U.S. 640 (2000); *Lawrence v. Texas*, 539 U.S. 558 (2003).

16 On media framing see William Gamson, "News as Framing," *American Behavioral Scientist* 33 (November 1992): 157–61; and William Gamson, David Croteau, William Hoynes, and Theodore Sasson, "Media Images and the Social Construction of Reality," *Annual Review of Sociology* 18 (1992): 373–93.

17 Michael J. Klarman, *From the Closet to the Altar: Courts, Backlash, and the Struggle for Same-Sex Marriage* (New York: Oxford University Press, 2013).

18 As figure 5.1 indicates, there were two spikes in opposition to decriminalization. The first was in 1986, when opposition to legal homosexual relations jumped from 43 percent to 57 percent. That spike followed the *Bowers* ruling, which maintained criminalization. The second spike followed *Lawrence*. Regardless of the direction of the Court's ruling, public opposition increases after a Court ruling. The uniformity in public response suggests an alternative possibility—that the poll captures sentiment about the Court's democratic deficit or its perceived "elitism." See Lino A. Graglia, "*Lawrence v. Texas*: Our Philosopher-Kings Adopt Libertarianism as Our Official National Philosophy and Reject Traditional Morality as a Basis for Law," *Ohio State Law Journal* 65 (2004): 1141. Perhaps the poll reflects a desire that decriminalization should be a policy matter left to the elected legislature. See Gregory A. Caldeira and James L. Gibson, "The Etiology of Public Support for the Supreme Court," *American Journal of Political Science* 36 (3) (1992): 635–64.

If this explanation were true, then public support of the Court's legitimacy should have declined around the time of the ruling. However, existing data do not support this expectation. At the time of *Lawrence*, there was no immediate change in public support for the Court. The approval rate in September 2002 was 60 percent. In the first week of July 2003, approval held at 59 percent. See Jeffrey Jones and Lydia Saad, "Gallup Poll Social Series: Governance," *Gallup. com*, 8–11 September 2011, http://www.gallup.com/poll/149906/Supreme-Court-Approval-Rating-Dips.aspx (accessed 15 February 2012).

19 Benjamin I. Page and Robert Shapiro, *The Rational Public: Fifty Years of Trends in Americans' Policy Preferences* (Chicago: University of Chicago Press, 1992), 386.

20 See James L. Gibson and Gregory A. Caldeira, "Knowing the Supreme Court? A Reconsideration of Public Ignorance of the High Court," *Journal of Politics* 71 (2) (2009): 429–41; Valerie J. Hoekstra, *Public Reaction to Supreme Court Decisions* (New York: Cambridge University Press, 2003); Jeffrey J. Mondak and Shannon Ishiyama Smithey, "Dynamics of Public Support for the Supreme Court," *Journal of Politics* 57 (4) (1997): 1114–42; Elliot E. Slotnick and Jennifer A. Segal, *Television News and the Supreme Court: All the News That's Fit to Air?* (New York: Cambridge University Press, 1998).

21 Rosalee A. Clawson and Eric N. Waltenburg, "Support for a Supreme Court Affirmative Action Decision: A Story in Black and White," *American Politics Research* 31 (3) (2003): 251–79.

22 *Lawrence v. Texas*, 539 U.S. 558 (2003), J. Scalia dissenting, 606, 599.

23 James W. Stoutenborough, Donald P. Haider-Merkel, and Mahalley D. Allen, "Reassessing the Impact of Supreme Court Decisions on Public Opinion: Gay Civil Rights Cases," *Political Research Quarterly* 59 (3) (2006): 419–33; see also Donald Haider-Merkel, *Media Coverage of* Lawrence v. Texas: *An Analysis of Content, Tone, and Frames in National and Local News Reporting* (New York: GLAAD Center for the Study of Media and Society, 2004).

24 *Lawrence v. Texas*, 539 U.S. 558 (2003), J. Scalia dissenting, 604, 605.

25 *Baehr v. Lewin*, 74 Haw. 530, 852 P.2d 44 (1993).

26 1996 Defense of Marriage Act (DOMA) (Pub.L. 104-199, 110 Stat. 2419), enacted 21 September 1996, 1 U.S.C § 1738C.

27 *Baker v. Vermont*, 744 A.2d 864 (Vt. 1999).

28 *Goodridge v. Department of Public Health*, 798 N.E. 2d 941 (Mass. 2003).

29 See generally Klarman (2013); see also William N. Eskridge and Darren R. Spedale, *Gay Marriage: For Better or for Worse? What We've Learned from the Evidence* (New York: Oxford University Press, 2006); Miriam Smith, *Political Institutions and Lesbian and Gay Rights in the United States and Canada* (New York: Routledge, 2008).

30 Various measures attest to broad support for gays and lesbians to have a right of personal freedom. For example, a vast majority of Americans, as of May 2003—88 percent—contended that gays and lesbians should have equal job opportunities; only 9 percent expressed opposition. Gallup Organization, 5–7 May 2003, margin of error +/- 3 percent. Question: "In general do you think homosexuals should or should not have equal rights in terms of job opportunities?" See Frank Newport, "Six out of 10 Americans Say Homosexual Relations Should Be Recognized as Legal," *Gallup News Service*, 15 May 2003, http://www.gallup.com/poll/8413/six-americans-say-homosexual-relations-should-recognized-legal.aspx (accessed 15 February 2012). And, by 2004, when the Don't Ask, Don't Tell policy reemerged at the forefront of media coverage, in part because of the possibility that the *Lawrence* ruling would compel the policy's repeal and in part because the country had become newly engaged in a war in Iraq, about 63 percent of Americans favored allowing gays and lesbians to serve openly in the military. Question: "Do you favor or oppose allowing openly gay men and lesbian women to serve in the military?" See Lymari Morales, "Conservatives Shift in Favor of Openly Gay Service Members," *Gallup Politics*, 5 June 2009, http://www.gallup.com/poll/8413/six-americans-say-homosexual-relations-should-recognized-legal.aspx (accessed 15 February 2012). Capping a trend of greater acceptance of the homosexual individual, about 60 percent supported Social Security and healthcare benefits for homosexual couples on a par with those of heterosexual married couples. Gallup Organization, 5–7 May 2003, margin of error +/- 3 percent. Question: "Do you think homosexual couples should or should not have the same legal rights as married couples regarding health care benefits and Social Security survivor benefits?" (Newport 2003).

31 Gary Mucciaroni, *Same-Sex Different Rights: Success and Failure in the Struggles over Gay Rights* (Chicago: University of Chicago Press, 2008), 89.

32 As of July 2003, 57 percent of Americans opposed civil unions that would confer upon gays and lesbians some of the legal rights and benefits of marriage. See David W. Moore and Joseph Carroll, "Support for Gay Marriage/Civil Unions Edges Upward," *Gallup News Service*, May 17, 2004, http://www.gallup.com/poll/11689/support-gay-marriagecivil-unions-edges-upward.aspx (accessed 15 February 2012); see also Karlyn Bowman and Bryan O'Keefe, "Attitudes about Homosexuality and Gay Marriage," *American Enterprise Institute for Public Policy Research* (Washington, DC, 2004); and Lydia Saad, "Americans Still Oppose Gay Marriage," *Gallup News Service*, May 22, 2006, http://www.gallup.com/poll/22882/americans-still-oppose-gay-marriage.aspx (accessed 15 February 2012). Only recently has support for same-sex marriage edged above 50 percent. At the time of the *Lawrence* decision, 50 percent of Americans were opposed to gay parenting. See Jennifer Robinson, "Homosexual Parenting Evenly Divides Americans," *Gallup News Service*, July 1, 2003, http://www.gallup.com/poll/8740/homosexual-parenting-evenly-divides-americans.aspx (accessed 15 February 2012). As of 2008, a *Newsweek* poll found that this opinion had changed little; only 53 percent of respondents supported gay adoption. See Princeton Survey Research Associates International, "Newsweek Poll: Gay and Lesbian Rights," December 3–4, 2008, http://www.pollingreport.com/civil.htm (accessed 15 February 2012). In short, the public, at the time of the *Lawrence* ruling, seemed to endorse the concept of gays and lesbians as free to be fully productive private citizens; however, when equality was extended to grant publicly sanctioned civil recognition, support fell.

33 Patrick J. Egan and Kenneth Sherrill, "Neither an In-Law nor an Outlaw Be: Trends in Americans' Attitudes toward Gay People," *Public Opinion Pros*, February 2005, http://www.publicopinionpros.norc.org/features/2005/feb/sherrill_egan.asp (last accessed 22 September 2015); Gary Hicks and Tien-Tsung Lee, "Public Attitudes toward Gays and Lesbians: Trends and Predictors," *Journal of Homosexuality* 51 (2) (2006): 57–77; Gary Mucciaroni, *Same Sex, Different Politics: Success and Failure in the Struggles over Gay Rights* (Chicago: University of Chicago Press, 2008).

34 Kenji Yoshino, *Covering: The Hidden Assault on Our Civil Rights* (New York: Random House, 2006), 89.

35 Ibid., 107.

36 Ian Ayres and Jennifer Brown, "Mark(et)ing Nondiscrimination," John M. Olin Center for Studies in Law, Economics, and Public Policy Working Papers, Paper 288 (2005), 3. One explanation for this resistance to public recognition of homosexual relations is the so-called ick factor, i.e., the alleged individual-level physical discomfort with homosexual sexual acts felt by the heterosexual majority. See William N. Eskridge, *The Case for Same-Sex Marriage: From Sexual Liberty to Civilized Commitment* (New York: Free Press, 1996); Matt Foreman, "Gay Is Good," *Nova Law Review* 32 (3) (2008): 557–72; Michael Nava and Robert Dav-

idoff, *Created Equal: Why Gay Rights Matter to America* (New York: St. Martin's Griffin, 1995).

37 Frank Baumgartner and Bryan Jones, *Agendas and Instability in American Politics* (Chicago: University of Chicago Press, 1993).

38 See Phillip E. Converse, "The Nature of Belief Systems in Mass Publics," in *Ideology and Discontent*, David E. Apter, ed. (New York: Free Press, 1964); Thomas E. Nelson, Rosalee A. Clawson, and Zoe M. Oxley, "Media Framing of a Civil Liberties Conflict and Its Effect on Tolerance," *American Political Science Review* 91 (September 1997): 567–83.

39 See Shanto Iyengar and Donald Kinder, *News That Matters* (Chicago: University of Chicago Press, 1987); and Jeffrey W. Koch, "Political Rhetoric and Political Persuasion: The Changing Structure of Citizens' Preferences on Health Insurance during Policy Debate," *Public Opinion Quarterly* 62 (2) (1998): 209–29.

40 Thomas F. Nelson and Donald Kinder, "Issue Frames and Group-Centrism in American Public Opinion," *Journal of Politics* 58 (4) (1996): 1074.

41 John R. Zaller, *The Nature and Origins of Mass Opinion* (New York: Cambridge University Press, 1992), 49.

42 To build a data set of television news coverage, this study used the holdings of the Vanderbilt Television News Archive. The archive contains coverage from the three broadcast networks (ABC, CBS, and NBC) and CNN. It does not have holdings for other networks such as Fox News or MSNBC prior to 2004; therefore, the sample may depress the level of popular exposure to the extent that certain conservative or more liberal viewpoints may be underrepresented. Although a study of "softer" news sources such as talk shows and blogs would be enlightening and would raise intriguing claims of audience fragmentation, a focus on more traditional media outlets is supported by Gallup polling that found that, as late as 2005, most Americans surveyed (56 percent) were not familiar with what an internet blog was, and only 26 percent considered themselves very familiar or somewhat familiar with a blog. See Lydia Saad, "Blogs Not Yet in the Media Big Leagues," *Gallup News Service*, 11 March 2005, http://www.gallup.com/poll/15217/Blogs-Yet-Media-Big-Leagues.aspx (accessed 15 February 2012).

43 Gary I. Lehring, *Officially Gay: The Political Construction of Sexuality by the U.S. Military* (Philadelphia: Temple University Press, 2003), 143.

44 David Rayside, *On the Fringe: Gays and Lesbians in Politics* (New York: Cambridge University Press, 1998), 219.

45 Francine D'Amico, "Sex/uality and Military Service," in *The Politics of Gay Rights*, Craig Rimmerman, Kenneth D. Wald, and Clyde Wilcox, eds., (Chicago: University of Chicago Press, 2000).

46 10 U.S.C. Section 654 (b)(1) (1994).

47 Ibid., Section 654(b)(2).

48 Ibid., Section 654(b)(3).

49 Dept. of Defense Directive No. 1304.26, encl. 1, Section B(8)(a).

50 Chai R. Feldblum, "The Federal Gay Rights Bill: From Bella to ENDA," in *Creating Change: Sexuality, Public Policy, and Civil Rights* (New York: St. Martin's, 2000), 175.

51 Tobias Barrington Wolff, "Political Representation and Accountability under Don't Ask, Don't Tell," *Iowa Law Review* 89 (2004): 1635–36.

52 Kenji Yoshino, "Assimilationist Bias in Equal Protection: The Visibility Presumption and the Case of 'Don't Ask, Don't Tell,'" *Yale Law Journal* 108 (3) (1998): 540.

53 *Romer v. Evans*, 517 U.S. 620 (1996), 627.

54 Ibid., 624.

55 Akhil Reed Amar, "Attainder and Amendment 2: *Romer's* Rightness," *Michigan Law Review* 95 (1996): 203–35.

56 *Plessy v. Ferguson*, 163 U. S. 537 (1896); *Romer v. Evans*, 517 U. S. 620 (1996), 623: One century ago, the first Justice Harlan admonished this Court that the Constitution "neither knows nor tolerates classes among citizens." *Plessy v. Ferguson*, 163 U. S. 537, 559 (1896) (dissenting opinion). Unheeded then, those words now are understood to state a commitment to the law's neutrality where the rights of persons are at stake. The Equal Protection Clause enforces this principle and today requires us to hold invalid a provision of Colorado's Constitution.

57 Although the Court invoked the error of *Plessy* and established sexuality as a status (like race) and not conduct, the race analogy did not compel the Court to apply explicitly a higher level of scrutiny when evaluating the Colorado constitutional amendment.

58 Robert H. Bork, *Slouching towards Gomorrah* (New York: Reagan Books, 1996); Ronald Dworkin, "Sex, Death, and the Courts," *New York Review of Books*, 8 August 1996, 48–50; Lino Graglia, "*Romer v. Evans*: The People Foiled Again by the Constitution," *University of Colorado Law Review* 68 (1997): 409–28; Thomas C. Grey, "*Bowers v. Hardwick* Diminished," *University of Colorado Law Review* 68 (1997): 373–86.

59 Klarman (2013), 68.

60 Note, however, that Gallup reports a slight dip in approval of homosexuality at the time of the *Romer* ruling; see figure 5.1.

61 Feldblum (2000).

62 See generally Mucciaroni (2008). As Mucciaroni writes, "The 'ick factor' reflects the taboo of gay sex, much of it fed by centuries of religious injunctions against sexual conduct between same-sex partners. Further normalizing gay relationships by legalizing their marriages, adoptions, and sexual behaviors may encourage gay couples to 'flaunt' their sexuality by engaging in public displays of affection" (23–24).

63 *Hurley v. Irish American Gay, Lesbian, and Bisexual Group of Boston*, 515 U.S. 557 (1995).

64 Ibid., 568, quoting S. Davis, *Parades and Power: Street Theatre in Nineteenth-Century Philadelphia* (Philadelphia: Temple University Press, 1986), 6.

65 Ibid., again quoting Davis (1986), 171.

66 Ibid., 561.

67 Ibid., 570.

68 Ibid., 574–75.

69 *Shelley v. Kraemer*, 334 U.S. 1 (1948), 13 ("Since the decision of this Court in the *Civil Rights Cases*, 109 U. S. 3 (1883), the principle has become firmly embedded in our constitutional law that the action inhibited by the first section of the Fourteenth Amendment is only such action as may fairly be said to be that of the States. That Amendment erects no shield against merely private conduct, however discriminatory or wrongful").

70 *Boy Scouts of America et al. v. Dale*, 530 U.S. 640 (2000). For detailed analysis of this case see Andrew Koppelman with Tobias Barrington Wolff, *A Right to Discriminate? How the Case of* Boy Scouts of America v. James Dale *Warped the Law of Free Association* (New Haven, CT: Yale University Press, 2009).

71 N. J. Stat. Ann. §§ 10:5–4 and 10:5–5 (West Supp. 2000).

72 *Dale v. Boy Scouts of America*, 734 A. 2d 1196 (1999); *Dale v. Boy Scouts of America*, 308 N.J. Super. 516 (1998).

73 Ibid., 653.

74 *Boy Scouts of America v. Dale*, 530 U.S. 640 (2000), 648.

75 Ibid., 649.

76 Ibid.

77 Ibid., 668.

78 Ibid., 651–52.

79 Ibid., 652.

80 Ibid.

81 Ibid., 653.

82 Ibid., 655–56.

83 Ibid., 666.

84 Ibid., 669.

85 Ibid., 670.

86 Ibid., 672.

87 Ibid., 675.

88 Ibid. Rulings against exclusionary membership policies include *Roberts v. United States Jaycees*, 468 U.S. 609 (1984) and *Board of Directors of Rotary Int'l v. Rotary Club of Duarte*, 481 U.S. 537 (1987).

89 Ibid., 676.

90 Ibid., 687.

91 Effective January 1, 2014, the BSA adopted a new membership guideline that no child may be denied membership in the BSA on the basis of sexual orientation alone.

92 Jason Pierceson, *Courts, Liberalism, and Rights: Gay Law and Politics in the United States and Canada* (Philadelphia: Temple University Press, 2005), 27.

93 David Eng, *The Feeling of Kinship: Queer Liberalism and the Racialization of Intimacy* (Durham, NC: Duke University Press, 2010), 17, 41; *Brown v. Board of Education*, 347 U.S. 483 (1954); *Loving v. Virginia*, 388 U.S. 1 (1967).

94 *Loving* contained an equal protection rationale and a due process fundamental rights rationale. The state law banning interracial marriage under review in *Loving* violated equal protection because the law only maintained white supremacy ("we reject the notion that the mere 'equal application' of a statute containing racial classifications is enough to remove the classifications from the Fourteenth Amendment's proscription of all invidious racial discriminations." *Loving v. Virginia*, 388 U.S. 1 [1967], 9). Additionally, as marriage constituted a fundamental right, the ban also violated a basic due process consideration ("These statutes also deprive the Lovings of liberty without due process of law in violation of the Due Process Clause of the Fourteenth Amendment. The freedom to marry has long been recognized as one of the vital personal rights essential to the orderly pursuit of happiness by free men. Marriage is one of the 'basic civil rights of man,' fundamental to our very existence and survival" [citations omitted], *Loving v. Virginia*, 388 U.S. 1 [1967], 13).

95 *Lawrence v. Texas*, 539 U.S. 558 (2003), 574–75.

96 Ibid., 575.

97 *Romer v. Evans*, 517 U. S. 620 (1996), 641.

98 Ibid.

99 See chapter 6 for further elaboration of suspect class and suspect classification.

100 Yoshino (2006), 188.

101 *Lawrence v. Texas*, 539 U. S. 558 (2003), 567.

102 Eng (2010), 24–25.

103 *Lawrence v. Texas*, 539 U. S. 558 (2003), 567.

104 Ibid., 578.

105 Alexander Bickel, *The Least Dangerous Branch: The Supreme Court at the Bar of Politics*, 2nd ed. (New Haven, CT: Yale University Press, 1986).

106 In *Federalist 78*, Hamilton characterizes the Court as "the least dangerous branch" since it lacks the executive's power of the sword and the legislature's power of the purse. It has "merely judgment." Gerald Rosenberg expands this "constrained Court" thesis in his *Hollow Hope: Can Courts Bring about Social Change?* 2nd ed. (Chicago: University of Chicago Press, 2008).

107 Erwin Chemerinsky called the countermajoritarian difficulty the "dominant paradigm of constitutional law and scholarship." See his "Supreme Court, 1988 Term—Foreword: The Vanishing Constitution," 103 *Harvard Law Review* 43 (1989): 61. On popular backlash against the Court see Klarman (2013) and Rosenberg (2008). On clashes between the Court and the elected branches see Charles Geyh, *When Courts and Congress Collide* (Ann Arbor: University of Michigan Press, 2006); and Stephen M. Engel, *American Politicians Confront the Court: Opposition Politics and Changing Responses to Judicial Power* (New York: Cambridge University Press, 2011).

108 See Mark A. Graber, "The Countermajoritarian Difficulty: From Courts to Congress to Constitutional Order," *Annual Review of Law and Social Science* 4 (2008): 361–84.

109 Robert Dahl, "Decision Making in a Democracy: The Supreme Court as a National Policy-Maker," *Journal of Public Law* 6 (1957), reprinted in the *Emory Law Journal* 50 (2001); Keith Whittington, *Political Foundations of Judicial Supremacy* (Princeton, NJ: Princeton University Press, 2007). For critical analysis and refutation of aspects of the regime thesis see Matthew E. K. Hall, "Rethinking Regime Politics," *Law & Social Inquiry* 37 (2012): 878–907.

110 Mark A. Graber, "The Nonmajoritarian Difficulty: Legislative Deference to the Judiciary," *Studies in American Political Development* 7 (Spring 1993): 35–73; George Lovell, *Legislative Deferrals: Statutory Ambiguity, Judicial Power, and American Democracy* (New York: Cambridge University Press, 2003); Howard Gillman, "How Political Parties Can Use the Courts to Advance Their Agendas: Federal Courts in the United States, 1875–1891," *American Political Science Review* 96 (September 2002): 511–24.

111 See Benjamin J. Rosech, "Crowd Control: The Majoritarian Court and the Reflection of Public Opinion in Doctrine," *Suffolk University Law Review* 39 (2006); Pamela S. Karlan, "The Supreme Court, 2011 Term—Foreword: Democracy and Disdain," *Harvard Law Review* 126 (2012); Neal Devins, "The Majoritarian Rehnquist Court?" *Law and Contemporary Problems* 67 (2004): 63–81; and, Barry Cushman, "Mr. Dooley and Mr. Gallup: Public Opinion and Constitutional Change in the 1930s," *Buffalo Law Review* 50 (2002): 7–102.

112 In an interview with Jeffrey Rosen, current Chief Justice John Roberts explicitly mentioned his objective to avoid backlash and maintain institutional legitimacy by attempting to avoid five-to-four rulings: "In Roberts's view, the most successful chief justices help their colleagues speak with one voice. Unanimous, or nearly unanimous, decisions are hard to overturn and contribute to the stability of the law and the continuity of the Court; by contrast, closely divided, 5-4 decisions make it harder for the public to respect the Court as an impartial institution that transcends partisan politics." Jeffrey Rose, "Robert's Rules," *Atlantic*, 1 January 2007.

113 Slip Opinion, *SmithKlineBeecham Corporation, DBA GlaxoSmithKline v. Abbott Laboratories* (issued on 21 January 2014), available at http://cdn.ca9.uscourts. gov/datastore/opinions/2014/01/20/11-17357.pdf; see also Adam Liptak, "Sexual Orientation Is No Basis for Jury Exclusion, a Federal Appeals Court Rules," *New York Times*, 21 January 2014, http://www.nytimes.com/2014/01/22/us/sexual-orientation-is-no-basis-for-jury-exclusion-a-federal-appeals-court-rules.html.

114 Clifford Geertz, *The Interpretations of Cultures: Selected Essays* (New York: Basic Books, 1973), 275; see also William N. Eskridge Jr., "Pluralism and Distrust: How Courts Can Support Democracy by Lowering the Stakes of Politics," *Yale Law Journal* 114 (2005): 1279–1328.

115 Paul Frymer, *Black and Blue: African Americans, the Labor Movement, and the Decline of the Democratic Party* (Princeton, NJ: Princeton University Press, 2008), 103.

116 Ibid., 105.

117 Deborah Stone, *Policy Paradox: The Art of Political Decision Making*, rev. ed. (New York: Norton, 2002), 381.

118 Karen Orren and Stephen Skowronek, *The Search for American Political Development* (New York: Cambridge University Press, 2004), 123.

119 See Brian J. Glenn, "The Two Schools of American Political Development," *Political Studies Review* 2 (2004): 153–65; and Robert Lieberman, "Ideas, Institutions, and Political Order: Explaining Political Change," *American Political Science Review* 96 (December 2002): 697–712.

CHAPTER 6. A HISTORY OF DISCRIMINATION

1 Letter from Attorney General to Congress on Litigation Involving the Defense of Marriage Act, 23 February 2011, *U.S. Department of Justice*, www.justice.gov/opa/pr/2011/February/11-ag-223.html (accessed 4 October 2013).

2 *SmithKline Beecham Corporation, DBA GlaxoSmithKline v. Abbott Laboratories*, No. 11-17357 (2014) 17, 19.

3 Jonathan Kaminsky, "Nevada Ends Fight to Ban Gay Marriage, Cites Changed Landscape," *Reuters.com*, 10 February 2014, http://www.reuters.com/article/2014/02/11/us-usa-nevada-gaymarriage-idUSBREA1A01F20140211 (accessed 11 February 2014).

4 *SmithKline Beecham Corp. v. Abbott Laboratories*, 740 F. 3d 471—Court of Appeals, 9th Circuit 2014.

5 This three-pronged test for the application of heightened scrutiny was articulated by the Supreme Court in *Bowen v. Gilliard*, 483 U.S. 587 (1987), 602–3. See Sonu Bedi, *Beyond Race, Sex, and Sexual Orientation: Legal Equality without Identity* (New York: Cambridge University Press, 2013) for a summary of this doctrine.

6 For a review of the development of the tiers of scrutiny framework as it applies to suspect classes for the purposes of Fourteenth Amendment equal protection consideration, see Richard H. Fallon Jr., *The Dynamic Constitution: An Introduction to American Constitutional Law and Practice*, 2nd ed. (New York: Cambridge University Press, 2013), 139–89.

7 Strict scrutiny is not always fatal to a statute. According to legal historian William Wiecek,

> Before the Reagan administration's assault on the achievements of the civil rights era, lawyers believed that strict scrutiny was always fatal to the statute or government practice if race was involved. And so it was—with the one troubling exception of *Korematsu*. Among the many lessons the case provides is the reminder that strict scrutiny is not necessarily fatal. This has enabled Justice Sandra Day O'Connor to impose a legal standard of strict scrutiny on state and federal affirmative action programs while maintaining that the Court was not necessarily condemning all efforts to overcome the effects of racial oppression (citations omitted).

William M. Wiecek, *The History of the Supreme Court*, Volume 12, *The Birth of the Modern Constitution: The United States Supreme Court, 1941–1953* (New York: Cambridge University Press, 2006), 358.

8 See Susan Gluck Mezey, *Queers in Court: Gay Rights Law and Public Policy* (Lanham, MD: Rowman & Littlefield, 2007). Eric Roberts argues that gays and lesbians qualify for suspect-class status under the three-pronged test articulated in *Bowen v. Gilliard*. See Eric A. Roberts, "Heightened Scrutiny under the Equal Protection Clause: A Remedy to Discrimination Based on Sexual Orientation," *Drake Law Review* 42 (1993): 496–97. See also Jeremy B. Smith, "The Flaws of Rational Basis with Bite: Why the Supreme Court Should Acknowledge Its Application of Heightened Scrutiny to Classifications Based on Sexual Orientation," *Fordham Law Review* 73 (2004–2005).

9 *United States v. Windsor*, 570 U.S. ___ (2013) (Docket No. 12-307).

10 As this chapter will argue, that tradition began with *Romer v. Evans*, 517 U.S. 620 (1996).

11 Media commentators and legal scholars were frustrated with the ruling's muddled language and lack of clarity on just how the Court majority evaluated DOMA. One called it "analytically unsatisfactory," yielding an "unstable solution"; another referred to it as "blather." See, for example, Andrew Sullivan, "The Method in Kennedy's Muddle," *Dish*, 27 June 2013, http://dish.andrewsullivan.com/2013/06/27/the-method-in-kennedys-muddle/ (accessed 11 February 2013); see also Michael McConnell, "Debating the Court's Gay Marriage Decisions," *New Republic*, 26 June 2013 ("I believe Justice Kennedy wrote the opinion the way he did because he was not prepared to impose a single answer on the entire nation, but he was not persuaded by the federalism argument. Well enough; he succeeded. But the analytically unsatisfactory nature of this holding renders it an unstable solution"); see also Sandy Levinson, "A Brief Comment on Justice Kennedy's Opinion in *Windsor*," *Balkinization*, 26 June 2012, http://balkin.blogspot.com/2013/06/a-brief-comment-on-justice-kennedys.html (accessed 11 February 2014):

> Already there is some of the same kind of nit-picking about the doctrinal problems with *Windsor* as there most certainly were [*sic*] with *Romer*, i.e., Kennedy wants to avoid a straight-forward equality argument that would inevitably mean that state prohibitions of same sex marriage are unconstitutional. . . . At the same time he no doubt realized that he couldn't get a single additional vote if he predicated the opinion on a "reserved powers of the state to define marriage" argument, though he certainly included some blather about traditional state sovereignty and marriage. So we get the combo that leaves many people who take legal doctrine overly seriously confused (though I presume we all predict that some time in the future the Court will go after the now-outlier states that are sticking to heterosexual marriage as the exclusive norm).

12 See Nancy F. Cott, *Public Vows: A History of Marriage and Nation* (Cambridge, MA: Harvard University Press, 2000); and Priscilla Yamin, *American Marriage: A Political Institution* (Philadelphia: University of Pennsylvania Press, 2012).

13 Amy L. Brandzel, "Queering Citizenship? Same-Sex Marriage and the State," *GLQ: A Journal of Lesbian and Gay Studies* 11 (2): 172.

14 Ibid., 194.

15 Michael Warner, "Introduction," in *Fear of a Queer Planet: Queer Politics and Social Theory*, Michael Warner, ed. (Minneapolis: University of Minnesota Press, 1993), xix. This book does not engage the normative debate as to whether gays and lesbians should seek marriage. See, for example, J. Jack Halberstam, *Gaga Feminism: Sex, Gender, and the End of Normal* (Boston: Beacon, 2012). If marriage is a tool of state power, and if queer activism is aimed at destabilizing the institutions that maintain that power, then it follows that marriage would not be a queer objective. On the other hand, marriage might be queered insofar as it might involve different conceptions of love. Historically, marriage has been pursued as a goal since at least the 1950s, with active reflection by gays and lesbians on whether same-sex marriage fundamentally alters rather than just expands the institution. See Julie R. Enszer, "'Whatever Happens, This Is': Lesbians Engaging Marriage," *WSQ: Women's Studies Quarterly* 41 (3 & 4) (Fall/Winter 2013): 220–21.

16 For another discussion of the role of state attorneys general as creatively shaping state policy see Paul Nolette, "Litigating the 'Public Interest' in the Gilded Age: Common Law Business Regulation by Nineteenth-Century State Attorneys General," *Polity* 44 (July 2012): 373–99.

17 William J. Novak, "A State of Legislatures," *Polity* 40 (2008): 341.

18 Myles Snyder, "Auditor: Pa. Wasting Money on Same-Sex Marriage Fight," *WHTM, ABC News 27*, 8 May 2014, http://www.abc27.com/story/25466755/auditor-pa-wasting-money-on-same-sex-marriage-fight (accessed 19 May 2014).

19 DePasquale quoted in ibid.

20 Ibid. Emphasis added.

21 See Louis Fisher, *Constitutional Dialogues: Interpretation as Political Process* (Princeton, NJ: Princeton University Press, 1988).

22 *Marbury v. Madison*, 5 U.S. 137 (1803), 177.

23 *Cooper v. Aaron*, 538 U.S. 1 (1958), 18.

24 On popular antijudicial protest see Richard Ellis, *The Jeffersonian Crisis: Courts and Politics in the Young Republic* (New York: Oxford University Press, 1971); and William Ross, *A Muted Fury: Populists, Progressives, and Labor Unions Confront the Courts, 1890–1937* (Princeton, NJ: Princeton University Press, 1993); for a brief review of judicial supremacy, legislative supremacy, and presidential claims to constitutional interpretation, see Walter F. Murphy, "Who Shall Interpret? The Quest for the Ultimate Constitutional Interpreter," *Review of Politics* 48 (Summer 1986): 401–23.

25 According to Robert Bork, judicial supremacy stands for the idea that when the Supreme Court rules, "whether legitimately or not, as to that issue the democratic process is at an end." Robert Bork, *The Tempting of America* (New York: Free Press, 1993), 199. On departmentalism see Susan Burgess, *Contest for Constitutional Authority: The Abortion and War Powers Debates* (Lawrence: University Press of Kansas, 1992).

26 Keith Whittington, *Political Foundations of Judicial Supremacy* (Princeton, NJ: Princeton University Press, 2007).

27 Edwin Meese, "The Law of the Constitution," *Tulane Law Review* 61 (1987).

28 See Stephen M. Engel, *American Politicians Confront the Court: Opposition Politics and Changing Responses to Judicial Power* (New York: Cambridge University Press, 2011), 348–54.

29 Keith Whittington, "Extrajudicial Constitutional Interpretation: Three Objections and Responses," *North Carolina Law Review* (2002): 776–77.

30 Ibid.

31 Ibid. Emphasis added.

32 On executive refusals to defend existing statute, see Neal Devins and Saikrishna B. Prakash, "The Indefensible Duty to Defend," *Columbia Law Review* 112 (2012): 507–77 (supporting Obama's refusal to defend but not his commitment to continue to enforce DOMA); Stacy Pepper, "The Defenseless Marriage Act: The Legitimacy of President Obama's Refusal to Defend DOMA's Section 3," *Stanford Law & Policy Review* 24 (1) (2013): 1–34 (arguing that Obama's refusal to defend is both unconstitutional and normatively undesirable); and Carlos A. Ball, "When May a President Refuse to Defend a Statute: The Obama Administration and DOMA," *Northwestern University Law Review Colloquy* 106 (2011): 77–95 (defending a contextual approach for evaluating when a president may appropriately refuse to defend a statute).

33 *Lockyer v. City & County of S.F.*, 95 P.3d 459, 465 (Cal. 2004).

34 Shaila Dewan, "Awaiting a Big Day, and Recalling One in New Paltz," *New York Times*, 19 June 2011.

35 "Oregon County Issues Same-Sex Marriage Licenses," *CNN.com*, 3 March 2004, http://www.cnn.com/2004/US/West/03/03/same.sex.marriage/ (accessed 20 May 2014).

36 *Lockyer*, 95 P.3d at 467.

37 Newsom's letter is quoted in *Lockyer v. City & County of S.F.*, 95 P.3d 459, 465 (Cal. 2004).

38 "President Jackson's Veto Message Regarding the Bank of the United States; July 10, 1832," *Avalon Project: Documents in Law, History, and Diplomacy*, Yale University.

39 Ibid.

40 Newsom, 10 February 2004, quoted in *Lockyer v. City & County of S.F.*, 95 P.3d 459, 465 (Cal. 2004).

41 Robert Sullivan, "Mayor with a Mission," *New York Times*, 28 March 2004.

42 Sylvia A. Law, "Who Gets to Interpret the Constitution? The Case of Mayors and Marriage Equality," *Stanford Journal of Civil Rights & Civil Liberties* 3 (2007): 15.

43 Ibid., 22–27.

44 Memorandum from Agnes Sowle, County Attorney, Multnomah County, to Diane Linn, Chair, Multnomah County 2, 2 March 2004, quoted in Law (2007), 22.

45 The county attorney argued that not granting marriage licenses to same-sex couples violated Article I, Section 20 of the Oregon Constitution, which states, "no law shall be passed granting to any citizen or class of citizens privileges, or immunities, which, upon the same terms, shall not equally belong to all citizens." The county attorney memo cited *Tanner v. Oregon Health & Sciences University*, 871 P. 2d 435 (Or. Ct. App. 1998). See Law (2007), 23, fn. 128.

46 Dawn E. Johnsen, "Presidential Non-Enforcement of Constitutionally Objectionable Statutes," *Law & Contemporary Problems* 63 (2000): 22.

47 Johnsen's criteria are developed in the context of presidential action. Law applies them to mayoral action in Law (2007). For Johnson's criteria see ibid. See also Dawn E. Johnsen, "Functional Departmentalism and Nonjudicial Function: Who Determines Constitutional Meaning?" *Law & Contemporary Problems* 67 (2005); and Dawn E. Johnsen, "The Obama Administration's Decision to Defend Constitutional Equality Rather Than the Defense of Marriage Act," *Fordham Law Review* 81 (2012).

48 Law (2007), 37.

49 On Johnsen's disagreement with Law, see Law (2007), 37. For Johnsen's defense of Obama see Johnsen (2012).

50 Marty Lederman, "John Roberts and the SG's Refusal to Defend Federal Statutes in *Metro Broadcasting v. FCC*," *Balkinization*, 8 September 2005, http://balkin.blogspot.com/2005/09/john-roberts-and-sgs-refusal-to-defend.html (accessed 20 May 2014).

51 Johnsen (2012), 610.

52 For an argument as to why BLAG should not have been granted standing see Matthew I. Hall, "How Congress Could Defend DOMA in Court (and Why the BLAG Cannot)," *Stanford Law Review* 65 (January 2013).

53 Johnsen (2012), 610–11.

54 Niraj Choksi, "Seven Attorneys General Won't Defend Their Own State's Gay-Marriage Bans," *Washington Post*, 20 February 2014.

55 Holder quoted in Matt Apuzzo, "Holder Sees Way to Curb Bans on Gay Marriage," *New York Times*, 24 February 2014. On Holder's contention that these laws be held to the highest scrutiny by AGs, see Associated Press, "Eric Holder: State Attorney Generals Not Obligated to Defend Gay Marriage Bans," *Guardian*, 25 February 2014.

56 "Attorney General Herring Changes Virginia's Legal Position in Marriage Equality Case," *Virginia.gov: Office of the Attorney General*, 23 January 2014, http://www.oag.state.va.us/Media%20and%20News%20Releases/News_Releases/Herring/012314_Bostic_v_Rainey.html (accessed 20 May 2014).

57 "Attorney General Kamala D. Harris Issues Statement on Prop. 8 Arguments," *State of California Department of Justice: Office of the Attorney General*, 26 March

2013, http://oag.ca.gov/news/press-releases/attorney-general-kamala-d-harris-issues-statement-prop-8-arguments (accessed 20 May 2014).

58 Illinois Attorney General Lisa Madigan, 1 June 2012, quoted in Choksi (2014).

59 "Attorney General Kane Will Not Defend DOMA," *Pennsylvania Office of the Attorney General*, 11 July 2013, http://www.attorneygeneral.gov/press.aspx?id=7043 (accessed 20 May 2014).

60 John W. Suthers, "A 'Veto' Attorneys General Shouldn't Wield," *Washington Post*, 2 February 2014.

61 *In re Marriage Cases*, 43 Cal.4th 757 (2008).

62 The Hawaii Court did not hold that there exists a right to same-sex marriage or that this right must be afforded the plaintiffs. It ruled only that should the state want to sustain its current policy of refusing marriage licenses to same-sex couples, it must demonstrate a compelling interest to do so. *Baehr v. Lewin*, 842 P.2d 44 (Hawaii 1993), 66–67.

63 See *Richard John Baker v. Gerald R. Nelson*, 291 Minn. 310, 191 N.W.2d 185 (1971); *Jones v. Hallahan*, 501 S.W.2d 588 (1973); *Singer v. Hara*, 11 Wash.App.247, 522 P. 2d 1187 (1974).

64 Judge James Burns discussed sexual orientation in a short concurrence in which he contended that there must be a finding of fact that sexual orientation is "biologically fated," such that sex would then include sexual orientation. If it were not traceable to biology, Burns contended, "then each person's 'sex' does not include the sexual orientation difference, and the Hawaii constitution may permit the State to encourage heterosexuality and discourage homosexuality, bisexuality, and asexuality by permitting opposite-sex Hawaii Civil Law Marriages and not permitting same-sex Hawaii Civil Law Marriages." Of course, sexual orientation remains subsumed as a characteristic of sex difference rather than a trait wholly distinct from sex, and thus the treatment of sexual orientation by this concurrence is not an evaluation of sexual orientation as a distinct suspect classification. *Baehr v. Lewin*, 842 P.2d 44 (Hawaii 1993), 70 (Burns concurring).

65 *Maynard v. Hill*, 125 U.S. 190,8 S. Ct. 723,31 L. Ed. 654 (1888), 726, 729.

66 *Meyer v. Nebraska*, 262 U.S. 390 (1923).

67 *Skinner v. State of Oklahoma, ex. rel. Williamson*, 316 U.S. 535 (1942).

68 Ibid., 542.

69 *Zablocki v. Redhail*, 434 U.S. 374 (1978).

70 *Baehr v. Lewin*, 842 P.2d 44 (Hawaii 1993), 56.

71 Ibid., 55–57.

72 Ibid., 58.

73 Ibid., 49.

74 Ibid., 52.

75 Ibid.

76 Ibid., 65.

77 Ibid.

78 *Frontiero v. Richardson*, 411 U.S. 677 (1973).

79 *Baehr v. Lewin*, 842 P.2d 44 (Hawaii 1993), 66–67.

80 Andrew Koppelman, "Why Discrimination against Lesbians and Gay Men Is Sex Discrimination," *New York University Law Review* 69 (May 1994): 203.

81 Cheshire Calhoun, "Separating Lesbian Theory from Feminist Theory," *Ethics* (1994): 562.

82 Edward Stein, "Evaluating the Sex Discrimination Argument for Lesbian and Gay Rights," *UCLA Law Review* (2001): 499.

83 Ibid., 499–500.

84 *Baker v. Vermont*, 744 A.2d 864 (Vt. 1999).

85 Ibid., 875.

86 Ibid., 870.

87 Ibid., 878.

88 Ibid.

89 Ibid., 879.

90 Ibid., citing *Washington v. Glucksburg*, 521 U.S. 702 (1997) (Souter concurring), 767 quoting *Poe v. Ullman*, 367 U.S. 497 (1961) (Harlan dissenting), 542.

91 *Baker v. Vermont*, 744 A.2d 864 (Vt. 1999) (Dooley concurring), 897.

92 Ibid., 890.

93 Ibid., 893.

94 Ibid., 891.

95 Ibid., 896.

96 Ibid.

97 *Baker v. Vermont*, 744 A.2d 864 (Vt. 1999) (Johnson concurring), 898.

98 Ibid., 905.

99 Ibid.

100 Ibid., 906. *Craig v. Boren*, 429 U.S. 190 (1976).

101 *Goodridge v. Department of Public Health,* 440 Mass. 309—Mass: Supreme Judicial Court (2003).

102 Ibid., 313.

103 Ibid., 312.

104 Ibid., 330 (citations omitted).

105 Ibid.

106 Ibid., 319–20, 331.

107 Ibid., 331.

108 Ibid., 344, 345 (Greaney concurring).

109 Ibid., 348–49 (Greaney concurring, citations omitted).

110 *Lewis v. Harris*, 188 N.J. 415, 908 A. 2d 196 (2006).

111 Ibid. (slip opinion, 5).

112 Ibid., 33.

113 *Goodridge v. Department of Public Health*, 440 Mass. 309—Mass: Supreme Judicial Court (2003), 331; *Lewis v. Harris*, 188 N.J. 415, 908 A. 2d 196 (2006) (slip opinion, 48–49).

114 Ibid., 37–43.

115 Ibid., 49.

116 Ibid. (Poritz concurring, 3).

117 Ibid.

118 Ibid., 7 quoting Martha Minnow, *Making All the Difference: Inclusion, Exclusion, and American Law* (Ithaca, NY: Cornell University Press, 1990), 4, 6.

119 Indeed, the claim against labels can be carried further. Suspect class requires labeling; it requires distinguishing groups of people as different as a matter of history, power, and democratic standing. It thereby has the potential to, as Sonu Bedi contends, reinscribe the oppression it seeks to compensate for and ultimately eradicate. Poritz's concern with labeling leads toward an anticlassification scheme, which follows from both his and Justice Kennedy's reduction of the questions before their Courts as fundamental matters of human dignity.

120 *Hernandez v. Robles*, 855 N.E.2d 1 (N.Y. 2006).

121 Ibid., 7.

122 *Lewis v. Harris*, 188 N.J. 415, 908 A. 2d 196 (2006) (slip opinion, 47).

123 *Hernandez v. Robles*, 855 N.E.2d 1 (N.Y. 2006), 7.

124 Ibid.

125 Ibid.

126 *Williamson v. Lee Optical, Inc.*, 348 U.S. 483 (1955), 488–89.

127 See, for example, Maura Dolan, "Gay Marriage Ban Overturned," *Los Angeles Times*, 17 May 2008 ("The California Supreme Court struck down the state's ban on same-sex marriage Thursday in a broadly worded decision that would invalidate virtually any law that discriminates on the basis of sexual orientation.").

128 *In re Marriage Cases*, 43 Cal.4th 757 (2008) (slip opinion, 3).

129 Ibid., 4–6; *Perez v. Sharp*, 32 Cal.2d 711, 198 P.2d 17 (1948).

130 Ibid., 6.

131 Ibid., 52.

132 Ibid., 63.

133 Ibid., 10.

134 Ibid.

135 Ibid., 11.

136 *Kerrigan v. Commissioner of Public Health*, 289 Conn. 135, 957 A.2d 407.

137 Ibid. (slip opinion, 10).

138 Ibid., 22–48.

139 Ibid., 27.

140 Ibid., 28.

141 Ibid.

142 *Varnum v. Brien*, 763 N.W.2d 862 (Iowa 2009).

143 On determination of suspect class and application of heightened scrutiny, see ibid., 889–98. The state's rationales for restricting marriage to cross-sex couples included (1) maintaining the definition of traditional marriage, (2) promoting an optimal environment in which to raise children, (3) promoting procreation, (4) promoting stability in opposite-sex relationships, and (5) conservation of fiscal resources. Ibid., 899–904.

144 Ibid., 885. Emphasis added.

145 *Perry v. Schwarzenegger*, 704 F.Supp.2d 921 (N. Dis. CA 2010).

146 Ibid. (slip opinion, 113).

147 Ibid., 119.

148 Ibid., 120.

149 Ibid., 121.

150 *Perry v. Brown*, 134 Cal. Rptr. 3d 499 (2011).

151 Ibid. (slip opinion, 5).

152 Ibid., 7.

153 Ibid., 33.

154 Ibid., 44.

155 Ibid.

156 Ibid., 45.

157 Ibid., 5.

158 Ibid., 34.

159 See, for example, James Taranto, "The Ball Heads for His Court: Same-Sex Marriage Looks Like a Sure Thing, at Least for California," *Wall Street Journal*, 7 February 2012 (predicting, "The court will not find a constitutional right to same-sex marriage in this case, but it will strike down Proposition 8 and thereby reimpose same-sex marriage in California. Reinhard's decision lays out a way in which Justice Kennedy can do so—and indeed makes it very difficult for Kennedy to uphold Proposition 8.")

160 *Hollingsworth v. Perry*, 570 U.S. ___ (2013) (Docket No. 12-144).

161 Writing for the majority, Chief Justice John Roberts contended, "We have never before upheld the standing of a private party to defend the constitutionality of a state statute when state officials have chosen not to. We decline to do so for the first time here." *Hollingsworth v. Perry*, 570 U.S. ___ (2013), 17. He maintained that only agents of the State of California could appeal the Ninth Circuit's ruling. Since no constituted governing body would defend Proposition 8 before the bench, the Court's denial of standing meant that the Circuit ruling was upheld.

162 *United States v. Windsor*, 570 U.S. ____ (2013).

163 Ibid., 22.

164 This count is taken from "Marriage Rulings in the Court," *Freedom to Marry*, http://www.freedomtomarry.org/pages/marriage-rulings-in-the-courts (accessed 10 November 2014).

165 *Borman v. Pyles-Borman* (2014), Circuit Court for Roane County, Tennessee (No.2014CV36); *Robicheaux, et al. v. Caldwell, et al.* (2014), U.S. District Court, Eastern District of Louisiana (No. 13-5090 C/W, No. 14-97, and No. 14-327); *Conde-Vidal, et al. v. Garcia-Padilla, et al.* (2014), U.S. District Court, District of Puerto Rico (No. 14-1253 [PG]); *DeBoar v. Snyder* (2014), U.S. Court of Appeals for the Sixth Circuit (Nos. 14-1341; 3057; 3464; 5291; 5297; 5818), all slip opinions.

166 *Kitchen et al. v. Herbert et al.*, Case No. 2:13-cv-217 (filed 20 December 2013) (slip opinion).

167 Ibid., 13.

168 Ibid., 30.

169 Ibid., 31.

170 Ibid., 32.

171 *Kitchen et al. v. Herbert et al.*, Case No. 13-4178. United States Tenth Circuit Court of Appeals (filed 25 June 2014) (slip opinion), J. Lucero ruling for the Court, *United States Court of Appeals for the Tenth Circuit*, https://www.ca10.uscourts. gov/opinions/13/13-4178.pdf (accessed 26 June 2014), 7.

172 The majority held that the Fourteenth Amendment protects the fundamental right to marry. Thus, the holding related only to the Fourteenth Amendment's due process clause; the mention of discrimination by sex constituted an equal protection violation, but nowhere did the majority engage in any close analysis of sex-based classifications as subject to intermediate scrutiny.

173 Kitchen quoting *Planned Parenthood v. Casey*, 505 U.S. 833, 846–47 (1992), 23.

174 Ibid., 23, 35.

175 Ibid., 40–41.

176 Ibid., 31, 33.

177 *Obergefell v. Hodges*, 576 U.S. _____ (2015)

CHAPTER 7. A JURISPRUDENCE OF BLINDNESS

1 *United States v. Windsor*, 570 U. S. _____ (2013), Scalia dissenting, 16–17. Citations omitted.

2 *M. Kendall Wright, et al. v. State of Arkansas, et al.* (Circuit Court of Pulaski, Arkansas, Second Division, Case No: 60CV-13-2662) (2014), 11.

3 *Obergefell v. Hodges*, 576 U.S. _____ (2015), Roberts dissenting, 23. Citations omitted.

4 *Bowers v. Hardwick*, 478 U.S. 186 (1986); *Romer v. Evans*, 517 U.S. 620 (1996); *Lawrence v. Texas*, 539 U.S. 558 (2003); *United States v. Windsor*, 570 U.S. ____ (2013) (Docket No. 12-307).

5 *Windsor's* singular focus on homosexuality as expressed through a coupled relationship has led some scholars to question whether the Court's move erases the gay or lesbian as an individual identity. See Noa Ben-Asher, "Conferring Dignity: The Metamorphosis of the Legal Homosexual," *Harvard Journal of Law and Gender* 37 (2) (2014).

6 Some legal scholars suggest that *Romer* raised the scrutiny level above rational basis but not quite to the tier of intermediate or heightened scrutiny. In so doing, *Romer* allegedly muddled the meaning of rational basis review. See Louis D. Bilionis, "The New Scrutiny," *Emory Law Journal* 51 (2002): 489–90 (noting how in *Romer*, "the linchpin of the Court's opinion was its identification of novel per se equal protection violation that allowed it to withhold the deferential courtesies traditionally associated with the rational basis test without fuller explanation"). See also Neelum J. Wadhwahni, "Rational Reviews, Irrational Results," *Texas Law Review* 84 (2005–2006): 808–9 ("Many commentators point out that there are ac-

tually two levels of rational basis review: good old-fashioned, deferential rational basis review and a more demanding heightened version—one with 'teeth'").

7 David Eng, *The Feeling of Kinship: Queer Liberalism and the Racialization of Intimacy* (Durham, NC: Duke University Press, 2010), 3, 2.

8 Muddled doctrine is hardly rare. State action doctrine, or the claim that the Fourteenth Amendment's requirements of equal protection and due process apply only to state action, with vague exceptions for private actors who serve a public function (see *Smith v. Allwright*, 321 U.S. 649 [1944], which held that elections are a public activity even if their operation is implemented by private party organization) and for state involvement extensively entangled with a private action, such as a neighborhood covenant (see *Shelley v. Kraemer*, 334 U.S. 1 [1948]) that must be enforced by state actors, has been called "a conceptual disaster area" and "a murky borderland of law." See Charles L. Black Jr., "The Supreme Court, 1966 Term—Foreword: 'State Action,' Equal Protection, and California's Proposition 14," *Harvard Law Review* 81 (1967): 95; and Paul Freund, "The 'State Action' Problem," *Proceedings of the American Philosophical Association* 135 (March 1991): 5. For an evaluation of how such murkiness develops see Christopher W. Schmidt, "On Doctrinal Confusion: The Case of the State Action Doctrine," unpublished essay on file with author.

9 *United States v. Carolene Products Company*, 304 U.S. 144 (1938).

10 Or Bassok, "The Supreme Court's New Source of Legitimacy," *Journal of Constitutional Law* 16 (October 2013): 168. As Bassok notes, such theories are hardly permanent, and the Court has "switched its legitimation theory several times over the years."

11 Ibid., 169, citing Thurman W. Arnold, *The Symbols of Government* (New Haven, CT: Yale University Press, 1935) ("Institutions . . . develop institutional habits, entirely separate from the personal habits of those who spend their working hours in their service" [xiv]).

12 Howard Gillman, "The Collapse of Constitutional Originalism and the Rise of the Notion of the 'Living Constitution' in the Course of American State-Building," *Studies in American Political Development* 11 (Fall 1997): 191–247. See also Johnathan O'Neill, *Originalism in American Law and Politics: A Constitutional History* (Baltimore, MD: Johns Hopkins University Press, 2005). For an assessment of the formalist-realist divide as far more porous and balanced than usually acknowledged, see Brian Z. Tamanaha, *Beyond the Formalist-Realist Divide: The Role of Politics in Judging* (Princeton, NJ: Princeton University Press, 2009).

13 See Stephen Skowronek, "The Reassociation of Ideas and Purposes: Racism, Liberalism, and the American Political Tradition," *American Political Science Review* 100 (3) (August 2006).

14 William G. Ross, *A Muted Fury: Populists, Progressives, and Labor Unions Confront the Court, 1890–1937* (Princeton, NJ: Princeton University Press, 1993).

15 William E. Leuchtenburg, *The Supreme Court Reborn: The Constitutional Revolution in the Age of Roosevelt* (New York: Oxford University Press, 1996); Jeff Shesol,

Supreme Power: Franklin Roosevelt vs. the Supreme Court (New York: Norton, 2010), and *Burt Solomon: FDR v. the Constitution: The Court-Packing Fight and the Triumph of Democracy* (New York: Walker, 2009). While the Court upheld some state legislation meant to mitigate the effects of the Great Depression, it struck down most federal measures that were part of the New Deal between 1934 and 1935.

16 Oliver Wendell Holmes Jr., *Collected Legal Papers* (New York: Harcourt, Brace, and Howe, 1920), 239.

17 Charles Beard, "The Living Constitution," *Annals of the American Academy of Political and Social Science* (May 1936), quoted in G. Edward White, *The Constitution and the New Deal* (Cambridge, MA: Harvard University Press, 2000), 216.

18 John Henry Schlegel, *American Legal Realism and Empirical Social Science* (Chapel Hill: University of North Carolina Press, 2011); Howard Gillman, "The Collapse of Constitutional Originalism and the Rise of the Notion of the 'Living Constitution' in the Course of American State-Building," *Studies in American Political Development* 11 (September 1997).

19 Justin Zaremby, *Legal Realism and American Law* (New York: Bloomsbury Academic, 2013).

20 Howard Lee McBain, *The Living Constitution* (New York: Macmillan, 1928), 2.

21 Ibid., 3.

22 Reconstituting milk with vegetable or coconut oils preserved the milk without refrigeration. Carolene Products was indicted in 1935 under the Filled Milk Act of 1923, which banned the interstate sale of any substance "in imitation or semblance of milk, cream, or skimmed milk" (c. 262, 42 Stat. 1486, 21 U.S.C. §§ 61–63).

23 *United States v. Carolene Products Co.*, 304 U.S. 144 (1938), 153.

24 Ibid., 152–53, n. 4 (citations omitted).

25 Louis Lusky, "Footnote Redux: A 'Carolene Products' Reminiscence," *Columbia Law Review* (October 1982): 1105.

26 This chapter is agnostic as to whether the impulse of footnote four describes how the Court has actually operated since it was drafted. Lucas A. Powe Jr. contends that the footnote, while elaborating a principle that the judiciary must oversee legitimate democratic processes, in no way captures what animated Supreme Court rulings since. L. A. Powe Jr., "Does Footnote Four Describe?" *Constitutional Commentary* 11 (1994): 197.

27 Democratic justice would require that when the cost of exit is high, voice is guaranteed, or when voice is not permitted, the barriers to exit are not high. See generally, Albert O. Hirschman, *Exit, Voice, and Loyalty: Responses to Decline in Firms, Organizations, and States* (Cambridge, MA: Harvard University Press, 1970); and Ian Shapiro, *Democratic Justice* (New Haven, CT: Yale University Press, 1999).

28 John Hart Ely, *Democracy and Distrust* (Cambridge, MA: Harvard University Press, 1980).

29 Ibid., 102.

30 Some scholars suggest that the Court exists to protect rights. Others contend that the Court should be originalist and embrace a position as experts on constitu-

tional history. Still others, like Ely, contend that judicial legitimacy rests in the Court's protection of process rather than in its defense of substantive claims. On rights protection see Martin Shapiro, "The United States," in *The Global Expansion of Judicial Power*, C. Neal Tate and Torbjorn Vallinder, eds. (Baltimore, MD: Johns Hopkins University Press, 1995), 46–47, noting, "The expansion of judicial power in the United States, and perhaps even worldwide, is essentially associated today with the great movement toward judicial protection of human rights." On judges as being expert constitutional historians, see Or Bassok, "The Two Countermajoritarian Difficulties," *Saint Louis University Public Law Review* 31 (2012). On process-based arguments for the Court's legitimacy see Ely (1980) and Samuel Estreicher, "Platonic Guardians of Democracy: John Hart Ely's Role for the Supreme Court in the Constitution's Open Texture," *New York University Law Review* 56 (1981).

31 In his elaboration of judicial legitimacy theories, Bassok writes, "My argument is not that certain Justices consciously adopted a certain legitimation theory, but how the Court and other institutions behaved." Bassok (2013), 168–69.

32 See Bruce Ackerman, "Beyond *Carolene Products*," *Harvard Law Review* (February 1985): 713–46.

33 On anticlassification versus antisubordination principles of the Fourteenth Amendment, see Jack M. Balkin and Reva Siegel, "The American Civil Rights Tradition: Anticlassification or Antisubordination," *University of Miami Law Review* 58 (2003): 9–14. For discussion of the anticlassification versus antisubordination debate as exemplified in the *Parents Involved* (2007) ruling and dissent, see Jonathan L. Entin, "*Parents Involved* and the Meaning of *Brown*: An Old Debate Renewed," *Seattle University Law Review* 31 (2008).

34 Mary Kathryn Nagle, "*Parents Involved* and the Myth of the Colorblind Constitution," *Harvard Journal of Racial and Ethnic Justice* 26 (2010) ("Together the plurality and Justice Thomas, in his concurrence, put forth a strict application of the anti-classification principle, advocating a contemporary colorblind view of the Constitution" [215–16]).

35 *Parents Involved v. Seattle School District No. 1*, 551 U.S. 701, 703 n14, 748 (2007).

36 *Plessy v. Ferguson*, 163 U.S. 537 (1896), 559 (Harlan dissenting).

37 *Brown v. Board of Education*, 347 U.S. 483 (1954).

38 *Parents Involved v. Seattle School District No. 1*, 551 U.S. 701 (2007), 772 (Thomas concurring) (citing *Plessy v. Ferguson*, 163 U.S. 537 [1896], 559 [Harlan dissenting]) (other internal citations omitted).

39 See Andrew Kull's discussion of how an explicitly color-blind text of the Fourteenth Amendment, offered by Wendell Phillips as an alternative to Representative John Bingham's adopted text, was rejected. Andrew Kull, *The Color-Blind Constitution* (Cambridge, MA: Harvard University Press, 1992), 53–87.

40 Joel K. Goldstein, "Not Hearing History: A Critique of Chief Justice Roberts's Reinterpretation of *Brown*," *Ohio State Law Journal* 69 (2008): 793.

41 Nagle (2010), 218.

42 *Strauder v. West Virginia*, 100 U.S. 303 (1880).

43 *Plessy v. Ferguson*, 163 U.S. 537 (1896), 556 (Harlan dissenting) (citing *Strauder v. West Virginia*, 100 U.S. 303 [1979], 306).

44 *United States v. Jefferson County Board of Education*, 372 F. 2d 836 (5th Cir. 1967), 876.

45 For an excellent discussion of the historical context of the *Slaughterhouse* decision as well as of the ruling and dissents, see Ronald M. Labbe and Jonathan Lurie, *The Slaughterhouse Cases: Regulation, Reconstruction, and the Fourteenth Amendment* (Lawrence: University Press of Kansas, 2005).

46 *The Slaughter-House Cases*, 83 U.S. 36 (1873), 68, 72, 73.

47 See Jed Rubenfeld, "Affirmative Action," *Yale Law Journal* 107 (1997): 430–32.

48 Ibid., 430–31 (citing Act of July 28, 1866, ch. 296, 14 Stat. 310, at 317 and Resolution of March 16, 1867, No. 4, 15 Stat. 20).

49 See Eric Foner, *Reconstruction: America's Unfinished Revolution, 1863–1877* (New York: Harper & Row, 1988), 153–69.

50 On immutability and irrelevance, see *Frontiero v. Richardson*, 411 U.S. 677 (1973), 686 (arguing that sex is an "immutable characteristic determined solely by the accident of birth" and that "the sex characteristic frequently bears no relation to ability to perform or contribute to society"). On history of discrimination and political powerlessness, see *Frontiero*, 411 U.S., at 684–85 (describing the history of discrimination against women) and *San Antonio Independent School District v. Rodrigues*, 411 U.S. 1 (1973), 38 (discussing how children of poorer families challenging a property tax law constitutes a class "not saddled with such disabilities, or subject to a history of purposeful unequal treatment . . . as to command extraordinary protection from the majoritarian political process").

51 Sonu Bedi, "Collapsing Suspect Class with Suspect *Classification*: Why Strict Scrutiny Is Too Strict and Maybe Not Strict Enough," *Georgia Law Review* 47 (2) (Winter 2013): 319–30.

52 Christopher J. Schmidt, "Caught in a Paradox: Problems with *Grutter's* Expectation That Race-Conscious Admissions Programs Will End in Twenty-Five Years," *Northern Illinois University Law Review* 24 (2003–2004): 775.

53 See Schmidt (2003–2004).

54 *City of Richmond v. J.A. Croson Co.*, 488 U.S. 469 (1989). See Bedi (2013) on the conflation of suspect-class doctrine, which compels an antisubordination principle, and suspect classification, which compels an anticlassification principle, as applied to race-based affirmative action in education and employment.

55 *City of Richmond v. J.A. Croson Co.*, 488 U.S. 469 (1989), 495.

56 Ibid.

57 Ibid., 519 (Kennedy concurring).

58 Ibid., 521 (Scalia concurring).

59 Ibid., 552–53 (Marshall dissenting).

60 Ibid., 496.

61 Ibid., 554 (Marshall dissenting) (citations omitted).

62 Skowronek (2006), 386.

63 *Reed v. Reed*, 404 U.S. 71 (1971).

64 *Frontiero v. Richardson*, 411 U.S. 677 (1973).

65 *Craig v. Boren*, 429 U.S. 190 (1976).

66 *United States v. Virginia*, 518 U.S. 515 (1996), 532–23.

67 Ibid., 571, 573 (Scalia dissenting) .

68 Ibid., 559 (Rehnquist concurring) (Rehnquist contended that the language of exceedingly persuasive justification was introduced in *Massachusetts v. Feeney*, which stated, "precedents dictate that any state law overtly or covertly designed to prefer males over females in public employment would require an exceedingly persuasive justification to withstand a constitutional challenge under the Equal Protection Clause of the Fourteenth Amendment." *Personnel Administrator of Massachusetts v. Feeney*, 442 U.S. 256 (1979), 273.

69 Kathryn A. Lee, "Intermediate Review with Teeth in Gender Discrimination Cases: The New Standard in *United States v. Virginia*," *Temple Political & Civil Rights Law Review* 7 (Fall 1997).

70 Ibid., 243–44.

71 *Romer v. Evans*, 517 U.S. 620 (1996).

72 Ibid., 632.

73 Ibid.

74 Ibid., 635.

75 Ibid., 644 (Scalia dissenting).

76 Tobias Barrington Wolff, "Case Note: Principled Silence," *Yale Law Journal* 106 (1996): 250–52.

77 Cass R. Sunstein, "Foreword: Leaving Things Undecided," *Harvard Law Review* 110 (1996): 62.

78 Kevin H. Lewis, "Note: Equal Protection after *Romer v. Evans*: Implications for the Defense of Marriage Act and Other Laws," *Hastings Law Journal* 49 (1997).

79 Sunstein (1996), 63. See also Daniel Farber and Suzanna Sherry, "The Pariah Principle," *Constitutional Commentary* 13 (1996): 275.

80 Jeremy B. Smith, "The Flaws of Rational Basis with Bite: Why the Supreme Court Should Acknowledge Its Application of Heightened Scrutiny to Classifications Based on Sexual Orientation," *Fordham Law Review* 73 (2004–2005): 2770.

81 The Court has repeatedly claimed that there is a fundamental right to sexual privacy. See *Skinner v. State of Oklahoma, ex. rel. Williamson*, 316 U.S. 535 (1942) (ruling that compulsory sterilization could not be punishment for a crime), *Griswold v. Connecticut*, 381 U.S. 479 (1965) (finding a constitutional right to privacy that included access to contraception for married couples), *Eisenstadt v. Baird*, 405 U.S. 438 (1972) (extending right to privacy and contraception to single people), *Roe v. Wade*, 410 U.S. 113 (1973) (extending privacy to include access to abortion), and *Planned Parenthood v. Casey*, 505 U.S. 833 (1992) (maintaining *Roe* but altering the standard applied when evaluating statutory restrictions on abortion access). *Gonzales v. Carhart*, 550 U.S. 124 (2007), which upheld a federal

ban on late-term abortion procedures, did not apply strict scrutiny, upending doctrinal tradition, as noted by Justice Ginsburg in dissent, and instead Justice Kennedy applied only rational basis review as he framed the question at stake to be the regulation of a medical procedure rather than a statutory infringement on the right to privacy.

82 *Lawrence v. Texas*, 539 U.S. 558 (2003), 586 (Scalia dissenting).

83 Ibid., 567.

84 *Gonzales v. Carhart*, 550 U.S. 124 (2007).

85 Partial-Birth Abortion Ban Act of 2003, 18 U.S.C. § 1531.

86 *Gonzales v. Carhart*, 550 U.S. 124 (2007), 152.

87 Ibid., 151.

88 David D. Meyer, "*Gonzales v. Carhart* and the Hazards of Muddled Scrutiny," *Journal of Law and Policy* 17 (1) (2007–2008): 59.

89 Joanna Grossman and Linda McClain, "*Gonzales v. Carhart*: How the Supreme Court's Validation of the Federal Partial-Birth Abortion Ban Act Affects Women's Constitutional Liberty and Equality: Part Two in a Two-Part Series," *Findlaw*, 7 May 2007, http://writ.news.findlaw.com/commentary/20070507_mcclain.html (accessed 5 March 2014).

90 *Gonzales v. Carhart*, 550 U.S. 124 (2007), 175.

91 *United States v. Windsor*, 570 U.S. _____ (2013), 13.

92 Ibid., 18.

93 Ibid.

94 Ibid., 19.

95 Ibid., 20.

96 Ibid., 21.

97 Ibid., 22.

98 Ibid., 25–26.

99 *United States v. Windsor*, 570 U. S. _____ (2013), 20–21.

100 *Obergefell v. Hodges*, 576 U.S. _____ (2015), 22–23.

101 Ibid., 3.

102 Ibid., 19.

103 Ibid., 22.

104 Ibid., 7.

105 Ibid., 4. Emphasis added.

106 Ibid., 10.

107 Ibid., 18.

108 Indeed, there was not even a concurrence that offered a more traditional application of scrutiny doctrine, which could further suggest how much the doctrine is being avoided.

109 *Obergefell v. Hodges*, 576 U.S. _____ (2015), 22–23.

110 Bedi (2013), 123–24.

111 Jodi Melamed, "The Spirit of Neoliberalism: From Racial Liberalism to Neoliberal Multiculturalism," *Social Text* 24 (4) (2006): 1.

112 *Gratz v. Bollinger*, 539 U.S. 244 (2003).

113 Eng (2010), 38.

114 See President Obama's 2012 inaugural:

> We, the people, declare today that the most evident of truths—that all of us are created equal—is the star that guides us still; just as it guided our forebears through Seneca Falls, and Selma, and Stonewall; just as it guided all those men and women, sung and unsung, who left footprints along this great Mall, to hear a preacher say that we cannot walk alone; to hear a King proclaim that our individual freedom is inextricably bound to the freedom of every soul on Earth.

Barack Obama, "Inaugural Address," 21 January 2013. Online by Gerhard Peters and John T. Woolley, *American Presidency Project*, http://www.presidency.ucsb.edu/ws/?pid=102827.

115 Eng (2010), 17.

116 Kenji Yoshino, *Covering: The Hidden Assault on Our Civil Rights* (New York: Random House, 2006), 188.

117 As Katherine Franke contends,

> The problem with dignity-based arguments is that they don't come free— someone else pays the price. Dignity does its work by shifting stigma from one group to another, in this case from same-sex couples to other groups who, by contrast, are not deserving of similar ennoblement. These others include "less-deserving" groups like unmarried mothers, the sexually "promiscuous," or those whose relationships don't fit the respectable form of marriage.

Katherine Franke, "'Dignity' Could Be Dangerous at the Supreme Court," *Slate*, 25 June 2015, http://www.slate.com/blogs/outward/2015/06/25/in_the_scotus_same_sex_marriage_case_a_dignity_rationale_could_be_dangerous.html (accessed 25 June 2015).

118 Taking note of the Court's turn from suspect-class designation and scrutiny doctrine, Kenji Yoshino writes, "Over the past decades, the Court has systematically denied constitutional protections to new groups, curtailed it for already-covered groups, and limited Congress's capacity to protect groups through civil rights legislation. The Court has repeatedly justified these limitations by adverting to pluralism anxiety. These cases signal the end of equality doctrine as we have known it." Yoshino, "The New Equal Protection," *Harvard Law Review* 124 (2011): 748.

119 Even this conclusion remains highly contingent. While the controversy created by Justice Sonia Sotomayor's famous "wise Latina" comment and President Obama's aspiration to appoint a judge with empathy pointed to an intention to consider the importance of context, opposition clung to Chief Justice Roberts's judge-as-umpire analogy, which he articulated during his own confirmation hearings. The most recently appointed justice, Elena Kagan, backed off the umpire analogy, signaling some intention to adhere to Progressive liberalism's emphasis on context: "There are cases where it is difficult to determine what the law requires. Judging

is not a robotic or automatic enterprise, especially on cases that come before the Supreme Court." Yet later in the hearings, Kagan informed the committee that "'it's law all the way down' when judges make decisions." Jonathan H. Adler, "The Judiciary Committee Grills Elena Kagan," *Washington Post*, 29 June 2010. See also Charlie Savage, "A Judge's View of Judging Is on the Record," *New York Times*, 14 May 2009; Sheryl Gay Stolberg, "In Court Pick, Obama Seeks Experience in Real World," *New York Times*, 23 May 2009; Dahlia Lithwick, "The Kagan Hearings: Elena Kagan's Relaxed and Charming Performance at Her Confirmation Hearing," *Slate.com*, 29 June 2010, http://www.slate.com/articles/news_and_politics/juris-prudence/features/2010/the_kagan_hearings/a_woman_in_full.html (accessed 24 March 2014).

CONCLUSION

1 Ross Douthat, "The Terms of Our Surrender," *New York Times*, 1 March 2014.

2 Niraj Chockshi, "Timeline: The 13 Federal Rulings against Gay Marriage Bans since June," *Washington Post*, 19 May 2014.

3 E. J. Schultz, "Honey Maid's Take on Wholesome Families Includes Gay Couple," *Ad Age*, 10 March 2014.

4 David Griner, "Ad of the Day: Honey Maid Celebrates Single Dads, Gay Dads, Punk Dads, and More, Reclaiming the Word 'Wholesome,'" *Ad Week*, 10 March 2014.

5 Quotation is from Andrew Sullivan, "Erick Erickson Has a Point," *Daily Dish*, 24 February 2014, http://dish.andrewsullivan.com/2014/02/24/erick-erickson-has-a-point/ (accessed 6 June 2014).

6 Lenhardt quoted in Julian Berman, "Apple, Delta, Petsmart Join Fight against Arizona's Anti-Gay Bill," *Huffington Post*, 26 February 2014, http://www.huffing-tonpost.com/2014/02/26/companies-arizona-gay-bill_n_4857964.html (accessed 6 June 2014).

7 *Burwell v. Hobby Lobby Stores, Inc.*, 573 U.S. _____ (2014) (slip opinion).

8 Ibid.

9 For commentary on this possibility, see "Room for Debate: If Gays Can Marry, and Be Fired for Doing So," *New York Times*, 24 March 2014.

10 Ibid., 46.

11 *Obergefell v. Hodges*, 576 U.S. _____ (2000), 27.

12 In a 2012 decision, the EEOC ruled that transgender discrimination was banned under existing Title VII language. See Chris Geidner, "Sexual-Orientation Discrimination Is Barred by Existing Law, Federal Commission Rules," *Buzzfeed*, 16 July 2015, http://www.buzzfeed.com/chrisgeidner/sexual-orientation-discrimination-is-barred-by-existing-law#.bdELLAjbm (accessed 17 July 2015).

13 *Complainant v. Anthony Foxx, Secretary, Department of Transportation* (Federal Aviation Administration), Agency. Appeal No. 0120133080, 17 July 2015, 14.

14 See *Hurley* (1995) and *Dale* (2000).

15 Alex Panisch, "Majority of Americans Think Gay Sex Is Immoral," *Out*, 4 March 2014.

16 An archive of ads from the United States and other countries featuring gay characters and themes is available at Accuracast Pink!

17 Sarah Posner, "Wave of New State Bills: Religious Freedom or License to Discriminate?" *Aljazeera America*, 7 February 2014, http://america.aljazeera.com/articles/2014/2/7/wave-of-new-statebillsreligiousfreedomorlicensetodiscriminate.html (accessed 24 November 2014).

18 *Deb Whitehead, et al. v. Michael Wolf*, United States District Court for the Middle District of Pennsylvania, 20 May 2014, slip opinion. The tweet is from the Task Force, @TheTaskForce, 20 May 2014, 3:08 PM EDT.

19 Judith N. Shklar, *American Citizenship: The Quest for Inclusion* (Cambridge, MA: Harvard University Press, 1991), 9.

20 Paisley Currah, "Homonationalism, State Rationalities, and Contradictions," *Theory & Event* 16 (1) (2013); Craig Wilse and D. Spade "Freedom in a Regulatory State? *Lawrence*, Marriage, and Biopolitics," *Widener Law Review* 11 (2005); Dorothy Roberts, *Killing the Black Body: Race, Reproduction, and the Meaning of Liberty* (New York: Pantheon, 1997).

21 Lisa Duggan, "The New Homonormativity: The Sexual Politics of Neoliberalism," *Materializing Democracy: Toward a Revitalized Cultural Politics,* Russ Castronovo and Dana D. Jelson, eds. (Durham, NC: Duke University Press, 2002); Susan Stryker, "Transgender History, Homonormativity, and Disciplinarity." *Radical History Review* (Winter) (2008).

22 On same-sex couples as entitled to equality but not as identical to cross-sex couples see Robert Leckey, "Must Equal Mean Identical? Same-Sex Couples and Marriage," *International Journal of Law in Context* 10 (1) (2014).

23 *Romer v. Evans*, 517 U.S. 620 (1996); *Lawrence v. Texas*, 539 U.S. 558 (2003).

INDEX

ABOUT THE AUTHOR

Stephen M. Engel is Associate Professor and Chair of Politics at Bates College and an Affiliated Scholar of the American Bar Foundation. His research and teaching focus on questions of American political development, U.S. constitutional law, and LGBTQ politics. He is the author of *American Politicians Confront the Courts: Opposition Politics and Changing Responses to Judicial Power* and *The Unfinished Revolution: Social Movement Theory and the Gay and Lesbian Movement*, as well as coeditor (with Stephen Skowronek and Bruce Ackerman) of the volume *The Progressives' Century: Political Reform, Constitutional Government, and the Modern American State*. He lives in Portland, Maine.